# Logic and Contemporary Rhetoric

## The Use of Reason in Everyday Life

**EIGHTH EDITION**

*Howard Kahane*

University of Maryland
Baltimore County

*Nancy Cavender*

College of Marin

**Wadsworth Publishing Company**

I(T)P   An International Thomson Publishing Company

Belmont • Albany • Bonn • Cincinnati • Detroit
London • Madrid • Melbourne • Mexico City • New York • Paris
San Francisco • Singapore • Tokyo • Toronto • Washington

Philosophy Editor: Peter Adams
Editorial Assistant: Kelly Zavislak
Production Editor: Hal Lockwood, Penmarin Books
Designer: Paula Shuhert and Image House
Print Buyer: Stacey Weinberger
Permissions Editor: Robert Kauser
Copy Editor: Kevin Gleason
Cover Designer: Stephen Rapley
Compositor: Janet Hansen, Alphatype
Printer: R. R. Donnelley & Sons
Cover Cartoon: Sydney Harris. Commissioned especially for this book.

Printed in the United States of America

1 2 3 4 5 6 7 8 9 10—04 03 02 01 00 99 98

For more information, contact Wadsworth Publishing Company, 10 Davis Drive, Belmont, CA 94002, or electronically at http://www.thomson.com/wadsworth.html

International Thomson Publishing Europe
Berkshire House 168-173
High Holborn
London, WC1V7AA
England

Thomas Nelson Australia
102 Dodds Street
South Melbourne 3205
Victoria, Australia

Nelson Canada
1120 Birchmount Road
Scarborough, Ontario
Canada M1K 5G4

International Thomson Publishing GmbH
Königswinterer Strasse 418
53227 Bonn, Germany

International Thomson Editores
Campos Eliseos 385, Piso 7
Col. Polanco
11560 México D.F. México

International Thomson Publishing Asia
221 Henderson Road
#05-10 Henderson Building
Singapore 0315

International Thomson Publishing Japan
Hirakawacho Kyowa Building, 3F
2-2-1 Hirakawacho-
Chiyoda-ku, Tokyo 102, Japan

International Thomson Publishing South Africa
Building 18, Constantia Park
240 Old Pretoria Road
Halfway House, 1685 South Africa

**Library of Congress Cataloging-in-Publication Data**

Kahane, Howard, 1928–
    Logic and contemporary rhetoric : the use of reason in everyday
life / Howard Kahane, Nancy Cavender. —8th ed.
     p.  cm.
    Includes bibliographical references and indexes.
    ISBN: 0-534-52470-2
    1. Reasoning.  2. Fallacies (Logic)  3. Judgment (Logic)  4. Mass
media.  I. Cavender, Nancy.  II. Title.
BC177.K34  1997
160—dc21                         97–19988

*For Bonny sweet Robin . . .*

# Contents

*I do not pretend to know what many ignorant men are sure of.*

— Clarence Darrow

*To know that we know what we know, and that we do not know what we do not know, that is true knowledge.*

— Henry David Thoreau

*We have met the enemy and he is us.*

— Walt Kelly's "Pogo"

*Education is not simply the world of abstract verbalized knowledge.*

— Aldous Huxley

*Many people would sooner die than think. In fact, they do.*

— Bertrand Russell

*You can fool too many of the people too much of the time.*

— James Thurber

# PREFACE

The purpose of this eighth edition of *Logic and Contemporary Rhetoric*, as of the previous seven, is to help students improve their ability to reason well about problems they encounter in everyday life and about issues that are debated in the social/political arena. The intent is not to move to students to the right or left on the political spectrum but rather to help them move *up* on the scale measuring rational sophistication.

The text contains examples and exercise items drawn from a broad range of sources—television programs, advertisements, literary works, political speeches, newspaper columns, and so on. Students get to sharpen their ability to think critically by reasoning about important topics and issues—abortion, astrology, capitalism, corruption, drugs, diets, doublespeak—instead of examples concerning sophomores dating seniors or all Greeks being mortal. It quotes from the writings, comments, and testimony of Aristotle, Molefi Kete Asante, Woody Allen, Muhammed Ali, Saint Augustine, Candice Bergen, Joyce Brothers, Ambrose Bierce, Winston Churchill, Ray Charles, Linda Chavez, William Shakespeare, O. J. Simpson, Adlai Stevenson, and hundreds of others. Examples are drawn from astrological predictions, Budweiser commercials, Clinton political doings, syndicated columnists, canned letters sent by members of Congress in response to constituent queries, works of literature, and hundreds of other sources. Instead of the made-to-order cartoons that appear in some other texts, *Logic and Contemporary Rhetoric* contains drawings by the likes of David Levine, Edward Sorel, Tom Toles, George Booth, Jules Feiffer, and many others, and comic strips featuring *Calvin and Hobbes, Andy Capp, Doonesbury, Beetle Bailey, Dennis the Menace*, and others to illustrate points in a lively and interesting manner. The trademark of *Logic and Contemporary Rhetoric* always has been, and still is, ease of comprehension and the presentation of up-to-date and interesting material. Textbooks need not be dull!

## NEW TO THE EIGHTH EDITION

The principal changes in this edition are these:

1. Hundreds of old examples have been replaced by more up-to-date items culled from the (sadly) thousands of new candidates.
2. Hundreds of old exercise items have been replaced by new ones.
3. Although much of the text again has been rewritten to improve organization, style, and flow, the general subject matter covered by this new edition has not changed. Several substantive changes have been made, however, including the following:
   a. The material concerning background beliefs and world views that constituted part of Chapter 1 has been expanded into a new chapter (Chapter 2). The point of this change is to emphasize the strong influence that background beliefs have on our ability to reason successfully about most of the problems encountered in everyday life and to stress the need to develop a large and accurate stock of background beliefs regularly checked for accuracy.
   b. Several examples have been added from important literary works—for example, by Conrad and Forster—as a way of nicely illustrating how world views influence reasoning in daily life.
   c. The chapter on evaluating and constructing extended argumentative works (essays) has been divided into two separate chapters, so that these two different (even if related) skills can be addressed separately. The material on constructing effective argumentative essays has been sharply increased.
   d. A section on new marketing wrinkles has been added to the chapter on advertising (Chapter 10), the point being to better educate students concerning the ways advertisers attempt to manipulate consumers—all of us   and thus to help students to become more savvy consumers.
   e. A new section on recent media developments has been added to the chapter on managing the news (Chapter 11), including a discussion about the import of the increasing concentration of mass media ownership in the hands of a very few megacorporations.
   f. A new section on how politics affects the selection of public school textbooks has been added to the textbook chapter (Chapter 12), the point being to improve the explanation as to how politics affects the content, tone, accuracy, and slant of public school textbooks.
   g. Several new sections have been added to the Appendix, including one dealing with the concepts of cause and effect and one on the nature of scientific method. Note also that the section on gambling fallacies and the calculation of probabilities has been moved to the Appendix.

## ORGANIZATION OF THE TEXT

The thought that sparked the original organization of material in *Logic and Contemporary Rhetoric* way back in 1969–1970 was that student reasoning about everyday topics could be improved by acquainting them with a few basic principles of good reasoning and, in particular, by enlightening them concerning common ways in which people are taken in by fallacious arguments and reasoning in everyday life. But a close examination of the ways in which reasoning in fact goes wrong in everyday life showed that it does so in a majority of cases first because of a lack of sufficient (or sufficiently accurate) background information; second, because of all of the psychological impediments (wishful thinking, rationalization, prejudice, superstition, provincialism, and so on) that stand in the way of cogent reasoning; and third, because of a poor understanding of the nature and quality of the various information sources.

Taking account of this insight has resulted in a book that divides into eight parts, as follows:

1. *Good and Bad Reasoning*: Chapter 1 introduces students to some basic ideas about good and bad reasoning, including some rudimentary remarks about deduction and induction and the three overarching fallacy categories.
2. *Background Beliefs*: Chapter 2 discusses the importance of background beliefs and world views for cogent reasoning.
3. *Fallacious Reasoning*: Chapters 3, 4, and 5 discuss fallacious reasoning, concentrating on how to avoid fallacies by becoming familiar with the types most frequently encountered in everyday life. The point is to help students increase their ability to spot fallacious reasoning by discussing the most common types of fallacious argument and by providing students with examples drawn from everyday life on which to practice.
4. *Impediments to Cogent Reasoning*: Chapter 6 talks about wishful thinking, rationalization, provincialism, denial, and so on, and how to overcome them. It explains the attractiveness and mistaken nature of belief in the paranormal and other pseudosciences. (Some instructors pass over this chapter on the grounds that the topic is more appropriately taught in psychology classes, not in classes primarily concerned with critical reasoning. But the reality here is that many students do not take the relevant psychology classes and that those who do often are provided with a purely theoretical account divorced from the students' own reasoning in everyday life, not with a "how-to" discussion designed to help them overcome these obstacles to rational thought.)
5. *Language*: Chapter 7 discusses the ways in which language itself can be used to manipulate, for instance, via doubletalk or long-winded locutions. (This chapter also contains a section, not common in critical thinking texts, on the linguistic revolution that has tremendously reduced the use of sexist, racist, and other pejorative locutions in everyday discourse, and it also has a few things to say about the use of politically correct (PC) locutions.)
6. *Evaluating and Writing Cogent Essays*: Chapter 8 deals with the evaluation of extended argumentative passages—essays, editorials, political speeches, and so on. Chapter 9 addresses the writing of these kinds of argumentative passages. (Instructors are urged not to pass over Chapter 9 and are urged to have students write *at least* two argumentative papers during the semester. Writing is very likely the best way in which we all can learn to sharpen our ability to reason well.)
7. *Important Sources of Information*: Chapter 10 discusses advertising (singling out political ads for special scrutiny) as an information source; Chapter 11 the media (television, newspapers, radio, books, and magazines), in particular, the mass media; and Chapter 12 public school textbooks. (For many people,

these are the most important sources of information about how the world works. Instructors are urged not to pass over the chapter on the media too quickly: In this day and age, so much that happens in our lives depends on our being able to assess accurately what the media— in particular, the mass media—tell us.)

8. *More on Cogent Reasoning*: Additional material on deduction and induction, cause and effect, scientific method, and so on is provided in the Appendix, including a few words about syllogisms and about a common misconception concerning the difference between deductive and inductive reasoning.

Note also that a section at the back of the book provides answers to selected exercise items. It should be remembered, however, that most of the execise items in this text are drawn from everyday life, where shades of gray outnumber blacks and whites. The answers provided thus constitute author responses rather than definitive pronouncements. Similar remarks apply to the answers to the remaining exercise items provided in the *Instructor's Manual* designed to accompany *Logic and Contemporary Rhetoric*.

## The Unique Nature of *Logic* and *Contemporary Rhetoric*

This book is unique among critical reasoning texts in bringing together all of these apparently diverse elements, in particular, in stressing the importance of bringing to bear good background information when dealing with everyday problems and in so extensively discussing the most important information sources. In this complicated modern world, all of us are laypersons most of the time with respect to most topics; the ability to deal effectively with the "expert" information available to us via the media—to separate wheat from chaff—thus is crucial to our ability to reason well about everyday problems, whether of a personal or of a social/political nature.

Although the text contains much discussion of theory, this is *not* a treatise on the theory of cogent and fallacious reasoning. Rather, it is designed to help students learn *how* to reason well and *how* to avoid fallacious reasoning. That is why so many examples and exercise items have been included—arranged so as to increase student sophistication as they progress through the book—and why exercises and examples have been drawn primarily from everyday life. Learning how to reason well and how to evaluate the rhetoric of others is a skill that, like most others, requires practice, in this case practice on the genuine article—actual examples drawn from everyday life.

This text provides students with more than the usual supply of exercise items (many hundreds in fact), but perhaps the most important are those requiring them to do things on their own: find examples from the mass media; write letters to elected officials; do research on specified topics. (The *Instructor's Manual*, available to adopters of the text, suggests several other kinds of student activities—for example, classroom debates on issues of the day—that dovetail nicely with the spirit of the text.)

A true critical reasoning course, or textbook, is unthinkable in a closed or authoritarian society and antithetical to the indoctrination practiced in that kind of culture. The authors of this text take very seriously the admonition that eternal vigilance is the price of liberty. Citizens who think for themselves, rather than uncritically ingesting what their leaders and others with power tell them, are the absolutely necessary ingredient of a society that is to remain free.

## ACKNOWLEDGMENTS

Many thanks to the publisher's reviewers for this eighth edition: Anatole Anton, San Francisco State University; Joseph Keim Campbell, Washington State University; David Detmer, Purdue University, Calumet Campus; Frank Fair, Sam Houston State University; John L. King, University of North Carolina; Dr. Herschel L. Mack, Humboldt State University; and Donna Monahan, College of Marin.

Thanks also to the others who have aided in the preparation of this and previous editions, including Professors Thomas Allen, California Polytechnic University, San Luis Obispo; Don Anderson, Pierce College; Gary L. Baran, Los Angeles City College; Lawrence Beloof, West Hills Community College; William Bonis, California State University, Long Beach; Gene Booth, University of New Mexico; Donald Burrell, California State University, Los Angeles; Henry C. Byerly, University of Arizona; Monte Cook, University of Oklahoma; Rosemary Cook, Saybrook Institute; Wally Cox, Regent University; Leland Creer, Central Connecticut State University; Robert Cogan, Edinboro University; R. V. Dusek, University of New Hampshire; Frank Fair, Sam Houston State University; Dana R. Flint, Lincoln University; Marilyn M. Fry, Coastline Community College; Sidney Gendin, Eastern Michigan University; Norman L. Geisler, Liberty University; James A. Gould, University of South Florida; J. Anthony Greybasch, Central State University; Paul J. Haanstad, University of Utah; Max O. Hallman, Merced College; Alan Hausman, Southern Methodist University; James Heffernan, University of the Pacific; Mark Herron, National University; J. Thomas Howald, Franklin College; John King, University of North Carolina; Donald Lazere, California Polytechnic State University; Herschel L. Mack, Humboldt State University; Patrick Maher, University of Pittsburgh; Reed Markham, California Polytechnic University, Pamona; Thomas McKay, Syracuse University; David Morgan, University of Northern Iowa; Clayton Morgareidge, Lewis and Clark College; Gonzalo T. Palacios, University of the District of Columbia; Ray Perkins, Jr., Plymouth State University; Linda Plackowski, Delta College; Nelson Pole, Cleveland State University; Merrill Proudfoot, Park College; Vincent Riccardi, Orange Coast College; Paul O. Ricci, Cypress College; Paul A. Roth, University of Missouri; Arent H. Schuyler, Jr., University of California, Santa Barbara; Robert Schwartz, University of Wisconsin—Milwaukee; S. Samuel Shermis, Purdue University; Pamela Spoto, California State University, Chico; Douglas Stalker, University of Delaware; Ben Starr, Modesto Junior College; Joan Straumanis, Kenyon College; John Stroupe, Western Michigan University; Gregory P. Swartzentruber, Villanova University; Roye Templeton, University of Maryland, Baltimore County; John Titchener, University of Maryland, Baltimore County; and Perry Weddle, California State University, Sacramento.

Finally, our very special thanks to the students of Whitman College, the University of Kansas, Bernard Baruch College of CUNY, the University of Maryland, Baltimore County, and the College of Marin.

HOWARD KAHANE          NANCY CAVENDER
Asilomar, California      Cessola, Italy

What is the use of philosophy, if all it does is enable you to talk . . . about some abstruse questions of logic, etc., and if it does not improve your thinking about the important questions of everyday life?

— Ludwig Wittgenstein

"Congratulations, Dave! I don't think I've read a more beautifully evasive and subtly misleading public statement in all my years in government."

*Cartoon commentary on the state of contemporary rhetoric.*

*It's much easier to do and die than it is to reason why.*

— H. A. Studdert Kennedy

*Read not to contradict and confute, nor to believe and take for granted . . . but to weigh and consider.*

— Francis Bacon

*You can lead a man up to the university, but you can't make him think.*

— Finley Peter Dunne

*You can lead me to college . . . but you can't make me think.*

— Sweatshirt update seen at Duke University

*Chapter*

# 1

# GOOD AND BAD REASONING

There is much truth to the old saying that life is just one problem after another. That's why problem solving is one of life's major preoccupations. **Reasoning** is the essential ingredient in problem solving. When confronted with a problem, those of us who are rational reason from what we already know, or have good reason to believe, or can find out, to new beliefs useful in solving that problem. The trick, of course, is to reason well. This book is about good reasoning—about how to reason well in everyday life—whether dealing with personal problems or those of a social or political nature.

Fortunately, no one is an island. We all have available to us a great deal of knowledge others have gained through experience and good reasoning—accurate information and well-intended advice available to anyone who reaches out for it. Unfortunately, not all information is created equal. Charlatans and fools can speak as loudly as saints or Nobel prize winners. The trick when evaluating the mountain of verbiage we all are exposed to is to separate the nourishing wheat from the expendable chaff. One way to become good at doing this is to think a bit about what makes reasoning good (cogent), as opposed to bad (fallacious).

## 1. REASONING AND ARGUMENTS

Here is a simple example of reasoning about the nature/nurture issue:

> Identical twins sometimes have different IQ test scores. Yet these twins inherit exactly the same genes. So environment must play some part in determining a person's IQ.

1

Logicians call this kind of reasoning an **argument**. In this case, the argument consists of three statements:

1. Identical twins often have different IQ test scores.
2. Identical twins inherit the same genes.
3. So environment must play some part in determining IQ.

The first two statements in this argument give *reasons* for accepting the third. In logic talk, they are said to be **premises** of the argument; and the third statement, which asserts the *claim* made by the argument, is called the argument's **conclusion**.

In everyday life, few of us bother to label premises or conclusions. We usually don't even bother to distinguish one argument from another. But we do sometimes give clues. Words such as *because*, *since*, and *for* usually indicate that what follows is a premise of an argument. Terms like *therefore*, *thus*, *consequently*, and *so* generally signal conclusions. Similarly, expressions such as "It has been observed that . . . ," "In support of this . . . ," and "The relevant data are . . ." are used to introduce premises, while expressions such as "The point of all of this is . . . ," "The implication is . . . ," and "It follows that . . ." are used to signal conclusions. Here is a simple example:

> *Since* it's always wrong to kill a human being (premise), *it follows that* capital punishment is wrong (conclusion), *because* capital punishment takes the life of (kills) a human being (premise).

Put into textbook form, the argument looks like this:

1. It's always wrong to kill a human being.
2. Capital punishment takes the life of (kills) a human being.
∴ 3. Capital punishment is wrong.*

Of course, an argument may have any number of premises and may be surrounded by or embedded in other arguments or extraneous material.

In addition to using transitional words like *since*, *because*, and *therefore*, we sometimes employ sentence order—the last sentence in a series stating an argument's conclusion—and occasionally even express a conclusion in the form of a question. During the 1992 presidential election, for example, a Democratic party spokesperson gave all sorts of reasons for believing that, if elected, Bill Clinton would push Congress into passing a health care reform bill and then stated his conclusion in the form of a rhetorical question: "Can anyone doubt, then, that Bill Clinton will succeed in reforming health care in America?"

We should also note that, in daily life, premises and even the conclusions of arguments sometimes are omitted as understood. Life is short, and we don't always bother to spell out matters that are obvious or not at issue or can be taken for granted. In the IQ example given earlier, for instance, the premise that IQ differences must be due either to genetic or to environmental factors was omitted as generally understood. When assessing arguments, we should by all means add omitted premises of this kind when they are relevant.

---

*The symbol "∴" often is used as shorthand for the word *therefore* and thus indicates that a conclusion follows.

## EXERCISE 1-1

Identify the premises and conclusions in the following arguments (the last five are from student exams—modestly edited):*

**Example:**
> *Argument*
> The barometer is falling sharply, so the weather is going to change.
> *Argument Structure*
> *Premise:* The barometer is falling sharply.
> *Implied Premise:* Whenever the barometer falls sharply, the weather changes.
> *Conclusion:* The weather is going to change.

1. Thomas Szasz: Since there are no mental diseases, there can be no treatments for them.

2. *Chicago Daily News:* If marriages were really falling apart, divorced persons wouldn't be as eager as they are to find another partner as speedily as possible.

3. *The Economist:* It is difficult to gauge the pain felt by animals because pain is subjective and animals cannot talk.

*4. William Shakespeare: Forbear to judge, for we are sinners all.

5. Aristotle: The Earth has a spherical shape. For the night sky looks different in the northern and the southern parts of the earth, and that would be the case if the earth were spherical in shape.

*6. Marijuana has many medical benefits. It is significantly less harmful than many legal drugs. It should be legalized.

7. We should not judge Dr. Kevorkian guilty of murder. Murder should be defined so that it is committed only when you take the lives of people against their will or help those who are healthy to commit suicide. Dr. Kevorkian helped terminally ill patients who wanted to die rather than to suffer needlessly.

8. America is a society that values its freedoms. Censorship clearly has no place in a society that values its freedoms. It curtails independent thought, and it discourages people from examining societal problems.

*9. No, I was not prepared to take this critical thinking class. How can you expect me to understand the material when I never heard of most of the people and events you talk about in class? And that textbook is just way over my head, talking about people and events I've never heard of. What *did* happen at Watergate and who *is* Frank Lloyd Wright anyway? Have I proved my point? I was not prepared!

10. Yes, without a doubt the author of our textbook is prejudiced. You can tell because he uses all those examples against Ronald Reagan, Richard Nixon,

---

*Starred (*) items are answered in a section at the back of the book.

and George Bush, but only a very few that make any Democrats look bad. It's true, as you said in class, that Republicans have won five of the last six presidential elections [this was before the 1992 election], but he still could have found more anti-Democrat examples. And some of those about President Reagan were really cheap shots.

## Exposition and Argument

Of course, only those groups of statements that provide *reasons* for believing something form arguments. Thus, anecdotes are not usually arguments, nor are most other forms of *exposition*. But even in these cases, arguments often are implied. Here is a sales clerk talking about the difference between a 19-inch Sony TV set and the 21-inch house brand: "Well, Sony has a one-gun picture tube, while our own Supremacy set doesn't; so the Sony picture will be a bit better in areas where reception is good to start with. Of course, if reception isn't that good in your area, the picture won't be clear anyway—unless you have cable. On the other hand, our own brand, Supremacy, is $175 cheaper for a 21-inch set than Sony is for a 19-inch one."

Although the clerk's remarks contain no explicit argument because no conclusion is drawn, a conclusion definitely is *implied*: you should choose the Sony if you're willing to pay $175 more for a slightly better picture (especially if you're on cable); otherwise, you should choose the house brand.

The point is that talk generally is not aimless. A good deal of everyday talk, even gossip, is intended to influence the beliefs and actions of others, and thus constitutes a kind of argument. In the television set example, the clerk provided information intended to convince the customer to draw either the conclusion "I'll buy the 19-inch Sony, because a small picture improvement is worth $175 to me," or the conclusion "I'll buy the 21-inch Supremacy because the difference in picture quality isn't worth $175 to me." In other words, the point of the clerk's chatter was to *sell a TV set*. Similarly, advertisements often just provide product information rather than advance explicit arguments, yet clearly every such ad has an implied conclusion—that you should buy the advertised product.

Nevertheless, it is important to understand the difference between rhetoric that is primarily expository and discourse that is basically argumentative. An argument makes the claim, explicit or implicit, that one of its statements *follows from* some of its other statements. It at least implies that acceptance of its conclusion is justified if one accepts its premises. A passage that is purely expository gives us no reason to accept any "facts" it may contain (other than the implied authority of the writer or speaker, as, for example, when a friend tells us that she had a good time at the beach).

## EXERCISE 1-2

Here are several passages (the first eight are from student papers—again modestly edited). Indicate which contain arguments and which do not, label the premises and conclusions of those passages that do (as you did in the previous exercise), and explain why you think the other passages do not contain arguments.

**Example:**

*Passage from an Agatha Christie novel:* M. Hercule Poirot, having nothing better to do, amused himself by studying her without appearing to do so. She was, he judged, the kind of young woman who could take care of herself with perfect ease wherever she went. . . . He rather liked the severe regularity of her features and the delicate pallor of her skin. He liked the burnished black head with its neat waves of hair, and her eyes—cool, impersonal and gray. *Evaluation:* This is not an argument. The author says Poirot judged (reasoned) that the woman could take care of herself, but does not describe his reasoning. And the rest of the passage simply says that Poirot liked certain features of the young woman.

*1. At the present rate of consumption, the oil will be used up in 20–25 years. And we're sure not going to reduce consumption in the near future. So we'd better start developing solar power, windmills, and other "alternative energy sources" pretty soon.

2. My thesis is that the doomsayers are wrong to believe we're going to run out of oil in the near future, because necessity is the mother of discovery (ha, ha), and my geology text says we have only discovered a small fraction of the oil in the ground.

*3. I don't like big-time college football. I don't like pro football on TV either. In fact, I don't like sports, period.

4. Well, I have a special reason for believing in big-time college football. After all, I wouldn't have come here if Ohio State hadn't gone to the Rose Bowl, because that's how I heard about this place in the first place.

*5. Are we wasting billions of dollars on animal research? The answer must be yes. The use of vivisection actually impedes scientific progress by devoting less time and money to developing new technologies that would better serve our needs.

6. My summer vacation was spent working in Las Vegas. I worked as a waitress at the Desert Inn and made tons of money. But I guess I got addicted to the slots and didn't save too much. Next summer my friend Hal and I are going to work in Reno, if we can find jobs there.

7. We've had open admission here at KU [the University of Kansas] ever since living memory can remember, and things work swell here, don't they? I suppose that's because those that don't belong here flunk out, or don't come here in the first place. So who needs restricted enrollment?

8. I've often wondered how they make lead pencils. Of course, they don't use lead, they use graphite. But I mean how do they get the graphite into the wood? That's my problem. The only thing I can think of is maybe they cut the graphite into long round strips and then cut holes in the wood and slip in the graphite.

9. Muhammed Ali (when in Africa for his fight with George Foreman): There's no country as great as the smallest city in America. I mean, [here in Zaire] you can't watch television. The water won't even run right. The toilets won't flush. The roads, the cars—there's nothing as great as America.

*10. Descartes: Good sense is of all things in the world the most equally distributed, for everybody thinks himself so abundantly provided with it, that even those most difficult to please in all other matters do not commonly desire more of it than they already possess.

11.  Kurt Vonnegut, *Jailbird:* There was no European language that Ruth could not speak at least a little bit. She passed the time in the concentration camp, waiting for death, by getting other prisoners to teach her languages she did not know. Thus did she become fluent in Romany, the tongue of the gypsies.

12.  Michael H. Hart: It is worth noting that over the past fifteen years—a period during which U.S. women began using the pill regularly—the life expectancy among U.S. women has *increased* significantly. That fact alone should make it obvious that the pill is not a *major* health hazard.

## 2. COGENT REASONING

Reasoning can be either *cogent* (good) or *fallacious* (bad). We reason **cogently** when we have satisfied the following conditions:

1.  The premises of our reasoning are **believable (warranted, justified)**, given what we already know or believe
2.  We have considered all likely relevant information*
3.  Our reasoning is **valid**, or **correct**, which means that the premises we employ provide good grounds for accepting the conclusion we have drawn†

When all three of these conditions of cogent reasoning are not satisfied, reasoning is said to be **fallacious**.

Note, by the way, that in daily life, we often speak of *arguments* as being fallacious or cogent, even though, strictly speaking, it is reasoners—individuals—who reason either fallaciously or cogently. Life is short and we often speak imprecisely when context makes clear what is intended.

## Believable Premises

The first condition of cogent reasoning requires that we bring to bear whatever we already know or believe—our relevant **background beliefs** and information—to determine whether we should or shouldn't accept the premises of an argument being evaluated. Take, for instance, the first premise of the capital punishment argument discussed earlier, the premise making the claim that taking the life of a human being always is wrong. Most of us are not pacifists—we don't believe that it always is wrong to take a human life. Bringing that background belief to bear thus should make us see the first

---

*Satisfying this extremely stringent requirement is usually beyond the ability of most of us most of the time. The point is that good reasoners try to come as close as possible to satisfying it, taking into account the importance of drawing the right conclusion and the cost (in time, effort, or money) of obtaining or recalling relevant information. (One of the marks of genius is the ability to recognize that information is relevant when the rest of us fail to notice.)

†Provided we know nothing else relevant to the conclusion. Note that reasoning from an *unjustified* premise may still be cogent if it also employs justified premises that sufficiently support its conclusion. Note also that the term *valid* sometimes is used more broadly than we have used it here. For a more comprehensive account of valid reasoning, see Howard Kahane and Paul Tidman, *Logic and Philosophy*, 8th edition (Belmont, Calif.: Wadsworth, 1998).

premise of the capital punishment argument as *questionable*. So we should not accept the conclusion of that argument unless further reasons are presented in its support.

By way of contrast, consider the stated premise of the following argument:

> Paul McCartney must be a heck of a good musician. After all, he was one of the four Beatles. (The implied premise is that anyone who was a member of that great rock group must be a very good musician.)

Virtually every pop music fan (not to mention almost everyone else with ears) knows very well that McCartney was a member of the Beatles, so for them, this argument's stated premise (that McCartney was one of the four Beatles) is warranted by plenty of background information.

It's interesting to notice that, in effect, evaluating a premise of an argument by bringing background beliefs to bear entails constructing another argument whose conclusion is either that the premise in question is believable or that it isn't. For example, when evaluating the capital punishment argument discussed before, someone who is not a pacifist might construct the following argument: "I believe that it isn't wrong to kill in self-defense, or in wartime, or to kill those guilty of murder. So I should reject the premise that taking a human life always is wrong."

This brings to mind the fact that in daily life we often are exposed to **assertions**, or **claims**, that are not supported by reasons or arguments. Clearly, it is not rational to accept these assertions without evaluating them for believability, and, obviously, their correct evaluation requires us to do exactly what we do when evaluating the believability of the premises of an argument, namely, bring to bear what we already know or believe. Evaluating unsupported assertions thus involves just part of what is done when we evaluate arguments.

## No Relevant Information Excluded

The second criterion of cogent reasoning requires that we not pass over relevant information. In particular, it tells us to resist the temptation to neglect evidence contrary to what we want to believe.

Consider the following argument, voiced many years ago, and very much like ones we all have heard many times since then:

> We absolutely must start cutting down on the use of oil as an energy source. The World Resources Institute estimates that at the present rate of consumption, known reserves will be used up in just a bit more than 30 years.

Even supposing the institute's estimate had been on target, their reasoning still would not have been cogent, because it suppressed relevant information that most knowledgeable people have been well aware of all along—information that the World Resources Institute experts can be expected to have known about. Scare stories about running out of oil have circulated for at least fifty years now, but in spite of ever-rising consumption, known reserves continually increase anyway because new oil fields continue to be discovered. Prospecting for oil is expensive and chancy, so that when oil is a glut on the market (the usual situation over the years), exploration slows down; when reserves become lower relative to demand, exploration increases. That is why oil prices, excluding taxes and adjusted to account for inflation, are lower now than they were even in the 1930s. (Note, by the way, that only a few of the likely places to find oil have been thoroughly explored so far, and that even without direct efforts to reduce consumption of oil products.)

There are two morals to be drawn here. First, when we neglect relevant evidence, we do not reason cogently. Second, those who don't realize, or suspect, that relevant information has been passed over are fair game for more knowledgeable, less principled operators. Contrary to the old saying, what you don't know *can* hurt you.

## Valid Reasoning

The third criterion of cogent reasoning requires that the premises of an argument genuinely support its conclusion; or, as logicians like to say, it requires that an argument be *valid*, or *correct*. It is vitally important to understand that the validity of an argument has nothing whatever to do with the truth of its premises or conclusion. Validity concerns the nature of the *connection* between the premises and conclusion of an argument, not the truth or believability of its premises. Determining that an argument is valid tells us that *if* we are justified in believing in its premises, *then* we also are justified in believing in the truth of its conclusion. It doesn't tell us *whether* its premises are true. An argument thus can be perfectly valid and have completely false premises, and even have a false conclusion. Here is an example:

1. The Cleveland Indians have won more world series games than any other major league team. (False premise, alas!)
2. So they have won more world series games than the New York Yankees. (False conclusion.)

The argument is valid because if the beloved Indians *had* won more games than any other major league team, then, obviously (well, it's obvious to baseball fans), they *would have* won more world series games than the Yankees. The argument is valid, even though its premise and conclusion both are false. It's valid because anyone who is justified in believing its premise *thereby* is justified in believing its conclusion.

## 3. TWO BASIC KINDS OF VALID ARGUMENTS

There are two fundamentally different ways in which premises may correctly support conclusions. The first way yields *deductively valid* arguments; the second *inductively valid* (or *inductively correct* or *strong*) arguments.*

The fundamental property of a **deductively valid argument** is this: If all of its premises are true, then its conclusion *must* be true also, because the claim asserted by its conclusion already has been stated in its premises, although usually only implicitly.

Here is an example of a very simple deductively valid argument:

---

*Some authorities believe that there is at least one other kind of legitimate argument, namely, the kind in which various alternatives are evaluated. The authors of this text incline to the view that evaluative arguments fall into one or the other of the two basic kinds about to be mentioned. Note also that some authorities restrict the use of the term *valid* so that it refers only to *deductively* good arguments, even though in everyday life inductively strong arguments generally are said to be valid. In addition, note that the reasoning process called "mathematical induction" happens to be a kind of deductive reasoning. (Terminology sometimes is misleading.)

> Everything made of copper conducts electricity. (Premise)
> This wire is made of copper. (Premise)
> This wire will conduct electricity. (Conclusion)

Taken alone, neither premise makes the claim that the wire will conduct electricity; but taken together, they do, although not explicitly. We cannot imagine what it would be like for both premises of this argument to be true and yet its conclusion turn out to be false. Indeed, it would be contradictory to assert both of its premises and then to deny its conclusion.

Note again that the validity of an argument concerns the nature of the *connection* between the premises and conclusion of an argument, not the truth or believability of its premises. Determining that an argument is deductively valid thus tells us just that *if* its premises happen to be true, *then* its conclusion must be true also; it doesn't tell us *whether* its premises are true.

Here, for instance, is a deductively valid argument that contains one true and one very likely false premise and thus does not guarantee the truth of its conclusion:

> If more people read Agatha Christie's mystery novels than read Shakespeare's plays, then her novels must be better than his plays. (False premise?) And her novels are in fact read by a lot more people than read Shakespeare's plays. (True premise) So her novels must be better than his plays. (False conclusion?)

Of course, a deductively valid argument that contains a false premise may, luckily, have a true conclusion. But that would be a matter of luck, not of good reasoning.

The fact that a deductively valid argument cannot move from true premises to a false conclusion constitutes its chief characteristic and primary virtue. But deductive arguments are limited. They cannot yield conclusions that are not implicit (or explicit) in the premises from which they are derived. *Inductive* reasoning is needed to perform this task.

**Inductively valid**, or **correct**, **arguments**, unlike deductively valid ones, have conclusions that go beyond what is contained in their premises. The idea behind valid induction is that of *learning from experience*. We often observe *patterns, resemblances,* and other kinds of *regularities* in our experiences, some quite simple (sugar sweetening coffee), some very complicated (objects moving according to Newton's laws—well, Newton noticed this, anyway). Valid inductions simply project regularities of this kind noticed in our experiences so far onto other possible experiences.*

Here is a simple example of an inductively valid argument of the kind sometimes called *induction by enumeration*:

> I loaned my friend $50 last November and he failed to pay me back. (Premise) I loaned him another $50 just before Christmas, which he hasn't paid back (Premise), and yet another $25 in January, which is still unpaid. (Premise) I suppose it's time to face facts: He's never going to pay me back. (Conclusion)

We use inductive reasoning so frequently in everyday life that its nature generally goes unnoticed. Being informed about induction is a bit like being told that we've been speaking prose all our lives. We start drawing perfectly good inferences of this kind (and some klinkers) at a very early age. By age five or six, the use of induction

---

*As well as those experiences we can't have, but might have if we had lived millions of years ago or if, say, we could go into the interior of the sun without being incinerated.

has taught us a great many of the basic truths that guide everyday behavior—for instance, that some foods taste good and some don't, the sun rises every morning and sets every evening, very hot things burn the skin, some people are trustworthy and some aren't, and so on.

The great virtue of inductive reasoning is that it provides us with a way of reasoning to genuinely new beliefs, not just to psychologically new ones that are implicit in what we already know, as in the case of valid deductions. However, this benefit is purchased at the cost of an increase in the possibility of error. As remarked before, the truth of the premises of a deductively valid argument guarantees the truth of its conclusion; but the premises of a perfectly good induction may all be true and yet its conclusion be false. Even the best "inductive leap" may lead us astray, because the patterns noticed in our experiences up to a given point may not turn out to be the exact patterns of the whole universe. This happens all too often in daily life—for example, when a restaurant that has served excellent food many times in the past fails us on a special occasion. But it sometimes happens even in the lofty realm of theoretical science. Physicists, for instance, believed for a long time that asbestos does not conduct electricity—a belief supported by very good, very strong, inductive arguments—but then discovered that all substances, including asbestos, conduct electricity when cooled down close to absolute zero.

Nevertheless, rational people use induction in formulating their ideas about how things are going to turn out, whether in ordinary, everyday circumstances or in the rather special ones scientists bring about in the laboratory. Induction, to paraphrase Winston Churchill's famous remark about democracy, is the worst way to expand one's knowledge except for all of the other ways (guessing, wishful thinking, astrology, and so on).

## 4. DEDUCTIVE VALIDITY AND INVALIDITY

Different arguments may have the same **form**, or **structure**. Here are two arguments that have the same form:

> (1)    1. If it's spring, then the birds are chirping.
>         2. It is spring.
>      ∴3. The birds are chirping.
> (2)    1. If a world government doesn't evolve soon, then wars will continue to occur.
>         2. A world government isn't going to evolve soon.
>      ∴3. Wars will continue to occur.

And here is the form or structure they share:

> 1. If [some sentence] then [a second sentence].
> 2. The first sentence (or a grammatical variant).
> ∴3. The second sentence (or a grammatical variant).

Or, using $A$ and $B$ to stand for the two sentences, respectively:

> 1. If $A$ then $B$.
> 2. $A$.
> ∴3. $B$.

This deductively valid form is traditionally called **modus ponens**.

Now, here is another commonly occurring form, called **modus tollens**, that also is deductively valid:

*Form:*      1. If *A* then *B*.
            2. Not *B*.
          ∴3. Not *A*.

*Example:*    1. If it's spring, then the birds are chirping.
            2. The birds aren't chirping.
          ∴3. It isn't spring.

Here is another commonly occurring deductively valid argument form, usually called **hypothetical syllogism**:

*Form:*      1. If *A* then *B*.
            2. If *B* then *C*.
          ∴3. If *A* then *C*.

*Example:*    1. If we successfully develop nuclear fusion power, then power will become cheap and plentiful.
            2. If power becomes cheap and plentiful, then the economy will flourish.
          ∴3. If we successfully develop nuclear fusion power, then the economy will flourish.

And here is the deductively valid form called **disjunctive syllogism**:*

*Form:*      1. *A* or *B*.
            2. Not *A*.
          ∴3. *B*.

*Example:*    1. Either Dole won in 1996 or Clinton did.
            2. Dole didn't win.
          ∴3. Clinton did.

Finally, here are several argument forms of a different kind (all but the first two are called **syllogisms**):†

*Form:*      1. No *F*'s are *G*'s.
          ∴2. It's false that some *F*'s are *G*'s.

*Example:*    1. No police officers accept bribes.
          ∴2. It's false that some police officers accept bribes.

*Form:*      1. All *F*'s are *G*'s.
          ∴2. If this is an *F*, then this is a *G*.

*Example:*    1. All salamis are tasty.
          ∴2. If this is a salami, then it is tasty.

---

*Strictly speaking, in spite of their names, *disjunctive syllogism* and *hypothetical syllogism* are not syllogisms.

†See the Appendix and also Howard Kahane and Paul Tidman, *Logic and Philosophy*, 8th edition (Belmont, Calif.: Wadsworth, 1998) for additional material on deduction and induction.

*Form:*      1. All *F*'s are *G*'s.
       2. All *G*'s are *H*'s.
  ∴3. All *F*'s are *H*'s.

*Example:*   1. All TV evangelists have high moral standards.
       2. All who have high moral standards live up to those standards.
  ∴3. All TV evangelists live up to high moral standards.

*Form:*      1. All *F*'s are *G*'s.
       2. This is an *F*.
  ∴3. This is a *G*.

*Example:*   1. All elected officials always tell the truth.
       2. Bill Clinton is an elected official.
  ∴3. Bill Clinton always tells the truth.

*Form:*      1. All *F*'s are *G*'s.
       2. No *G*'s are *H*'s.
  ∴3. No *F*'s are *H*'s.

*Example:*   1. All males are chauvinist pigs.
       2. No chauvinist pigs are likeable.
  ∴3. No males are likeable.

*Form:*      1. No *F*'s are *G*'s.
       2. Some *H*'s are *F*'s.
  ∴3. Some *H*'s are not *G*'s.

*Example:*   1. No foreigners can be trusted.
       2. Some newborn babies are foreigners.
  ∴3. Some newborn babies cannot be trusted.

## Deductive Invalidity

Any argument that doesn't have a deductively valid form is said to be **deductively invalid**.\* The number of deductively invalid argument forms is legion, but a few occur so frequently that they've been given names. Here are two examples (to give the flavor):

**Fallacy of denying the antecedent:**
 *Form:*      1. If *A* then *B*.
       2. Not *A*.
  ∴3. Not *B*.

 *Example:*   1. If abortion is murder, then it's wrong.
       2. But abortion isn't murder.
  ∴3. Abortion isn't wrong.

The conclusion doesn't follow: Even supposing abortion isn't murder, it may be wrong for other reasons.

**Fallacy of asserting the consequent:**
 *Form:*      1. If *A* then *B*.
       2. *B*.
  ∴3. *A*.

---

\*A deductively invalid argument may still be a good argument if it is inductively correct. Arguments that have the forms about to be discussed are bad because they are neither deductively valid nor inductively correct.

*Beetle Bailey.* Reprinted by permission of King Features Syndicate, Inc.

*Humorous use of disjunctive syllogism. General Halftrack's reasoning is this: Either the box is too small or we're not running this camp right. But it's false that we're not running this camp right. So the box is too small. Build a bigger one. Just as we often do in daily life, Halftrack omits a premise as understood, namely, the premise that it's false that the camp is not being run right.*

> *Example:*   1. If Reagan is still president, then a liar is now president.
>               2. A liar is now president.
>          ∴. 3. Reagan is still president.

The conclusion doesn't follow: Some other liar may now be president.

## EXERCISE 1-3

Invent deductively valid arguments having the forms *modus ponens*, *modus tollens*, *disjunctive syllogism*, and *hypothetical syllogism*. Then invent arguments having the forms of the fallacies *denying the antecedent* and *asserting the consequent*, and show that they are deductively invalid by explaining how their premises might be true when their conclusions are false.

## 5. INDUCTIVE VALIDITY (CORRECTNESS) AND INVALIDITY (INCORRECTNESS)

As indicated before, we can think of induction as a kind of patterning. Perhaps the simplest form of induction is the one called **induction by enumeration**, previously mentioned. In this form of inductive reasoning, we infer from the fact that all *A*'s observed so far are *B*'s to the conclusion that all *A*'s whatsoever are *B*'s. For example, a study of 100 members of Congress no doubt would show that they all accept campaign contributions from lobbyists intent on influencing legislation, and finding this out would count as good evidence for the inductive conclusion that *all 535* members of Congress accept funds of this kind.

Obviously, some inductions of this kind are better than others and make their conclusions more *probable*. While there are several interesting theories about how to determine the probability of the conclusions of inductive arguments by enumeration, almost all agree on a few points.

*Greater sample size yields greater probability.* The more instances in a sample (the instances observed so far), the greater the probability of a conclusion based on that sample. A sample of 100 members of Congress who accept campaign contributions from lobbyists provides a higher degree of probability that all do than a smaller sample, say, of 50 members. The point is that more of the same sort of evidence doesn't change the conclusion of an induction; rather it changes the degree of probability of that conclusion, and thus changes the strength of belief a rational person should have in it.

*More representative samples yield higher probabilities.* The quality of a sample is even more important than its size. (Indeed, the higher its quality, the smaller a sample needs to be to yield a given degree of probability.) When sampling apples in a barrel, for instance, it won't do just to sample a few from the top (the classic case); after all, rotten apples are more likely to be at the bottom than at the top of a barrel. Samples that neglect possible rotten apples at the bottom of metaphorical barrels are said to be *biased*. Obviously, less biased, more *representative* samples yield higher degrees of probability for the conclusions drawn from them.

*One definite counterexample shoots down an enumerative induction.* The most important reason that inductive reasoning is superior to many other kinds (for example, of the superstitious or the pseudoscientific kinds to be discussed later) is that it does not allow us to pass over evidence that indicates a pet theory is false. For example, if one woman who takes a birth control pill as directed gets pregnant, then no valid enumerative induction about the pill's effectiveness can be drawn. (Note that it still may be possible to draw other kinds of valid inductive inferences, including the statistical kind to be discussed shortly.)

However, it often is hard to be sure that what looks like a counterexample really is one. A woman on birth control pills who becomes pregnant, for instance, may have accidentally neglected to take the pills properly, and we may not be aware of that fact. The moral is that it is risky to reject an enumerative induction on the basis of one counterexample, or even two, unless we are very sure that at least one is a genuine counterexample. But when we are sure, then an enumerative induction in question must be rejected.

## Reasoning by Analogy

Several other kinds of inductive reasoning are very similar to enumerative induction, including reasoning by **analogy**. In one version of this kind of inductive reasoning, we reason from the similarity of two things in several relevant respects to their similarity in another. Thus, if we know that two people have similar tastes in books, art, food, music, and TV programs, and find out that one likes to watch *Mystery!* on public television, we're justified in concluding by analogy that the other probably does also.

The trouble is that every two things resemble each other in an indefinitely large number of ways. Only *relevant* resemblances count in drawing correct analogies. But what makes a resemblance relevant? The answer is background beliefs about how, in general, things hang together. For example, if the stock market rises and falls in concert with ups and downs in the Olympic elk population over several years, only fools are likely to conclude that the two will fluctuate together in the future, because so much background information contradicts this idea. On the other hand, if stocks were to rise and fall over several years in concert with ups and downs in retail sales, we could reason by analogy that the next change in one will produce a similar change in the other. (Of course, given all of the other factors relevant to stock market prices, an induction of the kind just described would have to be assigned a very modest degree of probability.)

In another version of analogical induction, we reason from the fact that all examined items of a certain kind have a particular property to the conclusion that a particular as yet unexamined item of that kind will be found to have that property. Finding out that, say, 100 members of Congress accept money from lobbyists, we can conclude by this kind of analogy that a certain other member probably also does so.

Analogical inductions are much safer, and thus have a higher degree of probability, than their enumerative counterparts, because they have much weaker conclusions. Concluding, for example, that a particular member of Congress accepts money from lobbyists is a much weaker, hence safer, prediction than that all members of Congress do so.

## Statistical Induction

When drawing a sample from a population, we often find that not all of the examined *A*'s are *B*'s, so that we cannot draw a valid enumerative induction. But having found that a certain percentage of the *A*'s have the property in question, we can conclude by a **statistical induction** that the same percentage of the total population of *A*'s have that property. Having found, say, that 480 of the first 1,000 observed tosses of a given coin land face up, we can conclude that 48 percent of all of the tosses with that coin will land face up (thus learning, incidentally, that the coin probably is slightly biased in favor of tails, as many coins are).

Of course, what was said about the quality and, hence, the degree of probability of enumerative inductions also applies to the statistical variety. The larger the sample employed and the more representative it is, the higher the degree of probability of a statistical induction based on that sample.

## Higher-Level Induction

More general, **higher-level inductions** can be used to evaluate those that are less general. For example, we use higher-level induction when we conclude that an automobile engine eventually will wear out or need to be repaired, even though it has run perfectly for 100,000 miles. We overrule a low-level conclusion telling us that because the car has run perfectly so far, it will do so forever, by appeal to a higher-level, more general, induction such as this one: All mechanical devices with moving parts checked up on so far have eventually worn out or needed to be repaired; so *very* probably this particular mechanical device (the engine in question) also eventually will need to be repaired.

More general inferences, based on larger samples about more kinds of items, usually have higher degrees of probability than do those that are less general. That is why an enumerative induction about a particular automobile is overruled by a more general one about many mechanical devices. (There are, in fact, even higher-level reasons for tossing out this low-level induction by enumeration—for example, scientific inductions concerning basic principles of physics and chemistry having to do with the effects of friction.)

## Causal Connections

When we reason inductively, we often are looking for explanations, or **causes**. For instance, early investigators of the connection between cigarette smoking and lung cancer, emphysema, and heart disease wanted to determine by means of statistical induction whether smoking *causes* these death-dealing diseases. They found that smokers contract these diseases much more frequently than nonsmokers, and heavy smokers more than light. That is, they discovered a statistical link between smoking cigarettes and contracting these diseases. Finding no higher-level evidence to the contrary, they concluded that cigarette smoking does indeed cause these life-threatening illnesses. (That some people smoke like chimneys and never come down with these illnesses doesn't prove the contrary, but it does suggest that part of the cause of these diseases must be some other, very likely genetic, factor.*)

The inductive patterns discussed in this chapter are relatively neat and simple. Enumerative induction is an example. But in daily life, and in particular in scientific theorizing, inductive reasoning often is much more complicated, and may involve mathematical reasoning (a kind of deductive reasoning) as well. We believe cigarette smoking causes lung cancer, for example, not just because a certain percentage of those who smoke get that deadly disease but also because the percentage of those who do not smoke and get lung cancer is much lower than for those who do smoke. It is the comparison of the two groups that proves the point. (See pages 83–84 for more on this point.)

## Exercise 1-4

1. What is the difference between an *induction by enumeration* and *analogical reasoning*? Provide an example (not mentioned in the text) of each.

2. Explain in your own words what the difference is between an *induction by enumeration* and a *statistical induction*. Provide an example (not mentioned in the text) of a valid statistical induction.

3. What is meant by saying that an inference is a *higher-level induction*? Provide an example (not mentioned in the text).

## Are Argument Validity and Cogency Relative?

Having just presented three standards of cogent reasoning and having explained the nature of valid deduction and induction, perhaps we need to mention several recently voiced ideas about logic and good reasoning. According to these trendy ways of looking at the topic, what counts as good reasoning is "culturally relative," or "gender relative," or even (popular among students) "individually relative." We hear talk of "feminine logic," supposedly different from the "male logic" taught in logic classes (often by female logicians, but let that pass), and of "black intelligence," different from the "Eurocentric" variety foisted on us by white males, as though what makes reasoning good differs from group to group, race to race, or one sex to the other. We all too often hear students say "That may well be true for you, but it isn't true for me"; and academics talk of "Aristotelian linear reasoning," as opposed to a more "intuitive" type of reasoning; and so on.

But there is no truth to these new ideas about what constitutes good reasoning. It is the height of folly to conclude, say, that *modus ponens* is not valid or that arguments

---

*See the section in the Appendix concerning necessary and sufficient conditions.

"How can we know that no one can win a nuclear war unless we try it and see?"

*Most readers of* Playboy *magazine no doubt smiled when they read the caption under this cartoon. But few would have been able to explain the nature of the folly in the respondent's reasoning. He seems to assume that the only way to establish or justify factual beliefs is by low-level induction by enumeration (or perhaps by statistical induction)—trying out several nuclear wars to see whether any nation can win them. He overlooks higher-level induction (plus deductive reasoning), which many of us use to conclude that the destruction caused by an all-out nuclear war would leave neither side a winner.*

having the form of the fallacy *asserting the consequent* are valid. Think, for example, what it means to seriously assert that all human beings have a right to life and then in the next breath, equally seriously, to claim that a particular human being, Smith, has no right to life. What sense is there in first saying that if Jones has been to China, then he's been to Asia, and then asserting that he has indeed been to China but not to Asia. Yet accepting reasonings that violate the standards of deductive logic means precisely accepting some sorts of contradictory assertions or other, because the point of the principles of valid deduction (including the valid principles of mathematics) is to assure that we do not contradict ourselves when we reason from one thing to another. (That's why, to take just one of a thousand examples, double entry bookkeeping works.)

Similarly, what reason could there be for violating the standards of good inductive reasoning—for denying what experience teaches us? That a large majority of the scientists who laid the groundwork in physics, chemistry, and biology were white males is totally irrelevant to the truth of their basic ideas and theories. *The way the world works does not differ depending on the race or sex of those trying to discover the way the world works!*

That is why there simply is no truth whatsoever to the idea that standards of good reasoning differ from group to group, male to female, or person to person. There is, however, a good deal of truth to three somewhat different ideas. One is that self-interest and narrowmindedness frequently lead to reasoning that violates the standards of good reasoning; another is that self-interest often motivates us to neglect the values or interests of others, even when we share those values, so that some groups or individuals find their interests systematically ignored; the third is that the values and interests of one individual or group frequently conflict with those of another individual or group. In families where both parents work, for example, husbands notoriously tend to paper over their failure to share household and child-rearing duties; in the business world, high executives, while asserting their belief in equal rights for all, frequently overlook the ways in which women, or blacks, are passed over for corporate advancement; on Wall Street, rich investors care more for their own profits than for the interests of low-wage workers.

In all of these cases, the problem is not with the principles of good reasoning. It is with the fallacious nature of the ways in which these principles sometimes are employed—for example, when Western historians neglect evidence about the contributions of non-Western peoples; or with the use of different values in the premises from which reasoning starts—for instance, when male chauvinists reason from their belief in the inferior value of women compared to men; or with the self-interestedly motivated neglect of the interests of others—for example, when rich, well-fed officials ignore the plight of the poor and hungry at the bottom of the economic pecking order.

Those who champion other sorts of "logics" than the standard variety thus may well be mistaken in their target. They attack the principles of good reasoning rather than the failure of their opponents to correctly employ these perfectly good (indeed the only perfectly good) standards of reasoning, or rather than their opponents' differing political, or moral standards.

A good deal more will be said in later chapters on these matters. For now, the point is just that we must distinguish the principles of good reasoning, which are the same for all, from the ways in which these principles are employed (sometimes fallaciously), and from the differing values that enter into the premises of different reasonings.

## 6. FALLACIOUS REASONING: HOW REASONING GOES WRONG

We said earlier that to be cogent, reasoning must satisfy three conditions. It must (1) start with justified premises; (2) include all relevant information; and (3) be valid. Reasoning that fails to satisfy all three of these criteria is said to be **fallacious**.

Consider, for instance, the following argument overheard in a restaurant:

> We don't yet know who committed this senseless and vicious crime, but we will know some day. The wheels of justice may sometimes turn slowly, but eventually, sooner or later, vicious criminals get caught and punished.

Cast into textbook form, the relevant portion of the argument reads something like this:

1. Sooner or later, all vicious criminals get caught and punished.
∴2. Sooner or later, the person who committed this particular vicious crime will be caught and punished.

Put this way, the argument clearly is valid, indeed deductively valid: If something is true of all things of a certain kind, then it must be true of any particular thing of that kind. Nevertheless, those who are convinced by this argument reason fallaciously, because there is good reason for doubting its premise that all vicious criminals get caught sooner or later.* Let's call fallacies like this one by the name **questionable premise**.

Now consider the following headline on an American Automobile Association (AAA) advertisement:

OVER 23,000,000 CAN'T BE WRONG!
YOU OWE IT TO YOURSELF TO INVESTIGATE!

(The figure 23,000,000 refers to the number of AAA members.)

This time the error is not that of *questionable premise*. There were indeed over 23,000,000 AAA members. But the headline suppresses the fact (not mentioned anywhere in the body of the advertisement) that a large majority of motorists, lots more than 23,000,000, were not auto association members. Readers taken in by this advertisement who knew this suppressed fact, or should have suspected it, were guilty of fallacious reasoning. And let's say that those who neglect evidence in this way are guilty of the fallacy of **suppressed** (or **neglected**) **evidence**.

Finally, in a lighter vein, here is a portion of a discussion between a certain party and his aunt:

*How:* You mean you take this horoscope business seriously?
*Aunt:* Yes, of course. Don't you see how today's horoscope fits you to a T?
*How:* Yes, but . . .
*Aunt:* No buts. There must be something to horoscopes if this one fits you so well.

---

*This is true, at any rate, with respect to those who have paid the slightest attention to what goes on in the world. People who go through life with their eyes closed are another matter. If they accept the goody-goody idea that vicious criminals always get caught, they will not be guilty of fallacious reasoning in this case, but they still will have reasoned from a false premise to a false conclusion.

The form of Aunt's reasoning is this:

1. This horoscope fits you to a T.
2. Horoscopes in general must be accurate.

Put this way, it's clear Aunt's reasoning was fallacious. That one horoscope fits one individual on one occasion lends only the most insignificant amount of support to the idea that all, or even most, do so. A single instance rarely is sufficient to justify a generality, even though many such instances often do. (They do, for example, when we reason from the fact that in a great many cases sugar has sweetened coffee—and never has failed to do so—to the general conclusion that it will in every case.) So Aunt's argument doesn't provide sufficient evidence to justify acceptance of its conclusion. Her reasoning is *invalid*. So let's call the fallacy she has committed that of **invalid inference**.

A great deal more will be said about fallacious reasoning in Chapters 3, 4, and 5.

## EXERCISE 1-5

1. Invent an argument that, were you to accept it as cogent, would make you guilty of the fallacy of *questionable premise*. Explain why acceptance of this argument would make you guilty of this fallacy.

2. Do the same with respect to the fallacy of *suppressed evidence*.

3. Do the same with respect to the fallacy of *invalid inference*.

## SUMMARY OF CHAPTER 1

Reasoning is the essential ingredient in solving life's problems. This chapter discusses some of the fundamentals of good reasoning and presents an overview of the material to be covered later on the topic of reasoning well in everyday life.

1. Reasoning can be cast into *arguments*, which consist of one or more *premises* (reasons) offered in support of a *conclusion*. In real life (as opposed to in textbooks), arguments usually are not labeled and divided from surrounding rhetoric, nor are their premises and conclusions neatly specified. But clues generally are given. Words such as *because*, *since*, and *for* usually signal premises, and *hence*, *therefore*, and *so* conclusions. Remember, though, that not all groups of sentences form arguments. They may be anecdotes or other types of exposition or explanation.

2. Reasoning is either *cogent* (good) or *fallacious* (bad). Cogent reasoning must satisfy three criteria: It must (1) start with *justified* (*warranted*, *believable*) premises; (2) include all likely relevant information; and (3) be *valid* (*correct*).

3. There are two basic kinds of valid reasoning: *deductive* and *inductive*. The fundamental property of a *deductively valid* argument is this: If its premises are true, then its conclusion must be true also. This is so because the conclusion of a deductively valid argument already is contained in its premises, although usually implicitly, not explicitly. (Note that a deductively valid argument may have false premises. What makes it valid is that *if* its premises are true, then its conclusion must be also.)

Unlike deductively valid arguments, those that are *inductively valid (correct, strong)* have conclusions that go beyond the claims made by their premises, projecting patterns stated in the premises onto additional cases.

4. Different arguments may have the same form, or structure. *Modus ponens*, *modus tollens*, *hypothetical syllogism*, and so on, are deductively valid argument forms. *Asserting the consequent* and *denying the antecedent* are deductively *in*valid argument forms.

5. There are several kinds of valid, or correct, inductions. One is *induction by enumeration*, in which we infer from the fact that all *A*'s observed so far are *B*'s to the conclusion that all *A*'s whatsoever are *B*'s.

   In general, the larger or the more representative a sample, the greater the probability of an induction based on it. Note that one definite counterexample invalidates an induction. (But we have to be sure that it really is a counterexample.)

   *Analogical reasoning* is very much like induction by enumeration, the chief difference being that analogies yield conclusions about just one case (which is why they have higher degrees of probability than corresponding enumerative inductions), whereas enumerative inductions typically concern a great many.

   *Statistical inductions* also are similar to the enumerative variety, but move from the fact that a certain percentage of a sample has a given property to the conclusion that the same percentage in the population at large has that property.

   We can use more general, *higher-level* inductions to correct, or overrule, lower-level ones. If experience shows that all mechanical devices eventually wear out or need to be repaired, then it isn't reasonable to conclude that a particular engine will not, even though it has run perfectly for 100,000 miles.

   Inductive reasoning often is used to discover *causes*, as in the case of the statistical induction linking cigarette smoking and various life-threatening diseases.

   Note that there is no truth to claims about there being such things as "feminine logic" or "Eurocentric logic." Good reasoning does not differ from male to female, black to white, or in any way tied to ethnicity.

6. An argument is *fallacious* if either (1) its premises are not warranted; (2) relevant information has been passed over; or (3) the claims made by its premises do not justify accepting its conclusion (so that the argument is *invalid*). When a premise is not warranted, the fallacy is said to be that of *questionable premise*; when information has been overlooked, that of *suppressed (neglected) evidence*; when the argument is not valid, that of *invalid inference*.

*Calvin and Hobbes* by Bill Watterson. Copyright 1992 Universal Press Syndicate.
Reprinted with permission.

*Calvin is no match for Miss Wormwood, who easily reads between the lines of Calvin's attempt at ingratiation.*

*Truth is more of a stranger than fiction.*
— Mark Twain

*Every man is encompassed by a cloud of comforting convictions, which move with him like flies on a summer day.*
— Bertrand Russell

*The pure and simple truth is rarely pure and never simple.*
—Oscar Wilde

*Chapter*

# 2

# BACKGROUND BELIEFS AND WORLD VIEWS

Recall that in Chapter 1, we characterized cogent reasoning in terms of three conditions: the validity of connections between premises and conclusions; the believability of premises; and the discovery and use of relevant information. Clearly, satisfaction of the last two of these three conditions requires the employment of background beliefs. That is why it often is true that the most important task in evaluating an argument for cogency is to bring one's background beliefs to bear.

Consider, for example, the argument frequently heard in the early 1980s that AIDS is essentially a gay plague inflicted on homosexuals as punishment for their perverse sexual conduct. The key premise of this argument was that AIDS can be transmitted sexually only via homosexual conduct, a premise that was supported by the evidence that in America virtually all of those reported early on to have the disease were indeed homosexuals. But those with good background information did not accept this argument. For one thing, they knew that in other places around the world—for instance, in Haiti and parts of Africa—large numbers of heterosexuals also had contracted AIDS via sexual behavior. And for another, those familiar with some of the basic scientific ideas concerning disease had theoretical (which means higher-level inductive) reasons for believing that AIDS could be transmitted via heterosexual behavior, as are syphilis, hepatitis B, herpes, and so on.

The point is that contrary to the old saying, ignorance is *not* bliss. It just renders us incapable of intelligently evaluating claims, premises, arguments, and other sorts of rhetoric we all are subject to every day. When evaluating arguments and issues, we can't bring relevant beliefs to bear if we don't have any, or if what we believe is off the mark.

In daily life, the term *belief* is used in several ways. Sometimes this word is used rather narrowly, to refer just to what is accepted on faith ("I believe in God."), sometimes more broadly, to refer to anything whatever accepted as true ("I believe snow is white."). It also can be used in order to distinguish what is less firmly held ("I believe Dole is a better candidate than Clinton, but I may be wrong.") from what we claim to *know* ("I was there; I know she did it."). To believe something, in the sense intended here when we speak of background beliefs, is to accept it as true, or very likely true, or, in the case of value beliefs, to have it as a value or conviction ("I believe Nirvana's music is better than Pearl Jam's."). In this sense, all of the things, taken together, that we accept as true, or very likely true, or that we hold as values, make up our total package of background beliefs.

## 1. KINDS OF BACKGROUND BELIEFS

Background beliefs can be divided in many different ways, one important way being into beliefs about *matters of fact* and beliefs about *values*. It is a factual question, for example, whether capital punishment is practiced in every society (it isn't); it is a question of values whether capital punishment is morally justified (is it?).

In dealing with most social or political issues, it is important to separate claims that are about matters of fact from those concerning values, because these two different sorts of claims are defended, or justified, in different ways. The statement, for example, that a given state has a death penalty is proved true, or false, by an examination of relevant government records; the judgment that capital punishment is, or isn't, morally justified as the punishment for heinous crimes is determined by bringing to bear an accepted moral code, or subjective intuitions.*

Background beliefs also can be divided into those that are *true* and (unfortunately) those that are *false*. Someone who believes, for example, that capital punishment exists as a practice in every society has a false belief; those who believe that every society punishes murderers in one way or another has a belief that is true. The point of regularly testing our background beliefs in terms of our experiences and of what we learn from others is precisely to weed out background beliefs that are false.

Another important way in which background beliefs divide is in terms of how firmly they are or should be held. We feel completely sure, completely confident, of some beliefs—for example, that the sun will rise tomorrow; less sure, but still quite confident, of others —for example, that the United States will still be in existence in the year 2020; and a good deal less sure, but still mildly confident, of others—for example, that we won't get killed some day in an auto accident. The trick is to believe firmly what should be believed, given the evidence, and believe less firmly, or not at all, what is less well supported by evidence. The trouble, of course, is that, for one psychological reason or

---

*Philosophers and others disagree seriously concerning the question whether there are such things as *objective* moral principles that all clear-minded, rational individuals are bound to see as correct, or whether moral right and wrong is a matter of subjective opinion—of feelings that can, and perhaps do, differ from person to person. More will be said on the topic of values in Chapter 8.

another, we often believe what we have no business believing. Think of the millions of people who believe in astrology, or in the truth of everything they hear on the evening TV news, or in the pristine purity of the human soul.

There are, of course, indefinitely many other ways in which background beliefs can be divided. Perhaps one other important way needs to be mentioned here, namely, the degree of generality of what is believed. Some beliefs are about *particular* things or events; some deal with matters of a more *general* nature. The belief that a particular pot of water boiled when it was heated to 212°F is particular. The belief that water always boils at that temperature is general and that all fluids boil at some temperature or other is even more general.

These examples bring to mind the fact that some beliefs are more *precise* than others, as the belief that water boils at 212°F is more precise than that all fluids boil at some temperature or other. It often is useful to know and act on less-than-precise facts, in particular when more precise ones are not available or when great precision is not required. It also is important to notice that beliefs that are not 100 percent true may be close enough to being true under ordinary circumstances to make it sensible to regard them as completely true in everyday life. Water, for example, doesn't always boil at precisely 212°F, but for those of us who don't live at very high elevations, it's useful to regard this as a good enough approximation of the truth.

Of course, most of what we believe or know is not of great moment in the grand scheme of things. That is why, on the whole, very general, high level beliefs tend to be the most important. These very general background beliefs, including our **philosophical beliefs**,* make up our **world views** or **philosophies**. Because they are so general, these beliefs influence how we deal with every problem, every argument, encountered in everyday life. *World views* spell out our most important beliefs about what the world is like, about our moral convictions, about which reasoning principles are acceptable, and so on. Although most of these beliefs are general (as just stated)—for example, that murder always is morally wrong, that there is some good in virtually all human beings, or that we all die sooner or later—not all are. Belief in a deity, for example—certainly an important part of every believer's world view—is a particular belief.

More general beliefs usually (that is, generally!) are more important than beliefs that are particular, or less general, because they tell us about a wider range of cases and thus are more useful in everyday life. Believing that it rarely rains in July in Los Angeles, for instance, clearly is more useful than believing merely that it won't rain, say, on July 16, 1999. That is why most of the important beliefs in one's world view are general, and also why most important scientific pronouncements are general, indeed often extremely general. Newton's laws, for example, don't tell us just about apples falling from trees, or even just about items of all kinds falling toward the earth. They also tell us about the motion of the earth around the sun; indeed, about the motion of all planets around the sun, about how tides rise and fall, and, in fact, about the motions of all objects whatsoever. That is why it is so important, and useful, to expand our world views to contain at least a few modestly knowledgeable beliefs about important scientific theories; for example, about the evolution of all life on earth.

---

*Including religious beliefs in the case of those who have religious convictions.

> Knowledge not renewed, quickly becomes ignorance.
>
> —Peter Drucker

## 2. INSUFFICIENTLY GROUNDED BELIEFS

Most of us have strongly held beliefs about a great many controversial issues, and so tend to respond automatically to arguments about these matters. We feel confident that we know whether marijuana or cocaine should be legalized; whether a single-payer, nonprofit health plan would be better than the for-profit HMO systems that are currently mushrooming into existence; whether this candidate or that is more likely to do well if elected to office; and so on. We hold these beliefs, often very strongly, even though a good deal of the time we have insufficient background knowledge and have engaged in too little thought to be able to intelligently support our beliefs or defend them against informed objections. What, for example, do we usually know about candidates running for seats in the United States House of Representatives? (In 1996, a significant number of voters did not even know the names of both major party candidates for Congressional seats in their districts; fewer still could name both candidates for state legislatures in their districts. Could you?) Clearly, then, expanding our stock of background beliefs is vital if we are to improve our reasoning about important, to say nothing of relatively trivial, matters.

This is particularly true with respect to those basic background beliefs that make up our world views. World views are like lenses that cause us to see the world in a particular way, or like filters through which we process all new ideas and information. Reasoning based on a grossly inaccurate or shallow world view tends to yield grossly inaccurate, inappropriate, or self-defeating conclusions (except when we're just plain lucky), no matter how smart we otherwise may be. Sometimes the harm is relatively minor (gamblers wasting a few bucks playing "lucky" lottery combinations), but at other times it can have seriously harmful consequences (jury members in the O. J. Simpson murder trial who did not understand, and thus could not reasonably evaluate, the scientific evidence they heard concerning DNA—evidence that one TV talk show host referred to as "scientific mumbo jumbo").

Obviously, then, we need to examine our background beliefs, in particular, those that make up our world views, for consistency and believability, and need to amend them so as to square with newly acquired information. Believers in "close encounters of the third kind" (to mention a relatively trivial issue) might carefully consider the reasons scientists provide for their conclusion that there is no good evidence supporting the existence of these alleged encounters; to take a much more serious issue, those who believe in the superiority of capitalism as compared to socialism, or vice versa, might consider the reasons and evidence provided by those who believe otherwise.

The point is that acquiring a good supply of background beliefs is not just a matter of filling up one's "tank" with gallons of facts. It is at least equally important to improve one's existing stock of beliefs by weeding out those that experience proves to be false, to sharpen vague beliefs, and to replace crude beliefs with those that are more sophisticated—beliefs that penetrate more deeply into the complexities of life and the world.

# 3. Are Unexamined World Views Worth Having?

As we grow up from childhood into adults, we tend to absorb the beliefs and standards of those in the world around us. Our world views grow out of family values, religious training, peer group attitudes, cultural heritages, and the like. They tend to be the most deeply ingrained and most resistant to amendment of all of our background beliefs. They become so much a part of us that we often appeal to them without consciously realizing we have done so. They are so intricately woven into the fabric of our belief systems that we often find it hard to isolate and examine individual strands. And when we do examine them, our natural tendency is to reaffirm them without thought and to disparage conflicting claims and evidence, quickly dismissing evidence that might count against them.

Consider the claim in a recent article that the government should increase funding for public school education so that all students, rich or poor, are provided a high-quality education. This idea fits in nicely with several commonly held background beliefs—for example, that the continued freedom we enjoy in democratic countries depends on our having an educated citizenry; that those who are well off have an obligation to provide aid to those who are not; that democratic societies should provide equal opportunities, and therefore equal education, for everyone; and so on. Readers holding these beliefs will be inclined to accept the idea that we should increase funding for public schools because it dovetails nicely with important parts of their world views, and they may be resistant to different ideas about the matter.

Other readers, of course, may evaluate the thesis about funding for public education in terms of different background beliefs. Many successful people have worked very hard, sometimes against great odds, to accumulate their knowledge, their wealth, and their power. And they often come from the same educational background as do failures. They thus wonder why they should be expected to spend even more money on people who haven't taken advantage of the educational system. After all, they might say, we all have an equal opportunity to do well in this country if only we try hard enough. Besides, some students are just smarter or more highly motivated than others, and no amount of money will change that. Those who have these beliefs as part of their world views may tend to dismiss the claim that we should increase spending for public education without taking seriously the arguments in its favor.

Socrates is said to have claimed that the unexamined life is not worth living. By the same token, an unexamined world view is not likely to be worth holding, because it may well contain little more than the passive accumulation of the ideas and prejudices of others. Examining world views allows us to take control of our lives by actively sorting out our fundamental beliefs, testing them against ideas and information that point to conclusions contrary to what we already believe, and making whatever revisions are indicated in the light of what we have learned. Doing this helps us to become our own person rather than just a follower of others. The trouble, illustrated by the

---

Those who do not remember the past are condemned to relive it.

—George Santayana

At certain moments, . . . athletes have feelings of floating and weightlessness. Sometimes, in fact, they even have out-of-body experiences. Now we would like to consider the possibility that the athlete is literally able to suspend himself in midair. In the earlier chapters we discussed the athletes' subjective feelings that they were floating or outside themselves. But is there an objective reality involved, something that can be verified by others? We think that there is. We have collected many statements by sportswriters, coaches, and other observers that attest to the fact that some athletes actually can, for brief moments, remain suspended in the air. Basketball players and dancers, especially, seem to demonstrate this amazing ability.

—*Human Behavior* (March 1979)

*Clearly, if better evidence could have been obtained to prove this kind of levitation, it would have been—first, because really proving it would have created a sensation, and second, because, if true, it would have been so easy to obtain proof (motion pictures would do the trick). Since they didn't provide this proof, it is reasonable to suppose that they couldn't. As the basic laws of physics suggest, individuals cannot suspend themselves in midair, even for the briefest moment.*

school funding example just discussed, is that there is a natural human tendency (discussed further in Chapter 6) to hang on to old, comfortable beliefs in the face of disconfirming evidence or reasons, and even to ignore or deride such evidence. To reason cogently, we need to resist these natural human tendencies.

It is worth noting here that widespread failure to revise world views often results in serious political and social unrest and injustice. E. M. Forster captures this poignantly in his novel *A Passage to India*, in which he depicts intense conflicts in colonial India between English masters and their conquered Indian subjects. Believing themselves socially and racially superior, the English relegate the Indians to subordinate positions, never allowing them equality under the British Raj. The insensitivity of the British to the plight of their subjects is met with resentment, distrust, anger, and threats of violent retaliation by the Indians. (To make matters worse, the Indians are divided from each other by differing religious and cultural beliefs.) Very few of the British or Indians Forster depicts ever revise their biases and prejudices in the light of new information—for instance, in the light of obvious evidence about the competence of individual Indians, or the obvious and glaring prejudice of several English officials. The novel makes a compelling case for a widespread reexamination of world views and other background beliefs if human beings are to arrive at a peaceful, nonexploitative coexistence on planet Earth.

# Exercise 2-1

1. It often is said that the regular portrayal of violence on TV is a major cause of youth violence in the United States and that therefore laws should be passed limiting the amount of violence in TV programs. What sorts of background

---

*Here is a Japanese bar association official, Koji Yanase (quoted in* Newsweek, *February 26, 1996), explaining why there are half as many lawyers in his country as there are in the Greater Washington [D.C.] area alone:*

---

If an American is hit on the head by a ball at the ballpark, he sues. If a Japanese person is hit on the head he says, "It's my honor. It's my fault. I shouldn't have been standing there."

---

beliefs might be relevant in evaluating this claim intelligently? Bring your own background beliefs to bear on this issue and argue either for or against such laws. (Be brief. We're just in Chapter 2.)

2. A while back, we mentioned some of the background beliefs often brought to bear in evaluating the claim that we should increase spending for public education. Which of the background beliefs mentioned there do you hold? Do you feel confident about them after carefully thinking about them in the light of other ideas?

3. Find at least one item in the mass media (a newspaper or magazine article or a television program) that seems to be based on a world view contrary to the one you yourself hold. Explain your choice.

4. Find at least one item in the mass media that reflects a typically American point of view you happen to share, and explain what makes it typically American. (This is not as easy to do as it sounds. Recalling the short discussion of E. M. Forster's novel may help prod your memory.)

5. Describe a situation in which you changed your mind on some more or less fundamental belief, and explain what convinced you to do so. (This is a very difficult question for many people to answer, another bit of evidence for the fact that much of what goes on in the accumulation and emendation of important background beliefs happens only on the edge of consciousness.)

## EXERCISE 2-2

Here are the first two paragraphs from a George Will newspaper column (May 25, 1994) on President Clinton's record during his first four months in office:

> An administration defining itself by thousands of actions is like a pointillist painting: One must stand back to see the pattern. The Clinton administration's emerging self-portrait is not a pretty picture, but it is becoming a clear one. It is a picture of an aggressive and comprehensive power grab.
>
> Under the "motor voter" law, states are required to allow people to register to vote while applying for a driver's license or at welfare agencies. People who will get registered only at such places are apt to be disposed to vote for a giving government—for Democrats. [His point, then, is that Democratic party support

for the motor voter law was motivated by crass party politics and isn't justified on its merits.]

&ast;1. One way to evaluate a passage such as this one is to try to discern underlying background beliefs, so as to determine what you must believe in order to accept the writer's reasoning. What sort of background beliefs seem to underpin Will's argument in the above passage?

2. Do you find these background beliefs congenial? Do they fit in well with your own beliefs? Why, or why not?

## Exercise 2-3

How do the ideas expressed in the following excerpt from an essay by British philosopher Bertrand Russell compare with those in your own world view and other background beliefs?

> The aesthetic indictment of industrialism is perhaps the least serious. A much more serious feature is the way in which it forces men, women, and children to live a life against instinct, unnatural, unspontaneous, artificial. Where industry is thoroughly developed, men are deprived of the sight of green fields and the smell of earth after rain; they are cooped together in irksome proximity, surrounded by noise and dirt, compelled to spend many hours a day performing some utterly uninteresting and monotonous mechanical task. Women are, for the most part, obliged to work in factories, and to leave to others the care of their children. The children themselves, if they are preserved from work in the factories, are kept at work in school, with an intensity that is especially damaging to the best brains. The result of this life against instinct is that industrial populations tend to be listless and trivial, in constant search of excitement, delighted by a murder, and still more delighted by a war.

Russell's essay, by the way, appeared in the June 1921 issue of the *Atlantic Monthly*. (The more things change, the more they remain the same?)

## 4. Reading Between the Lines

Someone with a reasonably accurate world view and a wealth of background facts often can get more information from a statement or argument than it explicitly—or even implicitly—contains. Doing this is called **reading between the lines** and often is the essential ingredient in assessing political rhetoric and (interestingly) advertisements.

Take the Bufferin ad that states, "No regular aspirin product reduces fever better." Reading between the lines of this ad, we should conclude that Bufferin does *not* reduce fever better than some competing products, because if it did, the ad would make that stronger claim ("Bufferin reduces fever better than any other aspirin product")

---

A wise person hears one word and understands two.

—Jewish proverb

rather than the weaker one that none reduces fever better. The point is that our own background beliefs should lead us to expect an advertisement to make the strongest claim possible and thus lead us to conclude that a less strong claim is made because stronger claims would be false.

Reading between the lines is the linguistic equivalent of "sizing up" other people—for example, of gleaning information about their beliefs or likely actions from their overt behavior or way of saying something. A good poker player, for instance, looks for signs of bluffing—some players systematically signal a bluff by increasing chatter or by nervous behavior; others do so by feigning lack of concern. Similarly, intelligent voters try to size up political candidates by looking for nonverbal clues and by reading between the lines of campaign rhetoric. (More will be said about campaign rhetoric in Chapter 7.)

Reading between the lines often requires great sophistication or subtle reasoning, but sometimes it just requires adding or subtracting a few figures. The following passage (from *Inquiry* magazine, October 15, 1979) illustrates the point:

> Consider the state of agriculture between the Civil War and World War I, a period of immense growth in the American economy. Agriculture shared in that growth: The number of farms tripled, the number of acres of farmland doubled, the net farm income increased more than fourfold. Despite this growth, two stark figures stand out. Farm population decreased from 60 percent to 35 percent of the national population, and agriculture's share of the national income dropped from 31 percent to 22 percent. In other words, agriculture did not keep pace with the rest of the economy.

Interesting figures. But by doing a little calculating, we can come up with two additional interesting statistics. First, the average farm, contrary to what one might think, seems to have decreased in size during the period in question (figure out why). And second, while lots of farmers must have gone broke, those who remained seem to have improved their financial position compared to nonfarm workers, contrary to the claim of the article (again, figure out why).

## 5. TWO VITAL KINDS OF BACKGROUND BELIEFS

Among the extremely important background beliefs are the ones having to do with the fundamental nature of human nature. Indeed, these beliefs constitute a vital part of everyone's world view. Good theories about human nature—the way people are likely to behave as opposed to how we wish they would—are crucial in applying what we know to the problems encountered in everyday life, whether of a personal or a social nature. When can we trust our friends? Is an instructor to be believed who says that students are graded solely on the quality of their exams and not on agreement with the instructor's personal opinions? Will people be sufficiently motivated to work diligently under a socialistic system? Are a large majority of elected officials motivated by selfish interests that frequently override their sense of duty to those who have elected them?

Fortunately, we don't have to start constructing theories about human nature from scratch, since other people, including some of the great writers (Shakespeare, Aristotle, Darwin, Freud), have been at the task for some time now. (Of course, tapping these sources has its risks. Freud, for instance, had some way-off-target ideas on the subject to go along with some extremely penetrating ones.) But even common everyday sayings contain a mother lode of wisdom. Blood *is* thicker than water, and power *does* tend to corrupt, even if it is doubtful that the female of the species is any more vain than the male.*

Thoughts about the accuracy and truthfulness of information sources constitute a second vital kind of background belief. As with computers, so also with the human mind: "Garbage in, garbage out." We therefore need constantly to reassess the reliability of important information sources, in particular, television, newspapers, magazines, the Internet, teachers (!), and other alleged experts. Under what conditions are these sources likely to provide truthful or, at least, sensible information or opinions? When are they likely even to possess the truth, much less be motivated to tell it to us straight? When are they likely to be prejudiced in ways that may cloud their judgment? We can't assume automatically that a source is reliable without some *reason* for believing this. As lamented a while back, many people seem to think that if they read it in print or hear it on the TV evening news, then it must be true. Sophisticated reasoners, however, realize that these information sources do not always furnish "the truth, the whole truth, and nothing but the truth"; they don't necessarily provide us with "All the news that's fit to print" (the *New York Times* motto), instead sometimes shaving matters either out of ignorance or from self-serving motives. Intelligent viewers of the scene thus try to determine when these sources are likely to be reliable and when not. That is why a whole chapter in this text, Chapter 11, deals with the reliability of the media and another chapter, Chapter 12, with public textbooks as information sources.

## 6. Science to the Rescue

The mention of Darwin and Freud a while back brings to mind the central place that science plays in modern life and in the construction of accurate stocks of background beliefs—in particular in the formulation of sensible world views. Although no information source is absolutely reliable, and no theory exempt from at least a small measure of doubt, the most reliable, the most accurate information comes from the well-established sciences of physics, chemistry, biology, and, to a lesser extent, from psychology, the social sciences, and the applied sciences such as engineering.† The

---

*Of course, we must apply these saying in an intelligent manner. Sometimes it is indeed wise to look before you leap, but at other times, those who hesitate are as good as lost. Wisdom consists in part in knowing one sort of time from the other.

†History has generally been classified as a discipline in the humanities, but more and more it counts as a science: Historical theories disconfirmed by evidence tend to get tossed out; the principles of other disciplines—for example, of the social and biological sciences—are appealed to in the evaluation of evidence; historians who suppress evidence lose standing among others in the field; and so on. (In Nazi Germany and in Stalin's Soviet Union, scientists were restricted in what they could do and say with respect to certain politically sensitive topics; for instance, concerning race in Germany and agriculture in the Soviet Union. They were expected to adhere to theories in these areas forced on them by political agencies. The result was "science" that failed to gain acceptance in any scientific communities. There are still authoritarian countries—for example, China and Singapore—in which economists and political scientists are not free to pursue the truth wherever it may lead them. But virtually every society encourages unfettered research in the physical sciences.)

scientific enterprise is an organized, ongoing, worldwide activity that builds and corrects from generation to generation. The method of science is just the rigorous, systematic, dogged application of cogent inductive reasoning, mixed with all sorts of deductive—including mathematical—reasoning from what has so far been observed over many centuries to theories about how the universe and the many things in it have functioned and are likely to function. Theories falsified by experience are tossed out, no matter whose pet ideas happen to get stepped on. Absolutely no one, starting from scratch, could hope to obtain in one lifetime anything remotely resembling the sophisticated and accurate conclusions of any of the sciences, even if that person were a Galileo, Newton, Darwin, and Einstein all rolled into one. *It is foolish indeed to dismiss what science has to say on any topic without very careful thought and without having extremely important reasons for doing so!\** 

Indeed, one justification for requiring all high school students to take at least one course in a physical or biological science is to allow them to gain an understanding of the great rigor with which scientific principles are tested and proved. But another, easier way to come to understand the power of science as compared to other ways of finding out what the world is like is to think carefully about the thousands of everyday items available to us today that were not in existence 300 years ago, products that owe their existence to the tremendous advances in scientific theory that have been made since the days of Galileo and Newton. Without science, there would be no automobiles, no airplanes (not to mention spacecraft!), no telephones, electric light bulbs, air conditioning, or other electric devices of any kind (certainly no computers!), no batteries, no aspirin or other common painkillers, no anesthetics (alcohol used to be the painkiller used during amputations), no antibiotics (or even knowledge of the existence of microbes and thus the extreme importance of cleanliness), no way to purify drinking water, no indoor plumbing, no eyeglasses, no insulin for diabetics, . . . the list goes on and on. Instead there were plenty of mosquitoes and flies (and fly paper) everywhere on summer days, and people made do with commodes, outhouses, and well-drawn drinking and washing water. In those days, doctors could cure only a handful of ailments, horse dung and its foul smell were everywhere in every city and town, lighting after dark was furnished by candles or oil lamps, and so on. Before the existence of the scientific, modern, industrial world, the average life span almost everywhere was less than 50 years, much less in most societies.

Of course, to avoid having beliefs contradicted by scientific theory, to successfully apply scientific principles in dealing with everyday problems, one does have to have at least a casual acquaintance with what science has to say on various topics. The problem is that large numbers of people have no idea what science is up to and have only the tiniest stock of scientific facts about the nature of the world.

According to a 1996 National Science Foundation (NSF) study, most Americans realize that almost everything used in everyday life owes its existence to scientific research and theories, but they don't understand the general way in which scientists go about their business. Researchers found that 64 percent of Americans surveyed have no understanding of the nature of the scientific enterprise; only 34 percent have some

---

*Note, however, that economics is not called the "dismal science" for nothing and that psychology has just recently come out of its infancy.

*Here is Isaac Asimov, one of the best-known popularizers of science (also famous for his science fiction), explaining why cheating in science is so rare, why getting caught is almost inevitable sooner or later, and thus why scientists on the whole are so much more trustworthy (when they're doing science!) than, say, politicians and other "public servants."*

## Self-Correction

Every once in a while—not often—scientists discover that one of their number has published false data or has plagiarized someone else's work.

This is always deeply embarrassing, especially since these days such news usually receives wide publicity in the nonscientific world.

In some ways, however, these scandals actually reflect credit upon the world of science. Consider:

1) Scientists are, after all, human. There is enormous pressure and competition in the world of science. Promotion and status depend on how much you publish and how *soon* you publish, for the lion's share of credit comes if you are *first* with an important theory or observation. Under these circumstances, there is great temptation to rush things; to make up some data you are sure you will eventually find anyway that will support your theory; or to help yourself to someone else's work. The surprise, really, is not that it sometimes happens, but that it doesn't happen much more often. Scientists resist the pressure marvelously well.

2) When it does happen, the mere fact that it is so publicized is a tribute to scientists. If it were a common event, or if people expected scientists to be corrupt, it would make smaller headlines and drop out of sight sooner. Single cases of scientific corruption, however, will be talked about for years and inspire articles and books by the score. It's really a compliment.

3) Cases of scientific misbehavior point out how difficult it actually is to carry them out successfully, or even for very long. . . . [A] vital principle in scientific research is that nothing counts until observations can be repeated independently and there, almost inevitably, anything peculiar is uncovered. Science is *self-correcting* in a way that no other field of intellectual endeavor can match.

4) It is scientists themselves who catch the frauds; no one else is equipped to do so. The point is that scientists *do* catch them. There is never any cover-up on the grounds that science itself must not be disgraced. However embarrassing the facts may be, the culprit is exposed pitilessly and publicly. Science is *self-policing* in a way that no other field is.

5) Finally, the punishment is absolute. Anyone who proves to have violated the ethics of scientific endeavor is ruined for life. There is no second chance, no vestige of status. He or she must drop out, forever disgraced.

Add to all this the fact that scientific ethics requires all scientists to labor to find flaws in their *own* observations and theories—and to publicize these flaws when they find them—and you will understand how stern the requirements are and how astonishing it is that scandal is so infrequent.

—From *SciQuest* (February 1982).
Reprinted by permission of the author.

idea of what constitutes a scientific experiment; and only about 2 percent can provide a reasonable explanation of the scientific method. Only 48 percent correctly answered a true/false question as to whether the earliest human beings lived at the same time as the dinosaurs. (They didn't.) Only 44 percent knew the right answer to the question whether human beings developed from earlier animal species. (Is that one reason for the much greater acceptance in the United States than in other industrial nations of so-called "creation science"? See Chapter 12 and the Appendix for more on this topic.)

Unfortunately, it isn't just the average person (or average college graduate?) who is more or less illiterate when it comes to science. Even those who need to know about science in order to do their jobs adequately are frequently remiss in this way. During the recent and quite severe drought in California, one government official defended his inaction by stating that "One problem [in deciding whether to enact water rationing measures] is that we have only 110 years of [precipitation] records. Our statistics [on California droughts] aren't very good." Yet, just prior to that time, a U.S. Geological Survey study of giant Sequoia tree rings had yielded a record going back over 2,000 years.

Students sometimes defend their ignorance of science by arguing that they only need to know the science, if any, that is relevant to the job they will perform after graduation from college. But this is a serious mistake. For one thing, it isn't possible to know now what basic scientific ideas will be relevant to a job held several years down the pike. (It isn't really possible, except in unusual cases, to know what sort of job it will *be*, much less what kinds of knowledge are going to be relevant to it.) In this increasingly technological age, more and more jobs require at least a general idea of what science has to say on relevant topics.

Anyway, a rudimentary understanding of science also is of immeasurable value when dealing with all sorts of everyday problems that aren't related to earning a living. Consumers spend millions of dollars every year on over-the-counter nostrums that don't work or may even be harmful. (A friend of the authors of this text who had a hearing problem wasted six months having his back manipulated by a chiropractor before going to a physician who removed wax from his ear and restored normal hearing.) Every day, people throw their money away on get-rich-quick schemes that defy the most basic principles of economics. Large sums are wasted on fortune tellers, mediums, and other charlatans whom science has proved over and over again cannot deliver the promised goods. (This is discussed a bit more in Chapter 6.)

Students often are put off science by the sheer complexity of the subject matter. Biology, for example, has to be an extremely complicated science, given that the human body contains trillions of cells, each one of which contains millions of atoms and subatomic particles (did you know that?). So the bad news is that every science quickly gets over the heads of almost all lay people. But the good news is that with only modest perseverance, people who are reasonably intelligent can learn enough about science to greatly improve their everyday reasoning and thus their chances of success in everyday life. (Clearly, similar remarks apply to mathematics, particularly to arithmetic and simple algebra.)

## EXERCISE 2-4

The 1996 National Science Foundation study mentioned a while back was based in part on a quiz given to determine how much American adults know about the nature of the world. Answer the following questions that were part of this quiz. (The first five are true/false questions.)

1. The center of the Earth is very hot.
2. Electrons are smaller than atoms.
3. The earliest human beings lived at the same time as the dinosaurs. (Were you awake when reading earlier portions of this chapter? Don't look back now.)
4. The continents on which we live have been moving their location for millions of years and will continue to move in future.
5. Human beings, as we know them today, developed from earlier species of animals.
6. Which travels faster: light or sound?
7. How long does it take the Earth to go around the sun: one day, one month, or one year?
8. Explain in your own words what DNA is.
9. Explain in your own words what a molecule is.

If some of these are a bit difficult for you to answer, you might take comfort in the fact that only 44 percent of the adult Americans asked question number 2 answered it correctly and that just 48 percent did so for question number 3. *Et vous?*

## SUMMARY OF CHAPTER 2

When evaluating an argument for cogency, we need to employ background beliefs—first, when determining whether the premises of the argument are believable, and second, when bringing other relevant information we may know about to bear on the argument.

1. Background beliefs can be divided in many ways, one being into beliefs about *matters of fact* (snow is white) and beliefs about *values* (Jane Austen's novels are better than those of Henry James). (Note that when speaking of beliefs here, we have in mind a broad sense covering everything accepted as true, or very likely true, and all value judgments and convictions.)

   Beliefs also, of course, can be divided into those that happen to be true and those that are false, and can be differentiated in terms of how firmly they are or should be held, and with respect to whether they concern particular events (Jones went to the show last Wednesday) or those that are general (It's always colder in July in New Zealand than it is in January). Note also that some beliefs are more precise than others and that some not-quite-true beliefs still may be useful in daily life (for instance, that water boils at 212°F).

   Our most important beliefs, taken together, make up our *world views*, or *philosophies*. They are particularly important because they enter into decisions of all kinds—about what to do or what to believe—that we need to make in everyday life. *Examples:* We all die sooner or later; Western medicine is much superior to the Eastern variety; it's always wrong to betray a friend; the best way to find out about how things work is to use induction and deduction. Note that, although most beliefs in our world views are general—even extremely general—a few are not. *Example:* We don't know whether there is or isn't a God (part of the world views of agnostics).

2. Unfortunately, we all tend at least sometimes to hold a belief without sufficient reason for doing so; for example, when complicated social or political issues are discussed. This is true even with respect to some of the beliefs that make up our world views. But world views, just as any beliefs, need to be carefully examined: Does evidence support them? Do we really value this more than that? Having an accurate supply of background beliefs is not just a matter of regularly acquiring more beliefs but also of pruning those we already have.

3. We tend to absorb the beliefs of those around us as we mature from children into adults. Our world views, in particular, tend to grow out of family values, religious training, peer group attitudes, cultural heritages, and so on. We often hold these vital beliefs uncritically—indeed, often without realizing that we hold them. Good critical reasoners, on the contrary, try to become aware of and to critically evaluate their background beliefs, especially those making up their world views.

4. Those of us who have a good stock of accurate background beliefs often are able to use them to *read between the lines* so as to glean more information from what we are told or experience than is evident. We can do this, for example, when listening to a political speech or even when discussing local gossip with a neighbor. (Recall the proverb cited on page 30.)

5. Beliefs about human nature are of vital importance when reasoning in daily life, because the success or failure of everyday interactions depends on them. Whether we can trust this sort of person or that is an example. That is one reason why reading the writings of great literary and scientific figures is so useful (in addition to being entertaining).

   Beliefs about the accuracy and truthfulness of information sources also are of great importance, because, as the saying goes, "Garbage in, garbage out." We can't reason well from poor or false information. That is why later chapters in this book deal with several important information sources.

6. Because science plays such an important part in everyone's life these days, it behooves us to become as well acquainted as we can, and as time permits, with the scientific view of the world and with the ways in which scientists come to their conclusions. No one on their own could possibly discover even a tiny fraction of what scientists have learned over hundreds of years about the way the world works. (Those who don't see the importance of science in their own lives should reflect on how much we depend, every day, on the fruits of scientific investigations—for example, when using an electrical device, a painkiller or other modern medicine, or even toilet tissue.) Unfortunately, most people do not have even a reasonably good grasp of what science is up to.

"Having concluded, Your Highness, an exhaustive study of this nation's political, social and economic history, and after examining, Sire, the unfortunate events leading to the present deplorable state of the realm, the consensus of the council is that Your Majesty's only course, for the public good, must be to take the next step."

---

*Question-begging advice, following oracular rule number one: Make pronouncements as empty as possible to minimize the chance of being wrong.*

*Chapter*

# 3

# FALLACIOUS REASONING—1

W e said in Chapter 1 that we reason fallaciously when we fail to satisfy all three of the requirements of cogent reasoning. Accepting premises that we should doubt makes us guilty of the fallacy *questionable premise*; neglecting relevant evidence, guilty of the fallacy *suppressed evidence*; and drawing conclusions not sufficiently supported by evidence, guilty of the fallacy *invalid inference*.

Of course, we must remember that the arguments encountered in daily life tend to be vague, or ambiguous; and premises, and even conclusions, sometimes are omitted as understood. As a result, everyday arguments often can be construed in different ways. Consider the following key line in a TV beer commercial:

More people in America drink Budweiser than any other beer.

Taken literally, this isn't an argument, but it clearly implies that the listener also should drink Bud. So its import might be put this way:

1. More people in America drink Budweiser than any other beer. (Premise)
∴ 2. You, too, should drink Budweiser. (Implied conclusion)

Construed in this way, the ad does contain an argument, but the argument is defective because it contains an *invalid inference*. That a beer is the most popular does not mean you should drink it. The most popular beer may not be the best beer and, anyway, perhaps you should drink a cheaper beer and save money or not drink any beer at all. We could, however, just as well restate the argument this way:

1. More people in America drink Budweiser than any other beer. (Premise)
2. The most popular beer is the best beer. (Implied premise)
3. You should drink the best beer. (Implied premise)
∴. 4. You should drink Budweiser. (Implied conclusion)

Now the argument is valid but contains at least two *questionable premises*—that the most popular beer is the best beer and that you should drink the best beer.

Like the Budweiser example, most fallacious arguments can be stated in more ways than one. So there often isn't a single "right" label to apply to fallacious reasoning. This doesn't mean that there aren't plenty of wrong ones to apply, and it surely doesn't mean that merely applying a plausible label is sufficient. The point is to understand *why* an argument is fallacious, and why a particular label can be shown to be right. In the case of the Budweiser ad, for instance, it's important to see that being the most popular beer is not by itself sufficient reason to conclude that we should go out and buy it. Labeling just helps us to see that an argument is fallacious, if it is, and helps us to understand *why* it is fallacious.

Notice, by the way, that in calling the argument itself fallacious, rather than reasoners who may have been taken in by it, we have employed the shortcut way of talking mentioned in Chapter 1. To be precise, we should have said, for example, that anyone who was persuaded by it would be guilty of fallacious reasoning.

Although all fallacious reasoning falls into one or more of the three broad categories just mentioned, over the years a number of other narrower fallacy species have been identified that crosscut the three basic types.* These labels have come into common use because experience has shown them to be helpful in spotting fallacious reasoning.

Let's now discuss some of the more important of these common fallacy categories, and also add some comments concerning the broad fallacy category *questionable premise*.

## 1. APPEAL TO AUTHORITY

One of the most serious errors in reasoning is to accept the word of someone, in particular an alleged authority, when we should be suspicious. We all have to appeal to experts for information or advice—only fools don't do so with some regularity. In this technological age we all are nonexperts in most fields. Accepting the word of an authority, alleged or genuine, when we shouldn't makes us guilty of the fallacy called **appeal to authority**.

---

*That is, some instances of a narrower fallacy species may fall into one of the three broad genuses and some into another.

Several hundred fallacy categories have been discussed in the literature, but no single source discusses all of them. Only those that occur frequently are discussed in this text, which means that our list is not exhaustive by any means. But the division into the three broad master categories *questionable premise*, *suppressed evidence*, and *invalid inference* is exhaustive. For more on this master fallacy classification scheme, see Howard Kahane, "The Nature and Classification of Fallacies," *Informal Logic: The First International Symposium*, edited by J. Anthony Blair and Ralph H. Johnson (Inverness, Calif.: Edgepress, 1980). Perhaps the best book on the history of fallacy theory is C. L. Hamblin's *Fallacies* (Newport News, Va.: Vale Press, 1986—reprinted from an earlier edition).

But which appeals are proper and which fallacious? Clearly, it isn't a good idea to believe that an authority is reliable without having good reason for doing so. Some alleged authorities don't have the expertise they claim; others can't be relied upon to tell it to us straight rather than feed us something more self-serving; sometimes it is wise to do our own thinking and research.

So when seeking expert advice, three basic questions need to be addressed if we want to avoid committing the fallacy of *appeal to authority*:

1. Is the source likely to have the information or good judgment we need?
2. If so, can we trust the authority to tell it to us straight?
3. Do we have the time, desire, and ability to reason the matter out for ourselves (or to understand the expert's reasoning, so that we don't have to rely merely on the authority's word)?

We usually know right away whether we have the needed time and inclination, but the other questions often are rather difficult to answer. There are, however, a few rules of thumb that should prove helpful.

## Some Authorities Are More Trustworthy Than Others

All experts are not created equal. Some are smart, others stupid. Some are more or less honest (a completely honest person being a rarity in any case), others pretty much untrustworthy. Characters who are less than completely ethical are found in every profession, but some fields attract this type more than others. The fields of law, financial advising, and politics, for instance, notoriously attract sharp operators; but even the ministry is not without its Elmer Gantrys and Jim Bakkers; and doctors who prescribe unneeded surgery are not unknown in the history of medicine. Experts in the physical sciences are more likely to have correctly figured things out in their fields than those whose expertise is in the social or psychological sciences.

Anyway, the personal interests of experts are bound now and then to conflict with their duties to clients. Professionals are human, after all, just like the rest of us. Politicians elected to the United States Congress are bound to savor the perks, fame, power, and excitement that goes along with their jobs (as who wouldn't?), making it rather difficult for them to refuse the fat cat "campaign contributions" (bribes?) needed to gain reelection, and thus more difficult still for them to tell voters the straight truth on important issues.

So when considering expert reasoning or pronouncements, we always need to assess believability. Does the authority have an axe to grind, a personal interest that might be furthered? Lawyers who speak out against no-fault auto insurance, as they usually do, have to be looked at with a jaundiced eye precisely because the point of no-fault insurance is to reduce legal costs. When members of Congress speak in favor of funding a new weapon like the Stealth bomber or vote against "single payer" health insurance plans that eliminate insurance company middlemen, we aren't being overly skeptical if we wonder whether their judgment has been warped by campaign contributions from interested parties or by narrow constituent interests. Was Congressman Newt Gingrich influenced when speaking (and voting) in favor of funding manufacture of certain military aircraft by the fact that they would be made principally in his district? Did President Clinton tailor what he said about gays in the military in 1996 to placate certain voters and thus increase his chances of reelection? (And the answer to both of these questions is . . . ?)

On the other hand, we should be inclined, other things being equal, to accept the word of dentists who urge their patients to brush and floss regularly, and of doctors who exhort us to quit smoking cigarettes, precisely because dentists make money when patients get cavities, and doctors profit when people get cancer, have heart attacks, or come down with emphysema. (Sad but true.) Advice to brush regularly or to quit smoking thus is more likely to be motivated by a professional intent to serve the interests of clients rather than by a desire to further selfish interests.

## Authorities in One Field Aren't Necessarily Experts in Another

Famous athletes and movie stars who endorse all sorts of products in television commercials are good examples of professionals speaking outside their fields of expertise. There's no reason to suppose that someone who knows how to act, or to hit home runs, knows any more about washing machines, or shaving cream, than anyone else. The fact that Ray Charles is paid to endorse Pepsi Cola, or Steve Young to tout Wheaties, proves nothing about the quality of these products, nor is there any reason to suppose that Whoopi Goldberg or Candice Bergen has any special knowledge about telephone companies. Yet most of us, irrationally, are suckers when it comes to celebrity TV commercials.

Many people, of course, are persuaded by these commercials just because they want to imitate famous people. They don't reason that if a particular celebrity endorses a product then it must be good. Their main concern is fashion, not other sorts of quality. Looking "right" is vitally important to many people, and one way to "look right" is to follow the lead of trendsetters—the rich, the powerful, and the famous. So if a movie star wears Jordache designer jeans, others also will want to. The trouble, of course, is that endorsing a product and using it are two different things. It's very unlikely, for example, that members of the "famed British wine-tasting team" who endorsed Taylor Empire Cream Sherry actually serve that quite ordinary product when friends come over for dinner. Does Nancy Kerrigan really prefer Campbell's Chicken Noodle Soup? Celebrities rarely endorse products for nothing. So if you really want to know which products famous people favor, you'll have to find out in some way other than by watching TV commercials or looking at slick ads in *Vanity Fair*. (You'd also better have lots of spare cash if you intend to emulate the rich.)

## Learn How Best to Appeal to Authorities

It generally is easy to know which sorts of experts to appeal to. Sick people need to consult doctors, someone sued for divorce a lawyer. It's a lot more difficult to find experts who know their stuff and can be relied upon. But even after finding them, we need to become adept at picking their brains. Experts often throw up roadblocks to understanding, especially by overwhelming us with professional lingo. They frequently find it tedious to explain complicated matters to lay people, and anyway they may not want to spend the time and effort necessary to do so.

It also is true that lay people often are unable to follow the complicated reasonings of trained professionals, such as medical specialists, for example. But it usually is possible to get at least a rough idea of what authorities are up to *if* we are persistent, and *if* we insist that they translate their professional lingo into ordinary discourse. It's hard not to be intimidated by professional jargon, or by an authoritarian aura.

## Check the Past Records of Alleged Experts

In professional sports, there is a saying that when in doubt you should go with a winner. Similarly, when expert advice is needed, it makes sense to go with a winner—someone whose track record is good. Those who have been right in the past are more likely than others to be right in the future, other things being equal. Remember, however, that other things are not always equal. Auto mechanics get out of touch with the latest technology, lawyers who have made their pile become lazy, and textbook writers (with at least two obvious exceptions!) eventually go over the hill.

Of course, judging alleged experts by their track records requires that we *know* their records, not just their reputations. During the recent Gulf crisis and war, television viewers were inundated with the prognostications of well-known figures with high-flown titles, such as Henry Kissinger, Secretary of State under President Nixon, Zbignew Brzezinski, head of the National Security Council under President Carter, and Dean Rusk, Secretary of State under President Kennedy. Taken in by what some people have called the "halo effect," many viewers automatically accepted the words of these "elder statesmen" without checking up on their records while in office, a grave mistake given the dismal performance of so many highly placed government officials. (Dean Rusk, by the way, stated on television, "My guess is that this [Gulf] war will last as long as a year. . . . It could be a very bitter war with heavy casualties.")

## Understand What Authorities
## Can Be Expected to Know

All experts definitely are not created equal. It isn't just that some alleged authorities, as we mentioned before, don't know what they claim to know, or that some aren't completely on the up-and-up. It's also that a good deal more is known about some topics than about others and that some information is much more expensive to obtain than others. True experts in some fields thus are more reliable than those in other areas of endeavor.

We all are forced by the nature of modern life to seek advice and expert performance from doctors, lawyers, auto mechanics, and other kinds of trained (and often licensed) professionals. But we can't expect the same sorts of definitive answers to our questions or solutions to our problems when consulting these authorities as we can, say, when consulting physicists or chemists. Medicine, for example, while based on biological theory, still is an art: Doctors cannot always be sure of their diagnoses, or of how to treat an ailment; the best of them are bound to be mistaken in their judgments now and then. Lawyers cannot be sure how jurors or judges will respond to evidence (one reason why lawyers do not win every case they handle). Ministers do not have direct lines to a higher authority. The pronouncements of the hard sciences come with an implied certificate of much higher *probability* than do those of dentists, accountants, or other working professionals.

Of course, a good deal of what we learn about the worlds of science, medicine, politics, current affairs, and so on comes not from experts in these fields but rather from information sources that differ widely with respect to accuracy (a matter to be discussed in Chapters 10, 11, and 12). For now, let's just point out that economic considerations limit the amount, accuracy, and detail of information that these other information sources provide. This is true in particular with respect to the media—television, newspapers, radio, magazines, and now the Internet. It is very expensive, for example, to obtain information concerning graft, corruption, and inefficiency in government or shenanigans in the business world; obviously the guilty parties aren't inclined to provide damaging information voluntarily. Similarly, it's much too expensive for the media to hire experts in every field they cover; journalists thus must be generalists, always knowing less about the topics and events they report about than those more intimately involved.

The import of all of this with respect to the personal decisions we all have to make in everyday life is obvious. When doctors advise serious surgery, for example, a second or even third opinion may be in order, and even then we, not the experts, have to make the final decision. But knowledge of the limitations of professional advice and performance is equally important in the carrying out of our duties as citizens. Take, for example, the millions of dollars spent every year on questionable medical procedures, in particular, blood tests ordered by doctors intent on protecting themselves against malpractice suits. (In doctor lingo, the practice is referred to as "CYA," which has to go unexplained here.) Medical mistakes and oversights frequently are attributed by juries to malpractice rather than to limitations in the knowledge and judgment of even the best physicians. The result is higher medical costs for all of us, not just those involved in malpractice suits.

## Become Your Own Expert on Important Controversial Topics

When authorities disagree on a topic of importance, the rest of us need to become our own experts, turning to authorities for evidence, reasons, and arguments, but not for conclusions. This is especially true with respect to social and political matters, because experts themselves disagree so much on these issues and because we have to watch out for the intrusion of self-interest into their stated judgments and opinions. Politicians, for example, may be beholden to special interests (as we noted before) or simply be going along with a misguided tide of public opinion. Conservative commentators generally see things differently than do those who are liberal.*

But politics is not by any means the only topic where the reasons and reasonings of experts should count for much more than their conclusions. Judges and juries, for example, too often uncritically accept the opinions of psychologists concerning the sanity of those charged with crimes, rather than delving into the reasons behind those

---

*Although labels such as "conservative," "libertarian," "liberal," "right-wing," and "left-wing" tend to be vague and ambiguous, they still have some content: Those labeled by these terms do tend to differ in their viewpoints, and critical reasoners need to take these differences into account.

opinions. After all, different opinions often can be obtained just by consulting other psychologists.*

Note, by the way, that most fallacious appeals to authority fall under the broader category *questionable premise*, because underlying the acceptance of the word of an authority is the implicit premise that it is wise to do so. In other words, the fallacy *appeal to authority* is committed by acceptance of expert advice or information when it isn't wise to do so, perhaps because the authority isn't likely to have the information we desire or may have a serious conflict of interest.

Before going on to a discussion of other fallacies, perhaps notice should be taken of the flip side of the fallacy of *appeal to authority*, namely, failure to take the word of authorities when we should. After all, salespeople frequently do give us the relevant facts straight; TV news programs do provide us with a good deal of useful information, even if they don't provide us with "the whole truth, nothing but the truth"; politicians sometimes do put aside self-interest and speak out against powerful interests. Being careful when evaluating information sources does not mean becoming completely cynical; indeed, cynical disbelief in the word of authoritative pronouncements can have serious consequences. Think only of the growing disbelief among young people who, having for years heard supposed experts spout nonsense about the evils of smoking marijuana, often do not take seriously warnings about the dangers of contracting AIDS through unprotected sexual intercourse (one reason that the incidence of this dreadful disease is increasing in populations of young heterosexuals). The trick is to learn which experts can be trusted, and when; and which cannot.

## 2. INCONSISTENCY

We reason or argue **inconsistently** when we move from premises that contradict each other. Obviously, if premises are contradictory, if they are inconsistent, then one of them must be false. So even though the argument in which they occur is *valid*, we reason fallaciously if we accept the argument's conclusion.†

It should be clear that the fallacy of inconsistency falls into the larger fallacy category *questionable premise*, because a set of inconsistent statements should be questioned by anyone who is aware of their inconsistency.

In daily life, of course, premises and conclusions do not come neatly labeled; arguments blend into each other and often join together to form longer arguments; conclusions sometimes are only implied, not explicitly stated. Inconsistencies thus tend to become concealed in a mass of verbiage.

Consider, for example, the ways in which inconsistencies intrude into campaign rhetoric. (*Campaign rhetoric:* The pronouncements of most politicians most of the time.) Candidates for public office do not explicitly say *A* and then immediately assert *not-A*. Instead, the contradictory nature of their pronouncements is concealed in one

---

*This observation conforms to B. Duggan's Law of Expert Testimony: "For every Ph.D. there is an equal and opposite Ph.D." See Paul Dixon, *The Official Rules* (New York: Delacorte, 1978) for more on irreverent, pithy sayings like Duggan's Law.

†(See Howard Kahane and Paul Tidman, *Logic and Philosophy*, 8th ed. (Belmont, Calif.: Wadsworth, 1998), Chapter 5, for an explanation as to why all arguments containing contradictory premises are valid. We also reason inconsistently, by the way, when the conclusion of one of our arguments contradicts its premises; but in that case, the argument is invalid.

Mike Peters, 1986. Reprinted by permission of United Feature Syndicate/United Media.

way or another. For instance, in the same speech, a candidate may assure voters that various government services or payments will not be emasculated (to curry the favor of voters who will profit from them), promise significant tax reductions (to gain the support of those burdened by high taxes), and favor a reduction in the national debt (to appeal to voter beliefs about the virtues of governmental thrift).* In the 1990s, that is how virtually every successful candidate for high office, including President Clinton in 1992 and in 1996, has played the game. But government services and benefits cost money, and a majority of government expenses are fixed (most notably interest payments on previously contracted debts), so that a package of increased services and benefits coupled with significant tax and public debt reductions can be regarded as inconsistent in the absence of a plausible explanation as to how this amazing trick is going to be performed. (In recent times, extremely high military expenditures, lobbied

---

We have just gone to some lengths to describe inconsistency as a serious mistake. Yet others have railed against being consistent; witness Ralph Waldo Emerson's famous remark, "A foolish consistency is the hobgoblin of little minds, adored by little statesmen, philosophers and divines."

But there need be no inconsistency in accepting both sides of this coin, provided we notice that consistency is an ambiguous concept. One sense requires us to be consistent in what we believe at any given time. This is roughly the sense meant in this chapter. The other requires us to be consistent now and forever, to stick to our guns no matter what contrary evidence we encounter. This, one must suppose, is the kind of consistency Emerson intended to disparage.

---

*Their argument thus can be put this way: If elected, I won't destroy the government services and payments you want; I will significantly reduce taxes; and I will reduce the national debt. Therefore, you should vote for me.

for by the "military-industrial complex," have made this trick even more difficult than it otherwise would be.) Adding up the figures is one way of determining whether candidates are being consistent, and hence believable, when they promise us the moon.

One reason that politicians get away with inconsistent claims or arguments so often is that voters, being human, tend to see political issues from the point of view of their own self-interest, just as they see personal problems and conflicts with friends and family. Self-interest tends to make us more blind than usual both to fair play and to cogent reasoning. Lots of cigarette smokers, for example, argue against a ban on the sale of cigarettes, on the grounds that we all have a right to inject harmful substances if we are so inclined, but most of them also, inconsistently, argue against the legalization of heroin because it is harmful to health. Extremist African Americans who get on their high horses about prejudice against blacks have been known at the same time to inconsistently preach hatred of whites.

In evaluating the various kinds of rhetoric encountered in everyday life, it is important that we don't misjudge deliberately equivocal, ironic, or humorous rhetoric. It won't do, for example, to brand the literally contradictory bumper sticker that says "Good enough isn't good enough" as contradictory, since it isn't intended to be taken literally. It says, in a humorous way, that we should do better than merely minimally well.

## Inconsistency Over Time or From Place to Place

Another way in which to be guilty of *inconsistency* is by reasoning inconsistently over time or when talking to one person and then to another. Of course, there is nothing wrong with changing one's mind—of believing A at one time and *not-A* at another. That, after all, is the point of learning from experience. It is when we continue to hang on both to A and to *not-A*, trotting out one for use when reasoning about one thing and the other when reasoning about something else, that we are guilty of fallacious reasoning.

In politics, being inconsistent over time or from audience to audience is called "blowing with the wind." What is popular with constituents one year, or in one place, may not be in another. Circumstances thus push politicians into being inconsistent in order to keep up with the latest trends in public opinion, or to placate particular audiences. This is true, for example, when, being elected to higher office, they come to represent different constituencies with different interests.

Lyndon Johnson's position on civil rights legislation is a case in point. As a congressman and (for a while) as a senator from Texas, he consistently voted and spoke *against* civil rights legislation. But when he became a power in the Senate, his tune modified, and when he became president, it changed completely. As president, he pushed important civil rights legislation through Congress, including the 1965 Voting Rights Act that was central to the dramatic change in American society concerning race that occurred in the 1960s. (Interestingly, it may well be that Johnson personally favored civil rights from the beginning but considered it political suicide to work for them until he had attained high office and, coincidentally, the mood of the nation had dramatically altered on racial issues.)

Of course, the same sorts of political pressures Lyndon Johnson had to work under exist today. Human nature does tend to remain fairly constant, and the nature of human nature drives politics. In 1992, for example, Bill Clinton campaigned on the promise not to raise taxes levied on the poor and middle classes; but in 1993, the first budget proposal he sent to Congress specified increased taxes for the middle class. The Republicans, as could be expected, voted almost unanimously against Clinton's budget proposal, calling it tax and spend, forgetting that from 1981 through 1992, the Republican administrations of Ronald Reagan and George Bush outspent every administration in American history.

It's true, of course, that candidates for high office often are forced by political realities into backtracking on campaign promises, if for no other reason than the need to compromise with opposing politically powerful forces. The furious federal budget battles that went on in 1995 and 1996, shutting down the federal government several times, illustrate how necessary compromise sometimes can be. But it often is very difficult in particular cases to determine whether an elected official is being realistic, given the political climate at the time, or merely hypocritical or even just chicken. In 1992, for example, candidate Bill Clinton promised to lift the ban on gays in the military (as commander in chief of the armed forces, a president has that power), but when in office he issued a kind of "don't ask, don't tell" directive. It's hard to know whether he was forced to go back on his campaign promise or just didn't have his heart in it. In either case, citizens ought at least to take notice of his inconsistency.

Unfortunately, being inconsistent over time isn't just a political disease. We all need to be on guard against proving what we wish to prove (for instance, that we can afford a new car, or to take time off from work) by arguing from premises that we reject in other contexts.

## Organizational Inconsistency

Large organizations generally have more than one representative authorized to speak on their behalf. So let's stretch the concept of the fallacy of *inconsistency* just a little bit more and say that an organization is guilty of this fallacy when its representatives contradict each other in their pronouncements to the public. This makes good sense because we can think of an organization as constituting an artificial person, which happens to be what the law, in fact, considers business corporations to be.

Deliberate organizational inconsistency is useful in all of the usual ways, of course, but there are special advantages to governmental organizational inconsistency that need mentioning. One comes into play when a "trial balloon" gets shot down by popular disapproval. Supposing, for example, that a cabinet member floats an idea that is poorly received, the president may then deny that his administration ever seriously considered such a half-baked measure.

Another kind of organizational inconsistency results from the need to provide a chief executive with an out should a shady, illegal, or extremely unpopular secret action begin to surface. In 1987, for example, Admiral John Poindexter, President Reagan's National Security Agency advisor, testified before a congressional committee that it was the job of hired hands to lie about what was going on in the Iran-Contra caper (Reagan's so-called "Irangate") so that the president would have "plausible deniability"—the ability to deny that his administration was doing what in fact it was doing, or to deny knowledge of its being done. Colonel Oliver North was perhaps the most noteworthy of those who lied in this way.

*Moon Mullins*. Reprinted by permission of Tribune Media Services.

## Inconsistency Between Words and Actions

Another way to be inconsistent is to *say* one thing but *do* another. (Calling this a fallacy again stretches that concept to serve everyday purposes. Strictly speaking, saying one thing and doing another does not make one guilty of fallacy, because it does not involve an inconsistency between one claim, idea, or argument and another. We include this discussion here because some sort of inconsistency is involved in this sort of behavior, and, as the saying goes, actions often speak louder than words. Anyway, it is important to be on guard against those who engage in this sort of shady behavior.)

During the congressional hearings held before Gerald Ford was confirmed as the first unelected vice president in American history, he was asked, "If a president resigned his office before his term expired, would his successor have the power to prevent or to terminate any investigation or criminal prosecution charges against the former president?" His reply was: "I do not think the public would stand for it," a clear indication that he would not use such power. But soon after becoming president when Richard Nixon resigned, Ford pardoned Nixon. (President Bush's blanket pardon of Ronald Reagan, whatever one might think of its impropriety, wasn't similarly inconsistent, because Bush didn't say he would never do such a thing.)

Of course, presidents aren't more prone to this kind of inconsistency than are other politicians. Legislators, in particular, often say one thing in order to placate voters while then selling out to special interests. In 1990, for example, Representative Dan Rostenkowski (Democrat, Illinois) loudly touted higher income tax rates for millionaires, a measure popular with his mostly nonrich constituents, while quietly working (along with Senator Lloyd Bentsen, Democrat, Texas) to reopen loopholes that allowed private business owners to pass on large parts of their holdings to heirs without paying inheritance taxes on them.*

But enough, for the while, with politician bashing. The rest of us aren't exactly paragons of virtue where consistency is concerned. Feminists who argue against different "roles" for males and females yet don't reciprocate when given expensive engagement rings, or who always leave the driving to their husbands, along with the

---

*See, for instance, "The Secret Solution to the Deficit," by Paul Glastris in *The Washington Monthly* (January/February 1991). The article mentions other loopholes in inheritance tax laws designed to benefit the rich.

spanking of errant children, surely are inconsistent. So were the gaggle of callers to TV talk-show programs who, within minutes of the jury's verdict in the O. J. Simpson murder trial, expressed outrage that the jury had, in the words of one irate caller, "let free a multiple killer. How dare they deliberate for just three hours and return a not-guilty verdict?" (How long did these callers deliberate before returning a verdict of guilty?) And what about the regents of the University of California who voted in 1995 to roll back "affirmative action" admissions for minorities and women on grounds that they were unfair to other candidates, but, it later turned out, privately used their influence to get relatives, friends, and the children of business associates admitted into the university?*

Inconsistency often is connected in people's minds with *hypocrisy*—with pretending to believe what one in fact does not, or to be what one is not. Virtually all candidates for office in the United States during the 1960s, 1970s, and 1980s ran on platforms opposing legalization of drugs even though lots of them smoked dope or sniffed cocaine. (Forget about the fact that virtually all of them also drank alcohol or smoked cigarettes.) Should we say that those who were inconsistent in this way were guilty of the sin of hypocrisy? One way or the other, they were pikers at the game compared to Anthony Comstock, who in the 1930s led the fight against pornography, with some success, all the while amassing what one aficionado described as a "magnificent collection" of the stuff.

Readers may note, when they have completed reading the three fallacy chapters in this text, that a good deal more time is spent on the first two fallacies than on any of the others. The reason is that these two are very likely the most important. The importance of the fallacy of *appeal to authority* is obvious: We all are nonexperts about most of the things that matter in everyday life and therefore regularly have to appeal to authorities for information and advice. The importance of the fallacy of *inconsistency* also should be obvious: It lies in the crucial importance of consistency to cogent reasoning. *At least one of a set of inconsistent statements must be false!* So when we reason from inconsistent premises, we reason from at least one false assertion.†

In fact, trying to be consistent is very likely the best way to improve one's stock of background beliefs (a point to be discussed again later). Having come to a conclusion

---

*Don't do what I do. Do what I tell you to do.*

When the American Heart Association's Union, New Jersey, branch held its 1990 Annual Pancake Breakfast to raise funds to finance its campaign against heart disease and strokes, its menu also included eggs, bacon, ham, sausages, muffins, buttered toast, danish pastry, coffee, and tea.

Similarly, the employee cafeterias in many hospitals offer foods high in saturated fats, salt, and other ingredients that doctors tell their patients to avoid. Doctors, of course, these days almost unanimously advise their patients to give up tobacco, although doctors who smoke, while becoming rather scarce, still are not an extinct breed.

---

*See the article by Cynthia Tucker, *Atlanta Constitution* editorial page editor, that ran in many newspapers on March 30, 1996.
†It's also true that when we reason from inconsistent premises to a given conclusion, say *A*, we also could have reasoned validly to *not-A*, for the technical reason, alluded to before, that contradictory premises imply any and everything.

for a particular reason, consistency requires that we ask ourselves whether we would be willing to carry through that line of reasoning when it applies to other cases. If not, then we must give up that line of reasoning or admit to the intellectual crime of being inconsistent.

Take, for example, those who argue that we should not resume normal trade relations with Cuba so long as they violate human rights and yet say nothing about the fact that the United States has normal trade relations with many other countries that have equally bad, or worse, human rights records (China, Saudi Arabia, Kuwait, most of the countries in Africa, and several in South America quickly come to mind). Consistency requires that we either show what is different about Cuba's human rights record that *makes* a difference or stop using this reason as justification for being against normal trade relations with Cuba (or, perhaps, conclude that we should not trade with any country that has a poor human rights record?).

## 3. Straw Man

While the broad fallacy category *suppressed evidence* seldom is mentioned in traditional logic texts, several species of this genus are given great play. One of these is the fallacy **straw man**, which is committed when we misrepresent an opponent's position, or a competitor's product, or go after a weaker opponent or competitor while ignoring a stronger one.*

*Straw man* has always been a stock-in-trade of advertisers. A Holiday Inn TV spot run a few years ago was typical of the genre. It pictured someone telephoning a competitor to find out whether they had a motel in Fargo, North Dakota, and being told *no*, then asking if there happened to be one in the area and being told *yes*, in Cleveland, Ohio. (This spot wasn't as effective as it might have been because lots of viewers had no idea how far Cleveland is from Fargo.) In the same vein, a Post Office commercial once pictured competitors trying to deliver packages with rickety old planes that fell apart on camera; IBM once touted its laser printers by comparing them with those of a pseudo competing product unable to collate printed material and therefore not really in competition with the printers IBM was touting.

## 4. False Dilemma and the Either-Or Fallacy

In traditional logic, a *dilemma* is an argument that presents two alternatives, both claimed to be bad for someone, or some position. (Dilemmas are discussed further in the Appendix.)

The general form of a dilemma can be put this way:

Either $P$ or $Q$.

If $P$ then $R$.

If $Q$ then $S$.

Therefore, either $R$ or $S$.

---

*Note, however, that some cases of this fallacy do not fall into the category of suppressed evidence. Should we, by the way, replace the name "straw man" by, say, "straw person," or perhaps "false characterization"?

Sometimes $R$ and $S$ are identical, sometimes quite different. Here is an example in which they are not quite the same: "Either our fellow citizens are good or they're bad. If they're good, laws to deter crime aren't needed. But if they're bad, laws to deter crime won't succeed. So laws to deter crime either are not needed or won't succeed."

A **false dilemma** is a dilemma that can be shown to be false. One way to do this is to demonstrate that the premise having the form "Either $P$ or $Q$" is false by showing that there is at least one other viable possibility. This is called "going between the horns" of the dilemma. In the case of the dilemma just mentioned, a viable alternative is that our fellow citizens may be both good (in some ways) and bad (in others).

Another way to defeat a dilemma is to challenge one or both of its other two premises. This is called "grasping the horns" of the dilemma. We might challenge the crime law dilemma, for example, by arguing that even if some citizens are bad, they still can be deterred by laws specifying harsh penalties.

*False dilemmas* usually are a species of the genus *questionable premise* because any set of statements that set up a *false* dilemma needs to be questioned. (Note, by the way, that we can have *false trilemmas, false quadrilemmas*, and so on.)

The **either-or fallacy** (sometimes called the *black or white* fallacy) is very similar to that of *false dilemma*. We're guilty of this fallacy when we mistakenly reason from two alternatives, one claimed to be bad (that is, to be avoided) so that we ought to choose the other alternative. The general form of the fallacy is this:

Either $P$ or $Q$.

Not $P$.

Therefore $Q$,

where there is at least a third viable alternative, or it is questionable that $P$ is bad. For example, "You have to vote either for the Republican or for the Democratic candidate. But you shouldn't vote for the Republican. So you should vote for the Democrat." A third alternative in this case would be to vote, say, for the Libertarian party candidate (this is like going between the horns of a dilemma), and some people would challenge the claim that you shouldn't vote for the Republican candidate (this would be like grasping a dilemma by its horns).

## 5. BEGGING THE QUESTION

When arguing, either with ourselves or with others, we can't provide reasons for every assertion and then reasons for the reasons, and so on. Some of what we assert must go unjustified, at least for the moment. But when we assume as a premise some form of the very point that is at issue—the very conclusion we intend to prove—we are guilty of the fallacy of **begging the question**. After all, we can't prove something by simply asserting that it is true or by appealing to something similar that is equally questionable.*

---

*In a sense, all deductively valid arguments beg the question, because what is said by their conclusions already is said in their premises. In the typical case, part of an argument's conclusion is said in one premise, part in another. That is the point of valid deduction; anyone who accepts the premises of a deductively valid argument and yet rejects its conclusion is guilty of being inconsistent. The difference in the case of the fallacy of *begging the question* is that the premises state the claim of the conclusion in a way that those who reject the conclusion also will reject the premises for being just as questionable as the conclusion.

(The fallacy of *begging the question* usually falls into the broad category questionable premise because a statement that is questionable as a conclusion is equally questionable as a premise.)

In real life, of course, this fallacy is not going to have the form

A. Therefore A.

Few would be taken in by so obvious a mistake. Instead, a premise may state a conclusion in different but equivalent words, so that the conclusion is not so obviously begged. This is the way in which the question is begged in one of the classic textbook cases (from the nineteenth century—human gullibility tends to remain constant): "To allow every man unbounded freedom of speech must always be . . . advantageous to the state; for it is highly conducive to the interests of the community that each individual should enjoy a liberty, perfectly unlimited, of expressing his sentiments."*

Although the traditional fallacy of *begging the question* dealt primarily with questions that are at issue, say, as in a debate, over time it has come to have a broader range so as to cover other sorts of questions. Thus, to take a textbook example, we can be said to be guilty of this fallacy when, having asked why chloroform renders people unconscious, we accept the answer that it does so because it is a soporific (a soporific being defined as something that induces sleep).

Doctors and other sorts of professionals are frequent perpetrators of this version of *begging the question*, but they aren't by any means the only ones who set us up for it. Indeed, many times questions are begged quite innocently. Here is an example taken from a magazine interview:

> *Question:* How old is John Kenneth Galbraith, the Harvard economist, and why was he never awarded a Nobel Prize in economics?
> *Answer:* Galbraith, . . . [born in 1908] emeritus professor of economics at Harvard, is a learned and witty writer on many subjects including economics. Apparently the Nobel Memorial Prize committee has not judged his contributions to economics, at least at this point, to be sufficiently original to merit a laureateship.

Well, then, why hasn't the prize committee considered Galbraith's work good enough for a Nobel Prize? Because they judged it not sufficiently original to merit a laureateship.

This example is typical in that the question, while in general begged, was not completely overlooked. The answer to it at least mentions the possibility that lack of originality was the problem. Of course, only original contributions tend to be rewarded by Nobel Prizes, so being told this comes very close to having our question answered by being rephrased as a statement. ("Why wasn't his work good enough to earn the prize? Because it wasn't good enough to earn the prize.")

The fallacy *begging the question* also has been broadened over time so as to cover cases in which a premise is different from the conclusion but is controversial or questionable for the same reasons that typically might lead someone to question the conclusion.

---

*Cited by Richard Whately in his excellent book *Elements of Logic* (London, 1826). Whately's fallacy classification is more like the one used in this text than are those of any other text in use today.

## 6. QUESTIONABLE PREMISE—QUESTIONABLE STATEMENT

As we noted earlier, most examples of the fallacies discussed so far fall into the broader category of *questionable premise*. But not all species of *questionable premise* have received specific names in the literature. So when a premise that is not believable is spotted in an argument and none of these more specific labels apply, we have to fall back on the general term **questionable premise**. That is what we did earlier when we pointed out that a statement in a Budweiser commercial constituted a *questionable premise*.

Knowing for a fact that a statement is false obviously is a very good reason for questioning it, indeed, for dismissing it. Thus, when a colleague was alleged to be incompetent on grounds that she was an alcoholic, one of the authors of this text rejected the charge on the basis of personal knowledge that the allegation was false. But often we ought to question a statement just because we have no good reason to think it true, even though we also don't have any reason to doubt it. When evidence is lacking, reason requires holding judgment in abeyance.

Remember, though, that hearing something from a trustworthy expert often counts as a reason for believing it to be true. For example, the fact that the overwhelming majority of scientists believe the burning of fossil fuels such as oil and coal is polluting the air and causing a rise in worldwide temperatures ought to constitute good reason for believing that there is a "greenhouse effect" resulting from the use of these fuels.

## 7. SUPPRESSED (OVERLOOKED) EVIDENCE

The general fallacy category **suppressed evidence**, introduced earlier along with *questionable premise* and *invalid inference*, has not received much attention in the fallacy literature, perhaps because theorists tend to see the suppression of evidence as an error in reasoning but not as a fallacy (as they define that concept). Whether thought of as a fallacy or not, however, it is important that we learn how to bring relevant evidence to bear on an argument and how to avoid being taken in by others when they suppress evidence.

Of course, people who suppress evidence often do so inadvertently, one reason that a better label for the fallacy might be **overlooked evidence**, or perhaps *slighted evi-*

---

Shall I tell you what it is to know? It is to say you know when you know, and to say that you do not know when you do not know; that is knowledge.
—Attributed to Confucius (that is, we do not know for sure that he said it)

---

*We don't want to be too hasty, or too picky, in leveling a charge of* begging the question. *Although what Confucius is quoted as saying is literally question begging, it is very likely that what he meant to say is that a large part of wisdom is to know what you do and what you don't have good reason to believe, and, by implication, not to believe what you do not have good reason to believe. Excellent advice, indeed.*

> *Many people have trouble distinguishing between having no evidence or proof for a claim and having evidence or proof that the claim is false. But having no evidence, say, that vitamin C helps us fight the common cold is quite different from having evidence that it does not do so. Similarly, a lack of clinical proof that marijuana has certain medicinal benefits is much different from having clinical proof that it does not. Lack of clinical proof, by the way, also is quite different from having no good evidence whatsoever concerning marijuana's medicinal benefits. In fact, there is a good deal of such "anecdotal" evidence.*

*dence.* It's easy, when strongly committed to a particular side of an issue, to pass over arguments and reasons on the other side. In recent years, advocates on both sides of issues such as capital punishment, abortion, the legalization of marijuana, the depiction of violence on TV, and the legalization of prostitution frequently have been guilty of slighting evidence damning to their side of the issue. Those opposed to "three strikes and you're out" legislation, for instance, tend to neglect the ways in which this kind of law might protect society from repeat offenders; those in favor don't like to talk about the high costs associated with keeping people in jail long past the age at which the vast majority of criminals have ceased to commit violent crimes.

We all, of course, sometimes are motivated by more crass considerations than mere overzealousness. Selfishness, self-interest, is a powerful motivator of deliberately shady reasoning. (More will be said concerning this rather unfortunate fact about human nature in Chapter 6.)

Anyway, the point of becoming familiar with the fallacy *suppressed evidence* is to sharpen our ability to spot cases in which relevant evidence is being slighted, whether by others or by ourselves. We need, in particular, to learn how to carry through reasoning so as to see whether all likely relevant information has been considered. Take, for instance, the following item, paraphrased from the November 22, 1994, McNeil Lehrer PBS news hour:

> The 28 percent capital gains tax tends to keep people locked in to their investments rather than moving to perhaps more productive investments. For example, someone who buys a stock at 50 that now is at 100 is not as inclined to sell and move to another stock because of the 28 percent loss in taxes of the $50 capital gain. So some new corporations, new ventures, may not be financed.

The suppressed material that really sharp critical reasoners would have added to the reasoning about the issue is this: If Smith doesn't sell at $100, someone else doesn't spend $100 to buy, and thus that other person is free to invest $100 in "more productive investments." So overall, the same amount of money is available for more productive investments whether Smith does or doesn't sell. It's surprising how often politically or economically driven arguments can be shot down by carrying through a line of reasoning in this way.

This is true with respect not just to arguments themselves but also to proposals for action (which, in any case, do imply arguments). Consider, for example, the proposal (in a letter to the *San Francisco Chronicle*, October 5, 1991) that suggested instituting a

*Doonesbury* by Garry Trudeau. Copyright, 1973, G. B. Trudeau.
All rights reserved. Used by permission of Universal Press Syndicate.

**Tokenism:** *Note that Clint equates his notion of half way with fairness.*

higher bridge toll for the low-mileage, high-polluting cars generally driven by rich people than for high-mileage, low-polluting cars driven by others. The point was to raise money in a way that would be fair by hitting those who could afford it most and who pollute the most. But the writer neglected to consider the monstrous traffic jams that would result from requiring toll booth attendants to determine the rate of gas mileage of every car passing through their gates. So the writer's suggestion was completely impractical, as good critical reasoners would quickly figure out by bringing to bear the overlooked evidence just mentioned.

## 8. TOKENISM

**Tokenism**—mistaking a token gesture for the real thing, or accepting a token gesture in lieu of something more concrete—is another common fallacy.

Sometimes, of course, the token gesture is accepted because nothing else is likely to be forthcoming. A long-time corporation employee who is "retired" early might just as well accept the token gift of a gold watch. But we often accept token gestures because we fail to see their true nature—as some retirees do when they get the watch.

As might be expected, tokenism is one of the politician's best friends. When action is demanded by voters but is politically inexpedient or otherwise not self-serving, elected officials typically turn to token gestures to make it appear that something is being done. During the 1992 and 1996 presidential and congressional election campaigns, virtually all candidates shouted about campaign financing reform, because the

---

*In the Italian film* Il Postino (The Postman), *the big politician promises, again, that pipes will be built so that the people can have indoor running water, and he actually has construction begin before the election. People again vote him into office and—surprise—construction immediately stops. Voters have again been suckered by a token gesture and only wake up to that fact when it is too late to make a difference.*

electorate was fed up with the way in which large donors curry favor with public officials. But after a great deal of laboring, actual campaign reform legislation produced a mouse of legislation—a token gesture intended merely to placate voters. (Were voters taken in by all this folderol? Tune in to future election blather and watch many voters again favor candidates who—for the $n$th time—promise true campaign reform.)

## SUMMARY OF CHAPTER 3

All fallacious reasoning falls into one or more of the three broad categories of *questionable premise*, *suppressed evidence*, and *invalid inference*. But other fallacy categories, crosscutting these broad ones, have come into common use.

1. *Appeal to authority:* Accepting the word of alleged authorities when there is not sufficient reason to believe that they have the information we seek or that they can be trusted to provide it to us, or doing so when we ought to figure the matter out for ourselves. *Example:* Taking the word of power industry executives that nuclear plants are safe.

   When appeals must be made to authorities, we should remember that some are more trustworthy than others, and in particular, we should be wary of experts who have an axe to grind. We also should pay attention to the track records of alleged authorities.

2. *Inconsistency:* Using or accepting contradictory statements to support a conclusion or conclusions. These contradictory assertions may be made (1) by one person at one time and place; (2) by one person at different times or places (without explaining the contradiction as a change of mind based on reasons); or (3) by different representatives of one institution. While not, strictly speaking, a fallacy, we need to note when there is a contradiction between what someone says and what that person does. *Example:* President Clinton's campaign promise that he would lift the ban on gays in the military compared with his actual performance on the matter.

3. *Straw man:* Misrepresenting an opponent's position or a competitor's product in order to make it easier to attack them or to tout one's own product as superior, or attacking a weaker opponent while ignoring a stronger one. *Example:* A post office commercial that pictured a competitor's plane that fell apart on camera.

4. *False dilemma:* A dilemma that can be shown to be false, either by "going between the horns" of the dilemma or by "grasping its horns." *Example:* Refuting the dilemma about the futility of laws to deter crime by pointing out that there is a third alternative, namely, that many citizens are both good and bad.

   The *either-or* (*black or white*) variation occurs when an argument based on the assumption that there are just two viable alternatives, one of which is bad (so the other is to be chosen), although there is at least one other viable alternative. *Example:* Refuting the argument that you should vote Democratic because the only alternative (voting Republican) is bad by pointing to a third possibility, say, voting for the Libertarian candidate.

5. *Begging the question:* Assuming without proof the question, or a significant part of the question at issue, or answering a question by rephrasing it as a statement. *Example:* Why hasn't the prize committee considered Galbraith's work good enough for a Nobel Prize? Because they judged it not sufficiently original to merit a laureateship.

6. *Questionable premise—questionable statement:* Accepting a less than believable premise or other statement. *Example:* Accepting the claim that Budweiser is the best beer as a reason for deciding to switch to Bud. (Note that the five fallacies just described are variations of this broader fallacy, but that not all species of questionable premise have special names.)

7. *Suppressed (overlooked) evidence:* Failing to bring relevant evidence to bear on an argument. *Example:* Advocates on both sides of the debates about the merits of "three strikes and you're out" laws who slight sensible arguments of their opponents.

8. *Tokenism:* Accepting a token gesture as though it is the real thing. *Example:* Being satisfied with campaign rhetoric when there is little likelihood of serious intent to carry through.

## EXERCISE 3-1

Determine which fallacies (if any) occur in the following passages and state reasons for your answers. Note: Some items may contain more than one fallacy.

**Example:**
*Passage:* Heard in a debate concerning capital punishment: "Capital punishment is morally wrong. After all, murder is just as wrong when committed by a government as it is when done by an individual person."
*Evaluation:* The speaker *begged the question* at issue. To say that capital punishment is murder is to say that it is a morally wrong killing (note that only wrongful killings are considered to be murder). But the issue was whether capital punishment—governmental killing—*is* morally wrong, so to argue that it is begs the question.

*1. Overheard in a laundromat: What makes me think abortion is murder? When my pediatrician refused to perform an abortion for me, she said she wouldn't be a party to murder. Babies and childbirth are her business, you know.

*2. President Lyndon Johnson: I believe in the right to dissent, but I do not believe it should be exercised.

3. 1960s bumper sticker: America—Love It or Leave It!

4. Farm Bureau statistics report cited in the *Washington Monthly*: Low earnings seem to be the key reason why someone who usually works full time is a member of a poor family.

5. Joe Morgan, announcing a Giants-Marlins baseball game and commenting on the Marlin pitcher: He's been a little erratic, which explains why he hasn't been consistent.

6. Does this Tom Meyer political cartoon tie in with some things that were discussed in this chapter? Explain.

Cartoon by Tom Meyer. © *San Francisco Chronicle*. Reprinted by permission.

7. Eric Jubler, in an article in which he argued that America should "open up" its wilderness areas: The purist [conservationist] is, generally speaking, against everything . . . the purist believes that those who do not agree with him desire to "rape the land."

8. Calvin Coolidge is alleged to have been the first to say this: We must keep people working—with jobs—because when many people are out of work, unemployment results.

9. Notice from the Hyatt Regency Hotel in New Orleans (quoted in the *Quarterly Review of Doublespeak*, July 1988): We are pleased to confirm your reservation. It will be held on a space available basis.

10. It is reported that when Socrates was condemned to death his wife cried out that "Those wretched judges have condemned him to death unjustly!" To which Socrates is said to have replied, "Would you really prefer that I were justly condemned?"

11. An MIT ROTC colonel, explaining the military's ban on gays: "We don't discriminate. We simply exclude certain types of people."

12. Blurb on the envelope of a World Watch Institute fund raiser: We are at one of those watersheds in human history, invisible at the time, that change the way we live.

13. United States public school textbooks point with pride to the fact that the border between the United States and Canada, "our friendly neighbor to the North," is the longest unprotected border in the world.

*14. From a conversation with a certain party's aunt: "I asked the doctor why my mouth was so dry, and he said it was because my salivary glands are not producing enough saliva." Some doctor.

*15. From a Dr. Joyce Brothers newspaper column: *Question:* You should be more fearful of rape at home because rapes occur more frequently in private homes than in back alleys. *Answer:* TRUE. Studies indicate that more rapes are committed in the victim's home than in any other place. Almost half took place in either the victim's home or the assailant's; one fourth occurred in open spaces; one fifth in automobiles; one twelfth in other indoor locations.

16. From a *New Republic* review of the James Michener book *Iberia*: Michener leads off his chapter on bullfights with an argument between your quintessential American and Spaniard about brutal sports—which the Spaniard wins by pointing out that more young men get killed and maimed every year playing American football than in the bullring.

17. A TV commercial argued in favor of NAFTA (the North American Free Trade Agreement) in part by stating the fact that all living former U.S. presidents joined President Clinton in support of the agreement, while citing Pat Buchanan, Ross Perot, Jessie Jackson, Jerry Brown, and Ralph Nader as being opposed.

18. Paraphrase of part of a letter to the editor (*Washington Post National Weekly Edition*, March 13–19, 1989): It's true that the Ayatollah Khomeini has gone too far with his death sentence for author Salman Rushdie (because of his outrageous book *The Satanic Verses*), but Rushdie also has gone too far by offending all Moslems. I am a strong believer in the freedom of speech. However, books like Rushdie's only create hatred and division and weaken the ties of people to each other. Therefore, his book and others like it should be abolished.

19. Interview with Ronald Reagan (taken from the *New York Review of Books*): *Mr. Otis:* We would like to know . . . what the Bible really means to you. *President Reagan:* I have never had any doubt about it being of divine origin. And to those who . . . doubt it, I would like to have them point out to me any similar collection of writings that have lasted for as many thousands of years and is still the best seller worldwide. It had to be of divine origin.

*20. Sociologist James Q. Wilson: I am not about to argue [as sociobiologists do] that there is a "sympathy gene." But there must be some heritable disposition that helps us explain why sympathy is so common. . . .

21. From "Intelligence Report" by Lloyd Shearer in *Parade* magazine (November 5,1978): This past September, [Bob Hope] refused to cross a picket line at the Chicago Marriot Hotel, where 1500 guests were waiting for him at a dinner of the National Committee for the Prevention of Child Abuse. W. Clement Stone, the insurance tycoon who contributed $2 million to the Nixon campaign fund in 1972, tried to negotiate a temporary halt of picketing so that Hope could enter the hotel. When Stone failed, Hope returned to the

Drake Hotel, where he videotaped a 15-minute spot to be shown at the dinner. Hope, who belongs to four show business unions, later explained that he had crossed a picket line many years ago and subsequently had to apologize to labor leader George Meany. He promised then never to cross another.

*22. Start of a letter from The Heritage Foundation soliciting funds:
Dear Fellow American:
A Russian official recently told a Heritage Foundation staffer: "I'm honored to meet you. I've been praying for Heritage for seven years." "How did you know of us?" asked the Heritage man. Said the Russian: "All we could read was *Pravda* and the controlled press—and they kept attacking Heritage. Thus I knew that Heritage was good."

23. Ad for an International Correspondence School journalism course:
Every successful writer started that first story or article with no previous experience. William Shakespeare, Alexander Dumas, Harold Robbins, Danielle Steel, Barbara Cartland—any famous writer you can name started just like you.

24. Walter Burns, in an article in which he argues for capital punishment:
When abolitionists speak of the barbarity of capital punishment . . . they ought to be reminded that men whose moral sensitivity they would not question have supported [it]. Lincoln, for example, albeit with a befitting reluctance, authorized the execution of 267 persons during his presidency . . . and it was Shakespeare's sensitivity to the moral issues that required him to have Macbeth killed.

25. Phyllis Schlafley, an outspoken opponent of the women's liberation movement, in her book *The Power of Positive Women*: The second dogma of the women's liberationists is that, of all the injustices perpetrated upon women through the centuries, the most oppressive is the cruel fact that women have babies and men do not. Within the confines of women's liberationist ideology, the abolition of this overriding inequality becomes the primary goal.

26. Paraphrase of a letter to the editor: Everyone is always talking about race prejudice and how blacks in this country still don't get a fair shake. Baloney! It's just the other way around. Look at O. J. getting away with murder. Look at all the black teenagers getting welfare—paid for with mostly white tax money. Look at blacks getting into colleges and getting jobs because of affirmative action.

Drawing by H. Martin; © 1974 The New Yorker Magazine, Inc.

"If the coach and horses and the footmen and the beautiful clothes all turned back into the pumpkin and the mice and the rags, then how come the glass slipper didn't turn back, too?"

---

*Two important factors in critical or creative thinking are the ability to bring relevant background information to bear on a problem and to carry through the relevant implications of an argument or position to determine whether they hang together. The cartoon above illustrates the second of these factors: The child carries through the reasoning in the Cinderella story and finds it wanting. The first factor might be illustrated by a child who realizes there are millions of chimneys for Santa Claus to get down in one night and wonders how he could possibly manage to do so in time.*

How happy are the astrologers, who are believed if they tell one truth to a hundred lies, while other people lose all credit if they tell one lie to a hundred truths.

— Francesco Guicciardini

It ain't so much the things we don't know that get us into trouble. It's the things we know that ain't so.

— Artemus Ward

# *Chapter*

# 4

# FALLACIOUS REASONING—2

Most instances of the fallacies discussed in the previous chapter fall into the broad fallacy categories *questionable premise* or *suppressed evidence*. Most of the fallacies to be discussed in this and the next chapter belong to the genus *invalid inference*.

## 1. AD HOMINEM ARGUMENT

There is a famous and perhaps apocryphal story lawyers like to tell that nicely captures the flavor of this fallacy. In Great Britain, the practice of law is divided between solicitors, who prepare cases for trial, and barristers, who argue the cases in court. The story concerns a particular barrister who, depending on the solicitor to prepare his case, arrived in court with no prior knowledge of the case he was to plead, where he found an exceedingly thin brief, which when opened contained just one note: "No case; abuse the plaintiff's attorney." If the barrister did as instructed, he was guilty of arguing **ad hominem**—of attacking his opponent rather than his opponent's evidence and arguments. (An *ad hominem* argument, literally, is an argument "to the person.")

A rather infamous remark by Senator Jennings Randolph, uttered during the debate on the Equal Rights Amendment (ERA) to the Constitution illustrates the fallacy of *ad hominem* argument perfectly. Jennings dismissed arguments by feminists who testified before Congress by referring to these women as a "small band of bra-less bubble-heads." This remark, no doubt, was good for a laugh in the then almost-all-male Senate, but it was irrelevant to the arguments women's rights advocates had advanced.

Randolph's *ad hominem* was rather crude, to put it mildly, but others—including this well-known gem uttered by Vice President Spiro Agnew—have on occasion exhibited a good deal of literary merit:*

> A spirit of national masochism prevails, encouraged by an effete corps of impudent snobs who characterize themselves as intellectuals.

The intellectuals, of course, loved this spirited barb, as they did his comment about "nattering nabobs of negativism."

It is important not to confuse *ad hominem* arguments with those in which the fallacy is *straw man*. The difference is that *straw man* misrepresents an opponent's position, whereas *ad hominem* attacks an opponent directly.

## Attacks on Character or Credentials Sometimes Are Relevant

Although attacks on a person generally are irrelevant to the arguments that person may have put forth, sometimes they are very relevant indeed. Lawyers who attack the testimony of courtroom witnesses by questioning their expertise or character are not necessarily guilty of arguing *ad hominem*. In the O. J. Simpson case, for example, defense lawyers certainly were not guilty of arguing *ad hominem* when they showed detective Mark Fuhrman to have perjured himself on the witness stand. Fuhrman's lie about not having used racial epithets was not directly relevant to the case at hand (it had nothing to do with whether Simpson was guilty of murder), but it certainly was relevant to judgment about Fuhrman's credibility as an expert witness.

Similarly, courtroom witnesses often express opinions or arguments against which the typical lay person is unable to argue directly. When doctors, auto mechanics, lawyers, or other experts testify, often the best we can do is try to evaluate their honesty or judgment. Evidence that a psychologist testifying in court has been convicted of perjury, or spends a great deal of time testifying in court, would be good reason to prefer the conflicting testimony of experts on the other side of the case. In the O. J. Simpson case, for instance, the fact that several experts, for example, Dr. Henry Lee, were shown to spend a good deal of time testifying in court was a relevant fact to consider in weighing their testimony.

Of course, negative evidence concerning an expert rarely proves that the authority's pronouncements are false. At best, character attacks just provide grounds for disregarding expert opinion, not for deciding that it is false. If a doctor who advises operating on a patient turns out to be held in low esteem in the profession, it is rash to conclude that *therefore* no operation is necessary.

What has just been said about attacking the credentials of experts applies to organizations and their pronouncements as well. That a research organization receives most of its funds from a political party and also regularly issues reports favorable to that party constitutes a very good reason to be suspicious of its output. Similar remarks apply to

---

*In a speech delivered in October 1969 and believed to have been written for Agnew by Nixon administration speech writer William Safire.

The Handbook of Political Fallacies, *by British political philosopher and reformer Jeremy Bentham (1748–1832), is one of the classic works on political rhetoric and fallacies. Here are excerpts from his account of the first of four "causes of the utterance of [political] fallacies" (another excerpt appears in Chapter 6).*

## First Cause . . . : Self-Conscious Sinister Interest

[I]t is apparent that the mind of every public man is subject at all times to the operation of two distinct interests: a public and a private one. . . .

In the greater number of instances, these two interests . . . are not only distinct, but opposite, and that to such a degree that if either is exclusively pursued, the other must be sacrificed to it. Take for example pecuniary interest: it is to the personal interest of every public man who has at his disposal public money extracted from the whole community by taxes, that as large a share as possible . . . should remain available for his own use. At the same time it is to the interest of the public . . . that as small a share as possible . . . should remain in his hands for his personal or any other private use. . . .

Hence it is that any class of men who have an interest in the rise or continuance of any system of abuse no matter how flagrant will, with few or no exceptions, support such a system of abuse with any means they deem necessary, even at the cost of probity and sincerity. . . .

But it is one of the characteristics of abuse, that it can only be defended by fallacy. It is, therefore, to the interest of all the confederates of abuse to give the most extensive currency to fallacies. . . . It is of the utmost importance to such persons to keep the human mind in such a state of imbecility that shall render it incapable of distinguishing truth from error. . . .

*Students inclined to complain that too many of the fallacy examples in this text come from politicians should seriously reflect on Bentham's remarks, especially because government today deals with so many matters that determine the quality of all of our lives.*

institutes that can be suspected of being more or less in the pockets of tobacco manufacturers or pharmaceutical houses.

## Guilt by Association

One of the important variations on an *ad hominem* argument is that of **guilt by association**. According to an old saying, people can be judged by the company they keep. But is this true? Is it rational to judge people in this way?

The answer is that it is—up to a point and under certain circumstances. In the absence of contrary evidence, a man frequently seen in the company of several different women known to be prostitutes is rightly *suspected* of being connected with their occupation. Similarly, a person who frequently associates with known agents of a foreign government is rightly suspected of being an agent of that government.

But suspicion is very different from certitude. Judgments based on a person's associations rarely have a high degree of probability. Suspecting that someone uses the services of prostitutes is much different from knowing that he does. (It is, however, good reason to look further, assuming we care enough about the matter.) Someone frequently in the company of prostitutes may turn out to be a sociologist conducting an investigation. A person often seen in the company of foreign spies may turn out to be a friendly counterspy.

## 2. Two Wrongs Make a Right

Those who try to justify a wrong by pointing to a similar wrong perpetrated by others often are guilty of the fallacy sometimes called **two wrongs make a right** (traditional name: *tu quoque*—"you're another"). For example, Cynthia Tucker, editorial page editor of the *Atlanta Constitution*, was guilty of this fallacy when, after pointing out how the rich and powerful often are given special privileges, she wrote in a March 1996 article that "These revelations make the case for affirmative action. People of color, who rarely have power or connections, are just seeking the same favors available to those who [already] have them." Clearly, that the governor of California and several regents of the University of California had used their influence to get children admitted into state universities (one of Tucker's examples) does not justify special treatment for nonwhites who lack special access. The one kind of wrong doesn't make the other kind right.*

### Fighting Fire with Fire

Like most other fallacies, *two wrongs* seems plausible because of its resemblance to a more legitimate way of reasoning—in this case to the plausible idea that we sometimes are justified in "fighting fire with fire." The justification of killing in self-defense illustrates this nicely. We feel justified in fighting one evil (the unjustified attack on our own life) by doing what otherwise would constitute another evil (taking the life of the attacker).

The fallacy *two wrongs make a right* thus is not automatically committed every time one wrong is counteracted by another. The crucial question is whether the second wrong is genuinely needed to fight, or counteract, the first.†

---

*There may, of course, be other reasons for having affirmative action programs; for example, to make up for earlier harms perpetrated on the underprivileged—to "level the playing field." The point here is that it won't do to argue that because the other guy has special access, so should you, given the better solution that no one receives special treatment.

†This passes over questions concerning retributive justice. If retributivists are right, we sometimes are justified in punishing those guilty of unfairly harming others even though in doing so we fail to fight the original harm (or fail to rehabilitate the criminal or deter others from similar offenses).

## Two Wrongs and Hypocrisy

The fallacy *two wrongs make a right* also sometimes seems plausible—not fallacious—for another reason: Those who argue this way may intend to imply that their opponents are being hypocritical, and often this charge is accurate and may even have some merit. The town drunk isn't the one to tell us we've had one too many and are making fools of ourselves, even if we are. (That's the import of the reply, "You're a fine one to talk.") Similarly, the philanderer who finds out about his wife's infidelity is hardly the one to complain that she has deceived him. But when we become outraged at the "chutzpa" of our accusers, we shouldn't lose sight of the fact that their hypocrisy doesn't justify our own failures.

## Common Practice and Traditional Wisdom

As the traditional latin name *tu quoque* suggests, the fallacy *two wrongs make a right* originally was intended to cover only those cases in which an individual or group responds to a charge by charging the accuser or accusers with a similar crime. But over time, it has come to take in related, indeed overlapping, sorts of fallacious arguments. One of these is **common practice**, committed when a wrong is justified on the grounds not that one other, or one other group, but rather lots of, or most, or even all others do the same sort of thing. Here is a typical example (from the *San Franci.. Chronicle*, February 17, 1993):

> Bank of America Corp. Chief Executive Officer Richard Rosenberg yesterday said he was surprised by the public outcry about the bank's plan to cut branch employee hours and some benefits. [This was the bank's euphemistic way of disguising the reduction of full-time employees to the status of part-timers, with lower pay and reduced fringe benefits.] . . . The bank's CEO firmly defended the way the company was reducing staff following its merger with Security Pacific Corp. "I couldn't understand how we could be torn apart on this issue when we've been moving toward part-timers since 1985 and Wells Fargo and virtually every other retailer has been doing the same thing," he said. "To pick on us alone doesn't make sense."

Forgetting the fact that others also were "picked on," Bank of America's CEO can be seen as guilty of the fallacy of *common practice.**

A related fallacy, sometimes called traditional *wisdom*, is committed when a wrong or an unsuitable practice is justified because it follows the traditional or accepted way of doing things. We do, of course, want to learn from past experiences, but we shouldn't assume that *just because* things have been done certain ways in the past, they must be the right, or best, way now. All innovations go against past practices— from the introduction of plows that dig deeper furrows (resisted by North African farmers on

---

*In fairness, however, we should note that, as in many cases in everyday life, complications lurk under the surface. Bank of America might very well put itself into an uncompetitive position by failing to reduce employee salaries when other banks do so. The underlying issue here is whether we want to have a system in which market forces of this kind are allowed to play themselves out, no matter how individual citizens are affected.

the grounds that their fathers and grandfathers had farmed the traditional way) to the elimination of practices based on racial, religious, or gender bias in the United States and practices based on the caste system in India, which forced "untouchables" to do dirty work such as collecting "night soil." (Interestingly, new methods of planting seeds without plowing at all may make deep furrow plowing obsolete in its turn.)

In some cases, practices that once made perfect sense no longer do because of changing circumstances or increased knowledge. In others, the fallacy in arguing for the retention of common practices is due to the wrongheadedness or unfairness of those old ways of doing things. Those who benefit from these practices find it hard to entertain the idea that there could possibly be anything wrong with them (a matter to be mentioned again in Chapter 6, where impediments to cogent reasoning are discussed). In England, for instance, women for centuries had no legal rights under the common law. It wasn't just that women were disenfranchised. Fathers could marry a daughter to whomever they pleased, and after marriage a woman's husband became the owner of her property. It took a very long time for these and similar legal injustices to be rectified; they were fought, for one thing, on the grounds that women had no legal rights because they never had had any. (In nineteenth-century England and America, for instance, the idea that women should have the vote was met with great hilarity in all-male circles of power, and political cartoons in newspapers and magazines poked fun at "lady suffragettes.")

But, again, we don't want to go overboard. Every change brings with it risks that may not have been calculated correctly. The recently passed "three strikes and you're out" bills, for example, were generally enacted without careful consideration of the likely consequences of such a serious departure from past practice. The point of such a bill is to assure that those who repeatedly commit violent crimes are not released from jail to again commit heinous offenses. But most of these measures enacted so far fail to correctly distinguish between *violent* felons and others; or to consider the cost of incarcerating criminals long past the time when they are likely to commit violent crimes (most of which are committed by young men); or to take account of the motivation these bills provide for two-time losers to shoot to kill rather than allow themselves to be captured and tried a third time.

## 3. IRRELEVANT REASON (*NON SEQUITUR*)

Traditional logic textbooks often discuss a fallacy called *non sequitur* (literally, "it does not follow"), usually described as being committed when a conclusion does not follow logically from given premises. In this sense, any fallacy in the broad category *invalid inference* can be thought of as a *non sequitur*. But other writers describe this fallacy more narrowly.

Let's replace the ambiguous term *non sequitur* with the expression **irrelevant reason**, used to refer to reasons or premises that are irrelevant to a conclusion when the error doesn't fit a narrower fallacy category such as *ad hominem argument* or *two wrongs make a right*.

Both before and after the outbreak of the 1991 war in the Persian Gulf, many Americans railed against antiwar demonstrators on grounds that they were giving the Iraqi leaders the idea that Americans were too soft to go to war, or to take the number of casualties winning might require. (The same charge was leveled against Vietnam War protesters 20 years or so earlier.) This charge may well have been true (Iraq certainly misjudged American resolve), but was irrelevant to the protesters' arguments against waging war with Iraq.

Note, by the way, that a reason is not automatically irrelevant just because it is false. For example, the old superstition about walking under a ladder bringing bad luck is false, but it isn't irrelevant to the question whether a person should or shouldn't engage in this practice; were it true, it would be a very good reason indeed for not walking under ladders.

Note also that a reason may be irrelevant when looking at a matter from one point of view but not from another. Take, for example, the remark by a psychological clinician (quoted in *Science News*, March 5, 1994) that abandoning the old and standard ways of classifying mental disorder in favor of new ones "will result in denial of insurance coverage for treatment of serious psychological disturbances." Looked at from the point of view of psychiatric theory, this remark is irrelevant, but from the point of view of psychiatric *practice* it is very relevant indeed.

## 4. EQUIVOCATION

A term or expression is used *ambiguously* or *equivocally* in an argument when used to mean one thing in one place and another thing in another.* Accepting an argument that is invalid because of an equivocal use of language makes us guilty of the fallacy that you will not be surprised to learn is generally called **equivocation**.

When a TV evangelist said that we all should stop sinning and "be like Jesus," someone in the audience expressed doubt that he was up to that, pointing out that, after all, "Jesus is the son of God." In reply, the evangelist told the doubter that he could indeed stop sinning because, "You're the son of God, too." But the evangelist was guilty of *equivocation*, because the doubter meant that Jesus is the son of God in the special way that (according to Christian doctrine) only Jesus is held to be, while the evangelist had to mean that the doubter was the son of God in the metaphorical sense in which (again according to Christian theology) we all are children of God.

*Equivocation* is a common fallacy because it often is quite hard to notice that a shift in meaning has taken place. As might be expected, given human nature, less than completely ethical manipulators frequently take advantage of the ease with which people can be fooled in this way. The sugar industry, for instance, once advertised its product with the claim that "Sugar is an essential component of the body . . . a key material in all sorts of metabolic processes," neglecting the fact that it is glucose (blood sugar) not ordinary table sugar (sucrose) that is the vital nourishment. It's true, of course, that table sugar does turn into blood sugar in the body, but it provides that necessary ingredient without also providing the other sorts of vital nutrients found in fruits, grains, and other more complete food sources.

---

*As used in everyday life, the term *equivocation* often connotes the use of ambiguity to deceive. As used here, it does not necessarily carry this connotation. We do, of course, have to remember that ambiguity and equivocation are frequently employed in daily life to make invalid arguments appear to be valid.

> It is he that sitteth upon the circle of the earth.
>
> — Isaiah 40:22
>
> ---
>
> ## Ambiguity
>
> *Almost any statement can be interpreted in various ways if we have a mind to do so. The Bible is a happy hunting ground for those intent on taking advantage of the ambiguity of natural languages, because so many people take what it says to be the word of the Ultimate Authority. This passage from Isaiah was once used to prove that the earth is flat, but when the discoveries of Copernicus, Kepler, and Newton made the idea of a flat earth archaic, the Isaiah quote was reinterpreted to prove that those who wrote the Bible knew the earth is a sphere.*

Advertisements of this kind are successful because a large majority of consumers know very little about how the body functions—what sorts of food are required for good health and what sorts are unhealthy. They tend to get their information about these vital matters from television commercials, other advertisements, and TV talk shows. So they are ready-made suckers for every fad that comes down the pike. Recently, for example, many food products have been advertised as especially healthy because low in cholesterol, or even cholesterol free, while containing the usual (high) levels of fats, which the body then uses to make cholesterol. The ambiguity taken advantage of here is, again, the difference between what is in a food and what is in the bloodstream. Low blood cholesterol levels are good; low food cholesterol levels combined with high fat content are not good.

Interestingly, terms that can be used either relatively or absolutely, like *rich* and *poor*, sometimes cause trouble. Poverty, for instance, is exceedingly unpleasant anywhere, at any time. But the poor in the United States today are richer in absolute terms with respect to material wealth than the vast majority of people who lived in days of old or who live today in the so-called "third world" countries of Africa, Central and South America, and Asia. This important truth (Recall Muhammed Ali's remark quoted in Chapter 1) is masked by the fact that the term *poor*, in its relative sense, does apply to those Americans who are poor compared to other Americans, although rich compared to most people who lived in the past or who live in third world countries today.

## But Ambiguity Often Serves Useful Purposes

Students sometimes get the idea that ambiguity, certainly equivocation, always is bad. But that isn't true. Ambiguous uses of language, especially metaphorical ones, and even equivocations, can be employed for all kinds of good purposes. The well-known psychologist, Carl Rogers, for example, used equivocation very effectively in the following passage to emphasize a point:

As a boy I was rather sickly, and my parents have told me that it was predicted I would die young. This prediction has been proven completely wrong in one sense, but has come profoundly true in another sense. I think it is correct that I will never live to be old. So I now agree with the prediction that I will die young.*

Ambiguous uses of language also serve to grease the wheels of social intercourse. Benjamin Disraeli, the nineteenth-century British prime minister, often used ambiguity to soften his replies to letters, while still coming close to being truthful, as in his reply to an unsolicited amateur manuscript: "Many thanks; I shall lose no time in reading it." (In most other contexts, of course, equivocation of this kind is rightly considered to be rather sneaky.)

Ambiguity also serves very useful purposes in literature, particularly in metaphoric passages. It enables writers to quickly introduce multiple meanings into a text in a way that adds significance to what is being said by drawing attention to often rather subtle connections without hitting us over the head with them. For example, the title of Joseph Conrad's great novel *Heart of Darkness* doesn't just refer to the central part of the African jungle but also captures some of the moral horror of the principal character, Kurtz, succumbing to the dark temptations of African life, and by extension draws attention to the corruption and depravity "civilized" people are capable of when they give in to their base instincts. It also suggests the appalling abuses of power resulting from the exploitation of Africans and their lands by European colonials at the turn of the century. The ambiguity lurking in the title of Conrad's novel thus prepares us for the complex moral issues addressed in his classic work.

## 5. Appeal to Ignorance

When good reasons are lacking, the rational conclusion to draw is that we just don't know. But when we greatly desire to believe something, it is tempting to take the absence of evidence, and thus absence of refutation, as justification for believing that it is true. Doing this makes us guilty of the fallacy **appeal to ignorance** (traditionally known as *argumentum ad ignorantiam*). Some people have argued, for example, that we should believe there is no intelligent life on other planets anywhere in our galaxy, since no one has been able to prove that there is; indeed, until recently, when the existence of other planets was confirmed, it was sometimes argued that there are no planets anywhere other than our own tight little island.

The fallacy in this sort of reasoning can be seen by turning it on its head. If appeals to ignorance could prove that no life exists on other planets, then it equally well could prove just the opposite. After all, no one has proved that life does not exist on any of these planets. In the absence of good evidence for a claim, the right thing to do is to be *agnostic* on the issue and neither believe nor disbelieve. Ignorance proves nothing, except, of course, that we are ignorant.

There are, however, cases in which the failure of a search does count against a claim. That happens when whatever is searched for would very likely have been found if it existed. Given all the sky watching that has gone on in the past 10,000 years, the claim

---

*Carl Rogers, *Journal of Humanistic Psychology* (Fall 1980).

In 1950, when Senator Joseph R. McCarthy (Republican, Wisconsin), was asked about the fortieth name on a list of 81 names of people he claimed were communists working for the United States Department of State, he responded that "I do not have much information on this except the general statement of the agency that there is nothing in the files to disprove his communist connections."

*Many of McCarthy's followers took this absence of evidence as proof that the person in question was indeed a communist, a good example of the fallacy of* appeal to ignorance. *This example also illustrates the importance of not being taken in by this fallacy. No scrap of relevant evidence ever was presented against any of the people charged by Senator McCarthy, yet for several years he enjoyed great popularity and power; his "witch hunt" ruined many innocent lives before, finally, McCarthy and "McCarthyism" were brought down in congressional hearings that revealed the true character of this miserable person.*

that there exists a planet-sized object between Earth and Mars is disproved by the failure of anyone to observe it. Similarly, the failure to find evidence of a virus in a blood test justifies a doctor's conclusion that we aren't infected with that virus. These are not cases of reasoning from ignorance, but rather of reasoning from the *knowledge* that we would have found the item looked for if it had been there to find.

Note, however, the importance of *appropriately* searching. That telescopes have searched the sky for several hundred years, and naked eyes for thousands, without spotting a god up there proves absolutely nothing about the existence of a god in the sky, since deities are not conceived of as the kind of entities that can be seen in this way.

## 6. COMPOSITION AND DIVISION

The fallacy of **composition**, also called the *salesman's fallacy*, but more accurately the *consumer's fallacy*, is committed when someone assumes that a particular item must have a certain property because all of its parts have that property. Auto dealers, for example, frequently try to get prospective customers to fall for this fallacy by touting low monthly payments while neglecting total costs, hoping their marks will assume that if the monthly payments are low, then the total cost must be low also. Washers and dryers used to be sold by telling customers that it takes "only 50 cents a day" to buy one. Of course, 50 cents a day adds up to $365 in two years (a lot of money until rather recently), something buyers seldom thought to figure out even though the arithmetic involved is on the grade school level.

The fallacy of **division** is committed when we assume that all (or some) of the parts of an item have a particular property because the item as a whole has it. The fallacy of *division* thus is the mirror image of the fallacy of *composition*. While infrequently fallen for in everyday life, cases do happen. An example is concluding that the rooms in a large hotel are large, as guests often do when making reservations at large, fancy hotels such as the Plaza in New York (where in fact lots of rooms are rather tiny).

## 7. Slippery Slope

In a typical *slippery slope* argument, a course of action is objected to on the grounds that once it is taken, another, and then perhaps still another, is bound to be taken, down a "slippery slope," until some undesirable consequence results. According to a slightly different version, whatever would justify taking the first step would also justify all the others, but since the last step isn't justified, the first isn't either.

Arguing that a slope is slippery without providing good reason for thinking that it is makes us guilty of the *fallacy* of the **slippery slope**. For example, a Canadian style "single payer" health care system has often been objected to on grounds that it is a kind of socialized medicine and that its adoption would lead to socialized insurance of all kinds, socialized railroads, airlines, and so on, without sufficient reason being presented for believing this would be the case. It also sometimes is argued that whatever would justify a single payer system of health care also would justify all sorts of other socialistic measures, again without justifying this conclusion.

Note, however, that some slopes may well be slippery. The *slippery slope* fallacy is committed only when we accept *without further justification or argument* that once the first step is taken, the others are going to follow, or that whatever would justify the first step would in fact justify the rest. Note, also, that what some see as the undesirable consequence lurking at the bottom of the slope others may regard as very desirable indeed.

---

Earlier editions of this text at this point had a section on a variation of the fallacy *slippery slope* called the *domino theory*. Back in the nasty old Cold War days, dominoes were alleged to be in danger of falling all over the globe. Perhaps the chief reason advanced by the Johnson and Nixon administrations for our involvement in the war in Vietnam was that if Vietnam fell to the communists, the rest of Southeast Asia would also, and then countries in Central America (Nicaragua, El Salvador, and so on) and even parts of South America (in particular, Chile). Although we were defeated in Vietnam, it is primarily communist dominoes that have fallen, perhaps the reason that the *domino theory* has gone out of fashion.

---

## SUMMARY OF CHAPTER 4

1. *Ad hominem argument*: An irrelevant attack on an opponent rather than on the opponent's evidence or arguments. *Example*: Senator Jennings Randolph responding to proponents of the Equal Rights Amendment by calling them "braless bubbleheads." Note, however, that not all character attacks are fallacious, as they may not be when challenging the integrity of an allegedly expert witness.

   We're guilty of the variation on this fallacy called *guilt by association* when we judge someone guilty solely on the basis of the company that person keeps.

2. *Two wrongs make a right*: Justifying a wrong by pointing to a similar wrong perpetrated by others. *Example*: Defending affirmative action for "people of color"

on the grounds that privileged whites often get special treatment. Note, however, that when fighting fire with fire, what would otherwise be a wrong often isn't, as when someone kills in self-defense.

Although there is an air of hypocrisy to a charge coming from an equally guilty party, this doesn't make an accurate charge any less on target.

Variations: *Common practice*, in which a wrong is justified because commonly engaged in. *Traditional wisdom*, in which a wrong is justified because that's the way things always have been done.

3. *Irrelevant reason*: Trying to prove something with evidence that is or comes close to being irrelevant. (Some other term, such as *ad hominem argument* may also apply.) *Example*: Countering the claims of antiwar protesters by arguing that antiwar talk tells the enemy we don't have the resolve to fight.

4. *Equivocation*: Using a term or expression in an argument in one sense in one place and another sense in another. *Example*: The TV evangelist's use of the expression "son of God" to refer to Jesus Christ and to a parishioner. Note, however, that intentional ambiguity, even equivocation, is not always fallacious. It isn't, for example, when used for metaphoric effect.

5. *Appeal to ignorance*: Arguing that the failure to find evidence refuting a claim justifies believing that it is true. *Example*: Senator Joseph McCarthy's claim that 81 State Department employees were communists because there was no proof that they were not. Note, however, that the failure of appropriate searches sometimes does support rejection of a claim.

6. *Composition*: Assuming that an item has a certain property because all or most of its parts have that property. *Example*: Assuming a commodity is inexpensive because of low installment payments.

   *Division*: Assuming that all or most parts of an item have a property because the whole item has it. *Example*: Assuming the rooms in a large hotel are large.

7. *Slippery slope*: Accepting a claim that a slope is slippery when no or insufficient reason has been presented to justify that claim. *Example*: Arguing that adoption of a single payer health plan will lead to adoption of all sorts of other socialistic measures.

## EXERCISE 4-1

Determine which fallacies (if any) occur in the following short passages and justify your answers (as you did when working on Exercise 3-1). (Some of these passages may contain fallacies discussed in the previous chapter.)

1. Letter to the Editor, *San Francisco Chronicle*: What, again? Another jab at the CIA by [columnist and reporter] Jack Anderson? . . . All countries have spy organizations. Most of them sometimes overstep the bounds of propriety. Why single out our own outfit?

2. From a conversation overheard in early 1994 during a large social event: *She*: I don't see what's so bad about how the Clintons have done in the White

House. They're doing pretty good as far as I'm concerned. *He*: Boy, you are gullible. They've been playing dirty power politics since the day they, ah, he, took office. *She*: Really? How do you know? *He*: They're Arkansas politicians, aren't they? Arkies are next to Okies.

3. Article in a college newspaper: A committee on teaching evaluation in colleges is the coming thing. Most other colleges have formed such a committee.

*4. Football player Roger Craig, on George Seifert's promotion to head coach of the San Francisco 49ers: I think George will do an excellent job, because he's been searching for a head coaching job for some time, and what better place to start his head coaching job. (In fact, Seifert did have an excellent record with the 49ers before being canned.)

5. *HK:* Hey, what's with all this junk food you bought? You're always railing at me about eating healthy. *Aunt:* Don't fuss. It was on sale. *HK:* Oh.

*6. Bumper sticker seen in California when a handgun bill was before voters of that state:
Gun Registration Equals Mass Extermination
First Register Guns, Then Register the Jews

7. (In this case, the question is what fallacy, if any, Momma failed to put over on her son.)

*Momma* by Mell Lazarus. Courtesy of Mell Lazarus and Field Newspaper Syndicate.

8. Jan Berger in the *Baltimore Evening Sun*: Weeks of patient investigation have revealed that the gas leaked at Bhopal [India—with thousands of casualties] because something went wrong.

9. Claim made by opponents of an initiative to legalize marijuana for medicinal purposes: It would be foolish to permit the sale of marijuana to seriously ill people on the recommendation of their physicians. That just opens the floodgates to the complete legalization of that dangerous drug.

10. A letter to the editor of *Connoisseur* magazine (January 1992) defended a previous article favoring bullfighting from "the protesting letters you are sure to receive," by reminding readers that bulls selected for the arena live twice as long as those destined for McDonald's and die in a far more noble fashion.

11. *Hal*: Here you are late again, so we missed the start of the flick. You promised last time you were late that you'd always be on time in future.
    *Enn*: Now you know how I feel when you're late for our walks with Harriet.

12. Jacob Neusner in "The Speech the Graduates Didn't Hear": Few professors actually care whether or not they are liked by peer-paralyzed adolescents, fools so shallow as to imagine professors care not about education but about popularity.

*13. Indian mystic Vivekananda: There is no past or future even in thought, because to think it you have to make it present.

14. From a conversation with a friend (not verbatim): Sure, I've told you before that I believe everyone's opinion counts on moral matters like abortion. But not *everyone's* opinion counts—I wouldn't want Hitler's to count. Well, [name deleted] isn't a Hitler, but she sleeps around like sex were going out of style next week, or something. She's just a slut, and she's broken up at least one marriage I know about. Why should her opinion count on anything? Why should we listen to her opinion on the abortion business?

15. Argument heard all too frequently in introductory philosophy classes: We're perfectly entitled to believe there is a God. After all, every effort by atheists to prove otherwise has failed.

16. Lewis Carroll, in *Through the Looking Glass*: "You couldn't have it if you did want it," the Queen said. "The rule is jam tomorrow and jam yesterday—but never jam *today*." "It *must* sometimes come to jam today," Alice objected. "No it can't," said the Queen. "It's jam every *other* day: today isn't any *other* day, you know."

17. Senator Lloyd Bentsen (in October 1988, after his debate with rival vice presidential candidate Senator Dan Quayle): After listening to Dan Quayle for 90 minutes, I can understand why he kept talking about job training.

18. Robert Ringer in *The Tortoise Report* (September 1983) touting gold as an investment: Two thousand years after the human flesh had disappeared, the gold that adorned it [an ancient Egyptian corpse] remained virtually unchanged. That's a real hard act for paper money to follow.

19. Dialogue from the movie *Fun with Dick and Jane* about whether to keep the money Jane has stolen:
    *Jane Fonda*: We've always done things the straight way.
    *George Segal*: Yeah. Well, I'm tired of belonging to a minority group.

20. Overheard on the bus to Atlantic City: I just play the quarter slots when I go to Atlantic City. That way, I don't lose too much money.

21. Peter O'Rourke, California Office of Traffic Safety, *San Francisco Chronicle* (August 20,1989): It isn't that our freeway system can't handle the cars; it's that congestion bottlenecks the system and prevents the smooth flow of traffic.

*22. Sigmund Freud: Our own death is . . . unimaginable, and whenever we make the attempt to imagine it we can perceive that we really survive as spectators.

23. *The Washington Monthly* (November 1989): There are many reasons to suspect that the affluent are not only wealthier than the rest of us, they're also more selfish. The latest evidence comes from the economist James Henry, who has discovered that the richest 12 percent of individual taxpayers are responsible for 40 percent of tax underpayments. Of the returns actually audited by the IRS, more than 70 percent of those for incomes above $200,000 conceal unreported income.

24. St. Augustine, in *De Libero Arbitrio*: See how absurd and foolish it is to say: I should prefer nonexistence to miserable existence. He who says, I prefer this to that, chooses something. Nonexistence is not something; it is nothing. There can be no real choice when what you choose is nothing.

25. Michael Kinsley, well-known writer and former co-host of the TV program *Crossfire*, after admitting to doing paid speeches before various groups (the suggestion was that his fees were payola), declined to state how much he was paid, saying: I do staged debates—mini *Crossfires*—before business groups. If everyone [others in the media] disclosed, I would. (Quoted in the *New Yorker*, September 12, 1994.)

26. The November 21, 1991, *San Francisco Chronicle* contained a story about a doctor fired from his university position for having "doctored" statistics in one of his papers on AIDS. In response, he said, in part, that the university had "misinterpreted what happened." He claimed to be the victim of an "agenda." He stated that "they have other cases where they covered up misconduct, and this [firing] is an attempt to show they can prosecute."

27. A lobbyist, whose job is to get people to call or write to members of Congress, responding to the charge that this sort of activity makes the "political playing field" uneven (because big money can afford these endeavors much better than small): Everyone knows that the playing field isn't level in this country in the business arena, or in others for that matter. Nobody complains about that. Why fuss about the funding for what I do?

*Doonesbury* by Garry Trudeau. Copyright, 1975, G. B. Trudeau.
All rights reserved. Used by permission of Universal Press Syndicate.

*It's dangerous to conclude that A is the cause of B just because B follows A.*

*Figures don't lie, but liars figure.*
　　　　　　　　　— Old saying

*There are lies, damn lies, and statistics.*
　　　　　　　　　— Benjamin Disraeli

*It's very difficult to make predictions,
especially about the future.*
　　　　　　　　　— Casey Stengel

*Chapter*

# 5

# FALLACIOUS
# REASONING—3

Let's now continue our discussion of fallacious reasoning with several fallacies that
generally fall into the broad category *invalid inference*.

## 1. HASTY CONCLUSION

The fallacy of **hasty conclusion** is committed when we draw a conclusion from relevant
but insufficient evidence. This fallacy is committed in many different ways and circumstances, ranging from judging political candidates primarily on the basis of
30-second TV commercials to concluding a neighbor is having an affair on the basis
of one or two suspicious clues.

　　Of course, if we mere human beings were as lucky as J. B. Fletcher, Hercule Poirot,
Miss Marple, or the other famous fictional detectives, our overly hasty conclusions
would frequently turn out to be correct. Here, for example, is the archetype of the great
fictional detective, Sherlock Holmes, making one of his amazing "deductions" when
first introduced to Dr. Watson in Sir Arthur Conan Doyle's *A Study in Scarlet*:

> Here is a gentleman of the medical type, but with the air of a military man. Clearly
> an army doctor, then. He has just come from the tropics, for his face is dark, and
> that is not the natural tint of his skin, for his wrists are fair. He has undergone
> hardship and sickness, as his haggard face says clearly. His left arm has been
> injured. He holds it in a still and unnatural manner. Where in the tropics could
> an English army doctor have seen much hardship and gotten his arm wounded?
> Clearly in Afghanistan.

What Holmes observed about Watson was consistent with all sorts of other possibilities that in real life might have been actualities. Doctors don't look that much different from other professionals. Some men with a military air (whatever that might be) never have been in the military. Among Englishmen in those days, when Britain ruled the waves, naval military men were just as common as army types. Tanned faces can result from exposure to nontropical sunlight. A still and unnatural arm carriage may be the legacy of a childhood accident, a haggard expression due to anguish at the loss of a close relative. And even supposing the person in question were a military man who had been wounded in battle in Afghanistan, he still might just have come from a funeral in Italy, South Africa, Brighton, or Timbuktu. The conclusion drawn by Holmes may have been a good guess, but stated with the typical Holmes air of infallibility, it surely was hasty.

## 2. SMALL SAMPLE

Statistics frequently are used to project from a sample to the "population" from which it was drawn. This is the basic technique that underlies polls—including those conducted by Gallup and Harris, and the Nielsen television ratings—as well as other sorts of inductive reasoning. But when we accept a conclusion based on a sample that is too small to be a reliable measure of the population from which it was drawn, we are guilty of the fallacy of the **small sample**, a variety of the fallacy *hasty conclusion*. No sample of 100 voters, for instance, can possibly be depended on to accurately reflect the entire voting population of the United States.

Scientists, of all people, aren't supposed to commit statistical fallacies (or any fallacies, for that matter), but they're human, just like the rest of us. In an interesting example (*Human Nature*, March 1979), researchers drew a conclusion about the mating vocal responses of primate species based on a sample of three human couples (each observed engaged in sex exactly once), a pair of gibbons, and one troop of chacma baboons.

The general question as to when a sample is sufficiently large is extremely difficult to answer and is a matter of great interest to statisticians and other scientists.

## 3. UNREPRESENTATIVE SAMPLE

In addition to being large enough, a good sample must be *representative* of the population from which it is drawn. Indeed, the more representative it is, the smaller a sample can be and still be significant. When we reason from a sample that isn't sufficiently representative, we commit the fallacy of the **unrepresentative sample** (sometimes called the fallacy of *biased statistics*, although that name also applies to cases where known statistics that are unfavorable to a theory are deliberately suppressed).

---

Sample size does not overcome sample bias.

— Saying popular among statisticians

The example just mentioned, about primate mating responses, illustrates the fallacy of the *unrepresentative sample* as well as that of the *small sample*. For one thing, only three of the dozens of primate species were checked—chimps, gorillas, tarsiers, and so forth may be quite different. For another, there is plenty of reason for believing that no sample of three human couples could possibly be representative of all *Homo sapiens*, given the tremendous variety of sex practices engaged in by members of our species.

As usual, relevant background information is crucial when we try to determine whether a sample is likely to be representative of the population from which it was drawn (or is likely to be sufficiently large, for that matter). Good reasoning *always* requires good background information.

## 4. QUESTIONABLE CAUSE

We commit the fallacy of **questionable cause** when we label something as the cause of something else on the basis of insufficient or unrepresentative evidence, or when doing so contradicts well-established, high-level theories.* (*Questionable cause* is a broader version of the traditional fallacy *post hoc, ergo propter hoc*, literally "after this, therefore because of this.")

As just mentioned, it isn't easy to determine whether a sample is sufficiently large or representative. This is true in particular because judgments on these matters often depend on seeing the relevance of background information *and bringing it to bear*. All too often, people make judgments about causal connections on the basis of observed correlations, often quite small, that contradict very general and quite easily understood theories about what sorts of causes can result in what kinds of effects. Often they do so because they lack the relevant and *accurate* background information; sometimes they are motivated by wishful thinking to ignore contrary evidence or theories (a topic to be discussed at some length in the next chapter).

Many people have little or no understanding of the general way in which things work in this world. As they experience life, they don't try to figure out how things work in general, or attempt to gain some of the knowledge that has been gleaned over time by others. Instead, they attend almost exclusively to immediate events and problems. They may see science as some kind of magical box from which gadgets like television sets, computers, and jet planes are extracted by bearded drudges with German accents. Having relatively little background information to bring to bear on experience, they are unable to assess either the adequacy of evidence or the possibility that a general idea might be true. Think, for instance, of those who fall for regimens that supposedly reduce body fat in certain parts of the body (such as the hips) by exercising muscles in those locations, ignorant of the well-known fact that the body doesn't burn body fat in that way; or who believe in ESP in spite of the failure of every scientific test to confirm its existence.

---

*This doesn't mean that these higher-level theories are exempt from refutation. Evidence that persistently runs contrary to even the highest-level, most general scientific theories eventually, and sometimes rather swiftly, overturns them, as, for example, old ideas about the motions of continents, and related matters, were overturned by evidence favoring the currently held theory concerning plate tectonics.

*The Small Society.* Reprinted by permission of the Washington Star Syndicate, Inc.

*It isn't always easy to determine what is the cause of what.*

In any case, the fallacy *questionable cause* also sometimes is committed because items are incorrectly classified—poorly sorted into different kinds. Any items, no matter how different from each other, have some things in common, so that there always is some reason for grouping them together in our thoughts. When we classify items in order to discover cause/effect relationships, we need to make sure we have bunched together just the right sorts of cases. In some areas of the United States, for instance, a larger percentage of nonwhite children* do poorly in school compared to students who are white, a fact that has led some people to conclude that being nonwhite is the *cause* of their doing less well in school, an interesting and very serious example of the fallacy *questionable cause.*

As might be expected, the statistical variety of *questionable cause*, in which a mere statistical correlation is taken to provide proof of a causal connection, is quite common. It's true that every statistical correlation has some significance and, in the absence of reasons to the contrary, increases the likelihood (probability), however slightly, that there also is a causal connection between the things correlated. But when there are reasons to the contrary, or the statistical sample in question is too small or unrepresentative, we make a mistake in jumping to the conclusion that we've found a causal connection.

Sometimes alleged causal connections based on statistical surveys are too silly to take seriously, because they are so obviously contrary to well-supported background beliefs. An example is the theory that smoking marijuana causes college students to get better grades, based on one dubious statistical study in which marijuana smokers averaged slightly higher grades than nonsmokers. This theory actually gained modest acceptance in some, ah . . ., "high"-minded circles during the 1970s. (And what are the

---

*Notice that in the United States, nonwhite is an ethnic, not a racial, category. Most Americans who think of themselves as African American are racially both of white (European) and African American (African) descent; a few are of African and Asian stock; and a very few are descended from European, African, and Asian forebears (Tiger Woods being a well-known example).

The
General Surgeon
has determined that breathing
is dangerous to your health.
This conclusion
was drawn from a survey
of 100 Canadian rats
that have died
within the past 5 years.
All were
habitual breathers.

*Greeting card humor illustrating some fallacy or other, no doubt.*

background beliefs that should make you doubt smoking dope causes an increase in grades?)

But often the questionable connection is less obviously in conflict with background beliefs or perhaps does not conflict with them at all. Take the very serious question of the alleged connection between caffeine consumption and various kinds of cancer and heart disease. Some statistical studies have shown correlations of this kind and some have not, but the samples, and sometimes the populations from which they were drawn, were different in each case. Which, then, if any, truly represent, say, the whole population of the industrial world? Are any of the conclusions drawn from these studies to be believed? These are difficult questions to which lay people must take a "watch and wait" attitude, at least until the medical profession itself comes to some sort of agreement. (Obviously, prudence requires those at great risk, say, of heart disease to cut down on coffee just in case, because the risk, even if low, outweighs the pleasurable benefits of drinking coffee.)

It's often very hard, if not impossible, for the lay person to evaluate statistical claims on complicated or technical subjects. Sometimes, the best that nonexperts can do is try to find the best professional advice they can. But sometimes they can evaluate these claims by employing the method described in the following excerpt from a *Psychology Today* article on statistical reasoning:

> *"What do the other three cells look like?"* This slogan should always be invoked to assess covariation [the statistical connection] of events. . . . To determine the effectiveness of chiropractic treatment, for example, one needs numbers from four

"cells." How many people were cured after being treated by a chiropractor? How many were not cured after such treatment? How many people got better without treatment? How many didn't get better and went untreated?

Most of us are impressed when we see first cell statistics and fail to realize that we usually need to know about one or more of the others to determine whether we've found a causal connection or just a statistical one. Reading, say, that about two-thirds of those treated by chiropractors get better proves nothing about the effectiveness of chiropractors; it may be that two-thirds of those with similar complaints who were not so treated also got well, or even that three-quarters did (in which case we would have evidence that chiropractors harm patients more than they help them.)

## 5. QUESTIONABLE ANALOGY

We reason by *analogy* when we conclude from the observed similarity of two or more items in some respects to their similarity in another.* Sports fans, for example, reason by analogy when they conclude that the next Olympic games will be fun to watch, given that they were enjoyable in previous years. (But see Chapter 11 for a discussion of media coverage of the 1996 Olympic games!) Caffeine lovers do so when they reason from the fact that coffee has kept them awake several nights in a row to the conclusion that drinking it again tonight will keep them awake.† The general form of such reasoning is that the items mentioned are alike in certain respects, so they will be alike in some other way.

But we aren't always justified in reasoning by analogy. When we do so anyway, we are guilty of the fallacy of **questionable analogy**, sometimes referred to as **faulty comparison**.

Analogical reasoning can be fallacious for several different reasons. The sample on which it is based may be too small or not sufficiently representative (recall the recent discussions of sample size and representativeness); or it may conflict with conclusions drawn by higher-level reasoning; or there may be a lack of relevant similarity between the items implied to be alike. Here is an example based on a much too small sample:

> I've won at blackjack twice in a row by drawing a card when holding cards totaling 18, so I conclude by analogy that I'll win next time I draw on 18.

This analogy also is defective because it ignores the higher-level theory of probability, which says your chances of success when drawing on 18 are quite low.

In some cases, the unapt nature of an analogy should make it obviously questionable. We frequently hear arguments, for example, urging cessation of an alleged wrong by comparing it to the Nazi persecution of the Jews, where it is clear that the wrong in question bears little resemblance to that horrible catastrophe. In a press conference in February 1996, for instance, after a meeting with Iraqi leader Saddam Hussein, Nation

---

*Analogical reasoning thus is very similar to *induction by enumeration*. Indeed the latter can be thought of as a kind of analogical reasoning.
†Recall, though, the earlier discussion of the fallacy *questionable cause*. It isn't easy to be positive that it's coffee keeping us awake.

of Islam leader Louis Farrakhan argued that our policy toward Iraq made life miserable for Iraqi citizens and compared the situation in Iraq to that in Nazi concentration camps. (Comparing whoever, or whatever, one dislikes to the Nazis, or to Nazi atrocities, has become a favorite way of arguing *ad hominem* these days.)

The fallacy of *questionable analogy* often is concealed in reasoning that appears to be legitimate. During the Cold War, Congressman Charles Rose (Democrat, North Carolina) answered (in part) the arguments of those opposed to government-sponsored research to develop "remote viewing—the ability to see a distant place telepathically"— by stating that "It seems to me that it would be a hell of a cheap radar system, and if the Russians have it and we don't, we are in serious trouble. This country wasn't afraid to look into the strange physics behind lasers and semiconductors, and I don't think we should be afraid to look into this."

Rose's analogy was between the successful development of lasers and semiconductors and the creation of a long-range telepathic system. This analogy was fallacious because the items compared were not relevantly alike: The so-called "strange physics" behind lasers and semiconductors grew out of the main body of extremely well-confirmed physical scientific theory; there is no similar body of evidence or theory that lends the slightest support to telepathy. (One suspects that Rose had no idea about what science was up to. His mind-set was more political than realistic—his comment, "if the Russians have it and we don't, we are in serious trouble," reminds one of the "mineshaft gap" in the movie *Dr. Strangelove*.)

Before turning to a discussion of other fallacies, perhaps it should be noted that we need to distinguish between *explanatory* analogies used to explain and *argumentative* analogies used to prove a point. When we argue or reason analogically, we present evidence for a conclusion; when we use an analogy to explain, we merely liken the thing explained to something already familiar. In Plato's famous analogy of the cave, for example, the people in the cave who merely see the shadows of things are likened to those who restrict themselves to the ever-changing world of everyday experience, while the person who comes out into the sunlight and sees the objects themselves is likened to the philosophers who reason to the unchanging reality that lies behind everyday experiences. The analogy explains Plato's ideas about a world beyond that of mere everyday experiences, but it doesn't prove that there is such a world or in any way argue that there is. (Plato himself seems to have intended his cave myth to be explanatory, not argumentative, but it sometimes is construed otherwise.)

The point here is that we shouldn't accuse those whose analogies are intended to explain of being guilty of the fallacy *questionable analogy*. It's true, though, that explanatory analogies sometimes are mistakenly taken to prove what they merely explain, and in this case we are indeed justified in accusing those who do this of the fallacy *questionable analogy*.

Finally, we need to notice that in everyday life it often is difficult to determine whether an analogy is intended to explain or to prove; no doubt some are intended to serve both purposes. In any case, as with explanations in general, it is hard to separate the mere explanatory nature of an analogy from its power to persuade. (Recall, for example, the salesperson's explanation about TV sets in Chapter 1, where the intent was to persuade a customer to buy a TV set, not merely to explain the differences between one set and another.)

## 6. QUESTIONABLE STATISTICS

Statistics always seem so precise and *authoritative*. It sounds so much more believable, for instance, to claim that the typical child watches an average of 4,286 acts of violence on TV by age 18 rather than just that kids typically watch an awful lot of TV violence. But how could anyone know such an exact fact? There would have to be a lot of guesswork and extrapolation from very small samples to arrive even at an informed rough estimate as to these sorts of matters. This doesn't mean that we ought simply to dismiss these statistics; it just means that we have to understand their limitations.

Statistics on the state of the economy are a case in point. Take the ones published by the federal government on business conditions in the United States. One of the major problems with these statistics is that their *margin of error* (not always provided) often is greater than the "significant" differences they report. This becomes evident when we consider that the government's revisions of its own figures often show a change larger than the alleged margin of error.

---

*Reliable statistics concerning illegal activities are by their very nature hard to come by. During the past 30 or so years, we have been bombarded with statistics about drug-related crime (generally cited by those in favor of keeping certain drugs illegal) that do not go away in spite of regular refutation.*

*About 20 years ago, for example, dubious statistics concerning New York City's heroin-related crimes gained wide circulation. (New York City has more heroin addicts than any other city in America.) It was said that the "over 100,000 heroin addicts" were stealing about $5 billion worth of property every year, based on the idea that addicts were spending about $30 a day, or about $1.1 billion a year, to support their habits ($100,000 \times 365 \times \$30 = \$1.095$ billion) and fencing stolen goods at a bit less than one-fourth their value ($1.1 billion $\times 4 = \$4.4$ billion).*

*This particular bogus stat was skewered very nicely in an article by Max Singer, who noticed that all retail sales in New York City in those days amounted to about $15 billion. He divided this by the generally accepted figure of losses from theft and embezzlement—2 percent—and concluded that a total of $300 million was lost every year due to retail theft. Even assuming half of these thefts were drug related, we get only $150 million. He then very generously assumed that one in five New York City households were burglarized every year (far higher than the true rate); and multiplying this by police estimates that the average burglary loss was $200, concluded that the total burglary loss per year was at most $100 million. So even if every crime of this sort was committed by heroin addicts, a ridiculous assumption, the total amount involved in all shoplifting and burglary by addicts would be $250 million, or only one-twentieth of the claimed $5 billion. (This and similar examples were cited by George Will in one of his 1992 columns that was reprinted in the* Quarterly Review of Doublespeak, *July 1992.)*

*It might be expected that refutations of this kind would eventually win the day, but in fact similar statistics are still regularly cited by those intent on keeping heroin, opium, and other poppy derivatives illegal.*

# DOLLAR$ AND NON$EN$E™

"The Net National Product—the total output of all the goods and services minus the total output of all the bads and disservices—rose slightly last month."

In addition, problems arise from the need to use a base year in determining long-run trends. Those who want to show that a given year has had a high rate of growth can choose a low base year; those intent on proving a low rate of growth a high base year. Meanwhile, the precisely true rate of growth may remain in doubt.

In the case of figures concerning the gross national product, there are several other reasons for being suspicious. One is that a good deal of commerce in the United States today is illegal. Think only of racketeering, gambling, drug traffic, prostitution, and the hiring of illegal aliens to do migrant farm labor and other low-paying or back-breaking jobs. Calculating, say, commerce in illegal drugs has to be done indirectly, by reference to the sale of legal drug equipment, drug busts, and so on.

Another reason for suspicion is that a good deal of otherwise legal commerce is done "off the books," so that no taxes need to be paid or so that restrictive laws can be avoided. How are we to assess the value of goods when one kind is bartered for another?

The government's figures on unemployment also need to be viewed with a good deal of suspicion. These figures are calculated on the basis of information gathered via polls of "representative" individuals. How these people respond depends on the precise wording of the questions they are asked (a point soon to be discussed further), and this in part depends on what the government considers to be full-time, compared to part-time employment, and who is said to be seeking employment as compared to those who have given up the search. (It also depends on how truly representative the government's samples happen to be.) In 1994, for instance, the federal government started using a genuinely improved system for gathering unemployment statistics that placed unemployment in January 1994 at 6.7 percent, up from the 6.4 percent figure reported for December 1993; but government officials themselves stated that unemployment probably was down, rather than up, during that period (which means that unemployment for December 1993 probably was higher than 6.7 percent, not the reported 6.4 percent).

All of this does not mean that government statistics on commerce and employment should be tossed into the nearest wastebasket. But it does mean that precise official figures should be taken for what they are: the best *approximations* we have of business activity, valuable primarily in showing very-long-term trends, but often calculated so as to serve short-term political interests.*

By way of contrast, consider a correctly cautious claim typical of those frequently made by scientists (*Science News*, January 19, 1991): Scientists using sophisticated techniques to determine the age of ancient cliff drawings in west Texas *estimated* that the drawings were painted "3,865 years ago, *give or take a century*" (italics added).

Finally, it's important to have some idea as to which sorts of statistics can be known, even in theory. Some statistics simply are *unknowable*, at least by human beings. How, for instance, could Dr. Dean Edell (whose TV and radio programs usually provide excellent information about health and medical matters) know that the average person tells 13 lies per week, as he stated on one of his programs? How could anyone know? Anyway, here is a letter one of the authors of this text received several years ago that contains examples of unknowable statistics it would be hard to top:

> Dear Friend: In the past 5,000 years men have fought in 14,523 wars. One out of four persons living during this time have been war casualties. A nuclear war would add 1,245,000,000 men, women, and children to this tragic list.

It's ludicrous to present such precise figures as facts. No one knows (or could know) the exact number of wars fought so far, to say nothing of the number of war casualties. (Does anyone even know the true casualty rates just for all of the wars that have occurred in the past ten years?) As for the numbers in a nuclear conflict, it would depend on who fought such a war, and, in any event, is a matter on which even so-called experts can only engage in the wildest sorts of speculations.

## 7. QUESTIONABLE USES OF STATISTICS

As we've just seen, statistics that are obviously questionable are a problem. But perfectly good statistics also can cause trouble—for two reasons. The first is the inability of so many people to understand the significance of this statistic or that, made worse by the natural tendency in all of us to see statistics as favoring conclusions we already have drawn. The second is the ability of charlatans to bamboozle the rest of us via cleverly employed statistics. (That's the import of the old saying that figures don't lie, but liars figure.)

---

*Think, for instance, of the 1996–1997 political battles over how the consumer price index (CPI) should be calculated. Because Social Security payments are tied to the CPI, those who wanted to balance the budget by reducing Social Security payments argued for a method that generally lowered the CPI; those who did not want to reduce Social Security payments fought to keep the old (in fact, more accurate) way of calculating.

The ways in which we confuse ourselves seem to be limitless. A recent article, for example, stated that "Of the $30 billion annually that business spends on training, $27 billion comes from 15,000 employers, about one-half of one percent of U.S. businesses," implying that most businesses are not doing their part here. But the statistic cited does not prove the point. How much of the national economy is controlled by these 15,000 businesses? Surely a very large majority. General Motors, General Electric, Wal-mart, IBM, and Ford, for example, count as only five businesses, but employ a significant percentage of all the laborers in the United States. (Note, again, the vital role played by relevant background information in critical reasoning!)

An item in the famous *Harper's Index* (February 1994) indicated that the murder rate is twice as high in states that have a death penalty for major crimes as it is in other states. Those opposed to the death penalty on grounds that it does not deter took this to be evidence supporting that conclusion. But sophisticated critical reasoners wondered whether doing so made them guilty of the fallacy *questionable cause*. For it very well may be that states with death penalties had a higher rate of murder to start with and that perhaps they opted for this harsh penalty in order to try to reduce the amount of serious crime. To prove their point, those opposed to the death penalty on these grounds would have to present statistics showing that serious crime remained the same, or increased, after a death penalty was imposed in particular states. Otherwise, the comparison is of apples and oranges.

It's often easy to prove a point simply by choosing statistics carefully, making sure not to cite the figures that are most relevant. Charlatans do this regularly, but everyone does so on occasion. The respected economist Robert J. Samuelson, for instance, did so when he argued that the American people "never had it so good," citing the fact that virtually all economic statistical indicators—concerning wages, family income, poverty, and so on—show a dramatic improvement now compared to 1945 at the end of World War II. What he neglected to mention (let's assume not with intent to deceive) is that nearly all of the improvements these figures demonstrate were made from 1945 to 1973; statistics since that time show either no improvement or, as some economists would say, "negative improvement."

Those intent on proving their point via carefully selected statistics frequently cite just those in what earlier was called the "first cell." (Recall the item about chiropractors.) But there are similar, and harder to detect, tricks that we need to watch out for. During the O. J. Simpson murder trial, for instance, defense lawyer Alan Dershowitz argued against the admission of evidence about Simpson having beaten his wife, Nicole Brown Simpson, on the grounds that only 1 in 1,000 men who beat their wives also murder

---

*Statistics seem to baffle almost everyone. Several years ago, when 200 educators were asked what percentage of children read at grade level or below, 78 percent failed to provide the correct answer—50 percent. Even teachers have a hard time keeping straight on the difference between* comparative *and* absolute *scales.*

*Another comparative rating that causes confusion is the IQ rating: Half of those who take the test must be rated at 100 or below, given that 100 merely marks the halfway point in results.*

them—far too slight a connection to admit such "highly prejudicial evidence." Der-showitz's statistical sleight of hand was explained by Thomas W. Hazlett in an article in *Reason* magazine (February 1995):

> The 1-in-1,000 probability is nonsense, because it tosses out the most important and least disputed fact of the entire trial: Nicole Brown Simpson has been mur-dered. Instead of predicting what the chances are that a battered wife will be slain, we have two pieces of evidence and ponder a third: Given that Nicole was bat-tered and that she was murdered, what are the chances the crime was committed by the ex- who battered her? Of the 2,000 such victims per year, one would think an overwhelming proportion—90 percent? 99 percent?—are murdered by those who abused them. (Looked at another way: What are the chances that a person who is severely abused will be murdered by someone other than the abuser?)

The judge in the case, Lance Ito (we put it this way because there may be one or two readers who haven't heard that Ito was the judge in this astoundingly famous case), by the way, wasn't taken in by Dershowitz's statistical chicanery.

## 8. Polls: An Important Special Case

A well-conceived and well-executed poll can be a fruitful way to find out all sorts of things, from the voter strength of a political candidate to Fido's preferences in dog food. Unfortunately, not all polls are created equal.

One problem is that the way in which a question is asked seriously influences the answers one can expect. It is extremely difficult, if not impossible, to word a question in a way that is completely neutral. At the height of the Watergate scandal, for instance, a Gallup poll asked the question:

> Do you think President Nixon should be impeached and compelled to leave the presidency, or not?

Thirty percent said yes. But a Pat Caddell private poll asked the question this way:

> Do you think the President should be tried, and removed from office if found guilty?

Fifty-seven percent answered yes to that one. So 30 percent answered yes to the ques-tion worded one way, 57 percent when the same question was put another way.

This fact has not escaped those intent on skewing poll results one way or the other. Here, for example, is a loaded question in a "National Public Safety Survey" con-ducted by Handgun Control, Inc.:

> Chief lobbyist for the NRA, Tanya Metaksa, announced recently, "We have the assurances of the speaker [Gingrich] that there will be repeal" of the assault weapons ban. Do you agree that *concern for public safety* and the *will of the people* should matter more to Congress than the agenda of the National Rifle Association?

What sorts of unfeeling monsters would answer that they do not agree—that they are not concerned for public safety and care not for the will of the people?

Of course, when it comes to slanted poll questions, the Democratic and Republican parties take a back seat to no one. Here are four typical examples taken from 1995 and 1996 mailings conducted by the Democratic National Committee of the Democratic party:

> Do you favor or oppose Republican plans to make huge cuts in entitlement spending, including $270 billion in reductions in Medicare, which will force the average Social Security recipient to spend almost half of his or her COLA [cost of living allowance] just to cover resulting higher out-of-pocket Medicare costs?
>
> . . . [T]he Republicans have proposed a "new budget plan" which would provide large tax cuts for the rich, large increases in defense spending and cuts in social programs and entitlement. Republicans claim that their plan will reduce the deficit. What is your opinion?
>
> [How high a priority would you put on] closing tax loopholes for large corporations and ending the tax exemption that allows billionaires to avoid taxes by renouncing their U.S. citizenship?
>
> Do you believe that government has a right to make decisions about a woman's reproductive rights?

The principal point of asking biased questions in a political survey is to make one's positions, or candidates, seem more popular than in fact they are, because of the "bandwagon" effect of being popular (discussed in the next chapter). During the 1996 session of Congress, for instance, Bob Dole, then Senate Majority Leader, in an attempt to influence passage of a Republican-sponsored balanced budget amendment to the Constitution, repeatedly cited a survey indicating that 79 percent of Americans favored a balanced budget amendment. But he omitted the fact that support for this extremely serious change in the Constitution shrank to 32 percent when respondents were asked not simply whether they favored such an amendment but rather: "Do you favor a balanced budget amendment if it means cuts in Social Security?"

---

*An article in the* International Herald Tribune *(June 18, 1995) by Andrew Pollack showed how statistics can be used to support both sides of a dispute by the way that things are categorized. Specifically, he showed how the United States supported its claim that American auto makers were not being given a fair shake in their effort to sell cars in Japan and how Japan used statistics to prove just the opposite. Japan's statistics, for example, showed that U.S. automakers were marketing only two models in Japan with the steering wheel on the right side of the car (Japanese drive on the right side of the road, as do the English), whereas U.S. statistics placed the number at 59. How was this possible? As Pollack explains, The U.S., but not Japan, counted autos made by American manufacturers in Europe and also those made by Mazda in Japan that are sold in Japan by Ford. Further, the U.S. view as to what constitutes a car model was more liberal than the Japanese, for example, regarding the Telstar autos sold by Ford as 16 different models (Ford Telstar II, 18iEf, Telstar II 18iE, Telstar II, 18iX, and so on). Claims made by the two countries as to how many U.S. cars are sold in Japan were similarly defended by one country counting only passenger cars, the other including commercial vehicle. And so on.*

*Doonesbury* by Garry Trudeau. Copyright, 1980, G. B. Trudeau.
All rights reserved. Used by permission of Universal Press Syndicate.

Polls also can be manipulated by means of the choice of questions asked—or passed over—and by the answers from which those polled are instructed to choose. Here is a *Washington Monthly* item (November 1989) that makes this point nicely:

> A friend who is a Harvard alumnus recently received a questionnaire from his alma mater asking him to choose "the three most important issues facing Harvard" from a list of nine. None of the nine mentioned the high cost of tuition.

Another problem with polls is that respondents don't want to seem prejudiced, or stupid. A 1981 Cambridge Reports poll conducted for Union Carbide asked:

> Some experts say that there are 50,000 toxic and poisonous chemical waste sites around the country that pose serious health and safety threats to the public. Other

experts say that . . . only a few of these sites pose a risk to the public. . . . In general, which view is closer to your own?

Common sense tells us that most Americans in those days knew next to nothing about the number of such sites (as they don't today!), yet 52 percent answered that there were 50,000, 25 percent that there were hardly any, and only 23 percent admitted that they didn't know.

But the biggest problem with polls no doubt is the difficulty of tapping a truly representative sample. The 1936 *Literary Digest* poll, based on names lifted from telephone directories and auto registration lists, is perhaps the most famous example of an extremely biased poll. It predicted that Alf Landon would defeat Franklin Roosevelt, while the actual result was a tremendous landslide reelecting Roosevelt. The magazine (which went out of business shortly afterward —*questionable cause*?) failed to take into account the fact that few people in the bottom half of the American population had telephones or autos in those days, so that their sample was completely unrepresentative of American voters.

Of course, the art of polling has come a long way since 1936, or even 1948, when polls predicted an easy victory for Thomas E. Dewey over Harry Truman. (The *Chicago Tribune*—whose motto, incidentally, was and is "The World's Greatest Newspaper"— was so sure Dewey would win that it grossly misinterpreted early returns and printed one of the most infamous headlines in newspaper history—"Dewey Defeats Truman"— which an exultant Truman held up to the crowd at his victory celebration.) But it still is difficult to get a representative sample of the voting population by polling only 1,500 or so potential voters—the standard practice today. In theory, a very carefully selected sample of roughly this size should be almost as reliable as one of 15,000 (polls this large would be much too expensive and are never conducted). But in practice, for all sorts of reasons, it frequently doesn't work as planned. This doesn't mean that we should not pay attention to polls. They often are the best or even the only way we have of

---

*Poll results usually are announced with a statement concerning the "margin of error" of the poll. Whatever that may mean, it isn't true that such a poll can be off by no more than that amount. We know that this is so because polls frequently disagree with each other by a wider amount than their alleged margins of error. This was true, for example, of four polls conducted from August 15 to August 18 during the 1996 presidential race:*

| Poll | Clinton | Dole | Margin of Error |
|------|---------|------|-----------------|
| *New York Times*/CBS News: | 50% | 39% | 3% |
| Gallup: | 51% | 46% | 3% |
| ABC News: | 49% | 44% | 3% |
| Princeton Survey Research: | 48% | 45% | 4% |

*Note that the four differed from each other by more than their supposed margins of error.*

testing the water. It just means we have to pay heed to them in an intelligent manner. A presidential poll taken in September is of much less value, other things being equal, than one conducted in October; polls paid for by one side or the other are worth less than those conducted by truly independent organizations. But most importantly, we have to remember that even the best polls have a batting average well below 100 percent.

## 9. FALSE CHARGE OF FALLACY

It often is all too easy to charge others with fallacious reasoning. This is particularly true when people change their minds and embrace positions they previously denied. The temptation is to charge them with the fallacy of *inconsistency*. But making a given statement at one time and one that contradicts it at a later time does not necessarily indicate inconsistency; we may have, and express, good grounds for changing our minds.

Take the person who says, "I used to believe that women are not as creative as men, because most of the intellectually productive people I knew about were men; but I've changed my mind, because I believe now (as I didn't then) that environment (culture, surroundings), not native ability, has been responsible for the preponderance of intellectual men." Surely, that person cannot be accused of the fallacy of inconsistency, since

---

*The very nature of the polling process makes it more likely that respondents will tell the truth when asked certain sorts of questions than others. "Do you smoke marijuana?" is the kind of question people cannot be expected to answer as truthfully as "Do you eat a hot or a cold cereal for breakfast?" Polls regularly show alcohol consumption to be much lower than do producer and seller records.*

*But it is answers to questions about sexual conduct that are perhaps the most suspect. It would be interesting to know just how many people in the United States are homosexual, but polls so far have not provided a generally accepted answer. What they have done, though, is provide ammunition for those who have an axe to grind one way or another. Thus, when a 1993 survey by the Alan Guttmacher Institute indicated that only 1.1 percent of Americans are gay, a much lower figure than most estimates, their findings were widely reported in the media; and conservatives who champion "family values" as a political stance jumped on this low figure to buttress their claim that homosexuals are less deserving of civil rights protection than other minorities. But, overlooking the spurious nature of the logic these opponents of homosexuality employed, the Guttmacher poll itself was seriously flawed. For one thing, only those males whose sexual activity has been exclusively homosexual were counted as homosexual, so that a great many of those who consider themselves homosexual thereby did not qualify. But more to the point here, homosexual respondents, who in any case were naturally reluctant to "come out of the closet" with interviewers, had to be especially skittish about answering truthfully because they were asked to provide their Social Security numbers and other identifying material. Reporting on this poll, the news magazine* Extra! *(June 1993) stated, "Given the reality of job and housing discrimination, it's likely that many gay men chose not to disclose their sexual activity under such conditions."*

he (or she!) has explained the change of mind as, for example, Lyndon Johnson did not explain his switch on the question of civil rights.

Anyway, in good textbook style, let's say that those who falsely accuse others of fallacy are themselves guilty of the fallacy we'll call **false charge of fallacy**.

Of course, falsely accusing someone of *inconsistency* is not the only way in which someone might be guilty of *false charge of fallacy*. Recall, for example, the earlier discussion of the distinction between analogical reasoning and explanatory analogies; clearly, we are guilty of the fallacy *false charge of fallacy* if we accuse someone of a *questionable analogy* when his or her intent is not to prove something but merely, via an analogy, to explain it.

Note, by the way, that some of the alleged fallacies that have been discussed in logic textbooks since time immemorial are not generally fallacious. Take the fallacy called *appeal to force* (traditional name: *argumentum ad baculum*), committed, it is said, when a conclusion is accepted after a threat of force of one kind or another. Lawmakers, for instance, sometimes are charged with commission of this fallacy when they are convinced to vote a certain way by the implied threats of lobbyists to stop the flow of campaign contributions.

But legislators whose arms are twisted in this way generally are not guilty of a fallacy—the arm twisting doesn't convince them of the merits or demerits of particular legislation, but rather of the personal (career) benefits to be gained by voting as lobbyists "suggest" they should.

## Quibbling

When deciding whether someone has or has not committed a fallacy, we don't want to **quibble**. We don't want to take advantage, for instance, of the fact that life is short and, in everyday life, we don't usually bother to spell out every detail. Some things can, and should, be taken for granted.

---

*Exercise item from the second edition of a certain textbook on logic and contemporary rhetoric:*

*Newspaper story:* Thor Heyerdahl has done it again, crossing the Atlantic in a papyrus raft designed according to ancient Egyptian tomb carvings. Landing in the Western Hemisphere on the island of Barbados, he was greeted by the Barbados prime minister, Errol Barrow, who declared, "This has established Barbados was the first landing place for man in the Western World."

*This was a very "un-PC" remark by Barrow, but that is not the point here. The point is that the correct answer to this exercise item was supposed to be* hasty conclusion, *but a student from Barbados pointed out that the prime minister was known for his sense of humor. Another* false charge of fallacy, *this time by the (here nameless) author of the critical reasoning textbook in question.*

Consider the American Medical Association (AMA) ad that stated:

> 100,000 doctors have quit smoking.
> Maybe they know something you don't.

Students have called this ad fallacious because, among other reasons, it suppresses evidence as to what kind of doctors have quit. ("Maybe it was horse doctors." "They don't say if they were doctors of medicine.") But this sort of response amounts to nothing better than *quibbling*. It resembles the remark of a student who objected to Shakespeare's wonderful line, "He jests at scars that has never felt a wound" (*Romeo and Juliet*), on grounds that *he* (the student) had felt a wound—a mere scratch—and still jested at scars. (Other students have objected to the line on the grounds that Shakespeare incorrectly used "that" instead of "who," but they (the students!) were guilty of another, grammatical sort of quibbling.)

This (finally!) concludes our discussion of fallacies, unfortunately restricted to just a few of the more common varieties that are discussed in one place or another in the literature. While it is useful to become adept at aptly applying specific names to cases of fallacious reasoning, the point of acquiring this skill, after all, is to learn how to improve one's own reasoning and to be better able to spot the fallacious reasoning of others. But we'll soon see that spotting fallacies is only part of the larger enterprise of evaluating more complicated passages containing related arguments that are intended to form a coherent whole. *Extended arguments* of this kind—argumentative essays—are discussed in Chapters 8 and 9.

## SUMMARY OF CHAPTER 5

1.  *Hasty conclusion*: Accepting an argument on the basis of relevant but insufficient information or evidence. *Example*: Sherlock Holmes's conclusion that Dr. Watson was an army man just back from Afghanistan.

2.  *Small sample*: Drawing conclusions about a population on the basis of a sample that is too small to be a reliable measure of that population. *Example*: Conclusions drawn about primate mating habits based on a sample of three human couplings, a gibbon mating, and those of one troop of baboons.

3.  *Unrepresentative sample*: Reasoning from a sample that is not representative (typical) of the population from which it was drawn. *Example*: The sample of primates just mentioned.

4.  *Questionable cause*: Labeling A as the cause of B on evidence that is insufficient, negative, or unrepresentative, or in serious conflict with well-established high-level theories. *Example*: Reasoning from the fact that children classified as nonwhite do less well in school than whites to the conclusion that being nonwhite is the cause of this discrepancy.

5.  *Questionable analogy*: Drawing an analogical conclusion when the cases compared are not relevantly alike. *Example*: Congressman Rose's analogy between developing a mental telepathy system and the development of lasers and semiconductors.

Note, by the way, that the quality of statistics sometimes differs a great deal from time to time and place to place.

6. *Questionable statistics*: Employing statistics that are questionable without further support. *Example*: Accepting government statistics on short-term business trends as completely accurate rather than just educated approximations. *Extreme example*: Employing unknowable statistics about how may wars have been fought in the past 5,000 years and how many casualties there have been.

7. *Questionable uses of statistics*: Perfectly good statistics also sometimes are a problem—for two reasons. The first is the inability of so many people to understand the significance of this statistic or that, made worse by the natural tendency in all of us to see statistics as favoring conclusions we already have drawn. The second is the *ability* of charlatans to bamboozle the rest of us via cleverly employed statistics. *Example*: Accepting evidence that the murder rate in states that have adopted a death penalty for serious crimes is twice as high as in states that have not done so as proof that the death penalty does not deter crime, without further evidence that this statistical evidence has a causal foundation; it could well be, for example, that states adopting death penalties had even higher murder rates than other states and have adopted a death penalty for exactly that reason.

8. *Polls*: Although polls are an important source of information, they need to dealt with cautiously. Polls can be misleading: (1) because of the way in which questions are worded; (2) because they ask the wrong questions; (3) because respondents don't want to appear ignorant, immoral, odd, or prejudiced; or (4) most importantly, because they are based on a sample that is too small or unrepresentative. *Example*. The Harvard University poll that failed to list high tuition rates as one of the problems respondents could cite as most important.

9. *False charge of fallacy*: Erroneously accusing others of fallacious reasoning. *Example*: Accusing someone of fallacy who has changed his mind as to the creativity of women in the light of contrary evidence.

   Note that we don't want to be overly critical of the reasoning of others to the point that we are guilty of *quibbling*.

   Note also that some of the alleged fallacies that have been handed down to us in logic textbooks often are not fallacious. For example, legislators who vote so as to satisfy lobbyists are not usually guilty of the fallacy of *appeal to force*: They become convinced by the implied threats of the lobbyists to vote as "suggested" because of self-interest, not because they change their minds about the merits of the legislation.

# EXERCISE 5-1

1. In the section on polls in this chapter, we cited this question on a Democratic party survey:

   Do you believe that government has a right to make decisions about a woman's reproductive rights?

a. What was the answer the survey makers expected most people to give? What clues lead you to this answer?

b. Construct an alternative question designed to elicit the opposite answer from respondents, and explain why you think they would be more likely to answer that way.

2. Comment on the following item, with respect to what was discussed in this chapter: A survey reported in *Psychology Today* (March 1990) of 657 randomly selected respondents, queried by telephone shortly before Christmas, revealed that 90 percent of the married respondents said they have never had extramarital affairs; almost two-thirds are "very happy" in their marriages; three-fourths still find their spouses physically attractive; and four-fifths would marry the same person again, if they had to do it all over.

3. Here is a paraphrase of a letter to the editor of the *Nutrition Action Health Letter* (November 1993): I am a diabetic who has found the artificial sweetener NutraSweet to be "a total nightmare." I thought it would be a good substitute for sugar [diabetics have to severely limit their intake of sugar]. But when I started using it, I began to have serious headaches that my doctor could not account for. So under my doctor's supervision, I stopped using NutraSweet and my headaches stopped. Going back onto NutraSweet was followed by a renewal of my headaches. I did this back and forth three times and the scenario was the same each time: "no NutraSweet, no headache; NutraSweet, headache."

Do you agree with the unstated implication of this letter—that taking the NutraSweet was the cause of the headaches? Defend your answer against likely objections.

4. Earlier in this chapter, we questioned the use of *Harper's Index* statistics concerning the death penalty to show that that extreme form of punishment does not deter crime more than lesser penalties. What about the *Harper's Index* item indicating that the chances of a white teenager arrested on a drug charge being tried in adult court, rather than a juvenile court, are about 1 in 70, while for blacks the chances are 1 in 18? Is the implied conclusion that black teenage offenders are discriminated against compared to whites justified on the basis of this evidence?

*5. Here is an item from *The Washington Spectator* (October 1, 1992): The authoritative *New England Journal of Medicine* offers ways to ensure a healthy heart. *Examples*: stop smoking, which lowers the risk of heart attack 50–70 percent; lower cholesterol, if it is high, by diet and medicine, cutting the risk 20–40 percent; exercise for a 40 percent lower risk; watch your weight and keep it below high levels, 35–55 percent; take a low dose of aspirin if the doctor agrees, about a third; treat high blood pressure, 20–60 percent.

Commenting on this item, a student remarked that if these statistics were accurate, we could completely eliminate the risk of having a heart attack, and then some; but we can't do that, so the statistics must be completely wrong. Was the student on to something? Defend your answer. (This is a rather difficult question. Think carefully about it and try to figure it out before checking the suggested answer at the back of the book.)

## EXERCISE 5-2

Determine which fallacies (if any) occur in the following short passages and justify your answers (as you did when working on Exercises 3-1 and 4-1). (Note again that some of these passages may also contain fallacies discussed in previous chapters.)

1. *Bangkok Post* (June 7, 1990): In sweltering California, a Red Indian brave performed a water ceremony in Clarcmont in the middle of last month. Now everyone is raving about the fact that just nine days after he returned to his teepee, "the skies opened up and a 2.54 cm deluge soaked the region." Three Valleys Municipal Water District supremo Paul Stiglich insists there is a connection. "The Indians came, they danced, it rained," he said.

2. Candice Bergen, when queried about lending her name to a Spiegel summer catalog: I felt it my civic duty to put together this collection of summer essentials for all my fellow Americans out there.

3. From a Bob Schwabach "On computers" newspaper column: There aren't just a couple of brands [of IBM-compatible computers] for those [very low] prices; there are dozens. Do they work? Someone I know has been running one continuously for five months, and it's never missed a beat.

4. A while back, the National Highway Traffic Safety Administration placed a value on human life, for purposes of assessing the costs to society of an accidental death, of $287,175.

5. Smoking pot definitely leads to heroin use. A report by the U.S. Commissioner of Narcotics on a study of 2,213 hard-core narcotics addicts in the Lexington (Kentucky) Federal Hospital shows that 70.4 percent smoked marijuana *before* taking heroin.

6. From a student essay: It is wrong to criticize advertisers for manipulating people through psychological ploys because that's what makes ads effective.

7. Overheard in a local bar: You women are wrong to be for censoring pornography, even if it's true, and I'm pretty sure it isn't, that porno stuff makes a few men more likely to rape. Would you want to ban miniskirts, bikini outfits, low-cut dresses, and such—require women to wear Muslim-style outfits—if it's true that scanty clothes make some men more likely to rape?

8. The president of a college that shall go unnamed here justifying the reduction of salary for adjunct (part-time) teachers who are paid only 75 percent of the rate paid to full-time staff per course: I don't see the problem here. No other college in the state pays more than we do.

9. Molly Ivins' column, March 12, 1996, in which she urged people to vote in primary elections to make sure bad candidates aren't selected: Steve Forbes:

Forbes' Texas campaign manager is Diana Denman, who starred with Ronald Reagan in the 1951 movie *Bedtime for Bozo*, along with a chimp.

*10. From a student paper in a critical reasoning class: You said in class that we should pay attention to old sayings—blood is thicker than water and all that. I say old sayings are for the birds. Putting that into your kind of talk, they're often contradictory, so half of them must be wrong. A stitch in time saves nine; look before you leap; he who hesitates is lost, etc. Dumb stuff.

11. From a student paper—not in a critical reasoning class: Are we wasting billions of dollars on animal research? The answer must be yes. The use of vivisection actually impedes scientific progress by devoting less money to developing new technologies that would better serve our needs.

12. Is there a fallacy illustrated in the following cartoon?

*Rhymes with Orange* © 1996 Hilary B. Price.

*13. Here is an exercise item from the previous edition of this text:

After the Soviet Union refused to accept a U.S. note demanding compensation for relatives of those in the Korean jet shot down by the Russians, the U.S. appealed to the Soviets to accept the note on grounds that it had been diplomatic common practice to do so for several centuries.

And here is a student answer you are to evaluate:

The fallacy here is *two wrongs make a right*, or *common practice*. Just because it's always been done that way doesn't make it right.

14. In this case, the question is what fallacy, if any, this *Andy Capp* strip illustrates:

Reprinted with special permission of North America Syndicate, Inc.

15. Detroit Mayor Dennis Archer on why he accepted Louis Farrakhan's call to African-American men to take part in the 1996 Million Man March on Washington, D.C.: If somebody has a cure for cancer, would you reject it because it was somebody you may not like who came up with it?

*16. From a student paper in a critical reasoning class: I notice you say the *Washington Monthly* is your favorite magazine source for info on how the system works & doesn't work, and how to fix it; but I also notice you have more fallacies from *Wash Monthly* than from other sources you knock, including the very downplayed *National Review*. [This was true of the edition in question.] Something must be wrong someplace! I think you are guilty of the fallacy *inconsistency*, oh author of our textbook.

17. Paraphrase of part of a letter in a December 1990 Ann Landers advice column: My parents didn't give me much guidance about social behavior, morals, or sex. But I read your column—you were one person I learned from. You said not to go for looks and popularity, but to pay attention to "the quiet one in the corner." So about nine years ago, I married an average-looking guy who is a "great father and a good provider," and have been very happy. Thanks very much for your excellent advice.

*18. Wayne LaPierre, executive vice president, National Rifle Association: I think that [the ban on assault weapons] has as much to do with crime control as making a wish while you blow the candles out on a birthday cake. [He then provided reasons that he believed showed that such a ban would not reduce the crime rate.]

19. Student paper: According to U.S. Dept. of Justice statistics, between 1977 and 1990, only one female was executed, out of a total of 143 executions. Similar stat ratios apply since then [1990]. This shows the bias against males that exists in the U.S. contrary to PC [politically correct] claims.

    Another student's reply to this: You might just as well argue that there is a bias against young males, say, those under 30, as compared to older males, since the vast majority of those convicted of murder are under 30, as are their victims.

20. Susan Brownmiller, arguing against the legalization of pornography: Pornography, like rape, is a male invention designed to dehumanize women, to reduce the female to an object of sexual access, not to free sensuality from moralistic or paternal inhibition.

21. Paraphrase of part of a letter to the editor, Marin [California] *Independent Journal*: When the first heart transplant was done by Dr. Christian Barnard, he was praised, not his scalpel. It was Cain, according to the Bible, not a rock, that killed Abel. Why, then, listen to the pseudoliberals and other nitwits when they blame crimes on guns rather than on people who use guns?

## EXERCISE 5-3

Here are a few more short passages to be evaluated.

*1. A letter to the editor of *Consumer Reports* (January 1990) suggested that spending $1.35 billion to develop HDTV [high-density TV] is like buying a Ming vase to use as a garbage can.

*2. Although traditional Jewish practices forbid eating the meat of the pig, a large minority of Jews in Israel have developed a taste for bacon, pork, and the rest. This offended Orthodox Jews, who wanted to pass a law prohibiting the sale of these products. Explained Rabbi Avraham Shapira, a leader of Orthodox Jews (in the fall of 1985—a law concerning meat from the pig was passed in 1990): Our law is not to forbid people to eat pork. We are very democratic here. What we want is people not to be able to sell pork. It hurts every religious man when he passes through a city in Israel and he sees a shop with pork in the window.

3. Is there a fallacy or two in this antismoking blurb?

---

### Portrait of an Achiever

### Abraham Lincoln

| | |
|---|---|
| 1831 | Failed in Business—Bankruptcy. |
| 1832 | Defeated for Legislature. |
| 1834 | Failed in Business again—Bankruptcy. |
| 1835 | Sweetheart and Fiancee died. |
| 1836 | Nervous Breakdown. |
| 1838 | Defeated in an Election. |
| 1843 | Defeated for U.S. Congress. |
| 1846 | Defeated again for U.S. Congress. |
| 1848 | Defeated once again for U.S. Congress. |
| 1855 | Defeated for U.S. Senate. |
| 1858 | Defeated again for U.S. Senate. |
| **1860** | **Elected President of the United States.** |

*"You cannot fail . . . UNLESS you quit!"*

*A quitter never wins and a winner never quits.*
*(Unless that winner quits smoking.)*

---

*4. Ad for a debate at North Texas State University: The arena has been set. The contestants are preparing themselves. The event—the Warren-Barnhart debate. On the timely question of ethics and morality. Dr. Barnhart's position is that if an act brings pleasure, then it is right. If an act is unpleasant, then it is wrong. But if two actions bring pleasure, then the one with the greatest amount of pleasure should be adopted. Dr. Warren's position is that an act is right or wrong based upon God's word—the New Testament. The stances have been made. The time is drawing nigh for the confrontation. The only thing lacking now are the spectators. And their judgment of which position is right.

5. Newspaper Association of America's spokesperson Paul Luthringer (quoted in *Extra!*, September/October 1995), responding to a survey that found only 19 percent of sources quoted or referred to on newspaper front pages were women: The fact that women are quoted less than men has nothing to do with the state of journalism, but has more to do with who—male or female— is the first to return a reporter's call.

*6. From a *Science News* article (December 22–29, 1990):

[Scientists] produced their map of the vegetation existing 18,000 years ago by sifting through published reports on ancient pollen and other plant remains in sediments from around the world. They then estimated how much carbon dioxide was locked within the plants, soil and peat in specific regions. Continental vegetation and soils contained far less carbon dioxide during the Ice Age than they do today, researchers report. . . . Carbon storage on the continents totaled 968.1 billion tons 18,000 years ago, compared with 2,319.4 billion tons now, an increase of 140 percent.

7. *New York Times* (June 14, 1988): When several women's groups protested the Pakistani law that accords the legal testimony of women half the weight of the testimony of men, Qazi Hussain Ahmed, leader of the Islamic party, said, "These laws do not affect women adversely. Our system wants to protect women from unnecessary worry and save them the trouble of appearing in court."

*8. Article in *Science 80* (November/December 1979): The chief trouble with the word "superstition" is that it always applies to the beliefs of someone else, not your own. The entire history of science shows that, in varying degrees, much that even the greatest scientists believed to be fact is today either false or else somewhat less than factual, perhaps even superstitious. It follows that what the best scientists today believe to be fact will suffer the same fate.

9. Jane B. Lancaster, in "Carrying and Sharing in Human Evolution" (*Human Nature*, February 1978), supporting her claim that other primates are more vicious than *Homo sapiens*: During the five years of observing the habits of a community of chimpanzees . . . , researchers witnessed eight attacks between the community and neighboring groups. These fights resulted in the deaths of at least two elderly males, an adult female, and four infants, the equivalent of an annual murder rate of 1,400 per 100,000 chimpanzees. The murder rate in the United States, 88 per 100,000 people in 1976, becomes insignificant in comparison.

10. A letter to the *San Francisco Examiner* from a physician argued that if juries award sums like $10.5 million to plaintiffs who have contracted toxic shock syndrome—even though that disease wasn't known to medical science when the damage took place—perhaps we can now expect lawsuits against pharmaceutical companies and physicians by the relatives of people who died of

pneumonia before 1943, on the grounds that as-yet-undiscovered penicillin hadn't been prescribed.

*11. When it was pointed out to Stephen Schneider, a climatologist at Stanford's Institute for International Studies, that he was recommending action now even though he was only 90 percent sure that global warming was occurring because of atmospheric emissions, he replied, "Why do we need 99 percent certainty when nothing else is that certain? If there were only a 5 percent chance the chef slipped some poison in your dessert, would you eat it?"

12. Peter Singer in his book *Animal Liberation*: The racist violates the principle of equality by giving greater weight to the interests of members of his own race when there is a clash between their interests and the interests of those of another race. The sexist violates the principle of equality by favoring the interests of his own sex. Similarly, the speciesist allows the interests of his own species to override the greater interests of members of another species. The pattern is identical in each case.

13. Paraphrase of letter in the *San Francisco Chronicle* (March 31, 1988): The *Chronicle* editorial favoring the law requiring motorcyclists to wear helmets omitted the fact that there are at least 20 times as many people killed or injured in auto accidents as there are in motorcycle accidents. And remember that it costs the same per serious injury no matter how the accident occurs. Since helmets have been proved to reduce the number of deaths and injuries in cars as well as motorcycles, why single out motorcyclists? Shouldn't you be in favor of requiring that everyone from birth wear a helmet at all times?

*14. Paraphrased argument (from a lost source) voiced after the very light turnout for the 1988 elections: The principal reason people don't vote is not the low quality of candidates or polls projecting winners and losers. The main reason is the voter *registration* requirements that keep people from the polls. A University of Michigan study shows that since 1964, at least 86 percent of registered voters actually vote. Conclusion: not requiring any registration, or universal registration, would raise the percentage of people voting sharply.

15. Part of a political column by George Weigel (November 29, 1992), in which he argued against the *Roe vs. Wade* Supreme Court decision: The hard sociological fact is that abortion on demand (the regime established by *Roe*) has been the greatest deal for irresponsible or predatory men in American history. Why? Because whatever else is said, *Roe* frees men from responsibility for the sexual conduct they consensually enter. *Roe* is alleged to have empowered women; in fact, *Roe* legally disempowered women from holding men accountable for their sexual behavior where that behavior had unplanned results.

*16. From an article in the January/February 1994 issue of *Quill* magazine about the claim by Dr. John Pierce (University of California–San Diego) that the Joe Camel cigarette ads were responsible for "a sharp increase in teen smoking: His study shows that first-time smokers among Californians from the ages of 16 to 18 had steadily declined from 12.5 percent in 1975 to 6.2 percent in

1988, but then began sharply increasing again. Joe Camel, a cool-looking, cartoonish character, was introduced as the Camel symbol in 1988. Teenage smoking immediately began increasing by 0.7 percent a year, through 1990. In 1992, Pierce conducted another study that showed Joe Camel was as familiar a character as Mickey Mouse to children as young as six.

The *Quill* article also indicated that because of his research, Dr. Pierce stated that he believes we should ban all tobacco advertising. When asked whether this wasn't censorship contrary to the Constitution's First Amendment, he replied, "There is no free speech [issue] here. The issue is to protect our children from being influenced into an addiction that will cause cancer."

*17. Since the 55-mile-per-hour speed limit was introduced by President Carter, traffic fatalities in the United States have dropped almost in half. So now that the Republican Congress (in 1995) has repealed the 55-mph limit we can expect traffic fatalities to go back to where they were—almost double what they are now.

*18. The U.S. House of Representatives Whip, Tom DeLay, when asked by CNN how he could accept his congressional salary ($133,600 per year) during the federal budget impasse, when most federal government employees were not being paid: I am not a government employee. I am in the Constitution . . . .

19. Taken from a student's paper (paraphrased): The prohibition amendment, which made drinking alcohol illegal early in this century, reduced consumption by 50 percent. When the amendment was repealed, the consumption of alcohol almost tripled. This shows that Americans take the law seriously; when something is illegal, they tend to stay away from it.

Instructor's comment on the student's paper: This must be why we have no drug problems today.

*20. Taken from an item in *Extra!Update* (August 1996): *Commentary* editor and pundit-at-large Norman Podhoretz argued in *Time* magazine (June 10, 1996) that the press is wrong to say the Israeli election was tight: "If you subtract the Israeli-Arab vote, it means Netanyahu received 55.5 percent of the Jewish vote. It's like a landslide—not a close vote at all."

## EXERCISE 5-4

Michael J. Barrett argued in an *Atlantic Monthly* article (November 1990) that the most practical way, all things considered, to bridge the gap between the performance in science and mathematics of American youths and those of many countries in Europe and Asia would be to extend the school year from about 180 to 220 days. His principal evidence in favor of this idea was the information provided in the following two tables indicating that the school year in the United States is much shorter than in most other (chiefly developed) countries and that American students do poorly on math tests compared to the students of some of these other countries. (He did provide other evidence.) Your job is to evaluate these statistics to show how well they support the author's claim that a longer school year will yield improved math ability among American public school students. (This is a rather difficult exercise.)

## Number of Days in the Standard School Year (1990)

| | | | |
|---|---|---|---|
| Japan | 243 | New Zealand | 190 |
| West Germany | 226–240 | Nigeria | 190 |
| South Korea | 220 | British Columbia | 185 |
| Israel | 216 | France | 185 |
| Luxembourg | 216 | Ontario | 185 |
| Soviet Union | 211 | Ireland | 184 |
| Netherlands | 200 | New Brunswick | 182 |
| Scotland | 200 | Quebec | 180 |
| Thailand | 200 | Spain | 180 |
| Hong Kong | 195 | Sweden | 180 |
| England/Wales | 192 | **United States** | **180** |
| Hungary | 192 | French Belgium | 175 |
| Swaziland | 191 | Flemish Belgium | 160 |
| Finland | 190 | | |

## Student Achievement by Subject Area*
### *(U.S. Twelfth-Grade Equivalent)*

| Advanced Algebra | Functions/Calculus | Geometry |
|---|---|---|
| 1  Hong Kong | 1. Hong Kong | 1. Hong Kong |
| 2. Japan | 2. Japan | 2. Japan |
| 3. Finland | 3. England/Wales | 3. England/Wales |
| 4. England/Wales | 4. Finland | 4. Sweden |
| 5. Flemish Belgium | 5. Sweden | 5. Finland |
| 6. Israel | 6. New Zealand | 6. New Zealand |
| 7. Sweden | 7. Flemish Belgium | 7. Flemish Belgium |
| 8. Ontario | 8. Ontario | 8. Scotland |
| 9. New Zealand | 9. Israel | 9. Ontario |
| 10. French Belgium | 10. French Belgium | 10. French Belgium |
| 11. Scotland | 11. Scotland | 11. Israel |
| 12. British Columbia | **12. United States** | **12. United States** |
| 13. Hungary | 13. Thailand | 13. Hungary |
| **14. United States** | 14. Hungary | |
| 15. Thailand | 15. British Columbia | |

*Comparison of "twelfth-grade students from various countries who were engaged in the serious study of mathematics." A smaller percentage of U.S. twelfth-graders fell into this category than in most of the other countries listed here.

# EXERCISE 5-5

A customer, call her Mrs. Smith, signs a contract to purchase a new car for cash but is then offered the following deal (typical of deals described in a Jane Bryant Quinn article that appeared in many newspapers on March 24, 1990):

> The cost of her new car is $11,434. Instead of paying cash, it is suggested that she can save money by taking out a loan, the current auto loan rate being 12.75%. Mrs. Smith earns 8.5% on her bank deposits. It is explained to her that by leaving the $11,434 in the bank at 8.5%, instead of paying cash for the car, she will net $6,029 over the five-year period of a car loan, money she won't earn if she pays cash. During that five-year period, she is told, the interest on a loan at 12.75% will amount to $4,153 (given that this interest will be paid on the "declining balance" of money owed on the loan—declining because the amount owed decreases with every monthly payment). So Mrs. Smith is told she will come out ahead $1,876 ($6,029 minus $4,153) by putting the money in the bank and taking out a loan on the car.

There were other advantages claimed for taking out a loan as compared to paying cash, but your job is just to evaluate the alleged advantage described above. Will Mrs. Smith be ahead of the game by $1,876 if she takes out a loan instead of paying cash for the car? (The example is typical of deals offered by many car dealers in recent years.)

# EXERCISE 5-6

Find several fallacy examples of your own, perhaps gleaned from newspapers, magazines, television programs, textbooks (hopefully not this one, but anything is fair game), or what have you, provide a name in each case if you can, and carefully explain why the passage is fallacious.

*Calvin and Hobbes* by Bill Watterson. Copyright 1993 by Universal Press Syndicate. Reprinted with permission.

*Memory says, "I did that." Pride replies, "I could not have done that." Eventually, memory yields.*

— Nietzsche

*Every dogma has its day.*

— Abraham Rotstein

*Think with your head, not your guts.*

— Old saying

Populus vult decipi *(the people want to be deceived).*

— Ancient Roman saying

*Nothing is so firmly believed as what we least know.*

— Montaigne

*How strange it is to see with how much passion*

*People see things only in their own fashion.*

— Moliere

*I wouldn't have seen it if I hadn't believed it.*

— Insightful takeoff on an old saying

Chapter

6

# PSYCHOLOGICAL IMPEDIMENTS TO COGENT REASONING: SHOOTING OURSELVES IN THE FOOT

Good reasoning is a matter of *character* as well as brain power. If human beings were completely rational animals, learning how to reason well would be a relatively easy task. We would simply learn which patterns of reasoning are good and which bad, and then make all of our reasoning conform to good patterns while avoiding the bad. Even if we started out with poor background beliefs, repeated use of valid deductive and inductive inferences, based on all of what we have experienced so far, would soon set things straight.

Unfortunately, human beings are not completely rational, although rationality is an important part of our makeup. This chapter is concerned with that other part of human nature—the nonrational, emotional component that prevents us from being perfect reasoners. While no one can completely eliminate these nonrational impediments to cogent reasoning, any more than a leopard can change its spots, understanding how they work can help us to reduce the harm they do to our attempts at completely rational thought.

## 1.  LOYALTY, PROVINCIALISM, AND THE HERD INSTINCT

Throughout history, individual chances for success at most things—getting enough food, attracting and holding a mate, successfully raising children—have depended on two fundamental factors: The first is the success of the groups we belong to in their competitions with other groups. Members of primary in-groups (nations, tribes, cultures) defeated by competing out-groups generally suffer serious harm to their chances of having a good life. That is why we all feel a tug of **loyalty** to our own in-group; a society that has too many disloyal people has little chance against other, more cohesive groups. (Note, however, that the strength of this tug differs greatly from person to person.)

But being a member of a successful in-group is of little value if others in the group do not allow us reasonable chances for success in whatever it is we want to do. That is an important reason why we all are so anxious to get along with the other members of the groups to which we owe loyalty. The person who is completely out of step with everyone else is not likely to be successful, even if the group as a whole thrives and multiplies.* Enter the **herd instinct** that tends to keep our beliefs, and thus our actions, within the bounds of what society as a whole will accept. Finding ourselves in a culture in which everyone covers certain parts of the body, we feel uncomfortable leaving those parts naked. Those belonging to Moslem or Orthodox Jewish groups find eating the pig abhorrent. In Western societies, virtually everyone avoids eating the meat of horses and dogs; in China dog meat is a delicacy.

Of course, there is no harm in feeling embarrassed if caught in public with the wrong attire or in finding shellfish repugnant. But the herd instinct sometimes leads people to do horrendous things, as they do when mobs carry out "vigilante justice" or when whole nations acquiesce to unfair practices. Refraining from eating the flesh of the cow is one thing; branding one's compatriots as "untouchables" is another.

The point is that it is part of human nature to find it easy and natural to believe what everyone else in our society believes and foolish to believe what others find foolish. This is no doubt one reason for what sociologists call *cultural lag*, the tendency of practices and beliefs to persist long after whatever conditions made them useful or sensible have disappeared.

We all desire to have at least a minimal status in the groups that we belong to, for the reasons just mentioned. But the higher our status, the better our chances. That's why most of us have such a strong desire to make a better than minimally good appearance when in public. We want to look intelligent, informed, and decisive—to shine compared to others. And that is why, for instance, millions of Americans who had never heard of Saddam Hussein before Iraq invaded Kuwait, who had no idea where Kuwait was, and who knew next to nothing about Islam and the Muslim religion, formed almost instant

---

*For more on this way of looking at the human repertoire, see Howard Kahane, *Contract Ethics: Evolutionary Biology and the Moral Sentiments* (Lanham, Md., Rowman & Littlefield, 1995) and James Q. Wilson, *The Moral Sense* (New York and Toronto, Free Press, 1993).

> Man is a social animal; only in the herd is he happy. It is all one to him whether it is the profoundest nonsense or the greatest villainy—he feels completely at ease with it—so long as it is the view of the herd, and he is able to join the herd.
> — Søren Kierkegaard

opinions on how to handle the resulting crisis. After the war started, newspapers across the country were filled with letters to editors expressing demands for this action or that. The need to be in the swim, to talk "intelligently" about topics of the day, leads us to form and broadcast these quick opinions based on superficial evidence. And once we have pronounced them, the need to avoid appearing to have been wrong in public leads us to hang on to those beliefs, often in the face of conflicting evidence. The underlying psychological mechanism is the desire to gain, and retain, the status in the eyes of others in our group that is vital to success in everyday life.*

It also should be noted that hardly any of the large societies common in today's world are completely cohesive. Nations such as the United States, Canada, India, and Russia are composed of all sorts of diverse subgroups, the United States being one of the two most diverse cultures in history (the other was the Soviet Union before its disintegration). Most people are completely loyal to their own nation but also have a special interest in the fates of subgroups, and therefore tend to see things not just from the point of view of the mainstream culture but also from that of smaller groups within the primary culture. We see the results of this in current political rhetoric designed to appeal to "special interest" groups such as religious fundamentalists, African Americans, Latinos, Jews, and so on. (Note, by the way, that we all have a special interest in the welfare of members of our own families.)

**Provincialism** stems in large part from this natural tendency to identify with the ideas, interests, and kinds of behavior favored by those in groups with which we identify. That is why blacks are more likely to notice injustices perpetrated against blacks, Jews against Jews, and women against women. (Think only of polls that showed a majority of black Americans agreed with the verdict in the O. J. Simpson murder trial, while the reverse was true of white Americans, even though both groups were exposed to the same evidence.)

Of particular importance is the fact that we tend to see things from the point of view and interests of our primary culture—our primary in-group—especially when there is conflict with other groups. The result is a kind of *belief provincialism* operating at various levels—leading Americans, for example, to pay relatively little attention to what happens to the peoples of the rest of the world and to misconstrue what is happening there. That is why, although the United States was founded on the principles of democracy and fair play, a great many Americans have failed to notice that since World War II the United States government has helped to overturn several democratically elected governments around the world (for instance, in Chile) and attempted to murder Cuba's Fidel Castro. It is difficult to swallow unpleasant truths when loyalty and the herd instinct reinforce what others in our group vehemently assert, and when

---

*Erving Goffman's fascinating book *The Presentation of Self in Everyday Life* (New York: Doubleday, 1959; Penguin, 1969) still is an excellent source of information on these matters.

provincialism narrows our range of interests and tends to make us see everything in terms of the interests of our own primary group.*

## 2. PREJUDICE, STEREOTYPES, SCAPEGOATS, AND PARTISAN MIND-SETS

Loyalty and provincialism often lead to **prejudice**, including prejudice against all or almost all members of other groups, and to the thinking in terms of unverified **stereotypes** that supports prejudicial beliefs. But being prejudiced against others is quite different from simply having a bad opinion of them. We are prejudiced only when our nasty beliefs about others are not justified by sufficient evidence. So prejudice can be defined as *thinking ill of others without sufficient warrant.*

Of course, no group of any size is composed of people who resemble each other as do peas in a pod, so it is foolish to be prejudiced against every member of such a group. It's just silly to think that the French all are great lovers, that all Jews and Scots are unusually frugal, or that all women are more emotional than men.

It is true, though, that people in a given large social group generally are different in many ways from those in other groups. The French *as a group* are modestly different from Germans, as are Iranians from Pakistanis, something anyone can notice simply by going from one of these countries to the other. The trouble with stereotypic thinking is rather that, even when accurate with respect to groups as a whole (and they often are not), they fail to take account of the differences between individual members.

The flip side of prejudice and intolerance directed against members of other groups is overtolerance of, even blindness to, the defects and foibles of our own group and its members. Loyalty tends to make us see our own leaders as a good deal more intelligent, informed, and honest than in fact they are (or than it would be reasonable to expect the leaders of any society to be), and to regard the general run of our compatriots as better on average than the people in other societies. Clear thinkers need to overcome this reverse prejudice in favor of the in-group, especially of in-group leaders (an important reason for the inclusion in this text of so many examples illustrating the clay feet of quite a few elected officials).

Prejudice against members of other groups, in particular of minorities within a larger culture, often is reinforced by the need to find **scapegoats**—others we can blame for the ills of the world—when in fact we ourselves may bear a large measure of responsibility. That a group being trashed cannot possibly have produced the troubles it is charged with rarely makes a difference.

This tendency to put the blame elsewhere is captured with chilling effect by Shirley Jackson in "The Lottery," her classic story of scapegoating. The residents of a small village gather in the town square for the annual lottery, an archaic ritual performed for so many years that the people have forgotten its original purpose. They know that one of them must draw the fateful lot, but beyond that they only remember how to use the pile of stones that figures prominently in the story. Until the lot is drawn, the villagers behave in a decent, kindly manner to each other, but once the "winner" is known, they hover around her like vultures over a carcass and, stones in hand, pelt her viciously,

---

*Another reason for this difficulty is that public school textbooks and the mass media generally play down or try to justify these kinds of breaches of professed ethical ideals. See Chapters 11 and 12 for more on this topic.

driven by the herd instinct to satisfy a barbaric practice of scapegoating whose purpose they no longer understand. The story is an allegory for practices that have unfortunately prevailed for centuries.

The classic scapegoat in the Christian world has always been the Jews. In days of old, when Christian theology was interpreted to say that lending money at interest constituted usury (a sin), Jews therefore became important moneylenders. Blaming them for calamities then sometimes at least had the practical motive of serving as an excuse for the repudiation of outstanding loans. But at most times, the primary point of anti-Semitism has been simply to place the blame for ills elsewhere.

Everyone nowadays is familiar with the way in which the Nazis used the Jews as scapegoats and with their attempt to exterminate all European Jews. So it might be supposed that picking on the Jews would have little appeal these days. Yet anti-Semitism is still very common in many places. In Russia, to take one example, Jews are commonly held responsible for the ills produced by 70 years of Soviet communism. (The thin thread holding this together is that some of the high officials in the Communist party and in the Soviet government were Jews.) In other Eastern European countries, Jews are similarly often held responsible for the problems generated by Soviet domination. This is true even in Poland, where only about 10,000 out of over 3 million Jews survived the German attempt at genocide and still reside in Poland.

One might suppose that the murder of millions of Jews in Europe during World War II, and the still existing anti-Semitism just described, would make Jews, of all people, the least likely to relegate others to second-class citizenship. And yet, in Israel, the first primarily Jewish state in about 2,000 years, Israeli Arabs do not have the same status as Israeli Jews, and Arab lands in the West Bank have been taken from them and given to Jewish "settlers." Not that the Arabs have been paragons of virtue—think only of the stated objective of several surrounding Arab countries to destroy Israel.

And then there are the genocidal tribal battles going on in Africa, the mass destruction and murder in the former Yugoslavia, hostilities between Hindus and Moslems, and so on. In every case, those on both sides in these ethnic battles feel justified in their vindictive hatred and prejudice against the "enemy."

Prejudice and scapegoating, of course, also occur in the United States. As usual, small or less powerful groups tend to be the ones picked on, including people of African and Asian descent, Latinos, Native Americans (American Indians), and, naturally, Jews. (Now that the Muslim population in the United States is more than minuscule and Muslim terrorists have been at work, innocent members of that religious group also are becoming the victims of prejudice.)

Thinking in terms of unverified stereotypes and scapegoats often results from a **partisan mind-set** that leads people to perceive evidence and to judge arguments via an "us against them" or a "my right view against your wrong view" attitude. We all are tempted to arrange fact to fit our side of an issue and tend to be blind to the import of evidence supporting any other side. Good reasoners fight this tendency in all of us to favor ideas already held and to automatically see our side as right and the other guy's as wrong. Those with a partisan mind-set give in to this all too human tendency, generally without being aware that they have done so. This is true, for example, of some individuals who are vigorously engaged in the social or political arenas. That is why it can be so maddening to discuss touchy issues with some very committed people—they tend to be deaf to counterevidence and counterarguments. (Another reason, of course, is that we ourselves may be "hearing impaired" when it comes to *their* reasons and arguments.)

Consider, for example, the student in a critical thinking class some time back who complained vigorously about the required textbook—an earlier edition of this one—pointing out that in one place it said that the Soviets under Stalin had murdered millions of their own citizens and then a few pages later claimed that these same Soviets, not the Americans or British, had done the principal fighting and defeating of the Germans in World War II. "Which side is the text's author on, here?" the student wanted to know. He was genuinely confused. He couldn't grasp the idea that the author's intent was neither to champion communism nor to root for "our side" but rather to present the facts of the matter in order to make a completely different point (about how history is distorted in public school textbooks).

A really good critical reasoner has a mind-set that is completely different from those who see everything from a partisan point of view. *This does not mean that good reasoners lack a sense of loyalty!* It means simply that they have an *open mind* rather than a mind that sees everything from the point of view that "our side always is right and the other side always wrong"—a mind open to the truth, wherever it may lie.

## 3. SUPERSTITIOUS BELIEFS

Prejudice against members of other groups at least has group loyalty going for it. That can't be said about **superstitions**. It is true, though, that superstitions often are based on

---

*The foolishness of the superstitious beliefs of peoples in other societies is much easier to see than the irrational nature of our own. Superstition and provincialism go hand in hand. Here are two examples of superstitious beliefs common in Hong Kong today:*

---

The word for fish in some Chinese dialects looks very much like the word for surplus. So on the Chinese New Year, lots of businessmen eat fish in order to generate assurances of profit (surplus).

The number 8 is thought to be extremely lucky. The auto license plate bearing just that number was auctioned off recently for 5 million Hong Kong dollars (a bit over 640,000 U.S. dollars).

---

*These superstitious beliefs are rather harmless, but others have bad, even terrible consequences. For instance, women born in the year of the horse, which occurs every twelfth year, are believed by many Asians to be smart, active, impatient, and argumentative. Women who exhibit these qualities are not considered desirable mates by most Korean men. Women born in the year of the white horse, which comes around every 60 years, are believed to be particularly "bad" in these ways, so superstitious men, a large percentage of the population, shy away from marriage to women born in such a year. To save potential offspring from spinsterhood, when the year of the white horse rolled around in 1990, lots of pregnant women in Korea consulted obstetricians to find out whether they were carrying male or female fetuses, and abortions of female fetuses reached epidemic proportions.*

*In Chapter 4, we presented the first of four "causes of the utterance of falla-cies" that Jeremy Bentham described in his famous book* The Handbook of Polit-ical Fallacies. *Here is an excerpt from the second of the four, which happens to be relevant to the topics discussed in this chapter:*

## Second Cause: Interest-Begotten Prejudice

If every act of the will and hence every act of the hand is produced by interest, that is, by a motive of one sort or another, the same must be true, directly or indirectly, of every act of the intellectual faculty, although the influence of inter-est upon the latter is neither as direct or as perceptible as that upon the will.

But how, it may be asked, is it possible that the motive by which a man is actu-ated can be secret to himself? Nothing, actually, is easier; nothing is more frequent. Indeed, the rare case is not that of a man's not knowing, but that of his knowing . . .

When two persons have lived together in a state of intimacy, it happens not infrequently that either or each of them may possess a more correct and complete view of the motives by which the mind of the other is governed, than of those which control his own behavior. Many a woman has had in this way a more cor-rect and complete acquaintance with the internal causes by which the conduct of her husband has been determined, than he has had himself. The reason for this is easily pointed out. By interest, a man is continually prompted to make him-self as correctly and completely acquainted as possible with the springs of action which determine the conduct of those upon whom he is more or less dependent for the comfort of his life. But by interest he is at the same time diverted from any close examination into the springs by which his own conduct is determined. From such knowledge he would be more likely to find mortifica-tion than satisfaction.

When he looks at other men, he finds mentioned as a matter of praise the prevalence of . . . social motives. . . . It is by the supposed prevalence of these amiable motives that he finds reputation raised, and that respect and goodwill enhanced to which every man is obliged to look for so large a proportion of the comforts of his life. . . .

But the more closely he looks into the mechanism of his own mind, the less able he is to refer any of the mass of effects produced there to any of these ami-able and delightful causes. He finds nothing, therefore, to attract him towards this self-study; he finds much to repel him from it. . . .

Perhaps he is a man in whom a large proportion of the self-regarding motives may be mixed with a slight tincture of the social motives operating upon the pri-vate scale. In that case, what will he do? In investigating the source of a given action, he will in the first instance set down the whole of it to the account of the amiable and conciliatory motives, in a word, the social ones. This, in any study of his own mental physiology, will always be his first step; and it will commonly be his last also. Why should he look any further? Why take in hand the painful probe? Why undeceive himself, and substitute the whole truth, which would mor-tify him, for a half-truth which flatters him?

some small scrap of evidence or other. Bad things obviously do occasionally happen after a mirror is broken. Coincidences do happen. And even newspaper astrology columns are moderately accurate once every blue moon.

The difference between superstitious and sensible beliefs is that sensible beliefs are based on *sufficient evidence* that justifies those beliefs, not on carefully chosen scraps of support. Superstitious beliefs are generally based on *biased evidence* or on *small* or *unrepresentative samples* (discussed in Chapter 5)—evidence from which all negative cases have been removed. Bad things do happen on Friday the 13th, but so do lots of good things. And bad things happen on other days also, so that there is nothing remarkable about the fact that they happen on Friday the 13th. Superstitious people ignore facts of this sort and pay attention just to the evidence supporting their superstitious convictions.

The odd thing about superstitious beliefs is that their complete irrationality doesn't seem to stop even the most brilliant people from having them. Chess grand masters, for example, display amazing intelligence and insight when playing that great intellectual game, not to mention incredible memories. (The "grand old man of chess," George Koltanowsky, several times has played over 40 games simultaneously—blindfolded.) Yet the current world chess champion, Garry Kasparov, thinks the number 13 is his lucky number (he was born on April 13—well, he's Aries, so that explains his great ability—and he is the thirteenth world chess champion). The previous champion, Anatoly Karpov, changes his suit every time he loses a game.

## 4. WISHFUL THINKING AND SELF-DECEPTION

As we have just seen, loyalty, prejudice, stereotypic thinking, the herd instinct, and superstition tend to give us beliefs that do not square with reality. Beliefs acquired in these nonrational ways often result from **wishful thinking**—believing what we would like to be true, no matter what the evidence—or from **self-deception**—consciously believing what at a deeper level we know to be dubious. It is a very human trait indeed to believe that which we would like to be true and to deny those things we find unpalatable (or, as in the case of our own death, extremely hard to accept).

Most people admit that this is so with respect to others. We aren't surprised to learn, to mention a classic case, that in 1938, British Prime Minister Neville Chamberlain signed an agreement with Hitler to bring, in his words, "peace in our time."

Chamberlain was so conscious of the horror another world war would bring, and so desperately anxious to spare his nation and the civilized world from such a disaster, that his judgment was destroyed and he failed to see Hitler's intent in spite of all sorts of evidence that many others, including Winston Churchill, perceived for what it was.*

The difficulty is in catching ourselves in the act of believing what we want to believe rather than accepting what the evidence indicates to be the reality. Of course, most of us, luckily, have no opportunity to make mistakes of the kind that Chamberlain committed. Our self-deceptions tend to result in less global evils, although they still may have catastrophic consequences for ourselves or friends. Think of the large number of people who drink and then drive. Or consider the significant percentage of adults in every

---

*In fairness to Chamberlain, note that a very few historians claim, on rather sparse evidence, that Chamberlain knew chances for peace were not great and wanted to gain time for Britain to rearm.

industrial country who still smoke cigarettes or chew tobacco in the face of overwhelming evidence linking tobacco to all sorts of fatal illnesses, including heart disease, various kinds of cancer, and emphysema. Millions of people everywhere continue to puff or chew away, undeterred even by warning labels on tobacco products like this one:

> SURGEON GENERAL'S WARNING: Smoking
> Causes Lung Cancer, Heart Disease,
> Emphysema, And May Complicate Pregnancy.

## 5. RATIONALIZATION, DENIAL, AND PROCRASTINATION

Perhaps the most common forms of self-deception are **rationalization** and **denial**. We engage in these psychological ploys when we ignore or deny unpleasant evidence so as to feel justified in doing what we want to do or in believing what we find comfortable to believe. Rationalization is nicely illustrated by the old joke about the psychiatrist and a delusional patient who believes he is dead. To prove to the patient that he is alive, the psychiatrist first gets him to agree that dead men don't bleed and then makes a cut in the man's arm, which then bleeds. Smiling, the psychiatrist tilts his chair back and waits. "Well," says the dismayed patient, "I guess I was wrong. Dead men *do* bleed." He thus manages to sustain his delusion by rationalizing away undeniable proof to the contrary.

Another example, from the play *Cabaret*: a credulous German is reading the latest Nazi propaganda. Scowling, he announces, "The Jews own all the banks. And they're behind an international communist conspiracy too." Whereupon his clearer thinking companion observes, "But bankers are capitalists and communists are opposed to capitalism. How can Jews be both?" The first man pauses, temporarily stymied, then nods sagely and rationalizes: "They're very crafty."

---

*Samuel Pepys, rationalizing in his famous diary:*

Up and at my chamber all the morning doing business and also reading a little of *L'Escolle des filles*, which is a mighty lewd book, but yet not amiss for a sober man once read over to inform him in the villainy of the world.

*Samuel Pepys, later on in his famous diary:*

I burned it [the lewd book] that it might not be among my books to my shame.

*So was Pepys unconscious at one time of what to readers of his diary is so obvious, while at another time aware of his true motive in reading that pornographic work? Was he in some way conscious, deep down, of his true motive all along? When we deceive ourselves, do we in general really* know, *deep inside us, the truth we wish to conceal from ourselves? (Ain't human beings fascinating creatures?)*

*Rhymes with Orange* by Hilary B. Price.
Reprinted with special permission of King Features Syndicate.

Rationalization often leads to **procrastination**—to putting off for "tomorrow" what common sense tells us needs to be done today. Young smokers often tell themselves that they'll quit a few years down the pike before any serious harm is done; students are famous for delaying work on term papers until the day before they're due. (Recall the old song about how "Mañana is good enough for me," and the hispanic saying "Mañana será otro dia," "Tomorrow will be another day.") It is an all-too-human tendency to favor immediate gratification at the risk of possible long-term harm. In general, the more likely or more serious the long-term harm, the less likely that an intelligent person will choose immediate gratification. The trouble is that most of us tend to weigh long-term harms or losses too lightly when compared with short-run gains.

The unwillingness of human beings to face unpleasant reality often is revealed strikingly in important works of fiction. In his novel *Heart of Darkness*, for example, Joseph Conrad described the way in which Europeans who invaded Africa in the nineteenth century rationalized their exploitation and degradation of native populations. He thus chronicled a case of self-deception and rationalization engaged in by a whole group of people over an extended period of time. In his novel, set in the Belgian Congo (now Zaire) at the turn of the century, European invaders see their aim as to enlighten and civilize the African natives—to "wean those ignorant millions from their horrid ways." But it becomes evident as the story develops that the colonial traders have only one mission—to plunder the land for ivory.

Although a work of fiction, *Heart of Darkness* was based on the true conditions that existed in the Belgian Congo at the turn of the century. In 1876, when the Belgians began their colonization of the Congo, their monarch, King Leopold, who literally took personal ownership of the Congo, described his intent as "to open to civilization the only part of our globe where Christianity has not yet penetrated and to pierce the darkness which envelopes the entire population." But in fact the king was a tyrant, the colonials profiteers, and the Congolese virtual slaves. When news of the atrocities committed against African natives reached Europe, a vague uneasiness rippled across the continent, but Europeans managed to deal with these reports by rationalization. If the natives rebelled, the sentries had to defend themselves, didn't they? Weren't some natives bound to die in the civilizing process in any case? Et cetera.

In his book, Conrad punctured European rationalizations about what they were doing in Africa in a graphic way by concentrating on a few characters, whose development revealed the underlying truth that the European claim to be bringing civilization to the Africans was a smokescreen whose consequence (and unconscious intent?) was not to deceive the natives but rather to deceive the Europeans themselves.

Anyone who dismisses the *Heart of Darkness* portrayal of mass self-deception as just fiction—a story—or thinks that this sort of thing only happened a long time ago might reflect on the present-day confiscation of native lands in Brazil, Indonesia, and elsewhere, where the destruction of indiginous ways of life and peoples is justified in the name of "the integration of native populations into modern life" or "maximal uses of resources."

## 6. THE BENEFITS OF SELF-DECEPTION AND WISHFUL THINKING

Our account of human beings as self-deceivers, as well as rational agents, has been objected to on several grounds, perhaps the most important being that such a harmful device could not have evolved, and if it did, would long since have been weeded out by natural selection.* There are at least two important responses to this objection. First, whatever any theory may say, it seems clear that human beings do in fact deceive themselves and do engage in wishful thinking that sometimes results in harmful behavior. Those who accept a theory of evolution and natural selection have to make their theory conform to this fact—they cannot deny the fact because of their theory. (One of the great virtues of science is that scientists are not permitted to engage in this kind of monkey business.)

The second response is that self-deception and wishful thinking do in fact provide important survival benefits as well as harms; it thus makes sense to conclude that they evolved because of their beneficial effects. Although these benefits are not yet clearly understood, we now are beginning to grasp how this side of human nature works.

One important function of self-deception is to reduce *anxiety* or *stress*, giving us greater ability to make decisions and to *act* when delay might bring on disaster. One of the authors of this text, for example, was in a serious auto accident a few years ago during which he felt no fear whatsoever. He thus was able to control the car during the crucial moments in a way that would have been impossible had he been paralyzed by conscious fear. (After the accident was over, of course, he pretty much fell apart.) Psychologists would say that his fear was *repressed* during the crucial moments.

Anxiety reduction also is crucial with respect to long-term dangers and potential failures. Scientists are beginning to understand the biological effects of long-term anxiety on the body, and they are not good, to say the least. Stress is related to reduced effectiveness of the immune system and perhaps also to problems with other important body systems.† The relationship between anxiety or stress and belief systems is still not very well understood by psychologists, but this much seems to be true: Doubt, in particular, doubt about important matters, produces anxiety in most people. Settling doubt and coming to some belief or other thus reduces anxiety and makes us feel

---

*That the rational, intelligent side of our nature should have evolved seems quite natural, given its immense value in solving life's problems, and this idea was held even in the nineteenth century, for instance, by Charles Darwin and Charles Peirce, among many others.

†For an excellent and very readable account of the relationship of self-deception to anxiety reduction, and of how the unconscious mind selects what comes into consciousness, see Daniel Goleman's *Vital Lies, Simple Truths* (New York: Simon and Schuster, 1985). For a short account of one theory concerning the relationship between stress and the immune and endocrine systems, see the May 1987 *Scientific American*, pp. 68B–68D.

*Andy Capp* by Reggie Smythe. Reprinted with special permission of North America Syndicate.

*Self-deception at work.*

better. So it isn't only the need to act, to do something, that sometimes leads us to premature or unwarranted beliefs. Even when there is nothing to be done right now, doubt may produce ongoing anxiety (sometimes referred to as "generalized anxiety"), and wishful thinking that eliminates this doubt may reduce the anxiety.

Perhaps the classic case in which self-deception helps people to feel better and to act more effectively occurs when, in spite of medical evidence, the terminally ill deny the proximity of death, thus reducing the numbing effect of terrible fear. We all need defenses against the knowledge of the certainty of death; those close to it much more than the rest of us. Similarly, it may be useful to be able to deny the seriousness of ailments that are not life-threatening, as it was for Franklin D. Roosevelt, whose denial for some time of the permanence and debilitating nature of his paralysis may well have been an important reason that he was able to persevere and become president of the United States.

Self-deception also plays a positive role in life for those who tend to relive in memory the good experiences life has afforded them while tending to forget the bad ones. Why, years later, dwell on the bad? Why drag ourselves down in this way? (It's important, of course, to remember the mistakes one has made in order to make sure not to repeat them. The point is that nothing useful is accomplished by dwelling on them needlessly, as so many depressed people do.)

In some cases, however, there may be a serious difference of opinion concerning the benefits of the denial that death lurks nearby. It is notorious, for example, that most young men who find themselves in the lethal killing zones typical of modern wars are able to function even though terrified in a way that most of the rest of us can hardly imagine. They can fight (those who can—many cannot) in large part because they tend to see the flying bullets and exploding shells hitting the next guy, not themselves. Servicemen tell stories of the extreme surprise some men show when they realize that they have been hit and are dying. The people who send young men into battle rely on this ability of the young to deny consciously what in some sense they know all too well—that they may be the next one to get it. The obviously good function of this kind of self-deception is that it enables soldiers to fight for their country when outside forces threaten its existence. The not entirely good consequence is that tyrants and other megalomaniacal leaders find it easier to get the young to risk their lives in immoral or foolish endeavors.

## 7. THE PULL OF PSEUDOSCIENCE AND THE PARANORMAL

That scientists, in particular those in the "hard sciences," generally know what they're talking about is vouchsafed by the everyday miracles that science makes possible, from computers to automobiles, TV sets, electric light bulbs, nylon, toilet paper, eyeglasses, insulin, and clean water, hot or cold, flowing out of kitchen faucets. *Pseudoscientific* theories continue to be accepted by a significant minority of people in spite of the fact that they produce no results whatsoever. Why is that?

The answer lies in the strength of the various psychological mechanisms that we have been discussing in this chapter. Although science produces results, it doesn't always provide easy or satisfying answers to our problems. Instead, it often confirms what we would like very much to deny, including, unfortunately, the fact that we are not entirely rational animals; that the virtuous are not always rewarded, nor the guilty punished; that hard work is the fate of most of us; and that in the end we all die. (It also says nothing one way or the other about the possibility of life after death.)

Pseudoscience, on the other hand, while it often titillates with predictions of disasters others will experience, generally has rosy things to tell us about our own futures. It sometimes allays fears that it itself has generated; for instance, by transforming the fear that extraterrestrials lurk about by making them into benign cuddly creatures. It tends to be comforting, uplifting, optimistic. It often provides relatively easy solutions to our problems. Astrologers tell us that we too can be successful in business, provided, of course, that we schedule economic transactions on the "right" days. Fortune tellers predict success in romance and marriage. Mediums claim to put us into contact with departed loved ones (implying the happy thought, by the way, that we too will survive death). One astrologer told Nancy Reagan which days were safe for her president husband to do his business (Mrs. Reagan apparently insisted that the president alter his schedule accordingly).

Nevertheless, it is bound to seem odd that pseudosciences are so widely believed in, given that they are regularly proved worthless. Astrology, for example, has been disproved countless times over the centuries. Pliny the Elder (Roman scholar and naturalist, 23–79 A.D.), for instance, stated a simple yet devastating objection to astrology way back then when he said, "If a man's destiny is caused by the star under which he is born, then all men born under that star should have the same fortune. But masters and slaves and kings and beggars all are born under the same star." Can wishful thinking alone generate the considerable acceptance so many pseudosciences enjoy in the face of constant refutation? Whatever the answer to that question, it is clear that a pseudoscience like astrology retains much of its appeal in spite of crushing objections in part because charlatans have devised ways to make it seem plausible to the very suggestive (most of us in weak moments).

---

### Superstition Marries Pseudoscience?

Price a Paris boutique charges for an ounce of Yin Shen White Tea, "handpicked by Chinese virgins": $90.

*Harper's Index* item (September 1996)

*Those who doubt the widespread belief in "paranormal," pseudoscientific phe-nomena should pay close attention to the results of this June 1990 Gallup poll of 1,236 adults (as reported in* The Skeptical Inquirer, *Winter 1991):*

One of every four Americans believe in ghosts.

One of every four Americans believe they have had a telepathic experience in which they communicated with another person without using the traditional five senses.

One in six Americans have felt they have been in touch with someone who has died.

One in ten claim to have seen or been in the presence of a ghost.

*Three in four at least occasionally read their horoscopes in a newspaper, and one in four say they believe in the tenets of astrology.* [Italics added. Why, by the way, do the other two in four occasionally read newspaper horoscopes if they don't believe them? Is there a bit of self-deception in their claim that they don't?]

*Of course, belief in astrology is at least equally widespread in many other coun-tries. Here, for instance, is an excerpt from a* Skeptical Inquirer *article (Spring 1990) on this point:*

While France [a predominantly Catholic country] has fewer than 36,000 Roman Catholic clergy, there are more than 40,000 [!] professional astrologers who declare their income to tax authorities—which says nothing of the undoubt-edly far greater number of moonstruck stargazers, faith healers, mediums, necro-mancers, and fortune tellers of every imaginable stripe who choose not to declare their income. . . . Large and established companies turn to graphologists, birth-date interpreters, and plain old astrologers before hiring job candidates. A leading computer company only hires people after a tarot card reading. A big insurance company uses a swinging pendulum [!!] to judge whether a candidate is honest.

*Well, at least trial by fire has gone out of style.*

One weapon in the con artist's arsenal is what some psychologists call the "Barnum effect," after nineteenth-century circus magnate P. T. Barnum. Barnum is deservedly famous for remarking that "There's a sucker born every minute," but he also maintained that the secret of his immense success was in providing a little something for every-one. Con artists disguised as astrologers follow this advice very carefully. They word their horoscopes ambiguously, so that virtually everybody who wants to can see them-selves in the descriptions under their sign. Here is part of a "typical Barnum profile":

> You have a great need for other people to like you and admire you. You have a tendency to be critical of yourself. You have a great deal of unused capacity which you have not used to your advantage. While you have some personality weak-nesses, you are generally able to compensate for them. . . . You pride yourself on

being an independent thinker and do not accept others' statements without satisfactory proof.*

In fact, this description fits relatively few people, but it does fit how most of us *think* of ourselves, or *want* to think of ourselves.

However, not all statements in horoscope columns are of the Barnum type. The typical "Aries" is generally said to be "bold, energetic, assertive, selfish, insensitive, and aggressive." Only some of these characteristics are highly thought of. Typical horoscopes mix statements listing these kinds of character traits with statements of a general Barnum nature. "People tend to be impressed by the specific details that appear to fit (and pay less attention to those that do not), while the general Barnum-type statements provide readily acceptable 'padding'."

It's interesting, by the way, that horoscope-column writers don't base their predictions and advice on any theory that is even remotely astrological. To put it plainly, they just make the stuff up out of their own heads, something easily proved by comparing what one astrology columnist says on a given day with what others tell their readers. Consider, for example, what two different newspaper "astrologers" had to say was in store for those born from May 21 through June 20 (newspapers have no room for flourishes like being "on the cusp") on June 24, 1996. The first is by the best-known person in the trade: Jeane Dixon:†

> **Gemini** (May 21–June 20): Consider the best way to achieve a cherished goal. A trip may prove less useful than expected. Your artistic talents are honored and applauded.

Compare that with this stuff written by syndicated horoscopist Jacqueline Bigar:

> **Gemini** (May 21–June 20): **** A friendship or long-term desire may seem distant. On the contrary, it may be a lot closer to becoming a reality than before. Worry less, and let your creativity flow. Another responds to your romantic overtures. Stay focused on work. Tonight: So what if it's Monday?

Nice way to make a lucrative, if somewhat shady, living, isn't it? (Those stars, by the way, "Show the Kind of Day You'll Have: 5-Dynamic; 4-Positive; 3-Average; 2-So-so; 1-Difficult." How can anyone believe that all Libras were going to have a "Dynamic" day on June 24, 1996, while all Virgos would only have days that were average? Oh, yes, you will be pleased to know that Bigar has caught on to the advantages of having a 900 number; so if you'd like to know more about the love, luck, health, or money matters in your future, for a mere 99 cents, or $2.95, a minute, depending on the service rendered, you now can find out. Don't delay!)

*Extrasensory perception* (telepathy, clairvoyance, precognition, etc.) is another form of pseudoscience widely believed by the public. According to a Gallup poll, half the people in the United States believe in ESP (including 67 percent of those who are college-educated!) Gulled by sensational press reports about "scientific" studies, they

---

*Taken from a fascinating article by Christopher C. French, Mandy Fowler, Katy McCarthy, and Debbie Peers entitled "Belief in Astrology: A Test of the Barnum Effect," *Skeptical Inquirer* (Winter 1991). The quotes in the next two paragraphs are from this article.
†Dixon passed away in early 1997 without, it should be noted, predicting her own demise. Perhaps her finest work was her 1979 book *Horoscope for Dogs*.

*Con artists like Jeane Dixon and Uri Geller are pikers in the great sweep of things. They titillate, comfort, and do a small amount of harm, and that's about it. But the great mesmerizers, the Benito Mussolinis and Ruholla Khomeinis, who sell whole nations a bill of goods, are another matter. Here are a few pronouncements about mass propaganda by Adolf Hitler, an intuitive master at the game (culled from his writings by the* Secular Humanist Bulletin *[March 1988]):*

All propaganda must be popular and its intellectual level must be adjusted to the most limited intelligence among those it is addressed to.

All effective propaganda must be limited to a very few points and must harp on these slogans until the last member of the public understands what you want him to understand by your slogan. . . . [T]he masses are slow-moving, and they require a certain time before they are ready even to notice a thing, and only after the simplest ideas are repeated thousands of times will the masses finally remember them.

*Propaganda's effect . . . must be aimed at the emotions and only to a very limited degree at the so-called intellect.* [Italics added.]

The very first axiom of all propagandist activity: to wit, the basically subjective and one-sided attitude it must take toward every question it deals with. The function of propaganda is . . . not to weigh and ponder the rights of different people, but exclusively to emphasize the one right that it has set out to argue for. Its task is not to make an objective study of the truth, . . . its task is to serve our own right, always and unflinchingly.

Does this sound like the formula to which most political rhetoric in the United States today is tailored?

accept as evidence of psychic powers such flawed studies as the tests on Uri Geller performed at the Stanford Research Institute (definitely not affiliated with Stanford University!). Geller, by the way, has been exposed as a fraud countless times; the way in which he appears to bend spoons "psychically"—the trick for which he is most famous—has been demonstrated on several TV magic shows and can be learned by anyone sufficiently motivated to practice a bit.

In fact, over a century of research fails to confirm the existence of ESP in any of its alleged forms. After reviewing a large body of research in this area for the National Research Council, a scientific committee concluded that "despite a 130-year record of scientific research on such matters our committee could find no scientific justification for the existence of phenomena such as extrasensory perception, mental telepathy, or 'mind over matter' exercises. . . . Evaluation of the large body of the best available evidence simply does not support the contention that these phenomena exist" (*American Psychological Association Monitor*, January 1988).

In the face of such findings, why do people continue to believe in ESP? We mentioned a few reasons a few pages back, but Thomas Gilovich, a cognitive psychologist at Cornell University concludes (from surveys asking people to explain the origin of their beliefs) that personal experience also plays an important role. When by chance or coincidence people experience a run of good or bad luck they often attribute it to some special power. Gamblers who have streaks of luck at black jack or roulette have trouble accepting the fact that the theory of probability predicts that streaks of luck are likely to occur every once in a while. They often become convinced that some special power is at work—that unseen forces are on their side—rather than accept the fact that coincidences are bound to happen now and then.

In fact, coincidences that may seem quite extraordinary occur quite frequently in everyday life. Gilovich cites the "birthday problem" used in statistics courses as an example.

> When asked to consider the probability that at least two people in a group of a particular size were born the same day of the year, most people are shocked to learn that the odds are roughly 50–50 when the group is as small as 23. More shocking still is the probability of a matching birthday is 85% when the group size is only 35. Thus, many people will be surprised by an outcome (a pair of matching birthdays) that is not unusual at all. . . . When people attribute coincidence to some kind of special power, they usually do so from ignorance. They would be much less gullible if they understood the likelihood of coincidence from a statistical perspective.*

*Premonitions* fall into the same category. A premonition is really a coincidence that occurs between someone's thoughts and actual events in the real world. A young man dreams about his ex-girlfriend, and lo and behold, she calls him the next day. If he thinks his dream is a premonition, he has forgotten for the moment the many times he has dreamed about her when she didn't call. After all, people frequently dream about ex-lovers, but rarely do they telephone the next day. When they do, it's coincidental. This element of chance applies as well to extraordinary premonitions that foretell an important event that really does occur. A woman has a dream that a TWA DC 6 will crash in the Florida Everglades—and it does! Of what significance is this? The question to ask is whether such events occur more often than we would expect them to by chance. People have an unfortunate tendency to believe premonitions that come true and to forget those that don't. This, by the way, nicely illustrates the difference between pseudoscience and science. Pseudoscience pays attention to successes and ignores failures; science never ignores failures. It puts its hypotheses to severe tests, requiring independent repetition of observations and experiments rather than relying simply on coincidence and anecdote.

# 8. LACK OF A GOOD SENSE OF PROPORTION

The kinds of irrationality catalogued in this chapter so far—provincialism, self-deception, and so on—seem to have evolved primarily because they are advantageous in certain kinds of circumstances. Self-deception, as mentioned before, may reduce stress, and provincialism tends to increase group cohesiveness. But explanations as to

---

*Thomas Gilovich, *How We Know What Isn't So* (New York: Free Press, 1991).

why so many of us lack a good **sense of proportion** are much harder to come by.* In any case, there can be no doubt that on occasion we all lack a good sense of proportion when we make decisions and come to conclusions in everyday life. The trick is to learn how to minimize this natural impediment to cogent reasoning.

**Prudence** is one of the chief components of a good sense of proportion. In the sense intended here, prudence consists in being provident—of tempering what we do today in order to maximize our overall, long-run interests. Of course, being prudent does not mean becoming a drudge, or a workaholic. It doesn't mean always putting off till tomorrow pleasures that could have been had today. But it does mean carefully weighing today's pleasures against long-term interests.

Note, though, that imprudence frequently is not a factor when people lack a sense of proportion. The impediments to cogent reasoning already discussed certainly play an important role here. A sense of loyalty, for example, sometimes clouds the perspective of even the most level-headed among us, leading us to exaggerate the wonders of our own society while neglecting its defects. And wishful thinking certainly plays an important role. People play state lotteries not just because they have little understanding of what it means to say the odds are a million, or a hundred thousand, to one against winning the big prize, but also because of wishful thinking. ("This is my lucky day," or "I was born on 1/23/45, so 12345 is my lucky number.")

But there are plenty of cases, some of a much more serious nature, in which wishful thinking or self-deception plays little or no role. During the 1991 Gulf War, for instance, thousands of Israelis moved from the Tel Aviv area to avoid being killed by Scud missiles directed at that city, although they had lived with much less panic in the face of the much greater threat of death via ordinary, everyday accidents. During that war, Westerners stopped flying to the Middle East and even to Europe because they feared terrorist retaliation, although the odds against being killed in this way are millions to one (again, driving to work every day is much more life-threatening). Many Americans refuse to fly commercial airplanes from one city to another even though driving is many times more dangerous. In fact, flying commercial airlines is just about the safest way to travel ever invented, yet lots of people, including one of the authors of this chapter on pseudoreasoning, have serious bouts with fear every time they fly.†

---

*Part of the explanation lies, no doubt, in the benefits of the psychological mechanisms already discussed. But perhaps another part lies in two important facts about human evolution. The first is that behavior guided by intelligence is a later arrival on the scene than responses motivated purely by desires and emotions (something that is confirmed by what is known about the development of the brains of vertebrate animals—in particular, mammals). Strong emotions that appropriately guided behavior at much earlier times now sometimes skew rational thought and motivate responses that are less than optimal. The second relevant fact is that until quite recently, very little was known about what philosophers used to call the "secret powers" that move things, and a great deal that was "known" has turned out to be false. (Think only of medicine until about 150 years ago, when practices such as bloodletting were common.) If we go back, say, just 10 or 20 thousand years in human history—an eye blink on the evolutionary timescale—we are back to a time when exceedingly few *accurate* general beliefs about cause-and-effect relationships can have been known. So it is only recently in the great sweep of things that it has slowly become increasingly beneficial to moderate the urges of immediate desire and strong emotions in terms of what intelligence can learn from experience. Perhaps, then, the lack of a better sense of proportion is partly explained as being due to a kind of "evolutionary lag."

†In some of these cases, psychologists understand the mechanisms leading to the poor sense of proportion; for example, a fear of unfamiliar threats as compared to the familiar and, in the case of airline flying, a lack of personal control of the plane (similar to fear felt when sitting in the back seat of a car). But they don't understand why people are prone to these kinds of irrationality.

> *It often is difficult to know whether someone is irrationally self-deceived, or perhaps imprudent, rather than being completely rational. Take the case of professional boxers and football players. Do they deceive themselves about the likelihood of permanent and serious damage to their bodies? Are they being extremely imprudent? Or do they so value their professional life (and its financial rewards) that to them it is worth the pain and suffering likely at a later date? Some retired professional football players, for instance, say that they were foolish to take the pounding week after week that has left them walking wounded; others say it was worth it. Are the latter still deceiving themselves?*

In fact, failure to see things in proper perspective is one of the most serious errors in reasoning that most of us are guilty of. This is true in particular concerning value judgments. For example, when "60 Minutes" aired a segment in January 1993 on animal research and another on the ill treatment of women, they received many more letters of complaint about cruelty to animals than to women. (We assume that most people, even "animal liberationists," value human welfare over that of other animals.) In a restaurant conversation overheard recently, someone defended a friend who had bilked an elderly couple of their life savings by pointing out the truth that we all break the law from time to time.

As might be expected, politicians frequently (one might say continually) take advantage of the failure of so many people to see things in a proper perspective. They know that people can be diverted from important issues and problems by being provided with "bread and circuses," and that, for instance, the best time to announce unpopular measures is when the minds of masses of people are riveted on the private lives of celebrities like Michael Jackson or Lady Di. It also is one reason why the mass media so frequently stretch the "human interest" angles to stories way out of proportion to their importance. (A good deal more on these topics needs to be, and will be said, in later chapters.)

## SUMMARY OF CHAPTER 6

Human beings are not completely rational animals. There also is a nonrational component to our makeup that often interferes with our ability to argue or reason cogently.

1. Our reasoning sometimes is skewed from the truth because of *loyalty*, which inclines us to see our own society and its beliefs in a more favorable light than the evidence may warrant; because of *provincialism*, which tends to narrow our interests and knowledge of what goes on in the world; and because of the *herd instinct*, which makes it easy and natural for us to believe what most others in our society believe. *Example*: failing to notice the undemocratic and nasty things our own government does on the international scene.

2. Loyalty and provincialism are related to *prejudice*, in particular, to prejudice against members of other groups, and to thinking in terms of *unverified stereotypes*. *Example*: the stereotype that was common in the United States until about the late 1950s, which pictured African Americans as foot-shuffling, obsequious

children. But believing bad things about others constitutes prejudice only when not justified by sufficient evidence.

Prejudice against others often is conjoined with an overtolerance of the defects and foibles of one's own group and its members, and may be reinforced by the need to find *scapegoats*—others who can be blamed for our own troubles and mistakes. *Example*: blaming the Jews for the transgressions of others.

Thinking in terms of stereotypes and scapegoats often stems from a *partisan mind-set*—viewing everything in terms of "us against them" or "my right opinions against your wrong ones." Good reasoners, by way of contrast, have minds open to the truth, wherever it may lead.

3. *Superstitions* often are supported by a small amount of evidence. What makes them superstitions is that we believe them on the basis of insufficient and, frequently, biased samples from which all negative evidence has been eliminated. *Example*: overlooking the fact that good things sometimes happen on Friday the 13th and bad things on other days.

4. Beliefs acquired in the irrational ways just described generally result from *wishful thinking*—believing what we want to believe, no matter what the evidence, or from its variant, called *self-deception*—consciously believing what, at some deeper level, we know to be dubious. *Example*: British Prime Minister Neville Chamberlain wishfully believing that the Munich agreement with Hitler had assured "peace in our time."

5. Two other important ways to cut the wishful thinking pie are *rationalization* and *denial*. *Example*: smoking cigarettes after being exposed to all sorts of evidence that they're bad for one's health. Rationalization often supports *procrastination* —putting off until tomorrow what ought to be done today. *Example*: starting to write a term paper the day before it's due.

6. While we can't yet be sure why nonrational mechanisms have evolved, scientists are beginning to understand some of their beneficial effects. Loyalty and provincialism increase group cohesiveness when there is competition or strife with other groups. The herd instinct helps individuals to work well with others in their group. And self-deception frequently aids in the reduction of *anxiety* and *stress*, both of which can be harmful to health. Prolonged doubt about serious matters tends to produce stress and anxiety; coming to firm beliefs about these matters tends to combat depression and thus be good for one's physical well-being. *Example*: denying the seriousness of a terminal illness, thereby reducing grief at the end of one's life.

7. *Pseudoscientific beliefs* are adopted, and endure, in spite of their failure to help us deal successfully with everyday problems, because of wishful thinking, self-deception, and similar psychological mechanisms. Pseudoscience is comforting and upbeat concerning our own welfare and the satisfaction of our deepest desires. *Example*: seances that practitioners claim can put us into contact with deceased friends and relatives.

But pseudosciences also gain widespread acceptance because charlatans have learned how to manipulate us in our unguarded or weak moments. *Example*:

alleged astrologers papering over the phoniness of their forecasts by larding them with "Barnum" profiles that tend to fit everybody. Note that the con artists who play on our weaknesses in this way are two-bit operators compared to such great political mesmerizers as Adolf Hitler, who expertly manipulate masses of their compatriots by clever and sophisticated appeals to the irrational side of the human psyche.

8. On occasion, most of us lack a good *sense of proportion*, a defect in reasoning that critical reasoners try to minimize. *Example*: being persuaded by political rhetoric to pay more attention to relatively unimportant matters than to those that are more serious. Being *prudent*, in the sense of *provident*—acting so as to maximize long-run interests—is an important component of a good sense of proportion that we often lack. *Example*: weighing today's small pleasure more highly than the long-run benefits of doing well on a final exam, thus not preparing until the last minute. But people often fail to see things in proper perspective for other reasons; for example, because of group loyalty or wishful thinking, or because of other emotional interferences with cogent reasoning. *Example*: being more afraid of small risks than of much bigger ones.

## EXERCISE 6-1

1. How, if at all, do the following items taken from the *Harper's Index* (March 1996) illustrate matters that were discussed in this chapter?

   Percentage of Americans earning less than $30,000 a year who believe "the meek shall inherit the earth": 61

   Percentage earning more than $60,000 who believe this: 36

2. How about this *Luann* cartoon?

*Luann* reprinted by permission of United Features Syndicate, Inc.

3. Overheard (expletives removed) in a restaurant during the 1996 presidential campaign: "I just heard another story about Bill Clinton's womanizing. That guy is unfit to be president of Waggawano, for Heaven's sake. We Republicans haven't a thing to worry about this time."

   The same character overheard about ten minutes later: So what if Bob Packwood was accused of a bit of sexual hanky panky. He shouldn't have been forced to resign. It's the great job he was doing in the Senate, not his private life, that should have counted."

Relate these remarks to at least two topics discussed in this book.

4. Explain how this conversation between a student and a teacher (not quite verbatim) relates to topics discussed in this chapter:

*Student*: I've come to your office to see about getting a B in this course. *Teacher*: But you're doing C work, the semester ends next week, and you missed two assignments. What makes you think you can get a B? *Student*: Well, I need to get a B to get into Berkeley [University of California at Berkeley] next fall. *Teacher*: But why didn't you come in sooner and talk to me about this and perhaps get help to do better work? *Student*: Yes. But I really need to get that B or I can't get into Berkeley.

5. Explain how this conversation between two students (again not quite verbatim, with names changed to protect the guilty) relates to topics discussed in this chapter:

*Smith*: Loan me twenty bucks. I'm strapped and have a heavy date with you know who. *Jones*: You're always asking me for favors, but you never do any for me. I always do the favors you ask of me; you regularly turn me down. Sorry, Charlie. *Smith*: Hey! What about last year when I got you a date with Charlene? You never got me a date with anyone. So how about it?

6. Do you believe that loyalty really does skew people's beliefs away from what the evidence will support? If so, support your belief with at least one example not mentioned in the text. If not, show that the examples given in the text are somehow mistaken.

7. Do human beings really have a herd instinct, or is that just true of cows and such? Defend you answer.

8. How does the text use the expression "belief provincialism"? Give some examples, other than those mentioned in the text, and explain why they are examples.

9. According to the text, what is wrong with categorizing, say, the French as great lovers, Germans as obedient automatons, and so on? After all, doesn't experience show that the members of a given group tend to be different from the members of other groups, as Greeks are different from Pakistanis and Mexicans from Nigerians?

10. Give at least two examples of other people engaging in self-deception or wishful thinking, and explain why you think their actions fit the relevant descriptions provided in the text. Do *you* ever engage in this sort of funny business? Explain and defend your answer. (Hint: You do.)

11. What are some of the good consequences of wishful thinking and self-deception that are mentioned in the text? Explain. Can you think of others?

12. Critically evaluate the following argument. (Does it contain a correct use of induction?): Several of my friends have been very lucky in life so far; and I've

read of quite a few other lucky souls. So when I say that my lucky friends will continue to have good luck, I'm basing my conclusion on experience, not wishful thinking.

13. If you had been interviewed for the Gallup poll discussed on page 122, would you have been among those expressing belief in at least one of the claims asked about by that poll? If so, explain. If not, you get a free ride on this question. (Note the temptation for those who would have been among those with the appropriate beliefs to engage in a tiny sort of lie of silent assertion by simply passing over this question!)

14. Carefully explain the so-called Barnum effect. How did the typical Barnum profile reprinted on pages 122–123 of this chapter fit you?

15. The box on page 124 lists some of the principles underlying Adolf Hitler's propaganda technique. Find at least two examples from the speeches of American presidents, members of the U.S. Congress, or Supreme Court justices that seem to be in accordance with these principles. Explain and defend your choices. (It's cheating to use examples that appear in this text.)

16. We all suffer to some extent from the impediments to rational thinking described in this chapter, the authors of this text not being exceptions. (Actually, one of us is an exception, but the other isn't.) Doesn't this textbook, for example, reflect the provincialism of its authors in some ways? If so, how? If not, why might some readers think otherwise? What about any other ways in which you think the text could be construed so as to indicate rational failures—of the kind discussed in this chapter—on the part of its authors? (Be brief!)

## EXERCISE 6-2

Here is a rather simple example of the way that numbers can be manipulated to con the unwary into thinking that something extraordinary is going on when it isn't. Your job is to explain the trick that produces this "amazing coincidence."

When you take the year of the birth of Bill Clinton and add to it the year he took office plus his age at his last birthday, and then subtract the number of full years he has been in office, you get the number 3986 (or 3985 depending on the time of year in which you calculate). Nothing surprising there. But when you add and subtract the similar figures for the leaders of Britain, France, Japan, China, and Saudi Arabia, you get 3986 (or 3985) in each case!

*Toles* by Tom Toles. Copyright 1989 *Buffalo News*.
Used by permission of Universal Press Syndicate.

---

*An important art of politicians is to find new names for institutions which under old names have become odious to the public.*

— Talleyrand

*If concepts are not clear, words do not fit. If words do not fit, the day's work cannot be accomplished, morals and art do not flourish. If morals and art do not flourish, punishments are not just. If punishments are not just, the people do not know where to put hand or foot.*
— Confucius, *Analects*, XIII, 3

*When an idea is wanting, a word can always be found to take its place.*
— Goethe

*He who defines the terms wins the argument.*
— Chinese proverb

*Beware of and eschew pompous prolixity.*
— Charles A. Beardsley

# Chapter
# 7

# LANGUAGE

Language is the indispensable tool used in formulating arguments. We all are familiar (or should be!) with the power of language when it is employed by fine writers of fiction—Shakespeare, Fielding, Austen, Conrad (to name just a few who wrote in the English language)—the list is very long. The principal point of literature classes is precisely to make this apparent. But good writing can be equally effective when used in the construction of argumentative essays and other argumentative passages. The trouble is that language also can be used effectively in the service of fallacious as well as cogent arguments, deceiving the unwary or unknowing into accepting arguments they should reject.

## 1. COGNITIVE AND EMOTIVE MEANINGS

If the purpose of a sentence is to inform or to state a fact, some of its words must refer to things, events, or properties of one kind or another. These words must thus have what is commonly called **cognitive meaning**. (The sentences they compose also are said to have cognitive meaning.)

But most words also have **emotive meaning**, which means that they have positive or negative overtones. The emotive charges of some words are obvious. Think of the terms *wop*, *kike*, *nigger*, and *fag*, or of the so-called four-letter words that rarely appear in textbooks, even in this permissive age.

The words just mentioned have negative emotive charges. But lots of words have positive overtones. Examples are *freedom*, *love*, *democracy*, *springtime*, and *peace*. And plenty of others have either neutral or mixed emotive force. *Pencil*, *run*, and *river* tend to be neutral words. *Socialism*, *politician*, and *whiskey* play to mixed audiences.

In fact, almost any word that is emotively positive for some people or in some contexts may be just the opposite for others. One person's meat often is indeed another's poison. Perhaps the paradigm case is the word *God*, which has one kind of overtone for true believers, another for agnostics, and still another for strident atheists.

Terms that on first glance may appear to be emotively neutral often turn out to have at least modest emotive overtones. The terms *bureaucrat*, *government official*, and *public servant*, for instance, all refer to the same group of people and thus have approximately the same cognitive import, but their emotive meanings are quite different. Of the three, only *government official* comes close to being neutral in tone.

## 2. EMOTIVE MEANING AND PERSUASIVE USES OF LANGUAGE

The fact that expressions have emotive as well as cognitive meanings has not escaped the notice of con artists, advertisers, politicians, and others whose stock in trade is the manipulation of attitudes, desires, and beliefs. Over the years, they have learned how to use the emotive side of language to further their own ends, whether benevolent or self-serving.

One common way in which the emotive force of language can be used to con, as Talleyrand observed some time ago, is to mask the odious nature of an institution or practice by giving it a nice name rather than a more accurate, nasty one. Why call the Chinese dictatorship by an accurate name when it can be called the *People's Republic of China*? When Saddam Hussein took control of Iraq, why should he have fiddled with the increasingly inaccurate name *Republic of Iraq*? The ruling clique in Burma surely has no reason to call its thugs who engage in mass murder and other kinds of nasty business anything other than the *State Law and Order Restoration Council*. In a slightly different vein, why call diluted beer *watered down beer* when it can be thought of as *lite*? Why should a minority political group call itself *The Moral Minority*, when it can puff itself up into *The Moral Majority*? (Note, by the way, the implication that the individuals in this group are more moral than other people.) And doesn't *Department of Defense* have a much sweeter ring to it than the original and accurate name *War Department*?

In any case, another way to trade on the emotive force of language is to use nasty terms when referring to items you wish to make appear less than desirable. Hippies often used the term *pig* to damn, ah, . . . peace officers. (Is the term *hippy*, by the way,

---

I am firm, you are obstinate, he is pigheaded.
                    — Bertrand Russell's example of words having similar
                       cognitive meanings but much different emotive senses

pejorative?) And, to take an example from closer to home, don't the authors of this text use the term *con artist* to sway reader sentiments against those who use language in ways they consider to be shady?

In recent years, manipulative uses of language have been given a spate of emotively negative names, each with a slightly different connotation, including *doublespeak* (deliberately ambiguous or evasive language), *bureaucratese* (governmental doublespeak), *newspeak* (media doublespeak), *academese* (the academic variety), *legalese* (lawyer talk), *gobbledygook*, *bafflegab*, and *jargon*.

Take *militaryese*. The military at all times and places has devised expressions intended as much as possible to hide the fact that war is, to put it mildly, unvarnished hell. Here are a few examples:

| | |
|---|---|
| Comfort women | Women of conquered countries forced to work as prostitutes "servicing" soldiers (term used by the Japanese during World War II) |
| Battle fatigue | Insanity suffered as a result of battle |
| Proximity fused rounds | Antipersonnel artillery shells designed to maim or kill |
| Friendly fire | Shelling friendly villages or troops by mistake |
| Protective reaction strike | Bombing |
| Pacification center | Concentration camp (itself originally doublespeak) |
| Termination | Killing (also used by the CIA, where *termination with prejudice* means *assassination*) |
| Selective ordnance | Napalm (used to kill by incineration) |
| The Final Solution | Plan of the Nazis to murder all European Jews |

During World War II—that most awful of all wars—the expression *dehousing industrial workers* was used by the British and Americans to mean killing civilians, including women and children via *saturation* air raids. The indescribably horrible massive air raids on Germany and Japan that created incredible firestorms (see the footnote on page 308) were said to result in *self-energized dislocation*, not widespread death by either incineration or asphyxiation. (When, during the Somalia "incident," a military spokesperson described women and children as *combatants*, Senator John McCain (Republican, Arizona) was moved to comment in disgust, "It reminds me of the soldier in Vietnam who said, 'We had to destroy the village in order to save it.'")

Of course, *bureaucratese*, *governmentese*, and *politicalese* (we all can play at this game) don't exactly suffer from a paucity of examples. In Philadelphia, the jail for juvenile "offenders" is called the "Youth Study Center." Florida chain gangs, for a short time, were called "restricted labor squads." San Francisco calls its garbage trucks "street environment service vehicles." Federal bureaucrats trying to make a case for the legitimacy of "nonstandard" English dialects referred to standard English as the "privileged dialect." And signers of the Republican party's uncontracted "Contract with America" called their proposed measure for a 50 percent reduction in the capital gains tax the "Job Creation and Wage Enhancement Act."

These examples illustrate the use of *euphemistic language*—locutions from which as much negative emotive content as possible has been removed—and the replacement of accurate names with more high-flown locutions. The point generally is to conceal or to mislead, which could be one reason that this kind of talk has become so popular with government officials, lawyers, military officers, doctors, and (alas!) a large number of academics. (Is this one reason why so many other[!] textbooks are so dull?)

In recent years, however, it's possible that doublespeak in the business world has managed to surpass even that of militaryese in its deviousness. Well, maybe not. But consider these examples of euphemisms used when someone is fired:

> *bumped, decruited, dehired, deselected, destaffed, discontinued, disemployed, dislocated, downsized, excessed, involuntarily separated, nonretained, non-renewed, severed, surplussed, transitioned, vocationally relocated.**

The place where you get downsized, by the way, is sometimes called the *outplacement office*.

Most large companies these days desperately want to avoid use of the f-word—*fired*—but at Bill Gates's Microsoft outfit, it's the b-word—*bug*—that is the no-no. Employees are required instead to speak of *undocumented beheavior*, or of a *design side effect*, *known*, *issue*, or *intermittent issue*. The fix for bugs in Microsoft's *Office 97* software—Microsoft's software is notorious for having bugs—was called an *Internet Mail Enhancement Patch*.

On a different note, NBC described its "tape delayed" coverage of the 1996 Atlanta Olympic Games as "plausibly live." The *International Herald Tribune* labels page ads (in small type at the top) "Sponsored Pages," which is a bit more honest than PBS stations (supposedly not carrying advertisements) that refer to their commercials as "expanded underwriting credits."

Interestingly, class differences have always been mirrored euphemistically. Average people *rent* apartments; the rich *lease* them. The nonrich talk of *social climbers*; social climbers like to think of themselves as *upwardly mobile* or (more recently) *changing course* and not as *pushy* but rather as *emphatic*. The wealthy don't earn a "salary"; they receive "compensation" or have an "income."

The deliberate use of euphemistic language has been going on at least since the beginning of recorded history, but it seems to have increased dramatically in recent years, perhaps because of the professionalization of most trades. Titled professionals want to sound objective and authoritative, not opinionated or biased.

It's true that euphemisms can and often do serve useful, nonmanipulative functions. Circumlocutions used to replace offensive four-letter words are good examples. Using expressions like *put to sleep*, *passed gas*, and *for the mature figure* often is just a matter of politeness. Why shock or offend when we don't have to? Nevertheless, all

---

*\*New York Times* Service (March 8, 1996). Mentioned in the July 1996 issue of the *Quarterly Review of Doublespeak*, the best source of information about doublespeak and other linguistic folderol.

*The popularity of the writings of George Orwell is an important reason that doublespeak has received more than a usual amount of attention in recent years. In this excerpt from his 1948 classic, "Politics and the English Language," he explains one reason why politicians favor this-less-than-straightforward kind of rhetoric:*

In our time, political speech and writing are largely the defence of the indefensible. . . . Thus political language has to consist largely of euphemism, question begging, and sheer cloudy vagueness. Defenceless villages are bombarded from the air, the inhabitants driven out into the countryside, the cattle machine-gunned, the huts set on fire with incendiary bullets: This is called *pacification.* Millions of peasants are robbed of their farms and sent trudging along the roads with no more than they can carry: This is called *transfer of population* or *rectification of frontiers.* . . .

The inflated style is itself a kind of euphemism. A mass of Latin words falls upon the facts like soft snow, blurring the outlines and covering up all the details. *The great enemy of clear language is insincerity. When there is a gap between one's real and one's declared aims, one turns as it were instinctively to long words and exhausted idioms, like a cuttlefish squirting out ink.* [These italics added.]

*Here, by the way, is Albert Joseph in the* Quarterly Review of Doublespeak *(July 1981) suggesting three more mundane reasons why so many people, not just politicians, use obfuscatory language:*

People everywhere enjoy making their messages sound more complicated than necessary. In all professions, people enjoy using language to convey the feeling, "my field is so complex ordinary mortals could never understand it." Children establish superiority over peers with pig Latin. Lawyers do it with gobbledygook, truck drivers with citizens-band jargon, and scientists (and educators) with the language of grantsmanship.

Now my main point is this. Misrepresentation is not the only reason so many people write in impossibly difficult language. In fact, years of study have convinced me it is not even the main reason. Many perfectly honorable people write in heavy language because it is an ego trip; they are writing to impress, not to express. They may not be writing doublespeak, in the sense that they are not deliberately concealing weak information, but the effect on language style is the same.

But the most common reason for heavy writing style is still more innocent: *most people honestly think they are supposed to write that way.* Who can blame them? They see it all around them—in government regulations, legal documents, and in their professional books and journals. They see it, alas, even in the writings of their teachers of English, who set the model.

*Inside Woody Allen.* From *Non-Being and Something-Ness* by Woody Allen. Drawn by Stuart Hample. © 1978 by IWA Enterprises, Inc. and Hackenbush Productions, Inc. Reprinted by permission of Random House, Inc.

too often euphemisms are used to further Machiavellian purposes. Indeed, the nastier something is, the greater the need to clothe it in neutral garb.

Doublespeak is especially deadly when it comes in whole sentences or runs on for whole paragraphs. Academese illustrates this nicely. Here are two short snippets (heard at the December 1989 Modern Language Association [MLA] meetings) that give the flavor:

> History can be totalized when being reified only if it moves into the absence of the real.
> . . . the shift from expressive to structured totality cannot ground mediation.*

But academese also can be employed to make simple or obvious ideas sound more profound. Here, for example, is a tiny snippet from Zellig Harris's well-known text *Structural Linguistics*:

> Another consideration is the availability of simultaneity, in addition to successivity as a relation among linguistic elements.

What this seems to mean (there is a certain amount of vagueness here) is that we can do things like gesture while we talk. (You didn't know that, did you?)

Anyway, appetites having been whetted, how about a whole paragraph of the stuff, say, this gem (taken from a Harvard University art exhibition handout):

> Abstraction is by its nature an undervalued aporia, inserting doubt into the aesthetic discourse. This aporia appears as various lacunae demanding embraces, demanding contradictions, demanding rejections, but always impelling a reinscription that must rupture and collapse.

A very small survey revealed that three people out of twenty-three thought they sort of understood what this meant, but two of them then changed their minds.

All of these examples of academese are badly written in one way or another (usually several). They use inflated or obscure language and, of special note, are full of *jargon*. There are several senses of this term, one being nonsensical, incoherent, or meaningless talk, another the specialized language used by professionals when talking

---

*Cited in the *New Republic* (January 29, 1990) by Alex Heard.

(or writing) to each other. The trouble is that jargon intended in the professional sense can and often does turn out to be jargon in the meaningless or incoherent sense, making vacuous or otherwise simple and easily understood remarks appear to be profound. The MLA item quoted above may well illustrate the incoherent variety (who can be sure?); the Harris remark exemplifies the obvious made to seem important. Recall, also, what was said in the discussion of appeals to authorities about not being intimidated by professional lingo. Telling patients that they have a *malignant melanoma*, for example, may leave them ignorant of the fact that they have a form of skin cancer which, if untreated, quickly leads to death.

We need to remember, though, that technical terms used by professional people generally do have an important function, namely, to ensure precision when it counts. Lawyers want contracts to be airtight. Doctors need to be sure they understand each other when they talk about patient illnesses. It may be adequate for a lay person to talk, say, about rapid or irregular heartbeats, but cardiologists need a more precise way of distinguishing the various kinds—distinguishing, for example, *supra ventricular tachycardia* from *atrial flutter* or from the immediately life-threatening *ventricular fibrillation*. Use of these technical expressions quickly conveys rather precise and absolutely vital information from one doctor to another.

Unfortunately, human nature being what it is, even medicalese sometimes is used to conceal. For example, in March 1995, the *New York Times* reported that when Dr. Mark Siegler conducted a study of surgical errors, he discovered that he was not supposed to use the words *error* or *mistake*, because they "distressed the surgeons" and were "fraught with meaning." Instead, the term *E.R.E.* (*eyebrow-raising episode*) was substituted. So much for the slip of a knife or a twitch of the laser beam. (In defense of the surgeons, we might remember that when they make honest mistakes, as being human they occasionally must, they become open to unfair malpractice suits.)

Another common feature of jargon, by the way, is *padding*—adding significant-sounding sentences here and there that in fact say little or nothing. Here is an example typical of a common variety in psychological writings: "Although the effects of mental attitudes on bodily disease should not be exaggerated, neither should they be

---

*As the world changes, language inevitably changes with it. New words come into common use for things and procedures that didn't exist just a few years ago; old words take on new meanings. The computer age illustrates this nicely. We now talk glibly of an inanimate variety of* mouse, clipless *clipboards,* non-edible *menus, floppy and hard discs, RAM, ROM, bytes and even megabytes, and glassless windows. We cut and paste without scissors or glue, and not only delete but also unerase. We surf the (dry) net and zero in on spiderless web sites, navigating with a cursor.*

*Initially, these new locutions were used and understood primarily by nerds like Steve Jobs and functioned, as professionalese generally does, to exclude the uninitiated. But they quickly worked their way into the vocabularies of everyone who uses these newfangled devices—called computers, even though much of what we do with them is word processing or game playing, not mathematical computation. So it goes.*

minimized." True. And here is an example of another type: "As soon as there are behaviors you can't generate, then there are responses you can't elicit." Yes. And another: "In order to achieve products, outputs, and outcomes through processes, inputs are required." Absolutely.

## 3. OTHER COMMON RHETORICAL DEVICES

Let's now look at a few of the many other rhetorical devices that are frequently used to manipulate the unwary or less knowledgeable. (This does not mean that these devices cannot be used in the services of truth and justice!)

### Tone

Good writers or speakers try to choose the **tone** best suited to their audience, as students are taught to do in writing classes. Tone expresses attitudes or feelings—of compassion, anger, levity, humility, congeniality, and so on—and can be quite powerful when employed properly in argumentative passages. Using the proper tone, even though doing so clearly plays to emotions, isn't like arguing fallaciously, or from premises known to be false, but rather just a matter of common sense; arguments aren't won by unnecessarily ruffling the other guy's feathers.

But tone can be employed for nefarious purposes, not just virtuous ones. Lawyers addressing juries are masters of the art (think of Johnny Cochran addressing the O. J. Simpson jury), as are politicians addressing constituents (Liddy Dole addressing the Republican National Convention). Success in politics, at least until the millennium arrives, requires knowing how to use the tone of "mom and apple pie" rhetoric when addressing, say, families of soldiers returning from overseas duty, and humor when dealing with matters of a lighter nature. Here, for instance, is an excerpt from the veto by Adlai Stevenson, then governor of Illinois, of a bill to protect birds by restraining the roaming of cats:

> It is in the nature of cats to do a certain amount of unescorted roaming. . . . That cats destroy some birds, I well know, but I believe this legislation would further but little the worthy cause to which its proponents give such unselfish effort. The problem of the cat versus the bird is as old as time. If we attempt to resolve it by legislation who knows but what we may be called upon to take sides as well in the age-old problem of dog versus cat, bird versus bird, or even bird versus worm. In my opinion, the state of Illinois . . . already has enough to do without trying to control feline delinquency.

Just the right touch to put the quash on a bill that members of the legislature cared little about anyway. By using elevated language to explain his decision on a rather minor matter, and by carrying the consequences of the vetoed bill's logic to ridiculous lengths, Stevenson managed to undermine the opposition with gentle humor and without offending anyone. (Stevenson, by the way, was rightly famous for his ironic humor; witness his remark when accused of being an "egghead": "Eggheads of the world unite; all we have to lose are our yolks.")

Contrast the tone of the Stevenson veto with the following excerpt from the best-known speech by Winston Churchill, a master at the trade. It is taken from the end of an address to the British parliament in the summer of 1940, during the darkest days of World War II, when the British expected to be invaded by German armies flush with recent and spectacular victories in France—a time when most observers believed Britain was about to be crushed by German military power:

> We shall not flag nor fail. We shall go on to the end. We shall fight . . . on the seas and oceans; we shall fight with growing confidence and growing strength in the air. We shall defend our island whatever the cost may be; we shall fight on beaches, landing grounds, in fields, in streets and on the hills. We shall never surrender and even if, which I do not for the moment believe, this island or a large part of it were subjugated and starving, then our empire beyond the seas, armed and guarded by the British fleet, will carry on the struggle until in God's good time the New World, with all its power and might, sets forth to the liberation and rescue of the Old.

The point of Churchill's rhetoric was to buck up the courage of the British people—to stiffen their resolve to fight in the face of terrible odds—and the tone of his speech, not to mention the content, accomplished exactly that.

## Slanting

**Slanting** is a form of misrepresentation. In one version, a true statement is made so as to imply or suggest something else (usually either false or not known to be true). For

---

*Monroe C. Beardsley was one of the first to write a textbook dealing strictly with critical reasoning (as opposed to formal logic). In this excerpt from his book* Thinking Straight, *he explains an example of suggestion:*

---

On November 30, 1968, the *New York Times* reported on the construction site for a new jetport in the Everglades, 40 miles from Miami:

> Populated now by deer, alligators, wild turkeys, and a tribe of Indians who annually perform a rite known as the Green Corn Dance, the tract could someday accommodate a super jetport twice the size of Kennedy International in New York and still have a one-mile buffer on every side to minimize intrusion in the lives of any eventual residents.

A more horrible example of suggestion could hardly be found. First, note that by putting the Indians in a list with deer, alligators, and wild turkeys, the writer suggests that they belong in the same category as these subhuman species. This impression is reinforced by the allusion to the "Green Corn Dance," which (since it is irrelevant to the rest of the story) can only suggest that this kind of silly superstitious activity sums up their lives. And the impression is driven home sharply at the end when we get to the need to "minimize intrusions on the lives of any *eventual* residents"—the Indians, of course, can hardly be counted as real residents.

*Thinking Straight*, 4th ed. Englewood Cliffs, N.J.: Prentice-Hall, 1975.

example, a defense lawyer may try to blunt damaging testimony by stating, "All this proves is that . . ." or "Since we willingly admit that . . . ," implying that the testimony is of little importance when in fact it is quite damaging. Or an advertisement may say, "Try our best-quality knife, *only* $9.95," implying that the price is very low.

Slanting also can be accomplished by a careful selection of facts. (So slanting often invites the fallacy of *suppressed evidence*, discussed in Chapter 3.) For example, the authors of most United States history texts used in public schools select facts so as to sanitize American history as much as they can (given the general stricture against wan-

---

*Here are excerpts from a pamphlet sent in 1990 to Republican candidates running for state offices by a conservative group called Gopac.\**

---

This list is prepared so that you might have a directory of words to use in writing literature and letters, in preparing speeches, and in producing material for the electronic media. The words and phrases are powerful.

### OPTIMISTIC POSITIVE GOVERNING WORDS

Use the list below to help define your campaign and your vision of public service. These words can help give extra power to your message.

| | | |
|---|---|---|
| common sense | hard work | principle(d) |
| courage | help | pro-environment |
| crusade | liberty | prosperity |
| dream | moral | reform |
| duty | peace | rights |
| empower(ment) | pioneer | strength |
| fair | precious | truth |
| family | pride | vision |
| freedom | | |

### CONTRASTING WORDS

Often we search hard for words to define our opponents. Sometimes we are hesitant to use contrast. These are powerful words that can create a clear and easily understood contrast. Apply these to the opponent, his record, proposals, and party.

| | | |
|---|---|---|
| anti-child | greed | self-serving |
| anti-flag | hypocrisy | sensationalists |
| betray | incompetent | shallow |
| cheat | liberal | status quo |
| collapse | lie | steal |
| corruption | obsolete | taxes |
| disgrace | pathetic | traitors |
| excuses | radical | welfare |
| failure | red tape | |

*\*Reprinted in* Harper's *(November 1990).*

dering too far from the straight and narrow). The point of public school history texts, after all, is not to produce disaffected citizens. (More is said on this topic in Chapter 12.)

Slanting sometimes goes under the name *suggestion* or, in some cases, the more pejorative name *innuendo*. The latter term might well be applied to the politician who responded to a statement by then Vice President Dan Quayle, "Well, I admit he wasn't lying *this time*." The nice thing about slanting, so far as practitioners of the art are concerned, is that you can always deny that you implied or suggested what you in fact have implied or suggested.

## Weasel Words

**Weasel words** (or phrases) appear to make little or no change in the content of a statement while in fact sucking out all or most of its content.* Typical is the use of the terms *may* or *may be*, as in this example from a student paper: "Economic success *may be* the explanation of male dominance over females" (italics added). Using the expression *may be* instead of the straightforward verb *is* protected the student from error by reducing the content of her statement close to zero. What she said is consistent with the economic success of males not being the reason for male dominance. By the way, note the assumption that males do dominate females in the last analysis, a contention some males (and females!) would deny.

The term *arguably* is another weasel word frequently employed to spruce up weak arguments. The student quoted above might just as well have protected herself by stating that "Economic success *arguably* is the explanation for male dominance over females."

## Fine-Print Disclaimers

Another common trick is to take back unobtrusively in the (usually) unread fine print what is claimed in the most easily read part of a document. Schlock insurance policies are notorious for their use of this device. They tout wonderful coverage in large type while taking it away in the fine print. After having their property damaged by the big hurricane of 1992, for instance, lots of Floridians who thought they were sufficiently insured against hurricane damage discovered to their chagrin that up-front promises of replacement cash were severely limited in the fine print of their insurance policies. Advertisers regularly use very small asterisks to direct readers to the bottom of ads, where they find out, say, that to get the "low-low" airline fare, tickets must be purchased 21 days in advance and cover a stay over at least one Saturday, and also learn that "other restrictions may apply" (note that weasel word *may*, hiding the fact that they do).

Fine-print disclaimers have become so odious that advertisers have begun to play on the fact with a bit of humor, announcing (as Lexus auto commercials did) that their lawyers have gone into paroxysms of joy while writing the fine print that is then scrolled across the TV screen (very quickly, so it can't be read—but that's part of the humor).

---

*Weasels often suck out the content of eggs without breaking their shells. The expression, by the way, was first used by Theodore Roosevelt.

One of President Clinton's campaign promises was to stop the "revolving door" between government and the lobbying industry, and on taking office he seemed in fact to make good on this promise: He announced a new ethics standard that forbade government officials from lobbying their former agencies for five years after departing government service. But a year or so later, when two of the president's advisors quit and went to work for the lobbying industry at about $500,000 per year, it turned out that Clinton's new rules prohibited lobbying but not the *supervision* of lobbyists, which is what the two departing public servants would be doing. (You say this is a difference that should make no difference?)

An interesting variation on the *fine-print disclaimer* gambit is the *reinterpretation ploy* mentioned when discussing fallacies of *inconsistency*. Having said what turns out to be unpopular, or perhaps offensive, the best strategy for a politician often is just to reinterpret the ill-advised remark. On one of the tapes released by Gennifer Flowers, Bill Clinton is heard making a remark that clearly implies Mario Cuomo (governor of New York) acts like a mafioso. When the tapes became public, an embarrassed Clinton apologized, which is the right thing to do when caught with . . . uh . . . one's pants down, but also stated that "I meant simply to imply that Governor Cuomo is a tough, worthy competitor," which was a clever, but somewhat shady, reinterpretation of his remarks.

## Blending Value Claims into Factual Assertions

One way to get value judgments across to others without justifying them is to slip them in with factual statements and hope they won't be noticed. The fewer the words used to do this, the better. Here is an interesting example from a 1994 CBS radio report (italic emphasis added) in which only one even mildly value-tinged word is used and yet the point gets across:

> *Leftist* state [of California] Senator Tom Hayden of Chicago Seven and Jane
> Fonda fame has announced his intention to run for governor of California.

Anyone who knows about either the Chicago Seven or Jane Fonda's reputation because of her anti-Vietnam war stance will get the suggestion that Hayden is a bad guy. (*San Francisco Chronicle* columnist Herb Caen remarked about this CBS report: ". . . does CBS refer to Ronnie Reagan, say, as a 'rightist'? Or Ollie North as a 'fascist'? "Notice, by the way, the evaluative implication of Caen's remark that North *is* a fascist.)

Or how about this somewhat more straightforward newspaper snippet: *Self-appointed* consumer advocate Ralph Nader . . . . (Italics added.)

## Obfuscation

Dictionaries tell us that to **obfuscate** is "to be so confused or opaque as to be difficult to perceive or understand," or "to render indistinct or dim." Let's stretch that definition a bit here to cover cases in which an issue or question has been *evaded* by *wandering from the point* or by snowing one's audience with an immense amount of detail in hope they either won't notice or at least won't press the point.

Here, for example, is conservative political pundit William Kristol, when asked what he meant by "proper sphere" in his remark that "Conservatives do of course favor an energetic government within its proper sphere.":

> What's most striking today is when there's a problem—spouse abuse, you name it—right away someone stands up and introduces federal legislation. There is something crazy about politics of this sort. It creates a politics that is so driven by the crisis of the day or the week that it's awfully hard to have a sensible debate about anything.

There certainly is some truth in this answer, but what there isn't is an answer to the question what Kristol meant by "proper sphere." What constitutes the proper sphere of government is, after all, an exceedingly difficult question—one might even call it "the mother of all political questions" (thank you, Saddam Hussein). Kristol took a tiny stab at it (he implied that spousal abuse is not a concern of government) and then retreated to the safety of obfuscatory issue evasion by wandering from the point while appearing to answer.

It isn't clear in this example whether Kristol was being wise—deliberately evading a hard question—or just being what political pundits often are—long-winded and overly fond of their own voices. In some cases, however, the intent to evade an issue is fairly obvious. In other cases—*academese* provides plenty of examples—we can be reasonably sure that there is no intent to obfuscate.

By the way, it needs to be said that not all wandering from the point constitutes obfuscation. We have to say this here because the many asides in this textbook ("Interestingly, . . ." and "By the way, . . . ," for example) definitely are not intended as obfuscations but merely as remarks about related or secondary matters that it is hoped the reader will find either interesting or informative.

## 4. THOSE WHO CONTROL THE DEFINITIONS . . .

Calling something by just the right name is crucial when you want to bend the law in your favor, influence public opinion, or justify funny business of one kind or another. For example, employers who want to pay employees less than the legal minimum wage or escape contractual obligations to provide health and other benefits to employees need only categorize them as *subcontractors* instead of *employees* and arrange paperwork accordingly. Minimum wage laws in the United States apply to employees but not to subcontractors; union-brokered agreements concerning employee health insurance don't cover subcontractors.* (Attempts at this kind of chicanery via definition occasionally have been overturned by the courts, but often they are successful.)

Closer to home, college administrators manage to cope with shrinking budgets by hiring lots of cheap labor, often referred to as *adjunct faculty* to distinguish them from "tenure line" professors. Teachers hired as adjunct faculty earn a good deal less per course than their tenured colleagues, receive many fewer, if any, fringe benefits, and

---

*While billionaire Bill Gates was becoming the richest person in the world, his Microsoft Corporation was using the subcontractor ploy to stiff over a thousand of his employees out of several perks other employees were entitled to. As this book goes to press, lower courts have held this nastiness to be illegal, but Microsoft is appealing that decision.

---

*Item from the February 1991* Harper's Index*:*

---

Number of times that the U.S. Congress has declared war: 5
Estimated [!] number of times that a U.S. president has sent troops into combat
situations: 130

---

don't enjoy similar job security. This division of labor can be thought of as an academic analogue to the "downsizing" that goes on in the business world.

Although the United States Constitution grants Congress the sole right to declare war, this has rarely deterred American presidents from waging war without obtaining any such declaration. They have simply renamed their escapades or simply declared them not to be wars. Assuming the December 1990 congressional measure allowing President Bush to carry out United Nations resolutions did indeed constitute a declaration of war, then the recent Gulf conflict is very likely the only legal war out of at least five fought by the United States since World War II.

From 1989 through 1991, the bailout of mismanaged savings-and-loan institutions cost taxpayers billions of dollars and this, coupled with "revenue shortfalls" caused by Reagan-years tax cuts, posed a serious problem for the federal government, namely, how to avoid exceeding the debt limit set by the Gramm-Rudman-Hollings bill. The solution was to move part of the federal budget "off budget." So, technically, which means not actually, the federal budget did not exceed the limit set by law. Yes, the U.S. government does work that way when it has to.

On a less vital note, here is a little item taken from *The Washington Monthly* (January/February 1996), illustrating how those who have power play the naming game for their own benefit:

> When it was disclosed that lunches served in the Army General Officers' mess cost six times the average the officers paid, the army announced that it was going to reform: "Meal prices must be sufficient to cover operating expenses and food costs." Did the generals give up their bargain? Not on your life. They redefined expenses to exclude such items as stoves, utilities, and the salaries of waiters and cooks.

Now here is an item that seems to have a certain amount of appeal:

> When the Swiss government determined that women who sold sexual favors practiced a "*therapeutic trade*," they were exempt from taxes. Now known as *prostitutes*, the same women must pay a 65% value-added tax.*

Happily for plain-speaking folk everywhere, not all attempts at victory via definition are successful. In 1987, an Alabama judge ordered several dozen textbooks removed from Alabama schools on the grounds that they favored the establishment of a particular religion—*secular humanism*—over Christianity, Judaism, Islam, and so on,

---

*Taken from the October 1995 *Quarterly Review of Doublespeak*, which credited the January 1995 *Playboy*. (Well, that figures.)

*In a letter to the editor of* Science News *(February 10, 1990), Russell Williams claimed that stories about drugs in the media "implicitly define 'abuse' differently for different drugs." In the case of alcohol, he said, it is used to refer to physical addiction or to being drunk on the job or when driving; but with respect to illegal drugs such as marijuana, to any kinds of "use." He also claimed that the word "abuse" is never used when discussing cigarettes or other tobacco products. Is Williams right about this? And, if so, has he pointed out an interesting example of shady language intended to manipulate public opinion?*

thus violating the provision in the Bill of Rights forbidding the establishment of a government-sanctioned religion. But his ruling was overturned by justices in higher courts who pointed out that secular humanism is a doctrine promoting moral principles and actions *not based on any religious doctrines*, so that it made no sense to call secular humanism a *religion*.*

Of course, Americans did not invent the practice of victory through definition. It has been employed frequently elsewhere, and throughout history. In Moslem Saudi Arabia, for example, where the commandment not to make graven images is taken very seriously, photography, therefore, was forbidden. But aerial photography was such a boon to oil exploration back in the 1970s that something had to be done. The result was that:

> King Ibn Saud convened the Ulema [a group of Moslem theologians who have great power over public morals] and eventually prevailed over them with the argument that photography was actually good because it was not an image, but a combination of light and shadow that depicted Allah's creations without violating them.†

The obvious reasons this sort of chicanery is so frequently gotten away with are self-interest and lack of careful attention. But a less obvious reason is that it isn't always easy to determine whether there is indeed some sort of sleight of hand going on. For years, the psychologist Thomas Szasz has been campaigning against the use of the expression *mental illness*, on grounds that there is no such thing as *mental* illness. Declaring John Hinkley "not guilty by reason of insanity" in his attempt to assassinate President Reagan was for Szasz just an extreme example of what happens when we take the analogy between physical illness and alleged mental illness seriously. (He does believe, however, that sometimes what is thought of as mental illness really is physical dysfunction.)

But Szasz is in the minority on this point, with the result, he claims, that various kinds of serious abuses of civil rights occur. One is that close relatives of the

---

*Interestingly, the American pragmatist philosopher and social activist John Dewey (1859–1952) stretched the term "religion" so that it would indeed make secular humanism a religion, and this still is the way many of today's pragmatists, including, for example, Richard Rorty, use that term.

†Peter A. Iseman, "The Arabian Ethos," *Harper's* (February 1978).

Reprinted by permission of Don Wright, Inc.

"mentally ill" often are able to have them "hospitalized for treatment" against their will. Forcing people into institutions in this way is a practice some see as not unlike the one that used to be common in the Soviet Union of confining political opponents in "mental institutions." In a similar vein, Szasz argues, "we call self-starvation either anorexia nervosa, a hunger strike, a suicide attempt, or some other name, depending on how we want to respond."

Well, then, is Szasz right about this? A number of psychologists (and half of this text-book's writing team) find his position modestly persuasive, while the majority (and the other half) do not. The reason for this split of opinion is that good arguments can be made on both sides of the issue, making it difficult to choose one over the other. Which choice we should make may well depend, as Szasz notes, on how we wish to deal with whatever circumstances our decisions affect. (Philosophy students might note the connection of this sort of case to the age-old conundrum about whether, when every part of an old ship has been replaced over the years by a new part, it is still the same ship.)

This does not mean clear-cut cases are not clear-cut. We did blockade Iraq before starting the Gulf War, thus engaging in warlike actions against that country without a congressional declaration; calling our action an "interdiction" or sky-blue-pink

> *Conservative*, n. A statesman who is enamored of existing evils, as distinguished from the Liberal, who wishes to replace them with others.
> — Ambrose Bierce (*The Devil's Dictionary*)

cannot change that fact. But it does mean that there are no easy or definite answers in every case.

## 5. THE REFORM OF SEXIST LANGUAGE

Languages aren't artificial products constructed by "linguistic experts" in some laboratory or "think tank." They are living, changing products of human intelligence designed to perform various functions, including not just communicating ideas from one person to another but also issuing commands, asking questions, and certifying relationships and bargains (as in wedding ceremonies). This being the case, languages tend to mirror the foibles, aspirations, loyalties, and (alas!) prejudices of those who speak them. English is no exception.

In the past 20 or 30 years, a minor revolution has taken place in the United States, as well as many other countries, in the attitudes of most people toward members of minority groups and women. Inevitably, this revolution has been mirrored in the linguistic practices of those caught up in it. The pejorative terms mentioned at the beginning of this chapter (*wop, nigger, kike, fag*) are not often heard in polite circles these days, and expressions like "free, white, and 21," common until about 30 years ago, are now as outdated as "23 skidoo."

But the most extensive linguistic changes of this kind have been those reflecting the changing attitudes of most people concerning relationships between men and women and the roles played by women in society. A large majority of previously common sexist locutions have disappeared from everyday speech. This linguistic change has occurred very quickly, as these things go, no doubt in part because of the persistent demands of women's rights advocates. But it also has happened quickly because of the swiftness with which attitudes toward women and their roles in society have changed and because of the speed with which women have entered fields previously reserved primarily for men.

Not so long ago, when the overwhelming majority of those in high offices were men, it may have made some sense to refer to these people as business*men* and congress*men*. But in this day and age, with increasing numbers of women taking on these roles, it makes much less sense. In addition, there is a general realization that these sexist terms imply not just that those holding these offices always are male but also, and wrongly, that only males are supposed to, or are competent to, fill them. The old sexist language implies in subtle but persuasive ways that positions of power should be *manned*, not *personed* or *womaned*, and this in turn implies that only men are capable of holding these important positions. Thus, substituting nonsexist words for the old sexist terms puts women on an equal linguistic footing with men that not only reflects their growing equality but helps make it possible. Our thoughts about the world—how it works and how it should work—always are framed in language; sexist locutions tend to introduce sexist thoughts into our minds.

So today, people who head committees or departments are generally called *chairs*, not *chairmen* ("I would like to address the chair about . . ." or "The chair has ruled that . . ."). Similarly, people who deliver the mail tend to get called *letter carriers*, not *mailmen*, and the term *man* and its many derivatives have been replaced by *people*, *person*, and the like. Publishers don't cotton to manuscripts that contain locutions like "Of course, a *man* might be described as taking a . . ." when it would be more accurate to say "*Someone* might be described as taking a . . ." or to phrases like "even if *he* is willing to allow . . . ," when what is meant is *he or she*.*

One of the more interesting language changes accompanying the feminist revolution has been the widespread use of the term *Ms.*, intended to serve when the marriage status of a woman is not considered relevant. The point of this change was to foster equal treatment of the sexes. Men, whether married or single, have always been referred to by the same term, *Mr.*, whereas women have had to be called either *Miss* or *Mrs.*, depending on their marital status. A similar, and perhaps much more significant change, is the fact that women nowadays don't always take on the last name of their mates, although, interestingly, they still usually do (while men rarely do). But even when women do adopt their husbands' last names, they often also hang on to their own, so that, for example, President Clinton's wife is referred to as Hillary *Rodham* Clinton, not just Hillary Clinton.

But an even more important language change may be the elimination of locutions like this one, once typical of the language encountered in all sorts of places, including public school history textbooks: "Pioneers moved west, taking their wives and children with them." That made all of the pioneers into men, while women and children were just accessories. A text written today would get it right and say something like "Pioneer families moved west."

*On the other hand*, things can get carried too far. It would be unnecessary, wouldn't it, for Germans to stop referring to their homeland as "*the Fatherland*," or Englishmen—that is, citizens of England—to their "*mother tongue*?" What purpose would be served by replacing *Uncle Sam* with *Aunt Sarah*? And why worry about using the term *manhole* when talking about those round excisions in streets and avenues, as did the Public Works Departments of several American cities? (Would it be wrong to change Biblical references to God from the *He* employed in the original versions to some more neutral term?)

In any case, the changes in linguistic style brought on by the feminist revolution have also raised questions of aesthetic taste—of what sounds right or wrong rolling off the tongue or when reading a book. The expression *her or his*, to take one example, rings false, perhaps because it calls attention to the avoidance of *his* (used to mean his or her), or of *his or her*, and thus detracts from what is being said. Consider the following excerpt from academic David Gauthier's book *Morals by Agreement* (Oxford: Oxford University Press, 1986), which occurs in a passage that started out talking about "the person who":

> The constrained maximizer considers (i) whether the outcome, should everyone do so, be nearly fair and optimal, and (ii) whether the outcome she realistically expects should she do so affords her greater utility than universal non-co-operation. If both these conditions are satisfied she bases her action on the joint strategy. The straightforward maximizer considers simply whether the outcome he realistically expects should he base his action on the joint strategy

---

*Both of these examples are taken, alas, from a journal article co-authored back in the bad old days by the male co-author of this text.

*In the past 15 or so years, various organizations have instituted guidelines for nonsexist uses of language that have gained wide acceptance. Here are a few excerpts from the American Philosophical Association (APA) list of examples of sexist language and nonsexist alternatives:*

| **Example** | **Preferred Alternative** |
| --- | --- |
| (1) The philosopher uses his reason to guide him. | The philosopher uses reason as a guide. |
| (3) The department chair must submit his budget by March 1st. | The department chair must submit a budget by March 1st. |
| (10) Reason is what distinguishes man from other animals. | Reason is what distinguishes humans (human beings) from other animals. |
| (12) the founding fathers | the Founders (founding leaders) |
| the father of relativity theory | the founder (initiator) of relativity theory* |
| (13) Dear Sir, Gentlemen (to an unknown person) | Dear Colleague, Dear Editor, Dear Professor, Dear Staff Member, etc. |
| Dear Mrs. Green (when a female's marital status is unknown) | Dear Ms. Green, Dear J. Green, Dear Jean Green |
| (14) man and wife | husband and wife |
| (15) husbands and wives | wives and husbands |
| descendants of Adam and Eve | descendants of Eve and Adam |
| his and her | her and his |
| (16) poetess, stewardess, fireman, lady lawyer, male nurse, woman doctor | poet, flight attendant, fire fighter, lawyer, nurse, doctor |

*The comment of the guidelines concerning the items in #15 is this:*

Varying the order (if the content does not require the conventional order) both counters the implication that males take priority over females, and enlivens discourse by avoiding cliche.

*Better, obviously, would be "the discoverer (or propounder) of relativity theory."

affords him greater utility than the outcome he would expect were he to act on any alternative strategy. (page 170)

In the next paragraph, the first personal pronoun used is *she*. Gauthier's heart clearly is in the right place, but his repeated shift from *she* to *he*, and vice versa, makes comprehension more difficult, because it shifts the reader's attention from content to style. (Note, by the way, the professional—and unnecessary—jargon employed by Gauthier.)

The point is that good taste sometimes dictates other sorts of moves, for instance, employing plural rather than singular pronouns, thus saying things like, "Constrained maximizers think of *their* rewards from . . ." rather than "A constrained maximizer thinks of *his* rewards from . . . ." (That's one reason for the plethora of plural expressions that occur in this textbook. Note, by the way, that the term "congressperson" nowhere appears on these pages, although "member of Congress" is used quite often.)

Interestingly, no one seems overwrought by the fact that Liberty always is portrayed as a woman (think, for instance, of the Statue of Liberty in New York harbor) and that, although there are lots of complaints about sexist terms like *waitress* and *actress*, no one seems bothered by the equally sexist term *widower*. Women still receive an award each year for "best *actress*." And freshmen still are called *freshmen*. Ah, well.

## 6. PC (POLITICALLY CORRECT) TERMINOLOGY

The revolution concerning gender rhetoric is part of a larger movement that also has dramatically changed the ways in which we speak of minorities. As attitudes have changed, language, inevitably, has followed suit.

---

*The* Los Angeles Times, *one of America's best newspapers, now has a guideline concerning "Ethnic, Racial, Sexual and Other Identification" that prohibits the use, among others, of the following words when describing individuals:*

---

Co-ed, deaf, deaf-mute, biddy, bra-burner, crazy, divorcee, gal, ghetto, gypped, handicapped person, hillbilly, Hispanic, holy rollers, Indians, inner city, lame, male nurse, normal, pow-wow, queer, WASP, welsher.

---

*Commenting on the* Times' *guidelines, syndicated columnist Robert Novak had this to say:*

---

The *Times* forbids reporters to write about a "Dutch treat" because this phrase is allegedly insulting to the Dutch. Nor can one report that a person "welshed on a bet" because that would be insulting to the Welsh. . . . I asked one of the *Los Angeles Times* editors, "How do you refer to Indian summer? Is it now Native American summer?" He replied that he would substitute "unseasonably warm weather late in the year." This is what political correctness can do to language; it destroys meaning. It also demeans the ethnic groups it supposedly protects. Do we really think that these groups are so unintelligent as to be unable to distinguish between conventional idioms and genuine prejudice? Is their identity so fragile that it must depend on censorship?

---

*Well, then, is Novak right about his thoughts concerning what he sees as overzealous PC?*

---

*This may be the PC term, but many, perhaps most, members of the group, for example, African-American politicians on television and students in many college classes, refer to themselves as *black*. (Interestingly, both of these terms conceal the fact that most of the people so labeled also are genetically part Caucasian, indeed often primarily Caucasian, or part Asian. The point is that both of these labels are social/political, not scientific, referring to class, not race.)

*Calvin and Hobbes* by Bill Watterson.
Copyright 1993 Universal Press Syndicate. Reprinted with permission.

The result is that certain locutions have become "in," while others are "out." Some are *politically correct*, some politically incorrect. Careers have been wrecked by publicly using expressions like "fat Jap" and "Nigra." It would be political suicide today to say publicly, as someone did in the 1970s when then Governor Tribbitt (Delaware) hired a woman as his press secretary at $20,000 a year, that "If he wants to pay $10,000 a mammary, that's his business." We aren't supposed to use phrases like *admitted homosexual* (because it implies that being a homosexual is bad) or *tidal wave of immigrants* (because of the negative implication concerning immigrants).

On the whole, of course, changes of this nature are all to the good and are applauded by just about everybody. But problems do arise, and it is quite possible that an excess of zeal causes some of them. One of the authors of this textbook, for example, received letters from students and teachers accusing him of race prejudice, or at least insensitivity, for having used the term *black* in the sixth edition of this textbook, on the grounds that the politically correct, nondenigrating, term for the minority in question is *African American*\*; but when the sixth edition was published, the politically correct term happened to be *black*. The compliment "She's so smart, and pretty too" was perceived by a student as sexual harassment, not as a very nice compliment. (Note that "He's so smart, and handsome too" would not be thought of as anything but a compliment.)

The University of Cincinnati Student Senate has declared that higher institution of learning "a Columbus-myth-free" campus." (The allusion, in case you missed it, is to the fact that Columbus could not possibly have "discovered" America—Native Americans having been here for at least ten thousand years before Columbus was born.) The Asian American Journalists Association handbook instructs reporters to avoid the term *industrious* when referring to those of "Asian-Pacific" heritage, and not to describe them as *reserved*, *quiet*, *philosophical*, *serene*, or *smiling*.

Well, then, are we getting a bit overzealous in our, shall we say, *linguistic cleansing*? It no doubt is a good idea, now that the children of unwed parents are not looked down upon, to refer to them as *nonmarital children* rather than *bastards*, thus getting rid of the unfair opprobrium of that nasty term. And why not change the name of the Italian Welfare Agency to the *Italian-American Community Service Agency*. But what is wrong with calling "mixed breed" dogs *mongrels*, "visually impaired" people *blind*, or the "psychologically impacted" *insane*? Don't those who call the *Sports Illustrated*

A *January 31, 1994,* San Francisco Chronicle *"Personals" column (by Leah Garchik) discussed the "Justice for John" committee formed by Howard G. Shaw, whose aim is to fight against "derogatory, disgraceful, disgusting, degrading, demoralizing and demeaning" abuses of the name John. Here is his "Shocking Seven" list of offensive uses:*

- "The John" is a toilet.
- "A John" is a prostitute's [. . . ah . . ., a sex worker's] customer.
- "Long johns" are ugly winter underwear.
- "John Doe" is an anonymous man named after a female deer.
- A "Dear John" letter means getting brushed off.
- A "Stage Door Johnny" is a pathetic guy who lusts after chorus girls.
- A "Johnny-Come-Lately" is a brash newcomer.

*So is this serious? Shaw himself says that "In our society, everybody who is offended by anything considers himself a victim. This is a sensitivity spoof." Shaw, of course, ought to have rephrased his remark into the plural so as to avoid that awkward term "himself."*

swimsuit issue *pornographic* rob that word of its legitimate meaning? (Is there a risk here that the door will be opened to wrongheaded legislation?) Was Newt Gingrich just being polite when he said President Clinton was "factually challenged" instead of calling him a liar? Anyway, has the First Amendment been bruised when the University of Michigan brought students before disciplinary hearings and then punished them for having uttered "hate speech" when they aired their belief in classroom discussion that homosexuality is a disease? And didn't certain Native Americans make some kind of mistake when they demonstrated during the 1995 World Series against the "demeaning symbols" used by the beloved Cleveland Indians and by the Atlanta Braves?

Speaking of demeaning symbols brings to mind the other kind—symbols of goodness and virtue—and their linguistic counterparts. During the 1996 political campaigns, *family values* were the magic words uttered by every candidate who seriously intended to win election. Voters thus were treated to the delicious irony of seeing politicians such as President Clinton and Newt Gingrich, both paragons of familial virtue, extolling the merits of this basic human grouping.*

---

*For those unacquainted with Gingrich's commitment to family values (we assume at least a modicum of reader acquaintance with Clinton's commitment), here is columnist Molly Ivins (November 16, 1994) with a little fill-in: In 1980 [Gingrich] filed for a divorce from his wife, Jacqueline, after 18 years of marriage. While they were separated, she had her second operation for cancer. Gingrich went to see her in the hospital to discuss the terms of their divorce. In 1993, Jacqueline sued Gingrich for failing to pay his $1,300 monthly alimony on a timely basis and for failing to pay the premiums on a life-insurance policy for her. He settled the lawsuit by agreeing to give Jacqueline the first $100,000 coverage in his life-insurance policy."

## SUMMARY OF CHAPTER 7

1. Most words have emotive meanings (in addition to cognitive meanings). Words like *oppression*, *kike*, and *bitch* have more or less negative (con) emotive overtones; words like *spring*, *free*, and *satisfaction* have positive (pro) emotive overtones; and words like *socialism*, *marijuana*, and *God* have mixed overtones.

2. Con artists use the emotive side of language (1) to mask cognitive meaning by whipping up emotions so that reason is overlooked and (2) to dull the force of language so as to make acceptable what otherwise might not be. The latter purpose often is accomplished by means of euphemisms (less offensive or duller expressions used in place of more offensive or emotively charged locutions).

3. Common rhetorical devices often are used in a slippery manner. *Examples: Slanting* words and expressions ("All this proves is that . . ."); *weasel words* that suck out all or part of the meaning of a sentence ("Economic success may be . . ."); *fine-print disclaimers* that take back part of what was originally asserted ("Tickets must be purchased 30 days in advance, subject to availability . . ."); *obfuscation* that, for example, may mask failure to respond to questions (William Kristol wandering from the point of the question about what he meant by "proper sphere" of government). Other devices include making unsupported value judgments that are inserted into primarily factual assertions (*Self-appointed* consumer advocate Ralph Nader . . .). Note that employing the right tone can be used to mask lack of cogent content or to sway audiences via emotional appeals (Gopac's list of terms Republican candidates should use when campaigning).

4. The meanings of words and expressions sometimes are changed so as either to get around or to take advantage of laws, rules, or customs. *Example*: Calling an employee a *subcontractor* to avoid paying a minimum wage or Social Security taxes. But it isn't always easy to determine whether terms have been used rightly or wrongly. *Example*: Psychologists disagree about whether it makes good sense to use the expression *mental illness*, because they disagree about whether the implied analogy to physical illness is useful or accurate.

5. The recent social revolution that changed the roles of women in society, as well as the attitudes of most Americans concerning male-female relationships, has resulted in matching linguistic changes. *Examples*: Replacing expressions in which the term *man* is used to refer to people in general by more neutral words such as *person*; using *Ms.* in some cases instead of *Miss* or *Mrs.*; not repeatedly using *his* to mean *his or her*; or switching to the plural form in order to avoid this use of *his*. (Note that when use of dechauvinized language may ring a bit false—*her or his* can sound somewhat forced—there always are aesthetically acceptable ways to avoid sexist locutions.) But do we go a bit too far when we start talking about, say, *personhole covers*?

6. The linguistic revolution that has replaced sexist language with locutions that are more congenial with today's attitudes and beliefs also has changed many of the ways in which we refer to members of minorities and other groups, as well as to activities in several important areas of life. Using current lingo, we can say that some ways of speaking are *politically correct (PC)*, others not. *Examples*:

The terms *Native American*, *physically challenged*, and *Latino* are "in"; *Indian*, *crippled* (or *handicapped*), and *Hispanic* (used to refer, say, to Mexican Americans) are "out." In some cases, the PC revolution may have gone a bit too far. *Examples*: Referring to women as *people of gender*; objecting to the use of Indian symbols by baseball teams.

## EXERCISE 7-1

1. Louisiana license plates feature the motto

   **SPORTSMAN'S PARADISE**

   Is this sexist? Defend your answer.

2. Comment on the following quote, heard during the 1992 election campaigns:

   Republicans are looking at Senator Gore's record to try to expose him as a liberal.

*3. Translate the following statement, found on the back of a Hallmark greeting card, into everyday lingo:

   Printed on recycled paper. Contains a minimum of 10% post-consumer and 40% pre-consumer material.

   Aside from the euphemistic use of language in this statement, is there something a bit sneaky going on here?

4. Here is a passage from a thankfully out-of-print edition of the United States history textbook *America: Its People and Values*:

   A friendly Indian named Squanto helped the colonists. He showed them how to plant corn and how to live in the wilderness. A soldier, Captain Miles Standish, taught the Pilgrims how to defend themselves against unfriendly Indians.

   How is language used to slant this account? In what other ways is it slanted? Rewrite the passage from the point of view of the unfriendly Indians in question.

5. Translate into plain English the following excerpt from a social science textbook:

   By social problem solving, we mean processes that are to eventuate in outcomes that by some standard are an improvement of the previously existing situation, or are presumed to so eventuate, or are conceived of as offering some possibility to so eventuate.

*6. Translate into plain English the following remark by Admiral Isaac C. Kidd when he was chief of Navy materiel:

   We have gone with teams of competent contract people from Washington to outlying field activities to look over their books with them . . . to see in what areas there is susceptibility to improved capability to commit funds.

# EXERCISE 7-2

1. Find at least one good example of an inappropriate name (for example, *subcontractor*) that is applied so that the law, a custom, or whatever deals with them differently, and explain the chicanery.

2. Check your local newspaper, or magazines, television programs, or some such; find at least two examples of doublespeak or jargon, and translate them back into plain English.

3. Do the same with a particularly obtuse example of academese from one of your textbooks (definitely not from this one!).

4. Do the same with respect to sexist locutions, but this time translate into PC language.

# EXERCISE 7-3

1. The authors of this text have received letters (happily only a very few) from students and instructors claiming that the use of the terms *PC* and *politically correct* are pejorative and therefore unsuitable for use in a textbook. Do you think they are right about this? Defend your answer.

*2. Each chapter in this text starts out with a few (hopefully) apt quotes. But doesn't one of the quotes that starts this language chapter use one of the devices railed against in this chapter? Which one might this be? If it doesn't, why doesn't it? If it does, wasn't it a mistake to use this quotation? Explain. (By the way, does a different one of these quotes commit the fallacy of *slippery slope*?)

3. Previous editions of this text have been criticized by some for implying that in some cases the recent linguistic revolution has gone a bit overboard. This edition contains the question "Why worry about using the term *manhole* when talking about those round excisions in streets and avenues, as did the Public Works Departments of several American cities?" Should we worry? Why, or why not?

4. The American Philosophical Association *Guidelines for Non-Sexist Use of Language* state that "Varying the order (if the content does not require the conventional order) [sometimes using *his or her* and sometimes *her or his*] both counters the implication that males take priority over females and enlivens discourse by avoiding cliche." The authors of this text, on the other hand, think that the use of *her or his* "rings false, perhaps because it calls attention to the avoidance of *his* (used to mean his or her) or of *his or her*, and thus distracts from what is being said." In your opinion, who is right on this question? Why? What about the suggestion that it's better just to employ the plural, where the gender question does not arise, rather than either *her or his* or *his or her*?

5. The writer of a letter to the editor of the *New Republic* (November 8, 1993) disagreed with the insistence of Native Americans that they be called *Native Americans* and not *American Indians*, stating that it is an "affront" to "the millions of native Americans of European, African and Asian descent." Is this writer on target? Defend your answer.

6. State and defend your opinion concerning the action described in the following AP news item:

SHAMOKIN, PA.—A plaque etched with a lesser-known Benjamin Franklin quotation was removed from a wall at a vocational school here at the order of the state civil rights coordinator, who said the slogan's use of "he" was sexist. The official, Glenn Dean Davis, was inspecting the Northumberland County Vocational-Technical School during the summer when he noticed the plaque, which reads, "He who hath a trade, hath an estate," said school director James Buggy.

Davis contended the use of "he" discriminated against women and the school removed it, Buggy said.

7. Explain what you think (and why, of course) of the following explanation (in Robert J. Ringer's irreverent book *Looking Out for Number One*) of President Kennedy's famous remark in his inauguration address, "And so, my fellow Americans, ask not what your country can do for you; ask what you can do for your country":

Ask what you can do for your country? Does this mean asking each of the more than 200 million individuals what you can do for him? No, individuals are not what Kennedy or any other politician has ever had in mind when using the word *country*. A country is an abstract entity, but in politicalese, it translates into "those in power." Restated in translated form, then, it becomes: "Ask not what those in power can do for you; ask what you can do for those in power."

*8. Why do you suppose the following excerpts from a 1993 newspaper article (*San Francisco Chronicle*) headlined **Joint Resolution to Release JFK Papers** are included in this exercise set?

Responding to the movie "JFK" and an anti-government mood in the land, key lawmakers yesterday proposed legislation to release secret documents about the assassination of President John F. Kennedy. . . .

Senator David Boren, D-Okla., said at a news conference he had no reason to believe that the files would reveal "any comprehensive government conspiracy or illegal activity." But because the public, "particularly the young people," distrusts the government's conclusion that Lee Harvey Oswald acted alone in killing Kennedy, the records must be opened, said Boren, chairman of the Intelligence Committee.

Oliver Stone, director of "JFK," said the legislation "could be the key that unlocks the answers to questions troubling Americans since 1963." . . .

Under the proposal, the U.S. Court of Appeals in Washington would appoint a five-member citizen board to review and decide on the release of assassination documents. In cases involving executive agencies such as the FBI or CIA, the president could overrule a decision by the review board. Boren said documents or parts of documents could be kept secret if the information might damage U.S. foreign relations, disclose intelligence sources or methods or invade an individual's privacy.

# Exercise 7-4

1. One good way to figure out the tone of a passage is to underline and then categorize its emotively charged words. In the Churchill excerpt on page 141, for example, he uses several charged words suggesting combat: *fight* is employed (several times); as are *defend, struggle, armed, and guarded*. He also favors phrases of cautious optimism: *growing confidence, growing strength, never surrender*, and *liberation*. The determination to carry on until victory is achieved is emphasized also by the effective use of parallel construction (a device used by virtually all great speech writers): "We shall not flag. . . . We shall go on. . . . We shall fight. . . . We shall defend. . . . We shall never surrender. . . ."

   Churchill's tone was forceful and expressed confidence and determination, thus furthering his aim, which was to buck up flagging confidence during one of the darkest moments in British history. Go to the library for a copy of Abraham Lincoln's Gettysburg Address and explain the tone of this famous speech and what sorts of linguistic devices were used to convey that tone.

2. Do the same with respect to the following excerpts from President Kennedy's famous 1961 inaugural address:

   . . . Let every nation know, whether it wishes us well or ill, that we shall pay any price, bear any burden, meet any hardship, support any friend, oppose any foe to assure the survival and the success of liberty.

   This much we pledge—and more. . . .

   So let us begin anew—remembering on both sides that civility is not a sign of weakness, and sincerity is always subject to proof. Let us never negotiate out of fear. But let us never fear to negotiate. . . .

   In the long history of the world, only a few generations have been granted the role of defending freedom in its hour of maximum danger. I do not shrink from this responsibility—I welcome it. I do not believe that any of us would exchange places with any other people or any other generation. The energy, the faith, the devotion which we bring to this endeavor will light our country and all who serve it—and the glow from that fire can truly light the world.

   And so, my fellow Americans, ask not what your country can do for you; ask what you can do for your country.

   My fellow citizens of the world, ask not what Americans will do for you, but what together we can do for the freedom of man.

*The prejudice against careful analytic procedure is part of the human impatience with technique which arises from the fact that men are interested in results and would like to attain them without the painful toil which is the essence of our moral finitude.*

— Morris R. Cohen

*There is no expedient to which a man will not resort to avoid the real labor of thinking.*

— Sir Joshua Reynolds

*Chapter*

# 8

# EVALUATING EXTENDED ARGUMENTS

Our principal topic in this chapter is the evaluation of extended passages, or *essays*, that argue to a conclusion. Up to this point, we've considered mainly short arguments, and these primarily to illustrate fallacious reasoning or manipulative uses of language. But in daily life, we frequently encounter longer passages, generally containing several related arguments, offered in support of a *thesis*—the overall conclusion of the passage.

We should recall, however, that there are other kinds of persuasive essays in addition to the argumentative variety. Even simple *description* or *narration* often is used for this purpose. For example, in his essay "A Hanging," George Orwell argued with some force against capital punishment simply by graphically describing a hanging and one person's gut-wrenching response to it. (The ongoing abortion debate is studded with detailed descriptions of aborted fetuses.) And just explaining something may effectively persuade others to our point of view. An article on chlorofluorocarbons, for instance, may simply describe how these chemicals deplete the ozone layer, thus increasing our chances of getting skin cancer, and yet convince readers of the implied conclusion that the use of Freon in refrigerators and other modern equipment should be stopped.

But our main concern in this chapter will be rhetoric in which there is an attempt to present reasons for conclusions. We need to remember, however, that a conclusion can be argued for in various ways. We may, for example, weigh the merits and demerits of a possible course of action, instead of just presenting favorable reasons. A **pro and con argument** of this kind can be very effective because it tends to answer questions the reader or listener may have about the thesis being argued for. This also is why essays often provide a **refutation to counterarguments**, as in the case of politicians who,

161

after arguing for their position, may then go on to say, "Now my opponent will no doubt respond _____; but I say _____," and then attempt to refute their opponent's objections. An essay may also argue for a course of action by showing that likely alternatives are less desirable, which means arguing by a **comparison of alternatives**.

Note, by the way, that a legitimate appeal to experts in a field may count as a reason for accepting their conclusions, even in the absence of an account of their reasoning processes. During World War II, for example, President Roosevelt accepted the conclusion of physicists Leo Szilard and Albert Einstein (conveyed to the president in a famous letter) that it was possible to build an atomic bomb, even though Roosevelt, like every other lay person, would have been unable to comprehend the reasoning behind their conclusion (which, no doubt, is why the two scientists didn't bother to provide it).

Finally, it needs to be mentioned that essay writers frequently employ more than one of the methods just mentioned. They first may argue, for instance, by a general comparison of alternatives and then, finding the alternative that seems to be the most attractive, zero in on it for a more careful analysis. Or they may provide reasons that support the essay's thesis and are in turn supported by expert opinion.

## 1. THE BASIC TASKS OF ESSAY EVALUATION

There are almost as many ways to evaluate extended passages as there are evaluators. What works best for one person may not work so well for others. And time and interest always need to be taken into account. Even so, there are guidelines that most people find of value, in particular, those who initially have a bit of trouble handling lengthy or complicated passages. (Most of the discussion that follows will deal with written passages, but applies also to those that are verbal.)

## Find the Thesis and Keep It in Mind

The most important thing, obviously, is to locate the **thesis**, the main conclusion of the argument. The thesis isn't always obvious because the passage may be poorly written, or because the thesis may be implied but not explicitly stated, or simply because the author may build up to it and reveal it only near the end of the work. The thesis is the point of an essay, so you have to keep it in mind to determine whether sufficient *reasons* are provided for accepting it. In many sports, the trick is to keep your eye on the ball; in evaluating extended passages, the trick is to keep your mind's eye on the thesis.

## Find the Reasons That Support the Thesis

The next task, obviously, is to find the *reasons*—the *premises*—that are provided in support of the thesis. Again, this will be hard or easy depending on the author's style and competence. But it may also be hard because the reasons themselves are supported by reasons, so that the sheer complexity of an extended passage makes analysis difficult.

But, typically, it isn't all that hard to see what the thesis of an essay is and to discover the principal reasons offered in its support. For example, a newspaper columnist arguing for the thesis that cigarettes should be made illegal supported his conclusion by pointing out that cigarette smoking kills millions of people; then supported that claim by presenting statistics concerning smoking and heart disease, cancer, and emphy-

sema; and then claimed that anything so bad for us should be illegal. The logical structure of his essay thus was something like this:

> *Thesis:* Cigarettes should be made illegal.
> *Reasons:* (1) Cigarette smoking is deadly.
>           (2) Anything so deadly should be illegal.
> *Support for (1):* Statistical proof linking smoking cigarettes with heart disease,
> cancer, and emphysema.

He assumed (wrongly) that most people would accept his second reason without further
justification.

## Identify the Evidence

Effective extended arguments often provide evidence, or support, for the reasons they
present. That is, they provide reasons for believing their reasons. In the cigarette example, statistical evidence was cited in support of the claim that cigarette smoking is
deadly. But many other sorts of evidence may be appealed to, including authoritative
pronouncements, examples, personal experiences, generally accepted facts or common
knowledge, and so on. In the Szilard/Einstein letter mentioned before, the evidence for
the conclusion that an atomic bomb could be built was just the authority of the letter's
authors. Someone might defend the claim that cigarette smoking is deadly simply by
appealing to what by now is the common knowledge that nicotine causes lung cancer,
heart disease, and so on. A powerful argument against war might well contain specific
examples of wars—for example, World War I—that produced incredible misery with
little else to show for them.

    In a sense, of course, all reasons or premises offered in support of a thesis consti-
tute evidence in its favor. The important point here is that reasons themselves often
need, and receive, supporting evidence. Indeed, good essay writers always support
reasons in this way except when confident that readers will accept them without further argument.

## Identify Responses to Likely
## Objections or Counterarguments

The sample essay concerning cigarette smoking did not discuss likely objections or
counterarguments, but essays often do. The cigarette essay, for instance, might have
raised and argued against the objection that we have a right to risk shortening our lives,
by smoking or taking other sorts of risks, if we want to. If this objection had been
included in the essay, then it would have been important to note and take account of it.

## Skip Whatever Doesn't Argue
## for (or Against) the Thesis

People write essays to persuade other people. So they often include irrelevant material
if they think it will help them to persuade others. This kind of "flavoring" material
makes reading more fun, but shouldn't influence the assessment of an argument.

## Add Relevant Information or Reasons

Everything needed to prove a thesis is *never* included in an essay, no matter how long it may be. There is no point in trying to prove things that are obvious or generally accepted. Good writers try to provide just the information their audiences will need in order to see the merit of the writer's point of view. Someone writing about education, say, for an audience of teachers, doesn't need to prove that plenty of students graduate from high school today without having attained the ability to read, write, and perform basic arithmetic calculations. Every teacher knows that.

Of course, writers, being human, often fail to do the best job of supporting their theses. They often overlook important evidence, or they reason incorrectly to a conclusion that can be supported by better logic. Good critical thinkers try to evaluate the best version of an argument, adding material, perhaps, that its author neglected. By the same token, of course, good reasoners also bring to bear whatever negative evidence or reasons they may know about.

## Come to an Evaluation

While evaluation is logically the last thing we need to do when dealing with an argumentative passage, good critical thinkers start evaluating from the word go. They keep in mind questions like: Do I already accept this thesis? Does it fit well with what I already know and believe? If not, what sort of reasons or evidence might change my mind? And they continue to evaluate as they go along, bearing in mind questions such as: Is this reason acceptable without further justification? Does that reason really defend the thesis at hand, or just a straw version of it? Do the facts alleged seem plausible, given my background beliefs? Has the writer forgotten a serious counterargument or omitted important counterevidence? It's true that a completely confident judgment about a work can't be reached until an essay has been thoroughly examined, but it still is useful to make provisional evaluations right from the start.

Successfully bringing relevant background information to bear clearly is the key to good evaluations, but other relevant thoughts often play an important role. We often simply don't know enough to come to a confident evaluation. But we still may speculate intelligently by thinking about the right questions that need to be raised either for or against a particular thesis. For example, one of the important reasons often given in favor of laws requiring capital punishment for heinous crimes is that these laws will act as a deterrent—criminals may think more carefully before committing murder if they know conviction means death. This sounds like a very plausible reason given the strength of the urge most of us have to stay alive. But does it in fact work this way? Not knowing the answer may be a good reason for withholding judgment, or for seeking further information, or at least for only *provisionally* assuming that the threat of death deters criminals more than do lesser penalties. The point here is that coming to a *justified* evaluation requires us to think of what it would be useful to know that we don't as yet know—it requires us to raise the right sorts of questions. (Raising questions of this kind, of course, also serves as a guide to research that might have to be undertaken.)

When the entire structure of an extended argument has been figured out, its relevant passages will divide into those that are argued for within the essay and those that are not. The latter are the writer's basic *assumptions—starting points—*assumed without being justified. When evaluating an extended passage, you need to ask and answer three basic questions, corresponding to the three basic requirements of cogent reasoning (discussed in Chapter 1):

1. Are the writer's assumptions and stated reasons justified by what you already believe?
2. Do you know other relevant reasons or arguments? (If so, then you need to add them before coming to a final conclusion as to the essay's cogency.)
3. Do the reasons (plus any relevant material you may have added) justify acceptance of the thesis—that is, is the reasoning valid?

If an assumption or reason is not supported by your background beliefs, if you know of relevant information that refutes or casts doubt on the thesis, or if the reasoning is not completely valid (taking into account material you may have added), then clearly you should not be convinced by that particular extended argument. It may be, of course, that your background beliefs neither support nor conflict with an argument's assumptions or reasons, in which case you can't either accept or reject the argument's thesis; you need to withhold judgment or to delve further into the matter.

*A note of caution*: It is common for some of the subsidiary arguments in a long essay to be cogent, while others are fallacious. When this is the case, reason dictates accepting only the untainted portions of the overall argument. But it would be wrong to automatically toss out the whole extended argument—wrong to reject the thesis of the essay—if that thesis can stand on the basis of the legitimate portions of the essay (along with relevant material you may have added from your background beliefs). This point often is characterized as one of *charity*—of being fair to the other side on an issue—but it also is an important requirement of good critical reasoning.

## Exercise 8-1

Here are several short passages (taken from longer works). Reveal the structure of each passage, including reasons that support the thesis, reasons for the reasons, counterarguments, extraneous material, and so on, as in this simple example.

**Example:**

*Original passage* (from an essay by Baruch Brody on the abortion issue): There is a continuity of development from the moment of conception on. There are constant changes in the foetal condition; the foetus is constantly acquiring new structure and characteristics, but there is no one state which is radically different from any other. Since this is so, there is no one stage in the process of foetal development after the moment of conception which could plausibly be picked out as the moment at which the foetus becomes a living human being. The moment of conception is, however, different in this respect. It marks the beginning of this continuous process of development and introduces something new which is radically discontinuous with what has come before it. Therefore, the moment of conception, and only it, is a plausible candidate for being that moment at which the foetus becomes a living human being.

**Rewritten passage:**

*Reason (premise)*: After the moment of conception, there is a continuous development of the human foetus, with no one state being much different from the next.

*Conclusion*: No moment after conception can be selected as the moment the foetus becomes a human being. (This conclusion then becomes a reason [premise] in the larger argument.)

*Reason (premise)*: But the moment of conception introduces something radically different from what came before.

*Conclusion (thesis)*: The moment of conception is the only plausible moment when the foetus becomes a human being.

1. Excerpt from a speech by then-President Reagan to the Congress: As many of you know, our administration has . . . strongly backed an amendment that will permit school children to hold prayer in our schools. [Applause] We believe that school children deserve the same protection, the same constitutional consensus that permits prayer in the House of Congress, chaplains in our armed services, and the motto on our coinage that says, "In God We Trust." [Applause] I grant you, possibly, we can make a case that prayer is needed more in Congress than in our schools, but . . . [Laughter, applause]

2. Then-Senator Lawton Chiles (Democrat, Florida) back in 1980 (things obviously haven't changed much since then): Citizens have the right to know how their government works; yet lobbying is largely hidden from public view even though it has enormous impact on legislation. Of an estimated 15,000 lobbyists in Washington, only about 2,000 are registered, and little of an estimated $2 billion a year spent for lobbying is being reported. This is allowed by current law loopholes, loopholes that legislation I am sponsoring would plug. The public understandably is suspicious of that which is hidden from it, and this suspicion creates doubt about the integrity of both lobbyists and the legislative process. We must have greater lobbying disclosure.

*3. Thomas Paine, in his classic *The Age of Reason*: Revelation is a communication of something which the person to whom that thing is revealed did not know before. For if I have done a thing, or seen it done, it needs no revelation to tell me I have done it or seen it, nor to enable me to tell it or to write it. Revelation, therefore, cannot be applied to anything done upon earth, of which man himself is the actor or the witness; and consequently, all the historical and anecdotal parts of the Bible, which is almost the whole of it, is not within the meaning and compass of the word "revelation," and therefore, is not the word of God.

4. Philosopher John Locke, in his classic *The Second Treatise on Government*: Though the earth and all inferior creatures be common to all men, yet every man has a property in his own person; this nobody has any right to but himself. The labor of his body and the work of his hands, we may say, are properly his. Whatsoever then he removes out of the state that nature has provided and left it in, he has mixed his labor with, and joined to it something that is his own, and thereby makes it his property. It being by him removed from the common state nature has placed it in, it has by this labor something annexed to it that excluded the common right of other men. For this labor being the unquestionable property of the laborer, no man but he can have a right to what that is once joined to, at least where there is enough and as good left in common for others.

5. Well-known author Ayn Rand: By what conceivable standard can the policy of price-fixing be a crime when practiced by businessmen, but a public benefit when practiced by government? There are many industries . . .whose prices are fixed by the government. If price-fixing is harmful to competition, to industry, to production, to consumers, to the whole economy, and to the "public interest"— as advocates of the antitrust laws have claimed—then how can that same harmful policy become beneficial in the hands of the government? Since there is no rational answer to this question, I suggest that you question the economic knowledge, the purpose and the motives of the champions of antitrust.

*6. From the 1954 U.S. Supreme Court decision in *Brown vs. Board of Education*, which declared segregated schools inherently unequal and thus unconstitutional: Segregation of white and colored children in public schools has a detrimental effect upon the colored children. The impact is greater when it has the sanction of the law; for the policy of separating the races is usually interpreted as denoting the inferiority of the negro group. A sense of inferiority affects the motivation of a child to learn. Segregation with the sanction of law, therefore, has a tendency to [retard] the education and mental development of negro children and to deprive them of some of the benefits they would receive in a racially integrated school system.

7. Psychologist B. F. Skinner: The concept of responsibility is particularly weak when behavior is traced to genetic determiners. We may admire beauty, grace, and sensitivity, but we do not blame a person because he is ugly, spastic, or color blind. Less conspicuous forms of genetic endowment nevertheless cause trouble. Individuals presumably differ, as species differ, in the extent to which they respond aggressively or are reinforced when they engage in sexual behavior or are affected by sexual reinforcement. Are they, therefore, equally responsible for controlling their aggressive or sexual behavior, and is it fair to punish them to the same extent? If we do not punish a person for a club foot, should we punish him for being quick to anger or highly susceptible to sexual reinforcement? The issue has recently been raised by the possibility that many criminals show an anomaly in their chromosomes. The concept of responsibility offers little help. The issue is controllability. We cannot change genetic defects by punishment; we can work only through genetic measures which operate on a much longer time scale. What must be changed is not the responsibility of autonomous man but the conditions, environmental or genetic, of which a person's behavior is a function.

8. Philosopher Sidney Hook, on recovering from a near-fatal stroke: A few years ago, I lay at the point of death [following a stroke]. . . . At one point my heart stopped beating; just as I lost consciousness, it was thumped back into action again. In one of my lucid intervals during those days of agony, I asked my physician to discontinue all life-supporting services or show how to do it. He refused. . . .

A month later I was discharged from the hospital. In six months I regained the use of my limbs [and voice]. . . . My experience . . . has been cited as an argument against honoring requests of stricken patients to be gently eased out of their pain and life. I cannot agree. . . . As an octogenarian, there is a reasonable likelihood that I may suffer another "cardiovascular accident" or worse. . . . It seems to me that I have already paid my dues to death—indeed . . . I suffered enough to warrant dying several times over. Why run the risk of more?

Secondly, I dread imposing on my family and friends another grim round of misery similar to the one my first attack occasioned. My wife and children endured enough for one lifetime. . . .

## EXERCISE 8-2

In general, we do not read poetry with the intent of constructing a summary and then evaluating for cogency. Nevertheless, it is a fact that poems often argue for a conclusion. Andrew Marvell's wonderful (one might say "Marvell-ous") poem "To His Coy Mistress" is a case in point. Clearly, there would be no point in constructing a detailed summary of this, or perhaps any, poem, citing every bit of support given for the reasons provided for its thesis. So in this case, simply state (in your own words) the poem's thesis; the reason, or reasons, provided in its support; and a rough idea of the support provided for the reason or reasons.

### To His Coy Mistress

Had we but world enough, and time,
This coyness, Lady, were no crime.
We would sit down and think which way
To walk and pass our long love's day.
Thou by the Indian Ganges' side
Shouldst rubies find: I by the tide
Of Humber would complain. I would
Love you ten years before the Flood,
And you should, if you please, refuse
Till the conversion of the Jews.
My vegetable love would grow
Vaster than empires and more slow;
An hundred years would go to praise
Thine eyes and on thy forehead gaze;
Two hundred to adore each breast,
But thirty thousand to the rest;
An age at least to every part,
And the last age should show your heart.
For, Lady, you deserve this state,
Nor would I love at lower rate.

But at my back I always hear
Time's winged chariot hurrying near;
And yonder all before us lie
Deserts of vast eternity.
Thy beauty shall no more be found,
Nor, in thy marble vault, shall sound
My echoing song; then worms shall try
That long preserved virginity,
And your quaint honor turn to dust,
And into ashes all my lust;
The grave's a fine and private place,
But none, I think do there embrace.

Now therefore, while the youthful hue
Sits on thy skin like morning dew,
And while thy willing soul transpires
At every pore with instant fires,
Now let us sport us while we may,
And now, like amorous birds of prey,
Rather at once our time devour
Than languish in his slow-chapped power.
Let us roll all our strength and all
Our sweetness up into one ball,
And tear our pleasures with rough strife
Through the iron gate of life,
Thus, though we cannot make our sun
Stand still, yet we will make him run.

## EXERCISE 8-3

The Declaration of Independence contains a thesis and reasons defending that thesis. Get a copy of that important document and (1) determine what its thesis is; and (2) list the reasons provided in defense of that thesis.

# 2. QUICK APPRAISALS

In real life, outside of the classroom, people seldom spend a great deal of time or effort on any particular extended argument. Exact analysis is regularly done only by lawyers, judges, and such types.

Many people, including the authors of this text, find it useful, when quickly appraising an essay, to make little notes or marks in the margins to indicate where the thesis, major reasons, and so on occur, so that after a quick read it is easy to go back and evaluate with some accuracy. (It's true, of course, that we can't be completely confident of an evaluation unless we have carefully laid out the structure of an essay, tried hard to think of other relevant material, and only then come to a firm evaluation. But life is short, we cannot have intense interest in every topic we think about, and other tasks often intrude. So acquiring the knack of quickly and competently appraising extended passages is of great value in everyday life. It also (this should come as no surprise) takes most people at least a modest amount of practice to develop this knack.

Of course, when doing quick appraisals, the point is to try to do swiftly the same things that must be accomplished when doing any good analysis. (That's why practice is required; we need to learn to keep several things in mind at the same time.) In particular, we need to keep an eye out for the thesis and the major reasons offered in its support.

# EXERCISE 8-4

1. Turn back to page 165 and reread the example excerpt from a Baruch Brody essay on abortion. What is your quick evaluation of that excerpt?
2. How about your evaluation of the Ayn Rand item on page 167.

# EXERCISE 8-5

What is your quick appraisal of the following items? Remember that you always need to defend your answers:

*1. Letter to the editor of the *San Francisco Chronicle* (February 4, 1987. Reprinted by permission of the author):

> The scare tactitioners [sic] have been getting so much space in your publication for their antismoking diatribes that I have come to the conclusion that you are using these articles to distract your readers from the disgusting antics of the Washington prevaricators. [The reference was to Irangate figures.]
>
> In 1955, I was working for an internist M.D. in Reno, Nevada. He received a request from Mutual of Omaha (I think) for statistical records of 100 lung cancer patients, deceased. The percentage of heavy smokers, light smokers and nonsmokers. It was my assignment to ferret out and submit our record. These numbers I recall clearly: 3 percent were heavy smokers, 15 percent were light smokers, and 82 percent were nonsmokers.
>
> I am now 70 years old and have smoked for 50 of my years and shall continue to do so. One distinct advantage for me has been the ability of the nicotine to curb my hyperactivity. Smoking has not wrinkled my skin unduly as had been predicted.
>
> I seem to recall a piece you printed some time ago that stated that a person standing on a street corner for five minutes waiting for a bus would inhale

more toxic fumes in five minutes than a cigarette smoker in a year. Or have the antismokers convinced you that you are not going to die?

Of course, you are going to die. We all are. Nonsmokers die of lung cancer, diabetes, heart failure, uremic poisoning, AIDS, peritonitis, influenza, etc. Fear of death is the driving force with its fear of retribution after death. The guilt trips fill the church's bank accounts. Salvation always seems to cost money. Death is as natural and necessary as birth to keep our species in balance. Smoking is not going to deter the inevitable one whit.

> Juneau A. Wilkinson
> Susanville, California

2. Letter to the editor of the *New York Times* (June 2, 1992):*

Everybody likes to complain about how big money has corrupted the political process, and our democratic institutions often do seem impotent before the bankbooks of the power elite. Presidential election campaigns in particular have become the purview almost exclusively of millionaires, and now billionaires. But the rich themselves are not to blame.

The wealthy have as much business being in politics as anyone else. Responsibility for big money's corruption of democracy must be laid at the news media's feet. . . .

The Libertarian Party, the third largest party in the country, has waged earnest Presidential campaigns since the 1960s. The party platform and position papers address all major public policy issues in detail. Libertarians hold local offices around the country; the party's Presidential candidate this year [1992], Andre Marrou, is a former state representative from Alaska.

The messages of the Libertarian Presidential candidates typically are as well thought out and articulated, at least, as those of their Republican and Democratic opponents. Nevertheless, the news media summarily ignore Libertarian candidacies. . . .

Along comes Ross Perot, billionaire celebrity. He merely floats the idea of a Presidential campaign, and the news media fawn before him. . . . And it is [the news editors] who determine the newsworthiness of candidacies and thereby define the viability of candidates.

The disparity between the dearth of attention given Mr. Marrou's typically Libertarian roll-up-the-sleeves campaign and the wealth of publicity given Mr. Perot's merely putative campaign illustrates the enfeebled condition of democracy in our country. But the lopsided coverage is easy to understand.

The news media have a vested interest in political campaigns, because they pump millions of dollars into media coffers via advertising. Mr. Perot has tens or hundreds of millions of dollars to spend on campaign ads. Mr. Marrou probably has six figures total to spend on his campaign. Guess whose bid is more likely to attract news coverage?

Until news editors change their criteria for determining the newsworthiness of campaigns, any engagement of the democratic process at the national

---

*Reprinted by permission of the author. Was this letter any less *a propos* the 1996 election?

level by a person or party without astronomical financial resources, no matter
how earnest, will remain quixotic.

Kenneth Jopp

St. Paul, Minnesota

3. Woody Allen on the colorizing of black and white films, in testimony before
the U.S. Senate Judiciary Subcommittee on Technology and the Law (May 12,
1987):

> . . . You might get the impression . . . that I am against colorization of black
> and white films, but . . . you'd be wrong. If a movie director wishes his film
> to be colorized, then I say by all means, let him color it. If he prefers it to
> remain in black and white then it is sinful to force him to change it. If the
> director is not alive and his work has been historically established in black
> and white it should remain true to its origin. . . .
>
> The colorizer will tell you that it's proven no one wants black and white
> but this is not true. . . . [A]nd even if it were—if audiences who have grown
> up on mindless television were so desensitized that a movie like *It Happened
> One Night*, which has been delighting people in black and white for genera-
> tions, now had to be viewed in color to be appreciated—then the task would
> be to cultivate the audience back to some level of maturity rather than to doc-
> tor the film artificially to keep up with lowered tastes. . . .
>
> The colorizers also tell us that a viewer can simply turn off the color
> and see the film [*The Maltese Falcon*] in black and white. The fact that the
> man who made the film wants no one at all to see it in color [because it
> would make this "hard-boiled Bogart film silly-looking"] means nothing
> to them. . . .
>
> If members of the public had the right to demand alterations to suit their
> taste the world would have no real art. Nothing would be safe. Picasso would
> have been changed years ago, and James Joyce and Stravinsky and the list
> goes on. . . .
>
> [T]he difference between color and black and white is often so wide it
> alters the meaning of scenes. If I had portrayed New York City in color rather
> than black and white in my movie *Manhattan*, all the nostalgic connotations
> would have vanished. All the evocation of the city from old photographs and
> films would have been impossible to achieve in glorious Technicolor. . . .
>
> If a producer insists on color and if a helpless director is forced to film it
> the studio's way, despite his own feelings that it should be black and while—
> well, a deal's a deal. But once a film exists in black and white and has been
> thrilling audiences for years, then to suddenly color it seems too great
> an insult. . . .
>
> Only in America are films so degraded. In other countries the artist is often
> protected by the government. No one can change a French film director's
> films without his consent. They have too much respect for people who con-
> tribute to the society by doing creative work to allow anyone to subvert their
> creations at random.
>
> My personal belief is of course that no one should ever be able to tamper
> with any artist's work in any medium against the artist's will. . . .

## 3. THE MARGIN NOTE AND SUMMARY METHOD

The *margin note and summary method* is a good method to use when an evaluation has to be right. The idea behind this method is that a summary can be more easily worked with than the longer work from which it is drawn, provided the summary is *accurate*. (Making a summary helps us to remember things better, and thus is a good study technique, one in fact that instructors often use when preparing class material.)

There are four basic steps in the margin note and summary method:

1. Read the material to be summarized.
2. Read it through again, this time marking the important passages with an indication of their content written in the margin. (The point of the first reading is to enable you to more accurately spot the important passages when you read through the material a second time. First readings often don't catch the drift.) Margin notes need not be full sentences, or grammatically correct. They may contain abbreviations, or whatever shorthand notes you care to employ.
3. Use the margin notes to construct a summary of the passage, indicating which statements are premises (reasons) and which conclusions, so that the structure of the passage's argument is laid bare.
4. Evaluate the essay by evaluating your summary, checking back and forth to be sure there are no significant differences between the essay and your summary.

Two things need to be remembered about the margin note and summary method. First, when we skip portions of a passage, we make a judgment that the passed over material is relatively unimportant. It takes practice and skill to know what to include and what to omit, and even those with a good deal of experience may differ on such matters. (This does not mean, however, that anything goes!) Second, margin notes and summaries are shorthand devices; they should be briefer than the passages they summarize—if possible, a good deal briefer. The risk in this process, obviously, is falsification. We don't want to commit the *straw man* fallacy by making judgments about the shortened version that would not be valid for the original.

## Evaluation

A summary restates the position of the author of an essay. The evaluation contains the reader's appraisal. Here is an example showing how the margin note and summary method can be used to evaluate an essay:

### How McDonald's Caved in to Environmental Yuppies

After building its colossus by feeding ordinary folks, the McDonald's restaurant chain has unaccountably allowed itself to be pressured by elitist yuppies of the Environmental Defense Fund.

*Statement of fact: EDF has pressured McDonald's into replacing polystyrene hamburger cartons with coated-paper ones.*

In the process, it has done serious harm to its customers and suppliers and, ironically, increased its net contribution to pollution. The incident, instead of building environmental credibility, heightens the growing perception of green silliness.

On November 1, McDonald's decided to abandon its recycling program on polystyrene foam hamburger cartons (clamshells) and replace them with coated paperboard containers. The three network anchors immediately saluted this decision as "good news for the environment." In fact, every scientist will tell you that the decision was, on balance, bad news for ecology.

*Thesis: This was an ecological mistake.*

Indeed, one of the main reasons that McDonald's chose to expand polystyrene foam for its hamburger packs was a nonpartisan 1975 Stanford Research Institute study, which said: "There appears to be no supportable basis for any claim that paper-related products are superior from an environmental standpoint to plastic-related ones, including polystyrene. The weight of existing evidence indicates that the favorable true environmental balance, if any, would be in the direction of the plastic-related product."

*Premise: Polystyrene is ecologically superior to paper.*

Or as scientist Jan Beyea of the National Audubon Society explained: "Using a lot more paper means a lot more pollution."

The reasons are obvious to any scientist or engineer. First, and most obvious, polystyrene is easily recyclable, while coated paper is not.

*Reasons in support:*
*1. Polystyrene easily recycled, but not coated paper.*

Second, comparable paper packaging requires on average 40 percent to 50 percent more energy, in part because the paperboard weighs more and consumes three times its weight in raw wood per pound of production—and that assumes no recycling of either product. That incidentally includes the energy value of the petrochemicals consumed in polystyrene manufacture.

*2. Paper uses 40–50% more energy to make.*

Third, the atmospheric emissions involved in producing paper are at least two to three times those for producing polystyrene, and the waterborne wastes and effluents are at least 70 percent higher.

*3. Paper manuf. produces more air & water pollution.*

Finally, coated paper is only slightly more biodegradable than polystyrene. While polystyrene takes up 50 percent more space in landfills than its paper substitutes, it still constitutes less than 0.4 percent of total landfill waste. Even a modestly successful polystyrene recycling program kills coated paper's advantage.

*4. Although paper slightly more biodegradable, polyst. recycling kills coated paper's advantage.*

*(Repeat)*

This means that the McDonald's decision to expand polystyrene use in 1975 was not only sound economically, but it was by far the most environmentally sensible approach. The decision to reverse course is not sound science, but ill-informed yuppie-ism.

The recent McDonald's decision is one more reason why serious scientists and economists now have almost universal contempt for the environmental advocacy

*(Extraneous)*

movement and what Senator Daniel Patrick Moynihan
called its "middle-class enthusiasms."
    Dumb, McDonald's, really dumb.*

Now here is a summary of the Brookes essay taken primarily from the margin notes:

The EDF has pressured McDonald's into replacing polystyrene containers with coated-paper ones.

*Thesis*: This was an ecological mistake.

*Premise*: Polystyrene is ecologically superior to paper.

*Reason (evidence) 1 (supporting this premise)*: Polystyrene is easily recycled; paper is not.

*Reason 2*: Making paper requires 40 to 50 percent more energy than does polystyrene. (The implied premise here is that increased uses of energy in the modern world are a threat to stable air and water temperatures, contribute to a greenhouse effect, and so on.)

*Reason 3*: Making paper products pollutes the air more than does manufacturing polystyrene. (Brookes clearly meant in ways other than merely by increasing air and water temperature.)

*Reason 4*: Although coated paper is slightly more biodegradable than polystyrene, a "modestly successful polystyrene recycling program kills coated paper's advantage."

And here is an evaluation of Brookes's argument:

Brookes presents no reasons in support of his claims that McDonald's switched from polystyrene to coated paper and that they did so because of pressure from environmental groups. But it was common knowledge at the time (well-known, for instance, to the authors of this text) that this was true.

Doing a modest bit of research indicates that polystyrene foam is indeed ecologically superior, according to experts in the field, to coated paper, and for pretty much the reasons Brookes cites. Readers are invited to do their own research on this question. (Note, however, that uncoated-paper products, which McDonald's could use instead of coated-paper containers, can be recycled! It's true, though, that they aren't as sturdy and don't hold in heat or moisture as well as the coated variety, making them more difficult and dangerous to use.) So Brookes's thesis seems on target.

It's worth noting that in trying to fight the good ecological fight, groups such as the EDF sometimes become overzealous or, as in this case, act on the basis of inaccurate, unscientific information (as movement enthusiasts often do—one of the authors of this text having often been a case in point . . . in the distant past, of course). But Brookes's denigration of his opponents as "elitist yuppies" and

---

*Reprinted by permission of Warren T. Brookes and Creators Syndicate.

his characterization of the environmentalist movement as "green silliness" are extremely unfair and uncalled for. The EDF and other environmentalist groups are trying to combat the callous disregard, in the absence of outside pressure, of corporate America (as of industry everywhere) for the environmental effects of their activities.

# EXERCISE 8-6

Using the margin note and summary method, construct a summary of each of the following essays, making sure to label premises (reasons) and conclusions, including the grand conclusion that constitutes the passage's thesis:

1. Political column by Frederick Willman:
   I was in a Greenwich [Connecticut] Hospital for six hours, two of them for anesthesia and surgery. I was home by 5:30 P.M.

    Now, I ask my friends, what do you think the hospital bill came to? Five hundred dollars, they guess. I prod them to go higher. A thousand? Three thousand?

    Then I let them have it: $11,865.76, including sales tax—reduced by a hospital discount to $11,450.46 for Empire Blue Cross and Blue Shield, which administers the fee-for-service health plan for I.B.M., my employer. . . .

    We're talking here about cost-shifting—hospitals passing along the costs of the uninsured, under-insured and cut-rate (managed care) insured to traditional fee-for-service patients and their employers.

    But cost-shifting slides into price gouging when you begin to look at the individual charges. The single biggest item in my bill is "medical and surgical supplies": $7,126. It took me three weeks to get the hospital to explain the two biggest items included in that charge.

    One, for $4,199, covers nine disposable cutting instruments and a 3-by-5-inch patch of plastic mesh. The nine small tools are a pair of scissors ("endo shears"), two clamps ("endo dissects"), a needle, a stapler, a staple reloader ("multi-fire endo hernia") and three instruments ("premium surgiports") into which dissecting tools are inserted. . . .

    The fundamental wrong in cost-shifting is not a hospital's obligation to balance the books but an out-of-control health care system that is depleting resources that could be used to offer coverage for everyone.*

2. *San Francisco Chronicle* editorial (November 20, 1995):
   The $243 billion Defense appropriation bill passed by the House and Senate last week makes a mockery of the high-stakes budget-cutting war that has virtually shut down the federal government [the reference is to the budget standoff during the fall of 1995]. It not only is obscenely bloated in terms of defense needs at a time when vital social and health programs are being slashed, but it also pushes the nation down a foolhardy defense planning path that will impede the best efforts of budget cutters for years to come, making the Republicans' goal of a balanced budget in the year 2002 a virtual impossibility. . . .

---

*New York Times* Service. Reprinted by permission.

[A]lmost five years after the Soviet Union disappeared from the face of the earth, Americans still pay more for defense than all our potential adversaries and neutral parties combined. . . .

Both Congress and the administration have passed up an historic opportunity to both downsize and rightsize the military budget—to eliminate expensive, Cold War era weapons programs such as the B-2 bomber, the Seawolf submarine and the ballistic missile defense system while shaping the tougher, leaner military forces and precision weapons systems required in this era of uncertain but lower-scale regional risks.

A serious effort to reshape the nation's defense program is long overdue. The process should begin right now, with a presidential veto and a demand that Congress stop treating the Pentagon as a make-work employment agency.*

3. Here, now, is a still-relevant 1970 essay by Gore Vidal:
**Drugs**
It is possible to stop most drug addiction in the United States within a very short time. Simply make all drugs available and sell them at cost. Label each drug with a precise description of what effect—good and bad—the drug will have on the taker. This will require heroic honesty. Don't say that marijuana is addictive or dangerous when it is neither, as millions of people know—unlike "speed," which kills most unpleasantly, or heroin, which is addictive and difficult to kick.

For the record, I have tried—once—almost every drug and liked none, disproving the popular Fu Manchu theory that a single whiff of opium will enslave the mind. Nevertheless, many drugs are bad for certain people to take and they should be told why in a sensible way.

Along with exhortation and warning, it might be good for our citizens to recall (or learn for the first time) that the United States was the creation of men who believed that each man has the right to do what he wants with his own life as long as he does not interfere with his neighbor's pursuit of happiness (that his neighbor's idea of happiness is persecuting others does confuse matters a bit).

This is a startling notion to the current generation of Americans. They reflect a system of public education which has made the Bill of Rights, literally, unacceptable to a majority of high school graduates (see the annual Purdue reports) who now form the "silent majority"—a phrase which that underestimated wit Richard Nixon took from Homer who used it to describe the dead.

Now one can hear the warning rumble begin: if everyone is allowed to take drugs, everyone will and the GNP will decrease, the Commies will stop us from making everyone free, and we shall end up a race of zombies, passively murmuring "groovy" to one another. Alarming thought. Yet it seems most unlikely that any reasonably sane person will become a drug addict if he knows in advance what addiction is going to be like.

Is everyone reasonably sane? Some people will always become drug addicts just as some people will always become alcoholics, and it is just too bad. Every man, however, has the power (and should have the legal right) to kill himself if he chooses. But since most men don't, they won't be mainliners either. Nevertheless, forbidding people things they like or think they might enjoy only makes

*Reprinted by permission of the *San Francisco Chronicle*.

them want those things all the more. This psychological insight is, for some mysterious reason, perennially denied our governors.

It is a lucky thing for the American moralist that our country has always existed in a kind of time-vacuum: we have no public memory of anything that happened before last Tuesday. No one in Washington today recalls what happened during the years alcohol was forbidden to the people by a Congress that thought it had a divine mission to stamp out Demon Rum—launching, in the process, the greatest crime wave in the country's history, causing thousands of deaths from bad alcohol, and creating a general (and persisting) contempt among the citizenry for the laws of the United States.

The same thing is happening today. But the government has learned nothing from past attempts at prohibition, not to mention repression.

Last year when the supply of Mexican marijuana was slightly curtailed by the Feds, the pushers got the kids hooked on heroin and deaths increased dramatically, particularly in New York. Whose fault? Evil men like the Mafiosi? Permissive Dr. Spock? Wild-eyed Dr. Leary? No.

The Government of the United States was responsible for those deaths. The bureaucratic machine has a vested interest in playing cops and robbers. Both the Bureau of Narcotics and the Mafia want strong laws against the sale and use of drugs because if drugs are sold at cost there would be no money in it for anyone.

If there was no money in it for the Mafia, there would be no friendly playground pushers, and addicts would not commit crimes to pay for the next fix. Finally, if there was no money in it, the Bureau of Narcotics would wither away, something they are not about to do without a struggle.

Will anything sensible be done? Of course not. The American people are as devoted to the idea of sin and its punishment as they are to making money—and fighting drugs is nearly as big a business as pushing them. Since the combination of sin and money is irresistible (particularly to the professional politician), the situation will only grow worse.*

## 4. DEALING WITH VALUE CLAIMS

By now, it should have become clear how often the reasons presented in favor of a thesis are at least in part about values, not facts. It is a *fact*, for example, that sugar sweetens coffee; it is a *value judgment* that sweetened coffee tastes better than unsweetened. It is a fact that the Earth goes around the sun once every 365 days or so; it is a value judgment that, other things being equal, those who give to the poor are better people than the Scrooges who don't.

When someone argues, say, that vacations are better taken in the spring, because spring is the best time of the year, that person uses a value judgment as a reason (premise) supporting the conclusion that vacations are best taken in the spring. (Note, by the way, that this conclusion is itself in part a value judgment, as are all conclusions that depend on at least one reason that is a value judgment.)

---

*Reprinted by permission of the William Morris Agency on behalf of the author. © 1970 by Gore Vidal. Originally published in the *New York Times*.

Value judgments typically are justified, or defended, in ways that are different from judgments about facts. Someone who claims, for example, that gold does not rust can support that claim by citing the fact that nothing made of gold has ever been observed to rust, and that all attempts to rust gold have failed. But the person who says that gold makes beautiful jewelry has to cite a different sort of evidence, for example, that people generally like the look of gold jewelry. That is why many philosophers say that value judgments concern matters that are subjective, while judgments about alleged facts deal with matters that are *objective*.

The idea that values are subjective is captured nicely by the saying that beauty is in the eyes of the beholder and by the old precept that there is no disputing about taste. According to these maxims, the fact that some people like string beans, or Bach fugues, while others don't, doesn't make those who do or those who don't wrong. By way of contrast, those who make a nonvalue, factual claim—for instance, that the Earth is flat (so-called "flat earthers")—are wrong; the rest of us who believe that it is (roughly) spherical are right. (Yes, there are people who still, in this day and age, believe that the Earth is flat. Recall the discussion of self-deception in Chapter 6.) Merely believing that something is a fact doesn't make it a fact; nor is such a belief justified in the absence of evidence (experience about something relevant) to support that belief.

It's true, of course, that lots of philosophers would argue against the idea that value judgments are by their nature subjective. Some would say, for example, that beauty is in the object, not just in the eyes of the beholder, so that the person who doesn't see the beauty in beautiful objects is like someone who is color-blind. (One of the points of a philosophy course in which value judgments are discussed is precisely to deal with disagreements of this kind.)

Fortunately, when the value judgments relevant to an argument are about beauty, or taste, or other aesthetic matters, we generally can come to an evaluation without having to deal with underlying philosophical issues like the one about objectivity versus subjectivity. Suppose, for example, that some people in a community want to make uncovered auto junkyards illegal, on the grounds that they constitute an "eyesore." Voters don't need to decide whether being an eyesore is an objective or a subjective property in order to figure out how to vote. They can just find out whether most people find them to be ugly, or at least whether they themselves see junkyards as a good deal less than attractive. (There may, of course, be good reasons against banning open auto graveyards, but that is another matter.) The point is that, in these cases, we can appeal to something subjective, namely, whether we see junkyards as ugly or not, without answering the underlying questions about whether the ugliness of something is in the thing itself or merely in the eyes of the beholder.

But other sorts of value cases are more problematic, the prime case being *moral* values. If it is true that moral values are subjective, then claims about them can be justified simply by appealing to evidence that most people hold these values. Enslaving people and working them to death then becomes morally wrong just because virtually everyone finds this sort of behavior repugnant. But if moral values are objective, judgments about them cannot be defended in this way. Subjective feelings become irrelevant if moral principles are objective—if there is something outside of us, be it Biblical commandments, natural rights, the greatest good for the greatest number, or whatever, that determines which actions are right and which wrong.* Thus, those who hold that moral

---

*All of these, and many other allegedly objective factors, have been argued for, and against, by philosophers and theologians.

standards are objective need to think carefully as to what sorts of justifications—appeal to cultural norms, natural rights, religious principles, or something else—they believe should count in assessing moral claims and whether these allegedly objective standards in turn can be justified without appeal to subjective values or standards.

The point here, however, where we are discussing the application of moral standards to the evaluation of arguments, is that when someone makes a moral value claim, it may be crucially important to find out what makes that person hold that value. Those who argue against legal abortions, for example, often present as their principal reason the claim that taking a human life is morally wrong; but if their justification is the Biblical commandment "Thou shalt not kill," then those who do not accept the Bible as the ultimate authority on moral matters have not been given a persuasive reason for accepting this claim about the immorality of taking a human life.* Similarly, those who argue in favor of legalizing prostitution often claim that a woman has a right to use her body in any way that she sees fit; but if their justification is a theory of objective natural rights, then those who reject the idea of objective rights have not been given a satisfactory reason for being in favor of legal prostitution.

In any case, good critical reasoners accept premises that contain moral value judgments only if those judgments conform to their own moral standards. Socialists, for instance, sometimes argue that it is not just impractical but also immoral to allow some workers in a community to earn thousands of times more than others (as is currently the case in the United States and most industrial countries), and they use this claim as a reason for overturning, or at least modifying, the free enterprise system now in place in most industrial countries. Good critical reasoners accept or reject moral claims of this sort by seeing how they fit with the moral principles they already accept.

This does not mean, of course, that moral standards and values are exempt from challenge. Those who believe, say, that it always is morally wrong to violate legally enacted legislation may see the matter differently if laws are enacted forbidding the practice of their own religion, or forcing acceptance of another faith.

It also needs to be noted that there often are no simple principles—say those like the Ten Commandments—to apply in determining moral right and wrong. It seems morally right to many people that income should be proportionate to what one produces, a standard encapsulated in the idea that one should reap what one sows. According to this *principle of just desserts*, the fruits of a cooperative effort ought to be distributed according to the relative contributions of the various parties, whether in labor, capital, or whatever. But even supposing this idea is accepted, how are just desserts to be determined in actual cases? How compare, for instance, the efforts of a corporate chief executive officer who oversees the successful introduction of a new product with the engineers who designed and perfected that product, or with workers on the line who actually produce the goods? How compare the contributions of those who put up the money (stockholders) with those of company executive or production line employees?†

---

*Note that appeals to documents such as the Bible can be tricky. With respect to the abortion case, for instance, it has been argued that the original Hebrew has been mistranslated and that what the commandment says is better translated as "Thou shalt not *murder*," so that the question remains as to whether abortion is murder— immoral killing. There also is the problem that most who deny the legitimacy of abortion believe certain kinds of killing are justified—for instance, in wartime or in self-defense; those who believe this would have to show why killing fetuses is not similarly sometimes justified.

†For more on this topic, see Howard Kahane, *Contract Ethics: Evolutionary Biology and the Moral Sentiments* (Lanham, Md: Rowman & Littlefield, 1995).

Finally, it is important to remember that those who go through life without carefully examining and questioning their moral principles run the same risk of mistake as do those who fail to acquire accurate factual beliefs about how things work in this complicated world of ours. This is true even if the subjectivist view of moral right and wrong is correct, for it still could well be that a person's unexamined feelings about this or that moral issue will fail to agree with how that individual might see the matter after careful thought, or after bringing to bear relevant background information. The first thought that virtually all of us have about infanticide, to take an interesting case, is that it is the worst sort of murder; but thinking carefully about the hard choices life presents to some parents has changed the minds of more than a few thinking and even compassionate individuals.*

## EXERCISE 8-7

A while back (Exercise 8-1, number 4), you were asked to summarize excerpts from the writings of philosopher John Locke.

1. Indicate which of his assertions, if any, in his essay concern values, moral or nonmoral.

2. Use the summary of the article that you constructed before, along with your beliefs about any value statements the essay in question may contain, to come to an evaluation of Locke's view on the matter, indicating where you think his argument is weak, where strong, and what your overall evaluation is, making sure, of course, to explain why you think so.

## EXERCISE 8-8

Follow the instructions for Exercise 8-7 with respect to the Andrew Marvell poem "To His Coy Mistress" on page 168.

## EXERCISE 8-9

Having now had a bit of practice, here is a rather difficult task: Evaluate the following excerpts from an article proposing an alternative to capitalistic economic systems.†

1. Using the margin note and summary method, or whatever method works best for you, construct a summary of the excerpt.

2. Critically evaluate the article, using your summary as your guide, making sure that your evaluation accurately reflects the excerpt itself, as well as your summary. You obviously will need to bring to bear large chunks of your world view, showing how it matches the one you believe underpins the excerpt. (The article from which the excerpt has been taken is a good deal longer, and provides quite

---

*It sometimes happens that the only alternatives open to parents in poor societies, or societies in the throes of famine, are to do away with a newborn child so as to be able to keep their other children alive or else to see all of their offspring slowly starve to death.
†By Michael Albert, Z magazine, April 1994. Reprinted by permission.

a few more arguments relevant to the general thesis of an alternative to our current economic system. You might obtain a copy of the article and consider some of the material contained in it relevant to the part excerpted here.)

## Economic Justice

[W]hether due to neoliberalism, the fall of the Soviet prison, or the ineptitude of many radicals who ought to know better—it is now *de rigueur* to claim that we've reached the end of the economic line. . . . A better capitalism . . . is all we can hope for. . . . In rebuttal, here are some arguments for a new economy. . . .

(1) There is no acceptable rationale for some people to consume significantly more than others. . . . A person concerned about economic justice either believes in equality or rejects it. Period.

We all have different desires and preferences. . . . Indeed, there is no need for conformity, and good reason to prefer diversity. . . . But—and this is where justice comes in—the sum of what Sue gets and the sum of what Bill gets ought to have essentially the same value. That's fair. . . . Moreover, if some people get more and some less, those with more will have means to exert greater influence. Not only fairness, therefore, but also democracy, requires material equality.

Okay, there is one caveat. If Sue puts out more effort as her contribution to society, or makes more personal sacrifices than Bill, Sue deserves to get just that much more back. That's fair. But that caveat doesn't allow for large differences in income. . . . Moreover, I didn't say Sue gets more if she produces more. If Sue is stronger, smarter, or quicker than Bill, but they both contribute the same effort, they get the same reward, even if Sue produces more. You don't get rewarded for genetic endowment, luck, . . . or anything more than your exertion.

(2) There is no acceptable rationale for some people to spend their time working in better conditions and doing intrinsically more fulfilling or empowering work than others. In assessing economic possibilities one either accepts that everyone should have (a) equal opportunity to fulfill their potentials, (b) an equal share of the pleasures and burdens of work at society's current technological and social level, and (c) an equally empowering position in the economy from which to participate in decision-making; or one believes that some people deserve superior circumstances compared to others. . . . It shouldn't be that John gets to spend his time doing interesting tasks that expand his personality and skills, while Sarah must spend her time doing onerous or dangerous tasks that stultify her potentials. Sarah and John should each get a fair share of enjoyable, fulfilling tasks, and of the more onerous or dangerous tasks that are still part of society's economic life. Fairness requires this. . . .

Overall material and circumstance equality comprise "economic justice." . . . I have heard two types of counterargument. One claims that either or both kinds of equity are not, in fact, good. . . .

[But], to believe that economic justice is itself bad requires a belief that independent of effort, some people deserve to have more or enjoy better circumstances than others. . . . [A]nyone who believes that some people are different than others, as all people are different than all dogs, will . . . claim that equity of circumstances and material reward for all people is intrinsically bad. However, anyone who doesn't think differences in skin color, gender, religion, personal perspective, weight, height, manual dexterity, beauty, strength, or cognitive aptitudes, justify one person getting more than another *for the same expenditure of effort*, must accept that economic justice as defined earlier is good. . . . [T]here is simply no remaining legitimate reason for inequality. . . .

The second objection to an egalitarian system [is] that equal . . . material and social circumstances for all would eliminate incentives to excel. We get equity, but lose productivity because people won't try hard anymore. "Why should people work hard if they can't get ahead?" . . .

Some say, . . . "people with exceptional skills won't be able to apply them solely where they are most beneficial, and that is wasteful.". . .

[In reply to the first objection], if we build our economy right, there will be incentives to work because, except where health or other socially recognized reasons interfere, work is required for getting an income. Moreover, there will also be three types of incentive to excel: (1) To improve society, and, by extension, since everyone gets a fair share of society's product, to improve one's own situation. (2) To win the admiration, esteem, and personal satisfaction that accompany accomplishment. And (3) to utilize one's powers to the fullest, which is generally recognized by most people as being fulfilling in and of itself. . . .

[In reply to the second objection: It is] true that those who now have only a few highly skilled or intellectual responsibilities and who work at them for long hours . . . would exert those for less time in a better society. But is this really a problem? . . . If you believe that among the gigantic pool of people who are not now employed in skilled and conceptual labors there is not enough talent for such tasks [assuming the proper education], then, yes, there would be a loss. But if you believe society's needs for these skills and creative capacities can be more than accommodated, even if everyone has to spend some of their worktime doing other balancing tasks, then there is no loss. . . .

Not everyone can be a surgeon, artist, musician, or . . . economist. But everyone who isn't suffering some pathology certainly does have the capacity . . . to engage in both conceptual and manual work, in both following a plan of action and developing a plan of action, . . . etc. That's what it means, in considerable part, to be a human and not a dog, isn't it? . . .

Finally, . . . what about the complaint that guaranteeing equality means precluding some people . . . from being richer and more powerful than others, and . . . from employing others? Isn't this a denial of "freedom"? Sure it is. Just like the denial of the freedom of some folks to buy and sell slaves, . . . employ children, . . . or rape others. . . . What we are talking about is creating institutions that preclude unjustified difference in circumstance and/or income. This doesn't subvert freedom but rather creates the conditions for real freedom, the freedom for every person to fulfill his or her capabilities . . . without running up against another person's perverted choice to . . . employ wage slaves, or amass a disproportionate share of society's product or decision-making influence for themselves.

So what is the implication of seeking economic justice for an alternative economy? There can't be [large private accumulations of] capital because profits can't be earned without subverting economic justice. There can't be reward according to the value of one's product, because this would cause those who are lucky, brilliant, exceptionally strong, or exceptionally quick to benefit more than others who work equally hard—thereby subverting economic justice. . . .

## 5. EVALUATING IRONIC WORKS

Jonathan Swift, author of *Gulliver's Travels*, wrote a famous satire called "A Modest Proposal" in which he suggested that the Irish should raise babies to be eaten in order to solve the myriad problems confronting that land back in the eighteenth century. But the point of his essay, of course, was completely other than that people should literally carry out the plan he proposed. He was, to be plain, writing in an *ironic* vein, saying one thing but meaning something entirely different. So when evaluating ironic works it is a mistake to take them literally; they need to be evaluated in terms of their underlying message. Swift's point was to force his British audience to face the mass starvation and misery in Ireland that British policies had produced; his ironic suggestions were intended to shock his audience into a recognition of what they were doing in Ireland.

Irony often is combined with humor or exaggeration to form a potent weapon in the hands of a master at the trade. Telling us what is true in a funny or exaggerated way makes it harder to deny than if it is put to us in a straightforward, serious manner. Ironic writing is particularly effective in penetrating the kinds of self-serving psychological defenses—denial, rationalization, and so on—that were discussed in Chapter 6.

When we are evaluating ironic or humorous essays, the first question we need to ask ourselves is whether what is literally said nevertheless contains at least a kernel of truth; the second question is whether this kernel is sufficient to carry the (often only implied) thesis of the work.

Here, for instance, is the beginning of an ironic essay, "What Radio Reports Are Coming to," published in 1926 in the now long-defunct *New York Sun*:

> This, ladies and gentlemen, is the annual Yale-Harvard game, sponsored by the Wiggins Vegetable Soup Company, makers of fine vegetable soups. The great bowl is crowded, and the scene, courtesy of the R. & J. H. Schwartz Salad Company, is a most impressive one.
>
> The officials are conferring with the two team captains at midfield under the auspices of the Ypsilanti Garter company of North America. They are ready for the kickoff. There it goes! Captain Boggs kicked off for Yale by courtesy of the Waddingham Player Piano Company, which invites you to inspect its wonderful showrooms. "Tex" Schmidt recovers the ball, by arrangement with the Minneapolis Oil Furnace Company, Inc., and runs it back twenty-three yards courtesy of Grodz, Grodz, & Grodz, manufacturers of . . .

## EXERCISE 8-10

1. What is the point of this item—its unstated thesis?

2. Clearly, things have changed a good deal since 1926. In your opinion, is the point of this ironic snippet relevant to what goes on today? Explain.

3. Does it make you take account of something you already knew, or that you hadn't paid sufficient attention to or appreciated the significance of? If so, explain. If not, why not?

Drawing by Weber. © 1996 The New Yorker Magazine, Inc.

"Before I pronounce you man and wife, a brief message from Archer Daniels Midland."

*Irony and exaggeration work well not only in written works but also in drawings and cartoons.*

## EXERCISE 8-11

Today, political columnists such as Art Buchwald and Russell Baker use a combination of irony and humor to make points about the current social/political scene. Here is an example, written by columnist Arthur Hoppe, perhaps the best in recent years at this game:

## The Sins That Count

POOR HORATIO ALGER. He seemed such a shoo-in for attorney general. Born in poverty, he had risen to become a universally respected financier, congressman and Washington corporate attorney.

The confirmation hearing before the Joint Washington Ethics Committee appeared at first to be routine. "Let me begin by asking a few preliminary questions, Mr. Alger," said the committee chairman, Commerce Secretary Ron Brown. "As a lobbyist, you represent a score of large corporations on Capitol Hill?"

"Yes, in fact they're sponsoring a ball in my honor," said Alger. "But of course this would never influence my conduct in a government office."

"I certainly understand that, Mr. Alger," said Brown, "and I'm sure the public would, too. You were also president of the now-defunct Sweetheart Savings & Loan, I believe."

"Yes, I'm afraid that little 'Sweetheart Deal,' as we called it, cost the government $1.2 billion," said Alger. "I'd be glad to explain the circumstances, if you'd like."

"No, no, I doubt the public is interested in such tangled complications," said Brown. "I assume the same could be said for your conduct as treasurer of BCCI?"

"Well, my statement to the SEC ran 32 pages," agreed Alger, "but I'm proud to say all charges of junk mail fraud were dropped."

"That's all well and good," said Brown as the committee members nodded. "But let's turn to substantive matters concerning your qualifications. Have you ever neglected to pay Social Security benefits?"

"Never," said Alger stalwartly. "Nor have I hired an undocumented alien."

"Did you ever sexually harass one?" asked Senator Robert Packwood, a bit wistfully.

"No, nor an American either," said Alger, his chin high.

"Now we're getting down to the nitty gritty," said Congressman Ron Dellums. "While you were in Congress, did you ever bounce a bad check?"

"Or cheat on your postage stamp fund?" asked Congressman Dan Rostenkowski.

"Or use a government car, airplane or FBI agent illegally?" added FBI chief William Sessions.

Alger raised his hand. "Gentlemen, I'm happy to say that I have committed none of these high crimes that would render me unfit for office. Furthermore, in answer to the questions you are about to ask, Senator Kennedy, I am a lifelong practicing monogamist who has never inhaled in a place where marijuana was being smoked."

As the audience rose to applaud, the committee members flocked about Alger to shake his hand and congratulate him for being, as Chairman Brown put it, "an appointee with an impeccable record."

Unfortunately, a legless WW II veteran wheeled his chair forward at this point to shake his fist angrily and cry: "What about May 24, 1961, when you borrowed my handicapped sticker to park in front of the Bijou Theater in Waco, Texas, Horatio Alger?"

Poor Alger! His face flushed guiltily. He collapsed in the witness chair. His head sank in his arms and one clenched hand beat feebly against the tabletop in frustration.

And so the search for an honest attorney general continues.*

1. What is Hoppe's point—his unstated thesis?

2. Why does Hoppe have Commerce Secretary Brown ask the particular questions—about neglecting to pay Social Security benefits, sexual harassment, the Sweetheart S&L, and so on—and mention Packwood, Rostenkowski, and others? (If you don't know, do some research.)

3. In your opinion, is he on target? Explain.

4. Does he make you take account of something you already knew, or that you hadn't paid sufficient attention to or appreciated the significance of? If so, explain. If not, why not?

## SUMMARY OF CHAPTER 8

Chapter 8 concerns the evaluation of extended arguments—essays.

1. Most types of essays are straightforwardly argumentative, but some—for instance, descriptive or explanatory essays—may mask their theses in one way or another. *Example*: Orwell's essay, "A Hanging."

Essays may argue by considering reasons *pro and con* a thesis, by providing a *refutation to counterarguments*, and by a *comparison of alternatives*, as well as simply by presenting *reasons (premises)* in support of a *thesis*.

There are several guidelines to use in evaluating argumentative passages: (1) Find the thesis and keep it in mind as you read; (2) find the reasons (premises) that support the thesis, and (when there are any) the reasons for the reasons, and so on, taking into account the evidence presented; (3) identify responses to likely objections or counterarguments; (4) skip whatever doesn't support (or argue against) the thesis; (5) add relevant information, pro or con, that you may know of; and (6) come to an evaluation.

Coming to an evaluation consists primarily in asking and answering three questions, corresponding to the three basic requirements of cogent reasoning introduced in Chapter 1: (1) Are the writer's (or speaker's) assumptions and stated reasons justified by what you already believe? (2) Do you know other relevant reasons or arguments? (If so, they need to be added to the mix.) (3) Do the reasons (plus any added material) justify acceptance of the thesis: that is, is the argument then valid?

2. In everyday life, there usually isn't time to thoroughly analyze an extended passage. So it's useful to develop the knack of *quick appraisal*. The trick is to learn

---

*Arthur Hoppe. © 1993 The Chronicle Publishing Co. Reprinted by permission of the author.

how to informally and quickly do the basic things just mentioned *as you read the passage*. In particular, it requires getting adept at bringing relevant background information to bear and learning how to evaluate effectively as a passage is being read.

3. When a more careful analysis is required, many people find the *margin note and summary method* to be very useful. There are four basic steps in the margin note and summary method: (1) Read the material carefully, (2) read it again and add margin notes at the relevant spots in the essay, (3) construct a summary from the margin notes, and (4) evaluate the summary, making sure to bring relevant information to bear.

4. Reasons offered in support of a thesis may be about facts or about values. Claims about values typically are justified differently than those about facts.

   It often is said that facts are *objective*, values *subjective*. On this view, the shape of a gold ring, for example, is an objective fact about the ring itself; the beauty of the ring is "in the eye of the beholder." A contrary view is that values inhere in valuable objects themselves, so that they too are objective.

   Among value claims, those about *moral* matters tend to be both controversial and important. If moral values are subjective, then moral claims can be justified by evidence that the writer or speaker, or most or even all people hold that value. But if moral right and wrong are objective facts, then how people *feel* about them is irrelevant, and something outside of our feelings—for example, Biblical commandments—need to be appealed to in order to justify a particular moral claim. So when one is evaluating arguments containing moral claims, it often is important to try to find out what makes the writer or speaker make such a claim and to then assess the claims in view of one's own moral standards, however one has arrived at them. Of course, one's own moral standards should not be exempt from challenge and improvement (for example, in subtlety). Those who accept, say, the Ten Commandments need to see that they do not automatically answer all questions—they don't answer all economic ones, for example—and thus are in need at the very least of interpretation and perhaps also augmentation. Careful consideration of a standard may lead to a change of mind, say, about abortion or infanticide in view of the dire situations some people find themselves in.

5. Ironic essays argue for a point indirectly and thus are not to be taken literally. (Swift did not espouse the eating of Irish babies.) The point in irony is not to present reasons for a conclusion so much as to get readers to see something clearly that they may have overlooked, or not paid sufficient attention to, or defended against by some sort of self-serving self-deception. An honest evaluation of ironic writing requires us to determine whether there is, as implicitly claimed, something important that we have overlooked or denied.

*Calvin and Hobbes* by Bill Watterson.
Copyright 1989 Universal Press Syndicate. Reprinted with permission.

*There are no dull subjects. There are only dull writers.*

— H. L. Mencken

*Learn as much by writing as by reading.*

— Lord Acton

*He can compress the most words into the smallest idea of any man I ever met.*

— Abraham Lincoln

*A deluge of words and a drop of sense.*

— John Ray

*Chapter*

# 9

# WRITING COGENT (AND PERSUASIVE) ESSAYS

The discussion in Chapter 8 should make clear the essential contents of an argumentative essay: a thesis (grand conclusion) and reasons (premises) supporting the thesis. It also should be clear that in most cases the reasons themselves need to be supported by evidence or secondary reasons and that it often is useful to consider and refute likely objections.

But it should quickly become evident that writing a cogent and effective essay is much more difficult than summarizing and evaluating someone else's effort. Writing is character forming; it does indeed make evident the truth that writing is nature's way of letting us know how sloppy our initial thoughts on a topic often are. There are three reasons for writing essays, and one is without doubt that it is the very best way to sharpen sloppy thoughts into ideas that are clear, sensible, and well supported by good reasons and evidence. (The other two are to convince others and—obviously—to satisfy course or other requirements.)

## 1. THE WRITING PROCESS

Experienced writers, according to investigators,* keep their basic goals firmly in mind as they write and, indeed, as they prepare to write. They usually develop a plan of attack

---

*See, for instance, John R. Hayes and Linda S. Flower, "Writing as Problem Solving," *Visible Language* 14:396–398.

designed to meet their goals, but they don't generally move relentlessly from one idea to the next. Rather they frequently revise their original plans in the light of new evidence or ideas, or in the face of unexpected difficulties.

But revision is not generally done in a linear manner. One task often interrupts another. (Interestingly, editing seems to have a higher priority with most experienced writers than any other writing task, and tends to interrupt others at any time. Having used an inaccurate word, for example, writers tend to put aside whatever they are doing and search for one that is more precise.)

For most people, then, essay writing is a convoluted process, not a straightforward, linear one.* Skilled writers constantly rework their ideas as they plan and then write. The process itself leads to discovery, including the discovery, alas, of the inadequacy of our previous thoughts.

## 2. PREPARING TO WRITE

Students generally are asked to write short argumentative essays on specific topics; for instance, literacy in the United States or legalizing marijuana. Suppose your assignment is to write an essay on the topic of regulating the possession of firearms.

The first task is to determine what the precise thesis of your essay will be. Gun regulation might involve restricting the carrying of handguns to specific places, or perhaps only to specified individuals. Your thesis might be for, or against, the legal possession of automatic, quick-firing weapons or might just focus on handguns such as pistols.

Once you have provisionally decided on a thesis, research and greater thought on the matter might well urge a change of mind, perhaps even a switch from pro to con, or vice versa. Unless a precise thesis is forced on you, say, by your instructor, the very process of thinking about the topic and investigating the evidence and the reasonings of others is likely to motivate you to revise your thesis in one way or another. Poor thinkers often decide on a thesis and hang on to it no matter what the evidence seems to indicate, as though changing one's mind indicates failure. Good thinkers realize that changing one's mind *for good reason* is the hallmark of intelligent thought. In the case of laws concerning firearms, for instance, evidence about the incredible destructive firepower of handheld automatic weapons such as "Uzis" might convince you to argue for the banning of these weapons.

After you have provisionally selected a thesis and have developed reasons and evidence in its favor, it often is useful to construct an outline of the essay that is to be the finished product. It's true, of course, that we all are different. Some people do better just starting out writing, doing research, and even altering their thesis as they go along rather than following the order suggested here. (Recall the earlier remark about writing being a convoluted process.) But most writers, in particular those with little experience, find it useful to do a good deal of preparation, including the construction of an outline, before

---

*There have been a very few exceptions to this rule, the philosopher Bertrand Russell, interestingly, being a case in point. His handwritten first drafts, with extremely few changes here and there, often were used by publishers to set final type. We ordinary writers can only examine these drafts with a sense of awe, not with the intent to acquire the knack ourselves.

WRITING IS NATURE'S WAY OF LETTING YOU KNOW HOW SLOPPY YOUR THINKING IS.

Reprinted by permission of the *Detroit Free Press*.

starting to write the essay itself. (That is an important reason why essays written the night before they're due seldom get good grades—their "off the top of the head" nature is obvious to instructors.) At the very least, an outline should include a provisional thesis and the reasons and supporting evidence expected to be presented in its favor. Outlines need not be written in whole, grammatically correct sentences. Phrases and key words often are sufficient. But it is a good idea for inexperienced writers to state the thesis and principal reasons in complete sentences.

Calvin (of the *Calvin and Hobbes* duo) found it overly tedious having both to write an essay about bats and to do research on the topic, but research—diligent research—almost always is essential. When doing research, take notes (including citations!) of pertinent evidence—statistics, examples, the opinions of experts, and so on. Regularly review what you have discovered in the light of your thoughts on the topic to see how the evidence supports, or undermines, your thesis and important reasons. If research undermines your thesis, you need to revise it (narrow it, perhaps) or change the reasons you intend to offer in its support. *Never simply ignore counterarguments or reasons!*

Of course, you don't want to snow readers with a mountain of reasons or evidence. Plan to stick to your best reasons—those that reflect your most convincing evidence.

Remember, though, that not all reasons are based on factual research or evidence. When relevant, moral convictions and standards, or beliefs about aesthetic or other values, constitute very good reasons indeed. For instance, the belief that taking the life of animals solely for our own purposes—for food or for furs—is morally wrong certainly is relevant to issues concerning the treatment of animals.

Finally, before starting to write an essay, make sure that its thesis follows logically from the reasons (premises) you intend to offer in its support. After all, validity—deductive or inductive—is an absolutely necessary condition of cogent argument. Reasons that do not genuinely support a thesis are useless.

## 3. WRITING THE ESSAY

Argumentative essays typically divide into three parts: an introduction (usually including the essay's thesis), the body of the essay, and a conclusion. Each part helps to develop, organize, and support the argument.

## The Introduction

A good introduction engages the reader's attention and lays the groundwork for an essay's thesis, which usually is stated toward the end of the introduction. It begins to persuade the reader of the thesis before it is even stated. (Remember, you have two goals in mind. One is to write an essay that is cogent. The other is to persuade readers to accept your thesis. A perfectly cogent essay that is not well written may very well not convince many readers.)

There are all sorts of ways in which an essay can be started, a good one being to quote from an authoritative source. For instance, an essay on the need for greater adult literacy might begin with the following quotation:

> Twenty-five million American adults cannot read the poison warnings on a can of pesticide, a letter from their child's teacher, or the front page of a daily paper. An additional 35 million read only on a level which is less than equal to the full survival needs of our society. Together 60 million people represent more than one-third of the entire [adult] population. [Jonathan Kozol, *Illiterate America* (New York: Anchor Books/Doubleday, 1985, p. 4.]

The essay might then tie this quote into the rest of the introduction:

> These alarming statistics, compiled from convincing evidence, suggest that there is something drastically wrong with a system . . .

and after a few more introductory remarks, provide readers with a clear statement of the essay's thesis, followed by an enunciation of the two major reasons that are offered in its support:

> It is imperative that we, as a nation, right this wrong by doing what is necessary to ensure a literate citizenry. This resolve is based not only on the need to improve the lot of those who suffer from illiteracy, although that certainly is reason enough, but on the necessity of reducing the costs to our society of having a third of its citizens functionally illiterate.

Starting the essay in this way prepares the audience to read the body of the essay intelligently. Although it isn't necessary to include the main reasons after the thesis, doing so helps to keep both the writer and the reader on track.

## The Body of an Essay

The body of an essay develops the reasons and evidence offered in support of the essay's thesis. How much support is needed depends on how resistant the intended audience is likely to be (or on how much space is available to make your case). You don't want to hit people over the head with what they already believe or know. The body of the essay on illiteracy might contain two subsidiary reasons offered in defense of the first major reason that illiterate individuals suffer personally:

> The humane argument for a completely literate population is quite simply that illiterate people suffer a great deal from their affliction. They suffer both on a psychological and on a practical level. Consider the man who is so embarrassed at being unable to read that he *pretends* to read . . . .

Note the use of an example to illustrate the first subsidiary reason.

After providing several examples that make the point about the psychological problems facing the illiterate, the essay might then argue for the second subsidiary reason:

> Personal humiliation, however, is only one consequence of illiteracy. Perhaps even more important are the ways in which the lives of functional illiterates are severely restricted. Imagine, for instance, how difficult perfectly ordinary everyday tasks become for those unable to read product labels, telephone books, . . .

Then, the second major reason—that society as a whole suffers when many of its citizens are illiterate—could be introduced as a way of countering a likely objection to the thesis that America should act to greatly reduce its rate of illiteracy:

> It may be argued that the expense of tracking down and stamping out illiteracy is more than our pocketbooks can bear. But that argument fails to take into account how much we as a society have to pay for the illiteracy of a third of our people. . . .

## The Conclusion

The conclusion of an argumentative essay often restates the thesis—perhaps with emphasis. If the essay is rather long or complicated, the main points may need to be summarized. Here, for instance, is part of what would make a good conclusion to the illiteracy essay:

> In sum, everyone will benefit from the eradication of functional illiteracy. Certainly the illiterate one-third of our adult population has a great deal to gain by learning to read. They will be better able to cope with such simple practical tasks as . . . . Those of us who enjoy the advantages of literacy will also benefit because . . . .

Here, now, is what the entire essay on illiteracy might look like. It is rather short as essays go, intended primarily to serve as an example, but it nevertheless does a satisfactory job of clearly presenting and defending an important thesis:

> "Twenty-five million American adults cannot read the poison warnings on a can of pesticide, a letter from their child's teacher, or the front page of a daily paper. An additional 35 million read only on a level which is less than equal to the full survival needs of our society. Together 60 million people represent more than one-third of the entire [adult] population." [Jonathan Kozol, *Illiterate America* (New York: Anchor Books/Doubleday, 1985, p. 4.]

> These alarming statistics, compiled from convincing evidence, suggest that there is something drastically wrong with a system of education that turns out so many students who cannot read well enough to function adequately in daily life. Some students cannot read at all. Others are "functionally illiterate"—they read on a level insufficient to satisfy the ordinary demands of everyday life. It is a tragedy that a country claiming to be among the most advanced in the world should allow over one-third of its adult population to remain illiterate and to rank 49th in literacy among the 158 members of the United Nations (Kozol,

p. 50). According to the National Commission on Excellence in Education, we are "a nation at risk."

It is imperative that we, as a nation, right this wrong by doing what is necessary to ensure a literate citizenry. This resolve is based not only on the need to improve the lot of those who suffer from illiteracy, although that certainly is reason enough, but on the necessity of reducing the costs to our society of having a third of its citizens functionally illiterate.

The humane argument for a completely literate population is quite simply that illiterate people suffer a great deal from their affliction. They suffer both on a psychological and on a practical level. Consider the man who is so embarrassed by being unable to read that he *pretends* to read books on buses and in restaurants, just to save face, or the woman who cannot read street signs when in an unfamiliar part of town and is ashamed to ask directions. Indeed, the functionally illiterate regularly suffer embarrassment because of their affliction. I once knew a young man who, to avoid ridicule, sometimes pretended to read and at other times had to go to great lengths to hide the fact that he could not do so. Although in constant fear of discovery, by friends, his boss, and others, he sometimes was forced to accept help, for instance, when filling out simple forms, to his complete humiliation.

Personal humiliation, however, is only one consequence of illiteracy. Perhaps even more important are the ways in which the lives of functional illiterates are severely restricted. Imagine, for instance, how difficult perfectly ordinary everyday tasks become for those unable to read product labels, telephone books, prescriptions, or even bills or letters from friends. Think of how illiteracy jeopardizes their ability to obtain any but the most menial jobs. As Robert Dentler and Mary Ellen Warshauer pointed out some time ago in *Big City Dropouts*, the economy is much less dependent on factory and farm workers than in days of old and much more on skilled or trainable service-producing workers, so that a young person's ability to gain employment depends more and more on his or her schooling (pp. 61–62). The dawn of the computer age has made this fact increasingly evident. These days it is a rare job that does not require reading ability.

It may be argued that the expense of tracking down and stamping out illiteracy is more than our pocketbooks can bear. But that argument fails to take into account how much we as a society have to pay for the illiteracy of a third of our people. In *Illiterate America*, Jonathan Kozol cites innumerable facts to support this contention. He estimates that direct costs to businesses and taxpayers were about $20 billion a year in the mid-1970s. Today they are astronomically higher. The functionally illiterate are disproportionately on welfare rolls, or in jail (Kozol, pp. 13–14). Unable to earn good incomes and often ignorant of simple preventive health or birth control measures, they increase the cost of programs such as Medicaid. Taxpayers, already heavily burdened by high taxes, can ill afford the additional expense of an illiterate population.

The private sector of the economy suffers as well as the public. The illiterate are much more likely to be injured on the job, costing employers several billion dollars every year in workmen's compensation and other insurance premiums and in the expense of replacing damaged equipment. At the same time that over

5% of the adult population is unable to find work, skilled jobs that require the ability to read and write go unfilled—think only of the shortages from time to time in computer programmers of various kinds. One New York insurance firm indicated that 70% of its dictated correspondence had to be redone because of spelling or punctuation errors (Kozol, p. 14), an expense hard to bear in a competitive economy.

In sum, everyone will benefit from the eradication of functional illiteracy. Certainly the illiterate one-third of our adult population has a great deal to gain by learning to read. They will be better able to find decent employment and to function well in everyday life. They will have reason to hold their heads high rather than to regularly feel embarrassment or humiliation. Those of us who enjoy the advantages of literacy will also benefit because the expense of supporting illiterates will be considerably reduced and we will have a more reliable, more efficient work force. We thus have everything to gain and nothing to lose by helping everyone to become literate, and we will have done a good deed in the bargain.

## BIBLIOGRAPHY

Dentler, Robert A., and Mary Ellen Warshauer. *Big City Dropouts*. New York: Center for Urban Education, 1965.

Kozol, Jonathan. *Illiterate America*. New York: Anchor Books/Doubleday, 1985.

---

## Good Writers Respect Their Audience

*F. L. Lucas, once fellow and lecturer at King's College, Cambridge University, stressed the writer's obligation to readers in his essay "What Is Style?," from which this excerpt is drawn:\**

The writer should respect his readers; therefore [he should behave with] courtesy. . . . From this follow several other basic principles of style. Clarity is one. For it is boorish to make your reader rack his brains to understand. One should aim at being impossible to misunderstand—though men's capacity for misunderstanding approaches infinity. Hence Moliere and Po Chu-i tried their work on their cooks; and Swift on his men-servants—"which, if they did not comprehend, he would alter and amend, until they understood it perfectly." Our bureaucrats and pundits, unfortunately, are less considerate.

Brevity is another basic principle. For it is boorish, also, to waste your reader's time. People who would not dream of stealing a penny of one's money turn not a hair at stealing hours of one's life. But that does not make them less exasperating. Therefore, there is no excuse for the sort of writer who takes as long as a marching army corps to pass a certain point. Besides, brevity is often more effective; . . . And because one is particularly apt to waste words on preambles before coming to the substance, there was sense in the Scots professor who always asked his pupils—"Did ye remember to tear up that fir-r-st page?"

*\*Holiday magazine, March 1960.*

## 4. SOME HINTS FOR EFFECTIVE WRITING

It is important to remember that the point of writing most essays is to persuade readers of your thesis. To do this, you have to write not just logically but also well. Poor writing generally does not hold an audience. But even when it does, it may well not be convincing.

### Help the Reader to Understand

That is why the most important writing task is to help readers to understand both what it is that you claim—your thesis—and why they should believe you. To start with, you want to be clear, concise, and to the point, including only whatever readers will need to become convinced. (But remember that audiences differ one from another in what they need to be told.) This may seem obvious, but what is obvious in theory often is very difficult to carry out in practice. In particular, it is human nature to spend a good deal of time explaining what we ourselves know best, while sliding more quickly over the parts of an argument we ourselves don't quite understand or are unsure of. What needs to be done, of course, is exactly the opposite. That we don't have a firm grasp on a point or aren't completely sure about an argument's cogency should convince us that readers also may have these problems. These are the points that need to be explained with great care (after, of course, we have sorted them out in our own minds).

But even being clear, concise, and to the point may not be sufficient. For instance, it may be useful to *compare* or to *contrast* a point with similar ones. But one of the best, most useful, ways to help readers understand is by providing *examples*. The student essay on illiteracy, for example, contained examples of situations in which the

---

### Block Those Metaphors!

*Metaphor is a time-honored linguistic device. In the hands of careful writers, it often can express ideas swiftly and more effectively than more literal language. The trouble is that writers often go overboard in their enthusiasm for this linguistic tool. Here is an example from the witings of Guy Gugliotta in the* Washington Post *(carried as one of the* New Yorker's *occasional metaphoric overkill items):*

---

There was no time, Acting Chairman Matthew F. McHugh (D-N.Y.) said last week, and the committee was tired of stoking public outrage with fortnightly gobbets of scandal. It decided to publish everything it had left, warts and all.

Now everyone is tarred with the same ugly brush, and the myth that forever simmers in the public consciousness—that the House shelters 435 parasitic, fat-cat deadbeats—has received another shot of adrenalin.

---

*This little snippet also illustrates another writing no-no: the use of obscure words few readers can be expected to understand. Or did you know what "gobbet" means without having to look it up?*

## Student Essay Bon Mots

Here are a few extreme examples from student essays to serve as a reminder that good writing requires care and—yes—extensive revision.

---

*The elementary school I first attended was racial towards minorities.*
  (Poorly expressed thought.)
*Women have sat on the back burner long enough.*
  (Unfortunate figure of speech.)
*I believe reality is inside of us if we aren't afraid to let it in.*
  (Confused thought.)
*Secondly, the American school system is more loose, thus encouraging students to be creative rather than Japanese.*
  (Faulty comparison.)
*Every day at 4:00 thousands of people evacuate on their jobs.*
  (Poor choice of words and construction.)
*The question of how a Sephardic language school in France and a privately owned airport in Texas benefits the economy as a whole boogles the mind.*
  (Subject verb disagreement plus lack of care in spelling.)
*Little towns seem to start out as little towns.*
  (First quick draft became final draft.)
*He usually settled arguments with fist-de-cuffs.*
  (Overly clever—or display of ignorance?)
*My mind is stereofoamed.*
  (Use of overly inventive word—or display of ignorance?)
*Do punctual errors count?*
  (Yes, they do.)
*A broader view also prevents the student from charging blindly into a brick wall of unconceptuality.*
  (Block that metaphor!)
*When you first meet someone for the first time, everything is so new.*
  (Playing it safe by being tautological or redundant.)
*Another aw inspiring example is the Sixteen Chapel.*
  (Double display of ignorance.)
*I am in favor of capital punishment particularly in cases of murder and rape and aggravated napping, child or otherwise.*
  (Unintended humor.)

---

*Ah, well, everyone can't go to the head of the class in this doggy dog world. But at least we all can have self-of-steam. (Our thanks to Fresh Person English students at Knownayme College.)*

— Courtesy of Alice Cleveland

illiterate themselves suffer and of ways in which society as a whole does so. (This last sentence, as a matter of fact, is an example intended to help readers to understand that they need to give examples to help readers to understand.) It isn't an accident that the most frequently used expressions in this book are *for example* and *for instance*.

## Summarize When Necessary

A short summary at the end of an essay helps readers to be sure that they understand what is being argued. This may mean doing part of your readers' evaluating work for them, which is a good idea because in everyday life not very many readers evaluate with great care. (In the U.S. Army, instructors are taught to tell the audience what they're going to tell them, tell it to them, and then tell them what they've told them.) That is why a summary was included in the essay about illiteracy.

## Provide Transition Locutions

A good essay obviously has to have a logical structure, but you also want to write so that one thought flows into another—so that the logical structure of your essays is easy to follow. Transition terms and expressions highlight the flow of an essay, helping readers to know what to expect next—to know which expressions serve as reasons and which as conclusions and, in general, how things hang together. Note the use, in the illiteracy essay, of the words *but*, *thus*, *however*, *consider*, *also*, *although*, and so on, and the expressions *think how*, *for instance*, *at the same time*, and *in sum*.

## Think Your Position Through Carefully

Having to write so as to convince others—much more than speaking extemporaneously—is an excellent way to get clear in your own mind as to where the truth lies. Writing a good argumentative essay requires mental discipline—the ability to see through the natural tendency to hang on to opinions once formed, even in the light of their inadequacy—to root out inconsistencies and fuzzy beliefs, and to arrange thoughts into a coherent whole.

## Rewrite! Rewrite! Rewrite!

The difficulty of arranging thoughts coherently is an important reason why rewriting almost always is necessary. When writing a critical essay, we often realize that our thoughts aren't as focused or penetrating as we supposed. The writing process itself constitutes an important part of the reasoning process.

That's why most writers, definitely including the authors of this text, construct the first draft of an essay as a learning, or thinking, device. They do the best job they can on the first draft and then critically evaluate it as they would an opponent's essay. The next draft then can take account of what has been learned by introducing new reasons and arguments that aren't open to the criticisms made of the first draft.

But one thing is clear. Only a few of the very best writers can construct a really good critical essay in one draft. Bertrand Russells are extremely rare in this world. The rest of us have to write at least two drafts, usually more, in order to get our thoughts into good order and to express them so they can be easily understood by others. And you shouldn't be surprised to find out that learning to do this well takes . . . practice, practice, practice.

If the need to practice, practice, practice has been mentioned, can lots of exercise chores be far behind? Here, therefore, are a whole bunch of exercises—just how many you will need to sweat over is a decision resting with your instructor.

## EXERICSE 9-1

One good way to get practice in writing well is to critique poor writing. Here is a tiny (142 words) tongue-in-cheek essay from the delightful book *Ordinary Money* by Louis B. Jones (New York: Viking, 1990). For many years, "Beynon" Jones was a reader for freshmen English and other college writing courses. As a warm-up exercise, explain the various writing bloopers, of the kind that might move your instructor to make negative margin comments—blunders that Jones constructed into his little "student-written" essay (described by one of the book's characters as "complete bull___, but Ohrbach— the instructor—never notices"):

> The comparison/contrast of the Greeks and Romans is a very important comparison/contrast. Since the beginning of time, people have pondered this question. In the hustle-bustle world of today, the comparison/contrast of the Greeks and Romans is very important and relevant. For example, the Romans were after the Greeks and therefore they had a more technology-oriented advancement. For example, they had plumbing and flush toilets and they had lead in the pipes which made everybody gradually insane. For example, Caligula, which caused the Decline and Fall of the Roman Empire. Another comparison/contrast of the Greeks and Romans is, the Greeks were very sane. For example, Plato and other world-famous philosophers pondered the greatest question of all time. Plato believed that everything was ideal. This is still true today.

## EXERCISE 9-2

Here are several issues that should be of some interest to college students. Select one and, bearing in mind the writing suggestions just discussed, write a short essay (about 500–1000 words), taking one side or the other of the issue. Then write a critical analysis in reply to your own essay (as though you were a competent—and fair!—opponent attacking your position). And then rewrite your original essay to take account of your own criticisms. Think of your fellow students, not your instructor, as your audience. Pick a topic that will let you show how well you can reason about a complicated issue. Do not pick an issue that you think has an obviously right solution to it. For example, do not select number 6 if all you are going to say is that of course everyone has a right to a college education and therefore tuition costs at state institutions should be affordable for all. Every issue is more complicated than that, and there always are serious pros and cons to consider. This is a difficult and very important assignment; it absolutely cannot be done satisfactorily the night before it is due—if for no other reason than that a certain amount of research very likely is in order.

1. Should all college students be required to take at least basic introductory courses in math and science? In a foreign language?

2. Should we have a military draft in peacetime? How about an age-18 nonmilitary draft to do other sorts of community service?

3. Should the government be an employer of last resort, so that everyone who is willing and able to work will have an opportunity to do so?

4. Should we keep the minimum wage law and peg it to a level so that everyone who works full-time will live above the poverty level?

5. Should affirmative action with respect to the education or employment of women and minorities be the law of the land? (If you write on this topic you must carefully explain what you mean by "affirmative action," and you should restrict your topic either to education or to employment.

6. Are tuition costs at state colleges and universities in your state too high?

7. Should colleges and universities have special schoolwide rules concerning sexual harassment, student-faculty dating, and/or offensive language (of the kind discussed in the chapter on language)?

8. Should the rule in college be that plagiarism is to be punished by an automatic failure in the course in question or perhaps even by expulsion from school, either after the first or the second offense?

9. Should we have sex education courses in high school?

10. Should we lower the legal drinking age?

11. Should convicted drunk drivers lose their licences for an extended period of time or even, for a second offense, forever?

12. Should we require every adult to be tested for the AIDS virus?

13. Should we institute corporal punishment (such as canings) for certain crimes or, perhaps, public humiliation (for example, signs indicating that a convicted sex offender lives here)? (If you argue for the affirmative, indicate for which crimes such punishments would be appropriate.)

14. Should animals be used in medical research?

## EXERCISE 9-3

Supreme Court Justice Antonin Scalia has become famous for dissenting opinions based on his belief that judges should not by their decisions become "illicit legislators" who substitute currently popular ideas or their own opinions for laws legally and democratically enacted. For instance, he refused to join the other Supreme Court justices in their decision that the (at that time) male-only Virginia Military Institute, because state-supported, could not reject students on grounds of sex. (The majority view was that doing so violated a woman's right to "equal protection of the law.") Scalia wrote that a democratic system "is destroyed if the smug assurances of each age are removed from the democratic process and written into the Constitution." He believed that the

Fourteenth Amendment requirement of equal protection did not overrule the decision of a properly elected legislature making a single-sex institution permissible. The Constitution, he said, "takes no sides in this educational debate." He saw what the majority of the court did in the VMI case as "not the interpretation of a constitution but the creation of one."

Write a paper either defending or attacking Scalia's opinion. (You might want to actually get and read a copy of his whole dissenting opinion.)


## EXERCISE 9-4

Here are excerpts from Adolf Hitler's *Mein Kampf,* a book in which he explained his philosophy and his goals for the "Thousand Year Reich."

   a. Construct a summary of Hitler's arguments.

 *b. Write an essay in which you critically evaluate these arguments. (In this case, the friendly authors of this text provide a summary in the answer section at the back of the book but not a critical evaluation. You should, of course, construct your own summary first, and then compare it with the authors' summary at the back of the book.)

**Nation and Race**
There are some truths which are so obvious that for this very reason they are not seen or at least not recognized by ordinary people. They sometimes pass by such truisms as though blind and are most astonished when someone suddenly discovers what everyone really ought to know. Columbus's eggs lie around by the hundreds of thousands, but Columbuses are met with less frequently.

   Thus men without exception wander about in the garden of Nature; they imagine that they know practically everything and with few exceptions pass blindly by one of the most patent principles of Nature's rule: the inner segregation of the species of all living beings on this earth.

   Even the most superficial observation shows that Nature's restricted form of propagation and increase is an almost rigid basic law of all the innumerable forms of expression of her vital urge. Every animal mates only with a member of the same species. The titmouse seeks the titmouse, the finch the finch, the stork the stork, the field mouse the field mouse, the dormouse the dormouse, the wolf the she-wolf, etc. . . .

   Any crossing of two beings not at exactly the same level produces a medium between the level of the two parents. This means: the offspring will probably stand higher than the racially lower parent, but not as high as the higher one. Consequently, it will later succumb in the struggle against the higher level. Such mating is contrary to the will of Nature for a higher breeding of all life. The precondition for this does not lie in associating superior and inferior, but in the total victory of the former. The stronger must dominate and not blend with the weaker, thus sacrificing his own greatness. Only the born weakling can view this as cruel, but he after all is only a weak and limited man; for if this law did not prevail, any conceivable higher development of organic living beings would be unthinkable.

The consequence of this urge toward racial purity, universally valid in Nature, is not only the sharp outward delimitation of the various races, but their uniform character in themselves. The fox is always a fox, the goose a goose, the tiger a tiger, etc., and the difference can lie at most in the varying measure of force, strength, intelligence, dexterity, endurance, etc., of the individual specimens. But you will never find a fox who in his inner attitude might, for example, show humanitarian tendencies toward geese, as similarly there is no cat with a friendly inclination toward mice.

Therefore, here, too, the struggle among themselves arises less from inner aversion than from hunger and love. In both cases, Nature looks on calmly, with satisfaction, in fact. In the struggle for daily bread all those who are weak and sickly or less determined succumb, while the struggle of the males for the female grants the right or opportunity to propagate only to the healthiest. And the struggle is always a means for improving a species' health and power of resistance and, therefore, a cause of its higher development. . . .

No more than Nature desires the mating of weaker with stronger individuals, even less does she desire the blending of a higher with a lower race, since, if she did, her whole work of higher breeding, over perhaps hundreds of thousands of years, might be ruined with one blow.

Historical experience offers countless proofs of this. It shows with terrifying clarity that in every mingling of Aryan blood with that of lower peoples the result was the end of the cultured people. North America, whose population consists in by far the largest part of Germanic elements who mixed but little with the lower colored peoples, shows a different humanity and culture from Central and South America, where the predominantly Latin immigrants often mixed with the aborigines on a large scale. By this one example, we can clearly and distinctly recognize the effect of racial mixture. The Germanic inhabitant of the American continent, who has remained racially pure and unmixed, rose to be master of the continent; he will remain the master as long as he does not fall a victim to defilement of the blood.*

## EXERCISE 9-5

Here are two additional essays on a topic concerning women's rights that also are of interest because they take opposite sides of an issue—whether private service clubs should be forced to open their membership rolls to women.
   a. Construct a summary of each of these two essays.
   b. Write an essay of your own taking one side or the other of the issue, making sure to take account of what was said in the two essays reprinted here.

---

*From Ralph Manheim's translation of *Mein Kampf* (Boston: Houghton Mifflin, 1971, pp. 284–287). Copyright 1943 and renewed 1971 by Houghton Mifflin Company. Reprinted by permission of Houghton Mifflin Company and The Random Century Group Ltd.

### Court Ruling Opens Doors for Women

Ten years ago, the men-only Rotary club in tiny Duarte, Calif., was languishing. Women had begun to occupy the community leadership slots that Rotary had traditionally turned to for members-to-be. So Duarte's Rotarians did the gentlemanly thing: They opened the door for the ladies.

And a very ungentlemanly squabble ensued.

Rotary International banished the club. Both sides went to court. The fisticuffs ended last week when the Supreme Court ruled 7-0 for the Duarte Rotarians.

Echoing an earlier ruling that ended the men-only status of the Jaycees, the court said states have the right to forbid sex discrimination by local Rotary clubs.

Why? Because, while truly private clubs have a constitutional right of free association, the Jaycees and the Rotary clubs aren't "private," the court said: They are too big, too business-related, too community service-oriented.

Does this spell the end to men-only clubs? The court said decisions must be made case by case. But across the USA, die-hard men's clubs are manning the barricades:

- In Salt Lake City, when a judge warned he would yank the beer license if the Alta Club didn't stop discriminating, the club quit selling beer—rather than admit women.
- In Bethesda, Md., the men-only Burning Tree Club forfeited $186,000 in tax breaks—rather than admit women.
- In New York City, the Century Association is so afraid that its income from non-members will jeopardize its private status that it is considering selling its art collection to substitute for that revenue—rather than admit women.

How *un*gentlemanly.

Professional and business people use private clubs to make contacts and clinch deals. Women should have the same opportunities. Today, 44 percent of the workforce is female. There are 130,000 women bankers, 104,000 women lawyers. It is unfair that they must stand outside while their male clients and competitors dine in the clubroom.

Now that the Supreme Court has sent the message that Rotary and the Jaycees must accept women, other men-only service groups should follow suit.

And what of the smaller, more exclusive private clubs where the socially prominent eat and play?

The court's message was less clear. But there's no mistaking the moral message: Closing the doors of opportunity to women is just plain wrong.

Clubs that have evolved into meeting places where members transact business must admit members without regard to race, religion, or sex.

The gentlemen of Duarte found that welcoming women helped their club. So did the men of Philadelphia's Union League Club, Washington's University Club, Pittsburgh's Duquesne Club, and others that have recently stopped discriminating. Old members say that since the ladies joined, the change has been negligible.

But for women, the change can be dramatic and positive. When opportunity knocks, they're there to answer.

It's time to open the door for the ladies.*

### This Ruling Threatens the Rights of Women

SPRINGFIELD, VA.—The latest feminist victory against discrimination—the Supreme Court's ruling that the state of California can force the Rotary club to admit women—is a major blow against everyone's freedom.

The government may still allow small, independent clubs to set their own admission standards if, in the court's words, the group involves "the kind of intimate or private relation that warrants constitutional protection." But organizations like the Lions, Kiwanis, and Elks apparently have lost control over their memberships.

While forcibly opening up such clubs obviously benefits women, it vastly increases state interference with the most minute and personal of social and business relationships.

Indeed, in the name of nondiscrimination, governments have banned discounts for women during "ladies' nights" at bars and restaurants. A children's hair salon in Los Angeles was sued for charging girls, who tend to have longer hair, more than boys. Price breaks for women at a car wash have been ruled discriminatory and illegal. One male patron even sued a night club that barred men, but not women, from wearing shorts.

In none of these cases was the discrimination invidious. Irritating, perhaps. But nothing like the old Jim Crow rules that treated blacks as subhumans.

And while there's no logical reason for organizations like Rotary to exclude women, human relationships are not logical. Which is why freedom of association—a right protected by the First Amendment—is so important.

Indeed, there are women's-only organizations, like the Cosmopolitan and Colony clubs in New York and the Spa Lady chain of fitness centers. They, along with establishments that cater to homosexuals, are threatened by rules that ban all discrimination.

In a free society like ours, the government should stay out of interpersonal relations whenever possible. Social change may take longer as a result, but it will still occur.

In fact, the Rotary case arose after the local club in Duarte, Calif., decided to induct women to help counteract a declining membership. Three dozen Kiwanis clubs have also defied their international organization by admitting women. And many women's colleges have gone coed because of economic pressure.

This sort of voluntary movement toward non-discrimination is preferable to heavy-handed government regulation. Where innocuous discrimination persists, whether it be men's business clubs or ladies' discount nights, it should be accepted as inevitable in a pluralistic society.

A free people must tolerate intolerance, for the cost to liberty of trying to expunge every last vestige of discrimination from society is too high.†

---

*USA Today* (May 12, 1987). Copyright 1987 *USA Today*. Reprinted by permission.
†*USA Today* (May 12, 1987). Copyright 1987 *USA Today*. Reprinted by permission.

# EXERCISE 9-6

The opinions written by high-court judges constitute a good source for essay topics because they often are written on matters of general concern and tend to be logical, or at least somewhat intelligent. Here are four short excerpts from opinions of judges of the U.S. Court of Appeals concerning suits challenging state laws against assisted suicides. Write an essay in which you evaluate the statements made in these excerpts, being sure to consider whether at least two remarks in them that might be thought to commit fallacies discussed earlier in this text in fact do so.

> *Judge Stephen Reinhardt, Ninth Circuit*: Those who believe strongly that death must come without physician assistance are free to follow that creed, be they doctors or patients. They are not free, however, to force their views, their religious convictions or their philosophies on all the other members of a democratic society, and to compel those whose values differ with theirs to die painful, protracted, and agonizing deaths.
>
> *Judge Roger Miner, Second Circuit*: Physicians do not fulfill the role of "killers" by prescribing drugs to hasten death any more than they do by disconnecting life-support systems.
>
> *Judge Andrew Kleinfeld, Ninth Circuit*: It is very difficult to judge what ought to be allowed in the care of terminally ill patients. The Constitution does not speak to the issue. People of varying views, including people with terrible illnesses and their relatives, physicians and clergy, can, through democratic institutions, obtain enlightened compromises of the complex and conflicting considerations. They can do so at least as well as we judges can.
>
> *Judge Robert Beezer, Ninth Circuit*: If physician-assisted suicide for mentally competent, terminally ill adults is made a constitutional right, voluntary euthanasia for weaker patients, unable to self-terminate, will soon follow. After voluntary euthanasia, it is but a short step to a "substituted judgment" or "best interest" analysis for terminally ill patients who have not yet expressed their constitutionally sanctioned desire to be dispatched from this world.

# EXERCISE 9-7

Here are excerpts from two essays that are interesting because they argue for more or less anti-PC theses—that is, they defend a currently very frowned on side of an issue.

1. Construct a short summary of each one.

2. Write an essay either attacking or defending the thesis of one of these anti-PC works, being sure to take account of what is said in the work in question, as well as in other writings that occur in this text. (Again, note that there is no law against doing outside research.)

**Gun Control Myths**
(Excerpted from a National Rifle Association (NRA) brochure, "Ten Myths.")
"The only way to discourage the gun culture is to remove the guns from the hands and shoulders of people who are not in the law enforcement business."
—*The New York Times*, September 24, 1975

That editorial conclusion by the nation's most influential news journal, one noted for its advocacy of individual liberties, represents the absolute extreme in the firearms controversy—that no citizen can be trusted to own any kind of firearm. This expressed attitude is particularly ironic since the overwhelming majority of the 60 million American firearms owners have done nothing to deserve such a sweeping condemnation. It is the product of a series of myths which—through incessant repetition—has been mistaken for truth. These myths are being exploited to generate fear and mistrust of the decent and responsible Americans who own firearms. . . .

### Gun Laws Do Not Reduce Crime

The greatest myth perpetrated by the advocates of repressive gun laws is that such laws reduce crime. They do not.

No empirical study of the effectiveness of gun laws has shown any positive effect—although, to the dismay of the prohibitionists, such studies have shown a negative effect. That is, in areas having lower levels of private firearms ownership, the robbery rates are almost invariably higher, presumably because criminals are aware that their intended victims are less likely to have the means with which to defend themselves.

Further, of all the gun laws enacted in the past 10 to 20 years—each promised by its advocates to result in a reduction of crime—not one city, not one state, not one nation, has experienced a reduction in crime rates, nor even a reduced rate of crime growth in comparison to its neighboring cities and states and nations without such laws.

If gun laws worked, the proponents of such laws would gleefully cite examples of lessened crime. Instead, they uniformly blame the absence of tougher or wider spread measures for the failures of the laws they advocated. Or they cite denials of license applications as evidence the law is doing something beyond preventing honest citizens from being able legally to acquire a firearm. And they cite two jurisdictions' gun laws as "working"—Massachusetts and the District of Columbia. Yet crime in Washington rose dramatically between 1976, the year before its handgun ban took effect, and 1982, the year the city's voters adopted an NRA-endorsed mandatory penalty for misuse of guns in violent crimes. The violent crime rate rose 43% during those years, and the murder rate rose 14%, while the national rates were rising 20% and 3%, respectively. After adopting a law to punish violent criminals, Washington's crime trends have been similar to the nation's.

With a crime rate rising twice as fast as big cities overall, Washington could not even claim a relative change in gun use in criminal violence. No wonder D.C. Police Chief Maurice Turner said, "What has the gun control law done to keep criminals from getting guns? Absolutely nothing. . . . [City residents] ought to have the opportunity to have a handgun."

Massachusetts is an odd example for anti-gunners to choose, since the much-vaunted Bartley-Fox law did not make it more difficult to obtain or carry any firearm legally; it made mandatory a one-year penalty for carrying a firearm without proper authority. For a time, gun-related street robberies rose, and non-gun crimes skyrocketed. Generally, however, the murder-rate fluctuations in the

Bay State have mirrored national trends with other violent crimes increasing somewhat faster than in the nation as a whole. . . .

Furthermore, restrictive gun laws create a Catch-22 for victims of violent crime. Under court decisions, the police have no legal obligation to protect any particular individual, and under restrictive gun laws, it may be illegal for the person to protect himself. A citizen is thus in the position of having to give up effective self-protection or risk arrest if he or she successfully wards off a violent criminal. In Washington, D.C., according to the author and key supporter of their gun law, self-defense use of handguns has fallen 62% since the virtual handgun ban was put into effect.

### Massive Noncompliance

But there is an invisible effect of gun laws that may prove far more important than the visible, direct costs—that is, the social costs of increasing numbers of normally law-abiding citizens disobeying unpopular, irritating or expensive gun laws. Such high social cost was paid during the era of the prohibition of alcohol when a significant portion, if not the majority of drinkers, simply ignored Federal law. That era produced a generation of scofflaws, and provided fertile ground for the growth of organized crime syndicates that plague the nation a half-century later.

The evidence that gun laws are creating scofflaws is evident to anyone willing to look. In New York City, there are fewer than 70,000 legally owned handguns, yet survey research suggests there are at least 750,000 handguns in the city, mostly in the hands of otherwise law-abiding citizens. In Chicago, a recent mandatory registration law has resulted in compliance by only a fraction of those who had previously registered their guns. The same massive noncompliance—not by criminals, whom no one expects will comply, but by the particular minority groups fearful of repression—is evident wherever stringent gun laws are enacted.

In exchange for such high costs, what have the nation's lawmakers achieved? Not an instance of a reduction in crimes of violence. There is evidence of increases in robberies and other offenses where potential victims are disarmed by governmental fiat.

### Stiffer Penalties for Criminals

And laws addressed directly to the question of misuse do work. When stiff, certain punishment is levied upon those who misuse firearms—even when it is merely threatened—crime rates go down, particularly for predatory crimes like murder and robbery.

After adopting a mandatory penalty for using a firearm in the commission of a violent crime in 1975, Virginia's murder rate dropped 36% and robbery 24% in 12 years. South Carolina recorded a 37% murder rate decline between 1975 and 1987, and a 9% robbery rate drop, with a similar law. Other impressive declines in homicide rates were recorded in other states using mandatory penalties, such as Arkansas (down 32% in 13 years), Delaware (down 26% in 15 years), Montana (down 18% in 11 years), and Maryland (down 23% in 15 years). And Florida, despite the "Cocaine Cowboys" and rapid urban growth, and with eased handgun purchase and carry laws, saw its homicide rate drop 22% in 13 years (1974–1987). . . .

There is ample evidence that there is a solution to the crime problem, and a solution to the problem of criminal misuse of guns. That solution lies in the promise, not the mere threat, of swift, certain punishment. So long as the law-makers refuse to apply that solution, and instead attempt to control crime by controlling law-abiding gun owners, the nation's problems with crime and criminals will only increase.

*The Real Task*
Our challenge: To reform and strengthen our federal and state criminal justice systems. We must bring about a sharp reversal in the trend toward undue leniency and "revolving door justice." We must insist upon speedier trials and upon punishments which are commensurate with the crimes. Rehabilitation should be tempered with a realization that not all can be rehabilitated.

The job ahead will not be an easy one. The longer gun control advocates distract the nation from this task by embracing that single siren song, the longer it will take and the more difficult our job will be.*

## Demystifying Multiculturalism
If you believe the multiculturalists' propaganda, whites are on the verge of becoming a minority in the United States. The multiculturalists predict that this demographic shift will fundamentally change American culture—indeed destroy the very idea that America has a single, unified culture. . . . But has America truly become a multicultural nation? And if not, will those who capitulate to these demands create a self-fulfilling prophecy?

At the heart of the argument is the assumption that the white population is rapidly declining in relation to the non-white population. . . .

In fact, white males will still constitute about 45 per cent—a plurality—of the workforce in the year 2000. The proportion of white men in the workforce is declining—it was nearly 51 per cent in 1980—but primarily because the proportion of white women is growing. They will make up 39 per cent of the workforce within ten years, according to government projections, up from 36 per cent in 1980. Together, white men and women will account for 84 per cent of all workers by 2000—hardly a minority share.

But the business world is behaving as if a demographic tidal wave is about to hit. A whole new industry of "diversity professionals" has emerged to help managers cope with the expected deluge of non-white workers. These consultants . . . train managers to "value diversity." [But what] precisely does valuing diversity mean? The underlying assumptions seem to be that non-whites are so different from whites that employers must make major changes to accommodate them, and that white workers will be naturally resistant to including non-whites in their ranks. Public-opinion polls don't bear out the latter. They show that support among whites for equal job opportunity for blacks is extraordinarily high, exceeding 90 per cent as early as 1975. As for accommodating different cultures, the problem is not culture—or race, or ethnicity—but education. Many

---

* Reprinted by permission of the National Rifle Association.

young people, in particular, are poorly prepared for work, and the problem is most severe among those who attended inner-city schools, most of them blacks and Hispanics.

Nevertheless, multiculturalists insist on treating race and ethnicity as if they were synonymous with culture. They presume that skin color and national origin, which are immutable traits, determine values, mores, language, and other cultural attributes, which, of course, are learned. In the multiculturalists' world view, African-Americans, Puerto Ricans, or Chinese-Americans living in New York City have more in common with persons of their ancestral group living in Lagos or San Juan or Hong Kong than they do with other New Yorkers who are white. Culture becomes a fixed entity, transmitted . . . in the genes, rather than through experience. Thus, "Afrocentricity," a variant of multiculturalism, is "a way of being," its exponents claim. According to a leader of the Afrocentric education movement, Molefi Kete Asante, there is "one African Cultural System manifested in diversities," whether one speaks of Afro-Brazilians, Cubans, or Nigerians (or, presumably, African-Americans). Exactly how this differs from the traditional racist notion that all blacks (Jews, Mexicans, Chinese, etc.) think alike is unclear. What is clear is that the multiculturalists have abandoned the ideal that all persons should be judged by the content of their character, not the color of their skin. Indeed, the multiculturalists seem to believe that a person's character is determined by the color of his skin and by his ancestry.

Such convictions lead multiculturalists to conclude that, again in the words of Asante, "[T]here is no common American culture." The logic is simple, but wrong-headed: Since Americans (or more often, their forebears) hail from many different places, each of which has its own specific culture, the argument goes, America must be multicultural. And it is becoming more so every day as new immigrants bring their cultures with them. . . .

The urge to assimilate has traditionally been overpowering in the United States, especially among the children of immigrants. Only groups that maintain strict rules against intermarriage with persons outside the group, such as Orthodox Jews and the Amish, have ever succeeded in preserving distinct, full-blown cultures within American society. (It is interesting to note that religion seems to be a more effective deterrent to full assimilation than the secular elements of culture, including language.) Although many Americans worry that Hispanic immigrants, for example, are not learning English and will therefore fail to assimilate into the American mainstream, little evidence supports the case. By the third generation in the United States, a majority of Hispanics, like other ethnic groups, speak only English and are closer to other Americans on most measures of social and economic status than they are to Hispanic immigrants. On one of the most rigorous gauges of assimilation—intermarriage—Hispanics rank high. About one-third of young third-generation Hispanics marry non-Hispanic whites, a pattern similar to that of young Asians. Even for blacks, exogamy rates, which have been quite low historically, are going up; about 3 per cent of blacks now marry outside their group. . . .

Affirmative-action programs make less and less sense as discrimination diminishes in this society—which it indisputably has—and as minorities improve their economic status. Racial and ethnic identity, too, might wane if there weren't such aggressive efforts to ensure that this not happen. . . .

Multiculturalism is not a grassroots movement. It was created, nurtured, and expanded through government policy. Without the expenditure of vast sums of public money, it would wither away and die. That is not to say that ethnic communities would disappear from the American scene or that groups would not retain some attachment to their ancestral roots. American assimilation has always entailed some give and take, and American culture has been enriched by what individual groups brought to it. The distinguishing characteristic of American culture is its ability to incorporate so many disparate groups, creating a new whole from the many parts. What could be more American, for example, than jazz and film, two distinctive art forms created, respectively, by blacks and immigrant Jews but which all Americans think of as their own? But in the past, government—especially public schools—saw it as a duty to try to bring newcomers into the fold by teaching them English, by introducing them to the great American heroes as their own, by instilling respect for American institutions. Lately, we have nearly reversed course, treating each group, new and old, as if what is most important is to preserve its separate identity and space.

It is easy to blame the ideologues and radicals who are pushing the disuniting of America, to use Arthur Schlesinger's phrase, but the real culprits are those who provide multiculturalists the money and the access to press their cause. Without the acquiescence of policy-makers and ordinary citizens, multiculturalism would be no threat. Unfortunately, most major institutions have little stomach for resisting the multicultural impulse—and many seem eager to comply with whatever demands the multiculturalists make. Americans should have learned by now that policy matters. We have only to look at the failure of our welfare and crime policies to know that providing perverse incentives can change the way individuals behave—for the worse. Who is to say that if we pour enough money into dividing Americans we won't succeed?*

## EXERCISE 9-8

Finally, in a very well-known, often reprinted lecture, "The Idea of a University," Cardinal John Henry Newman (1801–1890) argued that the principal work of the university is to provide a liberal education, not merely, or even primarily, professional training. He said that a liberal education:

> gives a man a clear conscious view of his own opinions and judgments, a truth in developing them, an eloquence in expressing them, and a force in urging them. . . . it prepares him to fill any post with credit and to master any subject with civility.

Do you agree with Cardinal Newman's assessment of a liberal education, and agree that the primary job of a university (or college) is to provide such an education? Write an essay defending your opinion.

---

## SUMMARY OF CHAPTER 9

The essential contents of an argumentative essay are a *thesis* and *reasons (premises)* supporting the thesis. Usually, reasons need to be supported in turn by evidence or secondary reasons.

1. Experienced writers usually keep their basic goals in mind as they prepare to write, developing a plan of attack to meet those goals, revising their original plans in the light of new evidence or unexpected difficulties. But they don't generally write in a linear fashion; writing tends to be a convoluted process.

2. The first task when preparing to write is to determine precisely what your thesis will be. Later, of course, you may change your mind, perhaps by narrowing the topic or zeroing in on it more carefully. Changing one's mind for good reasons, while preparing to write and during the writing process itself, is the hallmark of intelligent thought.

   After selecting a thesis and developing your principal reasons in its support, you may find it useful to construct an outline of the proposed finished product. When doing the generally inevitable research, be sure to take notes, including reference citations. If research undermines your thesis, or reasons in its support, you must revise. Never simply ignore counterarguments or reasons. Before starting to write, make sure your thesis follows logically from the reasons you intend to offer in its support.

3. Argumentative essays typically divide into three parts. The introduction generally states and lays the groundwork for the thesis, and may contain an authoritative quote. The *body* of the essay should contain the reasons and evidence, perhaps also reasons in support of the reasons, and is likely to be more convincing if it contains examples. If counterarguments are to be discussed, the right time to do so is in the body of an essay; similarly for comparing or contrasting with other ideas. The *conclusion* of your essay may restate the thesis or perhaps provide a short summary of the essay's most important points.

4. The point of writing an argumentative essay is to persuade readers to accept your thesis, and this requires not just cogent reasoning but also effective writing. The point is to help readers to understand what it is you claim—your thesis—and why they should accept it. In particular, it is important to carefully explain what readers are most likely to misunderstand, rather than concentrate on those most easily explained and understood. Comparing or contrasting may be useful, as, of course, are examples. A summary at the end of an essay also is helpful, so that readers can be sure what it is you have argued.

   Good writers also try to achieve a natural flow by providing readers with transition words and expressions such as *but, although, for instance*, and *nevertheless*.

   But (note the transition word), however well planned an essay may be, rewriting almost certainly will be necessary. A first draft may thus serve as a learning device, so that later drafts can take account of what has been learned.

Photo by Rita Nannini

A white-haired woman sits in an overstuffed chair and says, "All this talk of cutting Social Security is really making me nervous." She goes on to say that that's why she's voting for Barney Frank. "How can I be sure Barney will do the right thing by us older people?" She smiles. "Because he's my son." It's irresistible.

*This excerpt from a* Harper's *magazine article on TV spot commercials illustrates what has been happening to political campaigns in recent years. They are being won or lost primarily on television, and TV spots like this one are perhaps their most important component. Notice that the appeal of this commercial is to emotions, not reason. And notice that it is irresistible. We all are suckers for Mom and apple pie rhetoric. (Yes, Barney Frank won, and 16 years later still is a member of Congress.)* Source: Nicholas Lehman, "Barney Frank's Mother— And 500 Postmen." Copyright ©1983 by Harper's *magazine. All rights reserved. Reprinted from the April 1983 issue by special permission.*

*Chapter*

# 10

# ADVERTISING: SELLING THE PRODUCT

Advertising is so obviously useful that it's surprising it has such a bad name. Ads tell us what is new and what is available, where, when, and for how much. They tell us about a product's (alleged) quality and specifications. All for free, except for the effort of reading or paying attention.

Yet there are legitimate gripes about advertising. Ads don't tell us about product defects. They often mislead, either via exaggeration or, occasionally, downright lies. And because some products are advertised more heavily or more effectively than others, ads tend to skew our choices in unreasonable ways.

It also has been argued that advertising increases the costs of goods to consumers. It isn't uncommon for a quarter, or even a third, of the price of an item to be due to advertising costs, and critics have argued that this constitutes a tremendous waste.

But this charge is misleading. Advertising does cost a great deal of money, and this expense has to be factored into the costs of finished goods. Nevertheless, advertising

READ

Kristi
Yamaguchi
for America's
Libraries

American
Library
Association

*A good ad some of us need to heed.*

greatly reduces the prices of those goods in the marketplace, compared to what they would cost were advertising abolished or greatly restricted. It does so because it lowers production costs by making mass production profitable—it enables producers to obtain a mass market—and because it reduces the costs of *selling* goods. It is not an accident that virtually all businesses advertise; they do so because they don't know of a better or cheaper way to sell their products. Those who argue otherwise generally forget that if a company doesn't advertise, it will have to increase other selling costs, especially sales commissions. (Advertising also has been objected to on the grounds that it gives an unfair advantage to large organizations in competitions against smaller ones, but objections of this kind raise large issues best left unexplored here—for example, about the desirability of large versus small businesses.)

In any case, it is worth noting that advertising has become an important part of our lives in a way separate from its informative aspect. Ads become part of the common experience and knowledge of a culture, taking their place alongside myth and well-known stories. In every generation, ad slogans ("Where's the beef?", "You're in the Pepsi generation," "LSMFT") are instantly recognizable by virtually everyone.

# 1. Promise and Identification Advertisements

First of all, it is important to understand that virtually all ads are of two kinds (or a combination of the two). **Promise advertisements** promise to satisfy desires or allay fears. All you have to do is buy the product advertised (remove bad body odor by using Old Spice deodorant; enjoy life more by driving a Ford Explorer 4 × 4). Most promise ads provide "reasons why" the product will do the job, or do it better than competitors (Kleenex tissues are softer, Total cereal has more vitamins and minerals).

**Identification advertisements** sell the product by getting us to identify with the product. They are a kind of promise ad, since they promise that somehow or other you will be better off using the product. But the promise is made indirectly through identification with respected institutions or individuals. We all tend to identify with our own group and with those whom we respect—people who are famous, rich, accomplished, unusually brave, or powerful. Identification ads take advantage of this very human trait. Celebrity ads work precisely because we identify with the famous people they feature and thus with the products they tout; we become like them in some small way by using Chanel #5 (Catherine Deneuve), by playing basketball in a pair of Nikes (Michael Jordan), or by reading a good book (Kristi Yamaguchi—see page 214). (Note that some ads try to get us to identify not with a particular product but rather with the product manufacturer.)

Identification ads, indeed all ads, work, incidentally, for another interesting reason. When people shop, say, in a supermarket, they tend to purchase products whose brand names are familiar to them. Few of us, for example, will buy a brand of toothpaste we have never heard of or never seen advertised; we buy a brand we recognize even though we know no other "reason why" we should buy that product and not a competing one.

Among identification ads, those tailored to group identification are particularly interesting. Magazines often are chosen for these campaigns because they tend to tap specific markets. *Examples*: The Virginia Slims cigarette ads, built around the slogan "You've come a long way, baby!", featured dolled-up, foxy, white ladies in most magazines but pictured dolled up, foxy, *black* ladies in publications with primarily African-American readers such as *Essence*; the National Rifle Association (NRA) campaign that featured the slogan "I'm the NRA," and showed a macho state trooper in hunting magazines and a pediatrician and father in women's periodicals.

Occasionally, these ads border on the nauseating. *Example*: The TV commercials for Fidelity Investment Spartan U.S. Treasury Money Market Fund picturing students (10–12 years old?) answering questions about why people came to America back in the old days and, in effect, answering (correctly according to the teacher) to be able to acquire and safely save money. At least equally revolting was the D.C. (District of Columbia) Lottery ad featuring a picture of Martin Luther King, Jr., delivering a speech that was headlined:

**To Honor His Dream**
**We Must Live His Legacy**

Reprinted by permission of J. Walter Thompson USA.

*Many advertising executives subscribe to the idea, mentioned before, that there are just two ways to influence people: via promises and identification. This Marine Corps advertisement invites young men to identify with the Marines pictured handsomely decked out in fancy dress uniforms. It was so successful that it spawned several even more successful TV commercials, one showing a piece of steel being made into a sword that was then nicely placed into its scabbard by a handsome Marine in dress uniform, while the voiceover intoned: "We're looking for a few good men—with the mettle to be Marines!" An absolutely brilliant ad series.*

Below in small print, we read:

> He spoke to us of peace, equality and unity. Powerful words. Powerful actions. Every day, it's up to each of us to make his dream a reality.

By tossing money away on the D.C. Lottery, of course.

Ads also can be a bit annoying to those in the know when they encapsulate corporate hypocrisy, as did the Nike "women's empowerment" ad campaign—typical Nike laborers who make their shoes are "grossly underpaid women stuck in utterly powerless and often abusive circumstances."*

## 2. THINGS TO WATCH OUT FOR IN ADVERTISEMENTS

The good news about advertising, you will recall, is that it often provides true and useful information about products and entertains us with humor, storytelling, or just nice scenes or sentiments. Time enjoyably spent is time not completely wasted. *Examples*: The Budweiser Christmas TV commercials featuring their magnificent Clydesdales in winter scenes; Black and Decker's: "You don't have to be crazy to buy a Black and Decker cordless screwdriver. You just have to have a screw loose." Or the Billy Graham billboard ad:

---

*The quote is from the Laura Flanders article in the September/October 1996 issue of *Extra!*

You're born.
You suffer.
You die.
Fortunately, there's a loophole.

The bad news about advertising stems from the increasing ability of advertising geniuses—and some of them *are* geniuses—to manipulate audiences via sophisticated psychological ploys. Everyone realizes how others are sold by advertising, but most of us think that we somehow are exceptions. Young people, including college students, often deny that they are influenced by advertising. They typically say that they don't wear designer jeans or Adidas shoes because of advertising but rather that they just "like" these products, self-deceptively ignoring the effect of advertising on their preferences. In fact, *no one* is immune to the influence of advertisements. (A Madison Avenue bigwig was overheard recently saying, "Even I fall for the stuff.") So we all are faced with the problem of how best to use advertising without being used. One way is to become familiar with the advertising devices and gimmicks used to appeal to our weaknesses, prejudices, and emotions unguided by intelligence.

## Ads Invite Us to Reason Fallaciously

We've already noted that ads often feature celebrity endorsements to manipulate us into buying the product, thus inviting commission of the fallacy *appeal to authority*. We don't stop to think whether Ray Charles really does prefer Pepsi to Coca Cola or whether he just gets paid to say he does. Anyway, what difference would it make to you if he didn't drink soft drinks at all? (*Consumer Reports* taste tests, by the way, show hardly anyone can distinguish between Pepsi and Coke. Can Ray Charles?)

Ads generally are guilty of *suppressing evidence*. Ads tell us the good features of products and hide their warts. (Why should they do otherwise?) *Examples*: Ads for brand-name painkillers such as Tylenol acetaminophen tablets, Bayer aspirin, and Advil ibuprofen don't mention that drugstore and supermarket brands sell for much less and are pharmaceutically identical. TV spots for Pepcid AC, Tagamet, and other stomach acid reducers never mention the seriousness of interfering with the production of something as vital to good health as stomach acid. (They also neglect to mention that some people experience extremely unpleasant side effects when using these products.) These commercials just tell us how we can eat normally stomach-irritating foods without irritating stomach distress by popping a legal drug pill.

Advertising audiences also are invited to make *faulty* or *invidious comparisons*. *Examples*: Pizza Hut ads that compare their delivery service with dingbat pizza parlors that don't deliver at all, ignoring their true competitors, such as Domino's Pizza, that do; Wisk ads that claim their product is more powerful than Tide, so you need to use less,

---

*There is an art to making whole lies out of half truths.*
— Christy Mathewson (baseball hall of fame pitcher
who was paid to endorse Tuxedo pipe tobacco)

making it seem that it costs less to use Wisk than Tide, which is not true (figure out why).

## Advertisements Pound Home Slogans and Meaningless Jargon

In fact, ads run through the entire range of fallacies, challenging theorists to invent pigeonholes into which to put them all. How, for instance, should we categorize the fallacious reasoning that leads people to be swayed by endlessly repeated, mostly empty slogans? *Examples*: "Brut. Men are back." (Were they somewhere else?) "Nobody beats Midas. Nobody." "The World's Greatest Newspaper" (that's the *Chicago Tribune*, in case Chicago area readers didn't recognize it). "I love what you do for me, Toyota." And so on, *ad* infinitum.

Slogans run the range from the modestly informative ("Miller Light: Great taste, less filling") to the somewhat suggestive ("Chevrolet. Like a rock.") to the completely irrelevant ("Nike: Just do it."). In general, they work because they are repeated endlessly, so that they become ingrained in our minds. In the days before television, which is primarily a visual medium, singing commercials did the job on radio. There can be very few people over 60, for example, who could not at the drop of a hat sing the Rinso soap flakes jingle they heard belted out on radio countless times lo these many years ago: "Rinso white, Rinso bright; happy little washday song!"

Slogans that tout products as "the official" something or other are an interesting special case. In 1996, for example, Powerade advertised itself as "The official sports drink of the Atlanta Olympic Games." Puffs of this kind generally imply something that is false. The Powerade slogan implied that Olympic athletes preferred this brand to others, or even that drinking Powerade gave them an edge over competitors. In fact, becoming the official whatever merely means paying for the privilege of being identified with a name. Powerade paid through the nose to be identified with the Olympic Games, as did Delta (the official airline), Coca Cola (the official soft drink—neglecting the fact that Powerade is a soft drink?), and so on.

## Ads Play on Weaknesses, Emotions, Prejudices, and Fears

Advertising sells some products more easily than it does others. Those that play on weaknesses or fears are a case in point, one reason so many TV commercials are of

---

We don't want to give the impression that advertising people are perfect, just that the best of them are exceedingly good at their job. But even the best occasionally make mistakes. *Example*: The billboard effort of one ad agency on behalf of Aetna Insurance Company that had the headline "EKG A-O.K." but showed the EKG typical of individuals with ventricular tachycardia—definitely not A-O.K. (But then why should we suppose insurance companies know anything about medical matters?)

*Calvin and Hobbes* by Bill Watterson. Copyright 1993 Universal Press Syndicate.
Reprinted with permission.

this nature. *Examples*: The "ring around the collar" commercials; ads for mouthwashes, hair restorers, and hair colorers; "roach motels"; and so on. Some of these ads do have the virtue of being informative (Grecian Formula does darken gray hair), but in many cases the product doesn't do the job advertised (Listerine does very little if anything for bad breath, even though it does kill some mouth germs, since most bad breath originates elsewhere), and in most others it doesn't do the job any better than competing products (Mylanta isn't any better at counteracting stomach acidity than Maalox, Gelusil, or several other brands; Energizer and Duracell batteries are equally good).

## Ads Employ Sneaky Rhetoric

In particular, *weasel words* are quite common in advertising. When an ad says the product "*fights* bad breath," it's wise to assume it doesn't *cure* bad breath, because if it did, the ad would make this stronger, less weasely claim. Similar remarks apply to claims such as "*helps* control dandruff with regular use," "gets dishes *virtually* spotless," and so on.

We also need to watch out for sneaky uses of *comparative* and *evaluative* terms, like *good*, *better*, and (best of all) *best*. The term *best* often translates into "tied for first with all other leading brands." The "lowest fare to Europe" may turn out to be the standard fare every airline charges. And when an ad says "No one sells ___ for less," you can be pretty sure others sell for the same price. And then there is that wonderful term, *free*, itself perfectly unsneaky, but so often used to lure the gullible (all of us in weak moments) into thinking they're getting something for nothing.

But these kinds of ads aren't as sneaky as the "official sweepstakes" notifications that arrive regularly in the mail. Their fine-print disclaimers have reached a high art, as the one recently received from *Time*, Inc., that featured very large type showing through a transparent window in the envelope stating:

### THE RESULTS ARE NOW IN: HOWARD KAHANE
### HAS WON ONE OF OUR TWO $1,666,675.00 PRIZES!

Above this, on one line and in very tiny and easily overlooked type, came the fine-print disclaimer:

"Be it henceforth known that if you have and return the grand prize winning entry, we will be pleased to announce that . . ."

# All of us come from someplace else.

**Just once, you should walk down the same street your great-grandfather walked.**

Picture this if you will.

A man who's spent all his life in the United States gets on a plane, crosses a great ocean, lands.

He walks the same streets his family walked centuries ago.

He sees his name, which is rare in America, filling three pages in a phone book.

He speaks haltingly the language he wishes he had learned better as a child.

As America's airline to the world, Pan Am does a lot of things.

We help business travelers make meetings on the other side of the world. Our planes take goods to and from six continents. We take vacationers just about anywhere they want to go.

But nothing we do seems to have as much meaning as when we help somebody discover the second heritage that every American has.

**PAN AM**
America's airline to the world.

See your travel agent.

Courtesy of Pan American World Airways, Inc.

---

*Advertising tends to concentrate on marginal needs, desires, and fears at the expense of many more important ones. Indeed, a frequently heard charge against advertising is that it increases the already strong tendency of people in industrial countries to become preoccupied with buying and consuming goods. (Note the humorous bumper sticker* WHEN THE GOING GETS TOUGH, THE TOUGH GO SHOPPING.) *Occasionally, however, an ad comes along that reminds us of what (for most of us) are much more important values, even though we tend to forget them in the hustle and bustle of everyday life. This Pan Am ad is one of those rare ads that tend to push us in the right direction. Yes! If we can afford it (and more of us could if we spent less on lesser needs), just once, we should walk down the same street our great-grandfather walked. (Pan Am went belly up in the early 1990s, but for other reasons.)*

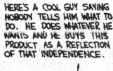

*Calvin and Hobbes* by Bill Watterson. Copyright 1993 Universal Press Syndicate.
Reprinted with permission.

All of which means that if HK happened to have been assigned the perhaps-one-chance-in-ten-million winning number, he would win the big bucks by returning the grand prize entry. (HK didn't waste time or a stamp finding out.) See the Appendix for more on this topic and on chances—probabilities—in general.

## Ads Play to Patriotism and Loyalty

If appeals to fears and prejudices can sell the product, why not patriotism and loyalty to one's country? *Example*: The Archer Daniels Midland ("supermarket to the world") ad that begins with a video of President Kennedy uttering his famous line "Ask not what your country can do for you but what you can do for your country," after which an announcer states in an authoritative voice, "At the Archer Daniels Midland Company, history has taught us that doing what's good for our country can also be good for business." (As the *New Republic* pointed out [June 18, 1990], ADM's "main line of business

---

*Advertisements for pain and sickness remedies, in particular, television commercials, are among the worst offenders against good taste, honesty, and good faith. Here is what the February 1991 issue of the University of California, Berkeley, Wellness Letter (clever title?) had to say about ads for flu and cold medicines:*

---

Over-the-counter flu medicines have invaded American's drugstores this winter. Does this mean there has been some victory over flu viruses? Unfortunately not. What drug makers are selling as flu preparations are basically the same old drugs they've marketed for colds. . . . Some of the new flu remedies are powders meant to be dissolved in hot water. The warm drink may have a soothing effect on a scratchy throat, but there's no evidence that it's any more effective than, say, tea. None of these ingredients have any effect against the flu or cold viruses. As a class, these remedies are expensive and of minimal use. They often contain ingredients that work against each other, or are present in less-than-effective dosages. Like colds, the flu . . . generally . . . goes away by itself.

— Excerpted from the University of California, Berkeley, *Wellness Letter*,
© Health Letter Associates, 1991

is refining corn into high-fructose corn sweetener and ethanol, a gasoline additive. Both products depend on massive government subsidies and trade protection." Compare this information from a knowledgeable source with what they tell us in TV commercials.)

## EXERCISE 10-1

Here are several advertising snippets (usually including the main ploy). Evaluate each of them for honesty, cogency, and the like and point out uses of the various kinds of gimmicks and devices (humor, jargon, etc.) discussed in the text.

1.  Dicker's Department Store (Redding, California) recently advertised its "47th Annual Once-in-a-Lifetime Sale."

2.  A Rolaids commercial showed a Rolaids user rejecting another brand: "Rolaids' active ingredient—medically recognized safe and effective."

*3.  A Lanocane ad claimed Lanocane is better at stopping itching from bites, swelling, etc., than Jergens and Vaseline Intensive Care lotions.

4.  Burger King sign: "10 FREE French Fry Certificates for only $1.00."

5.  BASF touted its video cassette tapes via the claim that these tapes last forever.

6.  Theme line in a French Government Tourist Office brochure touting the advantages of European travel originating in France: "The only European country that borders on six *other* countries, France brings you into the heart of Europe."

7.  Princess Cruises commercial: "It's more than a boat. It's the Love Boat," said by Gavin McCloud, captain in the "Love Boat" TV series.

8.  Calvert Gin ad: "Dry, Drier, Driest, Crisp."

9.  Safeway ad: "Nobody does it better than Safeway. Nobody."

10.  "Just as you can depend on the sun to rise, you can count on Metropolitan [Life Insurance Co.]."

11.  "Pontiac: We are driving excitement."

12.  "Cadillac: Creating a higher standard."

13.  "Ford Mustang: It is what it was, and more."

*14.  "Transamerica: The power of the pyramid is working for you."

15.  Mail order ad: "Special collector's edition. Priceless recordings. $6.98 per album."

*16.  "How'd you do it [get Kleenex softer]? We've got it down to a science."

17.  A Vancouver, British Columbia (Canada), KFC fast-food restaurant advertised:
Rediscover Original Recipe
now crispier and juicier

18. Ad depicting a rich elderly gentleman talking to another rich elderly gentleman between their palatial homes: "I was wondering if I could possibly borrow a cup of Johnny Walker Black Label?" This was a takeoff on the Grey Poupon commercials.

19. Ad for Wisk Away:

    Wisk Away
    with
    Penetron

*20. Part of a Nike commercial: "You don't win silver; you lose gold."

*21. Commercial for Dean Witter (investment brokers):

    We must plan for our client's future as if it were our own. . . .
    We measure success one investor at a time.

22. A full-page ad in the *New York Times* related how Ken Caminiti of the San Diego Padres "ate a Snickers bar and then hit two home runs against the New York Mets," and how in the next ten games he batted .472, hitting 7 home runs. Tony Gwynn was quoted as stating, "We all started screaming for . . . Snickers after that."

23. Budweiser commercial: A rooster very carefully crosses the road and then goes into a tavern where they serve Budweiser. A guy watching this then says to his buddy: "Well, I guess that answers that question."

*24. The principal part of a newspaper ad sponsored by the U.S. Council for Coconut Research/Information featuring a photo of Martin Agronsky: "The truth told by famous U.S. television personality: Whoever says coconut oil's 'poisoning' America isn't supported by facts. . . . In fact, an on-going medical study in a Boston hospital has turned out some strong evidence that the 'fatty acids' of coconut oil could be beneficial to human health. America's intake of coconut oil fats is a lot less than what you think [sic]. The FDA [Food and Drug Administration] commissioner testified recently before the U.S. Congress that less than 1.5% of U.S. total fat intake is made up of coconut oil. . . ."

25. Newspaper ad for the Massachusetts State Lottery: "There's a good chance you could win the Numbers Game today. Just ask the 12,000 people who won yesterday. . . . The only thing that's hard to do is lose. When this many people win, how can you lose?"

26. Denorex TV commercial, featuring a picture of a man with Denorex on one side of his head and Head and Shoulders on the other: *The man*: "This Denorex side really feels like it's doing a lot more than the Head and Shoulders side. It feels real cool and tingly over here." *Voiceover*: "Both have a dandruff ingredient, but Denorex adds an extra anti-itch medicine you can feel working." *The man*: "The tingle told me that Denorex is doing more for my hair."

27. Notice on the package of Elizabeth Arden Ceramide Time Complex Capsules: "Take your skin back in time to the future of a younger tomorrow."

28. The Budweiser "going to the fridge" TV commercial that ran during the 1994 Winter Olympics said that advertisers usually didn't like the fact that TV audiences tend to go to the fridge during commercial breaks but that the makers of Budweiser didn't at all mind if they did (while on screen we see someone go to the fridge and take out a Budweiser).

## EXERCISE 10-2

1. What is your opinion of the Nike commercial showing a woman struggling as she ran to the tape with the voiceover: "If you don't lose consciousness in the end, you could have run faster. FASTER! Nike Air."

2. How about the following excerpts (paraphrased) from a *Wall Street Journal* letter advertisement:

Twenty-five years ago, two very similar young men graduated from the same college and started work at the same company. Returning to college for their 25th reunion, they still were much alike—happily married, three children, and so on—but one was manager of a small department in the company, the other was the company's president.

The difference that made the difference was in what each of these two men knew and how they made use of that knowledge: one read the *Wall Street Journal*, the other did not.

*3. Here is a United Airlines TV commercial:

*Ben* (the boss, addressing his sales force): "I got a phone call this morning from one of our oldest customers. He fired us. After 20 years. He fired us. He said he didn't know us anymore. I think I know why. We used to do business with a handshake—face to face. Now it's a phone call and a fax—get back to you later. With another fax probably. Well folks, something's gotta change. That's why we're gonna get out with a little face-to-face chat with every customer we have." *Salesman*: "But Ben, that's gotta be over 200 cities." *Ben*: "I don't care. Edward, Ryan, Nicholas . . ." *Voiceover*: "If you're the kind of business that still believes personal service deserves a lot more than lip service, . . . welcome to United. That's the way we've been doing business for over 60 years." *Salesman*: "Ben, where're you going?" *Ben*: "To visit that old friend who fired us this morning." *Voiceover*: "United. Come fly the friendly skies." (Used by permission of Leo Burnett Co.)

Do you think this was a successful commercial? Why, or why not? Is this primarily a promise or an identification ad?

4. Respond to the following marketing major's comment: "Kahane's criticism of ads that manipulate via psychological ploys is mistaken, because that's what makes them effective."

5. One of the classic ads in the Pepsi-Coke advertising competition is set some time in the distant future and shows a teacher taking his students to an archeological site containing artifacts from the late twentieth century. He explains the various objects while his students drink cans of Pepsi. One of them holds up a bedraggled Coke bottle and asks the teacher what it is, to which the teacher responds,

after much puzzled thought, "I've no idea." A great commercial (why? what is its pulling power?), it brings to mind the way in which ordinary items from a time and place can reveal a great deal to discerning investigators (doing the archeological equivalent of reading between the lines).

Advertisements, if you can believe Marshall McLuhan, contain a treasure trove of clues about our times. If you were an investigator who came across records containing most of today's advertisements a thousand years hence, what might you learn from them about life in the latter part of the twentieth century? Explain.

6. Comment on the Security Pacific Bank notice that illustrated the reasonableness of a new $5-a-day charge on overdrawn accounts by showing that it represented "only" a 21.47 percent per year charge, assuming a one-day overdraft of $8,500.

## EXERCISE 10-3

1. Create a magazine ad for a product: (1) Decide which product it will be; (2) decide on an intended audience for your ad; and (3) design the picture and the copy.

   Use the ad to make a sales pitch to the class. Then ask students why they would or wouldn't buy the product, based on your ad, and analyze the ad's appeal, or lack of same.

2. Compare two ads for the same product in magazines with very different audiences (for instance, *Vogue* and *Time* magazine, or *Sports Illustrated*). Explain how the intended audience influenced the ad design and sales pitch.

## 3. NEW MARKETING WRINKLES

Although the advertising professionals are exceedingly good at their business, they are forced by increasing competition between advertisers, coupled with increased consumer sophistication, to do a good deal of market research. That is why, these days, there is an immense amount of research behind every successful advertising campaign. One way for consumers to defend themselves against the ad campaigns that result from sophisticated market research is to become familiar with some of the recent developments in the field.

Eric Clark notes, in *The Want Makers*,* that "virtually nothing appears from a major advertiser or agency until it has been opinion-polled, test-marketed or copy-tested, submitted on the way to panels of consumers whose words have been turned into statistical tables or analyzed by psychologists." Most large agencies have research staffs of their own, in addition to using specialist agencies like the A. C. Nielsen Company.

Types of research vary, depending on the method in favor at any given time, but roughly they can be divided into *qualitative research*—getting into people's heads to find out their thoughts and feelings—and *quantitative research*—gathering information by observation, experimentation, and surveys.

---

* New York: Viking, 1988. Some of what follows is summarized from this fascinating book.

Qualitative research grew out of Freud's theory that unconscious motivations often influence behavior. The underlying assumption, already stressed here, is that people make many decisions irrationally and often are not even aware of their reasons for making them. So researchers try to figure out how people really feel about products, not just how one might suppose they would feel. For example, on the basis of interviews with 300 mothers about how they fed their babies, researchers concluded the mothers were more concerned that feedings should be convenient and enjoyable for *themselves* than for their children, even though the mothers themselves said their baby's satisfaction was paramount. The resulting successful marketing ploy was to merely mention that babies would enjoy being fed the food but to stress that feeding time would be shortened.

Since all of us are motivated by unconscious desires at some time or other, these new marketing techniques make it more difficult for us to make rational decisions about the products we buy. We need to be more careful about what we buy and ask ourselves some commonsense questions before plunking down our money. Do we really need the product? Can we afford it? How does it compare with other similar products? Are we being conned—overly motivated—by advertising?

The quantitative approach to research has come a long way since the days when researchers asked people on the street what brand of soap or cereal they preferred. When you buy goods at most stores these days, the bar codes that are read at the checkout counter provide the retailer with a good deal of information concerning price, item purchased, and so on, that can be stored in computers; market researchers are now tapping into this information to find out what products people acually buy, not what they *say* they will buy. They are keeping track of the purchases made by carefully selected families, linking this information with further data concerning family income, number of children, and TV programs watched, including special test commercials. The result is that these marketing gurus can identify the ads that effectively sold the targeted products and plan large-scale ad campaigns accordingly. Perhaps an appropriate slogan these days would be that eternal vigilance is the price of economic solvency.

Helpful though research is, advertisers are up against a new set of problems. Increasingly sophisticated technology allows just about everyone to zap commercials with remote controls. Bob Goldstein, president of Proctor and Gamble in the mid-1980s, estimated that his company was losing 25 percent of its audience for commercials through zapping alone. And it's no news to anyone that the favorite time for a kitchen or bathroom break is during commercials (Recall the Budweiser ad that tried to make hay out of this practice.) Advertisers also have to contend with the growing popularity of relatively unadvertised generic products, and with the escalation of price wars that squeeze profit margins and advertising budgets. In response to this trend, advertisers regularly try new strategies.

In the November 16, 1992, issue of *Advertising Age*, America's leading advertising journal, Joe Capro, the publishing director, argued that the industry is undergoing a massive revolution that is changing the rules of marketing. Marketing money is shifting away from conventional media. He estimated that 65 percent of all marketing expenses in the United States go to nonmedia sectors, such as sales promotions, public relations, direct mail, catalog marketing, and trade promotions. Think, for instance, of the ever-mounting piles of junk mail just about everybody gets these days.

Databased marketing is another of the new advertising concepts. As Stan Rapp and Thomas L. Collins point out in *Beyond Maxi Marketing*,* advertisers are reducing their concentration on mass marketing in favor of more focused, less wasteful, individualized marketing, using precisely targeted database programs. For example, a Tennessee department store chain's database identified 1,400 customers who purchased clothes by high-fashion designers such as Anne Klein and Liz Claiborne only when they went on sale and then notified these customers when designer clothes went on sale, increasing two-day sale receipts on these items by 97 percent. Personalized marketing is much more likely to appeal to consumers than is mass marketing, making it harder to resist.

## The Shape of Things to Come

The Internet's noncommercial days are rapidly disappearing. A growing number of businesses are advertising their products on home pages on the World Wide Web. Viewers can click on to a commercial and read about and order the product in one fell swoop. Quick, easy, and tempting.

One problem Net advertisers face is that their ads can be easily clicked off. Another is that, as yet (!), they don't have a say concerning program content because they don't underwrite Net services. Anyway, there are a few insiders who doubt that the Internet will ever become a mecca for unsolicited advertisements because there is a charge, however slight, even to employ a scanner to screen out unwanted e-mail.

Visionaries also talk a lot about the "television/computer," which allows viewers to do things like switch from online programs to television, to films, to game-playing. In a few places even today, viewers using remote-control pads can play along with video quiz shows, select camera angles for sports events, and access detailed information about advertised products. These sophisticated telecomputers open up a whole new world for the advertising industry; consumers will be able to scroll through a Spiegel catalogue, order products instantaneously from the already-popular shopping channels, and access detailed information about the car they want to buy or the HMO they want to join. Which of these new marvels will turn out to be the wave of the future remains to be seen; billions are being spent by various competing parties intent on getting their feet in the doors they hope will be the right ones. But however these battles turn out, the danger is that lots of us will be pushed even more into the "consumer mode" and become even more likely to be talked into buying products it would be best for us to pass over.

## EXERCISE 10-4

1. Find an ad that has strong emotional appeal for you and try to figure out why you find it so engaging. Once you have done so, decide whether you would purchase the product, and explain your decision.

---

*New York: McGraw-Hill, 1994.

2. Show an ad to the members of your class and ask who would buy the product. Then interview the potential buyers and try to discover what motivated their choice. Once you have done so, figure out how you could persuade them *not* to buy the product.

3. Go through a series of ads on any items that interest you—cars, cosmetics, sports gear, etc.—and choose the one you would like to buy. Then do some research in *Consumer Reports, Consumers Digest,* or any number of books that specialize in product comparisons. On the basis of your research, decide whether you would still purchase the item you selected. Explain your decision.

4. Here is part of a comment made by John Kasson:

Advertising . . . has become . . . a way of telling us not just what we should buy but how we should live, how we should associate the advertised objects with ourselves.

Is Kasson right? Or do ads primarily appeal to already-existing desires and lifestyles? It is obvious, for example, that we cannot have a desire to play computer games like Nintendo before they exist, but do most ads touting products merely tell us about new ways to satisfy old desires, or do they create new ones, or perhaps just strengthen existing desires so that we spend more on them than we should? Do ads, say, for designer jeans and other fashion clothes just reinforce existing preferences? (Defend your answer.)

## 4. POLITICAL ADVERTISING

By now, just about everybody knows that political candidates and issues are marketed in pretty much the same way as breakfast foods and laundry detergents. This means that appeals to reason tend to be scarce, while devices designed to move emotions preempt the field.

In the old days, only candidates for local office could reach more than a tiny fraction of their prospective constituents—via "whistle stop" campaigns in which they made speeches before small audiences and "pressed the flesh." Billboards, lawn signs, newspaper ads, posters, patriotic bunting, and that sort of thing were extremely important parts of any successful campaign.

But the average voter never heard the actual voices of candidates running for high office or, except for some presidential candidates, ever saw their pictures or photographs. Political parties and platforms thus loomed much larger than they do today. Charisma didn't travel very widely.

Things began to change early in the twentieth century with the introduction of electronic and other scientific devices, starting with methods for printing pictures in newspapers and continuing with the widespread ownership of radios. Franklin Roosevelt was the first president to fully understand and gain significant political advantage from the miracle of radio; his "fireside chats" were an immensely successful public relations instrument, and his voice was instantly recognized by virtually everyone in America at the time.

But the changes in political rhetoric and tactics that came after World War II dwarfed those that preceded it. A large increase in the number of primary elections reduced the

> Orthodontics and the hair dryer have become vital to the achievement of political power.
>
> — Len Deighton

power of political parties and party "bosses" and, much more importantly, television (TV, the tube) brought candidates and their pitches into living rooms across the nation. Political campaigns were changed forever (as was pretty much everything else). Within a few years, image makers, which means advertising experts, reigned supreme. Names such as Roger Ailes became familiar to careful viewers of the political scene.

The first presidential candidate to make full and effective use of the new medium was Dwight D. Eisenhower. His successful 1952 campaign against Adlai Stevenson featured short television commercials like the following example, part of a series of TV spots in which General Eisenhower read from letters sent in by "citizens" asking questions that Eisenhower then "answered":

> *Citizen*: Mr. Eisenhower, what about the high cost of living?
> *General Eisenhower*: My wife, Mamie, worries about the same thing. I tell her it's our job to change that on November 14.*

No need for Eisenhower to tell viewers *how* he planned to change it.

Of course, Eisenhower conveyed an almost perfect *image*—war hero and father figure—and most people therefore strongly identified with him. War heroes, father figures, and candidates with *charisma*, John Kennedy being perhaps the best example, are very hard to beat. But candidates who project a less appealing image can, and frequently do, overcome their handicaps by hiring image makers to attractively tailor their campaigns *and their personalities*.

Eisenhower's TV spots were very effective, but image makers have honed their craft a great deal since then. They have learned, for example, that negative ads—attacking one's opponent—can be dynamite. One of the first TV spots to use this technique to full effect—the 1964 "Daisy/Girl/Peace" spot—also is probably the most famous of all political TV commercials. It ran just once as a paid advertisement but received so much comment that it was broadcast several times as a news item. (It was once believed that this commercial was never run again because of a public outcry against it, but in fact the original plan was to run it just once and then to garner free repeat TV coverage, which is exactly what happened.)

The spot starts by showing a very young girl picking petals from a daisy while counting "1, 2, 3, 4, 5, 7, 6, 6, 8, 9, 9," at which point there is the voiceover of a man counting "10, 9, 8, 7, 6, 5, 4, 3, 2, 1, 0," followed by the blast of an atomic bomb on the screen and the voice of President Lyndon Johnson saying, "These are the stakes—to make a world in which all God's children can live—or to go into the dark. We must either love

---

*David Ogilvy, in his *Confessions of an Advertising Man* (New York: Atheneum, 1963). Ogilvy quotes Eisenhower as moaning between takes, "To think that an old soldier should come to this." Note that the device used is a promise to satisfy a strong desire (for lower prices) without providing a single reason for believing that the promise would be kept.

*Here are three "awards" given by* Time *magazine (November 18, 1996) for political rhetoric in 1996:*

---

- **Most Vicious Ad:** In California's 3rd District, a television ad from Republican Tim LeFever morphed the face of Polly Klaas's killer, Richard Allen Davis, into that of Democratic incumbent Vic Fazio.
- **The Slight Inconsistency Medal:** To Al Gore, who left not a dry eye in the house at the Democratic Convention as he described his sister's death from smoking-induced lung cancer. Gore failed to mention that for some years following her death, his family continued to grow tobacco and that he continued to accept campaign money from tobacco interests.
- **Most Nauseating Spin:** Gore explained the above by saying, "I felt the numbness that prevented me from integrating into all aspects of my life the implications of what that tragedy really meant."

each other or we must die." Then another voiceover: "Vote President Johnson on November 3rd. The stakes are too high for you to stay home."

The point of this commercial was to picture Johnson's opponent, Republican Senator Barry Goldwater, as an extreme hawk all too willing to push the button, while Johnson is portrayed as a responsible "peace" candidate. Is it an accident that this best-known of all political spots also is one of the most vicious, inaccurate, and unfair?*

When it became clear to the media experts just how potent negative TV spots can be, they began to become a staple of many campaigns. Candidates had to face the reality that, however much they may find it odious to slam opponents in this way, victory often depends on doing so. In particular, a candidate far behind in the polls may feel compelled to resort to a bit of mud slinging.

In any case, attacking one's opponent via barbed humor has always been an acceptable part of the political process (going back, in fact, to the time of the ancient Greek democracy in Athens, where comic plays regularly made fun of well-known figures in all walks of life). Here is a rather appealing low blow from the 1996 campaign that traded on the fact that candidate Jack Kemp happened once to have been an NFL quarterback: "Jack Kemp held pro football's record for most recoveries by a player of his own fumbles." Equally cute was ex-president Gerald Ford's remark at the 1996 Republican National Convention: "When I was in the White House, I said I was a Ford, not a Lincoln. Today, what we have in the White House is neither a Ford or [sic] a Lincoln. What we have is a Dodge."

Of course, not all campaign advertisements feature mud slung at one's opponent. Tearing down the other guy is important, but propping up your own candidate is equally important. One way to do this is via image building and *identification*. During both the

---

*For more on this and other classic TV spots, see *A Viewer's Guide*, by David Beiler, a companion pamphlet to the fascinating videotape documentary *The Classics of Political Television Advertising* (Washington, D.C.: Campaigns & Elections, 1986), which contains a copy of the Daisy/Girl/Peace spot.

1992 and 1996 campaigns, for example, Al Gore was portrayed as a "rural youth" from Tennessee (thus suppressing the fact that he was brought up the son of a rich United States senator and throughout his life lived in very comfortable circumstances in places like Washington, D.C.). Bob Dole, in his 1996 run for the presidency, was touted as coming from the "heartland" of America (Russell, Kansas, in particular) and was identified with Ohio (through his father) and with several other states.

But candidates also need to be perceived as being on the "right" side of issues—as in support of measures favored by various constituencies. The trouble is that anyone running for high office needs to raise a great deal of money. Candidates thus are torn between the need to tell voters what they want to hear and the need to placate fat-cat campaign contributors. Candidate Dole, for example, had to tell silly lies about a lack of proof that cigarette smoking causes lung cancer, thus pandering to lobby money, although doing so alienated a great many potential voters.

Turning from presidential to local campaigns, the spot run by the California Democratic party's 1990 gubernatorial candidate, Diane Feinstein, featured video footage of her opponent, then Senator Pete Wilson, being pushed into the Senate chamber in a wheelchair, with the voiceover stating: "Republican Senate leader Robert Dole explains how they got Pete Wilson to vote against Social Security," followed by Dole jokingly stating: "Senator Pete Wilson had an appendectomy that morning. We rolled him from the hospital. He came up to the capitol. He was under heavy sedation. They rolled him on the floor. I said, 'vote yes'; he voted yes and we rolled him out again. He does better under sedation," at which point his audience erupts in laughter. Dole quickly demanded that Feinstein take the spot off the air, stating his remark was "a harmless joke that was made entirely in jest." Feinstein's spot made Dole's attempt at humor and Wilson's loyal effort on behalf of his party into one of the more offensive *ad hominem* attacks in recent years.

During that campaign, by the way, Feinstein came up with a humorous quip that paid off politically quite nicely. Taking clever advantage of Wilson's change of mind on the abortion issue, she remarked: "My opponent isn't pro-choice; he's multiple choice." But perhaps Ronald Reagan's put down of candidate Bill Clinton at the 1992 Republican convention was the best quip of the decade: "This fellow [Clinton] they've nominated claims he's the new Thomas Jefferson. Well, let me tell you something. I knew Thomas Jefferson. Thomas Jefferson was a friend of mine. And Governor, you're no Thomas Jefferson." (This was a takeoff on Lloyd Bentsen's famous put down in the 1988 vice-presidential debates of Dan Quayle's attempt to identify himself with Jack Kennedy.)

We also need to mention the *presidential debates* that have become a permanent part of the American electoral process. Political debates are hardly a new idea—think of

---

I'm not an old hand at politics. But I am now seasoned enough to have learned that the hardest thing about any political campaign is how to win without proving that you are unworthy of winning.

— Adlai Stevenson (1956)

---

*What one candidate learned from two (failed) runs at the presidency.*

the famous debates between Abraham Lincoln and Stephen Douglas. But the first presidential debates, between Richard Nixon and John Kennedy, did not take place until 1960. (Interestingly, these debates are still the most vividly remembered.) Kennedy is generally seen as the winner because he exhibited "vigor" and youth and exuded great charisma, whereas Nixon appeared to be overcautious and a bit sneaky. (Nixon later complained that his makeup was incorrectly applied—a very important point.) The debates generally are credited with being the crucial factor in Kennedy's extremely narrow victory.

In all of the presidential debates so far, just as in the Nixon-Kennedy debates, it has been *image*, not reasoning or displays of intelligence or character, that has determined the winners. (More will be said shortly on the topic of image building.) The 1988 debates between George Bush and Michael Dukakis illustrate this nicely. When Dukakis failed to respond with instant outrage to CNN commentator Bernard Shaw's famous question about what Dukakis would do if his wife were raped, his chances of winning election pretty much flew out the window.

Finally, no account of campaign rhetoric could be complete without mention of the role of polls in elections. No serious candidates for high office these days would open their mouths without having first tested the wind via polls. Whatever may be the case after they have won, when running for election, smart candidates make their pitches conform to what the polls indicate about voter sentiments and prejudices. During campaigns, at any rate, successful politicians generally are followers, not leaders. They waffle because they have to in order to get elected. It's always better to tell voters what they want to hear, not what the candidate genuinely intends to do if elected.

But what do presidential debates and polls have to do with advertising? Why discuss them in a chapter devoted to advertising? The answer is that political advertising campaigns are built around image making. Candidates see debates as a way to sharpen

---

In this day and age, in which political campaigns cost a great deal of money, most of it comes from fat-cat and PAC contributions, a sad state of affairs that constitutes one of the principal problems with the current political process. But an even worse scenario lurks on the horizon, namely, the buying of elections by multimillionaires, or billionaires, as happened in the last national election in Italy, in which the winner was the owner of all privately held TV stations in Italy. (He thus had vast sums to spend and his own private media to toot his own horn.)

Nothing quite that dramatic has happened in the United States, or is likely to happen, given the modestly broader ownership of the mass media here. But the successful 1992 campaign of California Republican Michael Huffington was rather ominous, because Huffington spent over $5 million of his own money and came from behind to win a seat in the U.S. House of Representatives. (In 1994, his attempt to buy a Senate seat with $24 million of his own money failed by a narrow margin.) And we shouldn't forget Ross Perot's 1992 run for the presidency in which he garnered 19 percent of the votes in spite of almost self-destructing on a "60 Minutes" TV program. His attempt in 1996 never had a chance, but the point cannot have been lost on the multirich that it is possible to spend oneself into victory. Woe for democracy.

their image with voters. The presidential debates provide candidates with the largest audiences they will be able to advertise to during a whole election campaign. (Nowadays, of course, a tradition has been established so that candidates pretty much are forced to debate or lose face.) And polls tell candidates how to advertise; their media experts build campaigns in terms of what they learn from polls; blind advertising bit the dust a long time ago.

Well, then, if virtually all political rhetoric is guided by expediency, why pay attention to it? If we can expect candidates to waffle, even to lie, why hear them out? The answer is that even waffling and lies can tell those of us who read between the lines a great deal about how candidates may perform if elected to office: Which sorts of lies they tell and what kinds of campaign promises they make tell us something about which groups and positions a candidate is likely to favor if elected. The promises made by Dole, Kemp, and their champions during the 1996 presidential campaign were somewhat different from those made by Clinton, Gore, and their advocates, because somewhat different constituencies were being appealed to. Clinton was forced to take a "center" position, Dole had to move to the right-of-center, both thus tipping their hands a bit as to which constituencies they would most favor if elected. Their pitches did, of course, overlap in many ways, in particular with respect to "family values"—a key mom-and-apple-pie concept these days—and concerning illegal drugs. (Interesting assignment: Try to determine the underlying messages being conveyed by the two major 1996 presidential candidates and their cohorts, and how their rhetoric might have been expected to translate into actions.) Nevertheless, it is true in the political arena at least as much as anywhere else that actions speak louder than words.

## Noncampaign "Campaign" Rhetoric

Politicians don't just campaign via advertisements or when they have thrown their hats into the ring. *Image building* is a day-in, day-out task—indeed, in terms of time spent, perhaps a successful politician's principal task. Of course, for those holding high office, in particular, for the leader of a nation, image building often coincides with ceremonial duties. At the start of the Gulf War, for example, President Bush was photographed going to church—symbolic of the seriousness of the step into war just taken—and evangelist Billy Graham was invited to spend the night with the Bush family in the White House. (Saddam Hussein prayed on camera virtually every day of that war in spite of being well-known as a nonbeliever.) Candidates challenging incumbents don't have the opportunity to improve their images via ceremonial activities, one reason incumbents are hard to unseat.

Another reason, of course, is that incumbents, at least of the United States Congress, can improve their images at taxpayer expense via their letter franking privilege. Members of Congress aren't supposed to use this privilege for campaign purposes, but they do it anyway, for instance, by sending franked letters containing "questionnaires" and by answering letters from constituents.

Senator Milton R. Young of North Dakota was one of the first members of Congress to take full advantage of the opportunities offered by letters from constituents. He was expert at tailoring his responses so that they expressed sentiments recipients would be pleased to hear and would appear to have been individually written by the

We've mentioned several times now that those running for high office tend to say whatever they think voters want to hear, whether or not the candidates actually intend to, or can, carry through and deliver the goods. During the 1992 campaign, Bill Clinton made quite a few promises that were popular with voters, although at least some of them were very likely to be impossible to deliver. He promised to cut the deficit within four years; reduce middle-class taxes; get Congress to pass genuine campaign finance reform; stop the use of federal funds to finance abortions; aid Haitian refugees and restore democratic government to that ill-fated country; integrate gays into the military; get the United Nations, with U.S. support, to do whatever is necessary, including perhaps the use of force, to stop the slaughter in Bosnia; and "have the bills ready the day after I'm inaugurated," so that we would have "the most productive 100-day period in modern history." So how did he do on these and his other campaign promises? How many did he seriously attempt to carry out? And what about his 1996 campaign promises?

senator himself.* Nowadays, this practice has been honed to the point that computer software is available to make letter composition almost automatic. (It isn't possible for members of Congress to write an individual reply to every letter received; they have to use standard replies classified by issue and position taken on the issue.) Here is the main part of Young's standard reply to antiabortion letter writers:

> I thought you would be pleased to know that I have strongly supported the position you take. I have been a co-sponsor of a resolution in the Senate proposing a Human Life Amendment since the Supreme Court issued its decision liberalizing abortion. . . .

But here is the sort of thing you got in reply to a pro-abortion letter:

> I appreciate hearing from you and receiving your views on this matter. . . .
> I agree with you that a woman should have a right to decide whether or not she wants an abortion.

All officeholders who want to win reelection have to do this sort of thing.

Incumbents also have an advantage when it comes to garnering media coverage via press conferences. President Roosevelt was perhaps the first American president to exploit this kind of image-building opportunity, but the technique was perfected by President Kennedy, who, unlike Roosevelt, had television at his beck and call. Since Kennedy's time, presidential news conferences have generally been scheduled so as to gain the president free exposure on evening TV news programs. (President Carter arranged the Begin-Sadat Camp David agreement between Israel and Egypt so that the three leaders would sign on the dotted line and congratulate each other on television programs planned to have large national and international audiences.) Presidents are

---

*His nearly record-breaking length of service in the Senate—from 1945 until his retirement in 1980—was often credited to his considerable ability to talk out of both sides of his mouth when answering letters from constituents. See the *Washington Monthly* (October 1979) article by Mark Feldstein for more details.

> *The fact that politicians cannot personally attend carefully to every constituent letter sometimes results in a bit of foot-in-mouth. In early 1997, when Amtrak planned to eliminate the train called the Texas Eagle from its schedule, Vice President Al Gore received many letters protesting this reduction in service; one of those letter writers received this letter in reply:*
>
> ---
>
> Thank you for your letter regarding the protection of the Texas Eagle. I share your view that the urgent problem of species extinction and the conservation of biological diversity should be addressed. . . . All animals and plants help make our natural surroundings more diverse and should be protected to ensure the preservation of a healthy environment. . . .

coached beforehand so that they have ready-made "answers" to all likely questions, and they rarely are forced into on-the-spot improvisations.

Of course, being a politician is not all sweetness and light, even for those who have managed to get elected. Being human, incumbents get into trouble now and then. Enter what columnist Richard Cohen referred to as the "totally insincere gesture."\* For example, during the 1988 presidential campaign, when the Democratic party vice presidential candidate, Texas Senator Lloyd Bentsen, resigned from three private clubs, two of which had no black members, it wasn't because of a change of heart on the issue of restricted clubs. It was just a totally insincere gesture. After losing the election, he promptly rejoined all three clubs.

## Recent Developments

The world does not stand still. New ways of doing things crop up now and then, mostly now these days.

Many years ago, virtually all political advertising was for candidates running for office. But with the advent of ballot initiatives and referendums—propositions put before voters for their direct decision—issue advertising entered the scene, and during the past few years it has become an extremely important kind of political advertising because voters in many states and localities now are regularly asked to decide all kinds of controversial issues. Interested parties now spend millions advertising their views on these measures. Philip Morris, for example, spent big bucks on a referendum measure that appeared to be antismoking but whose actual effect would have been to weaken existing antismoking legislation. (Unfortunately for Philip Morris, its originally concealed part in the campaign was revealed to the public, which then turned against the measure.) Another big change in political advertising stems from the increased ability of media experts to target specific audiences. This has enabled special interests to indirectly influence legislators by generating floods of letters and calls to their elected representatives. In 1993 and 1994, for instance, the health insurance industry spent millions on TV spots directed against the Clinton health plan (which was defeated). Seventeen

---

\*See the *Washington Post National Weekly*, December 4–10, 1989.

million dollars was spent on the "Harry and Louise" TV spots, which generated over 500,000 letters to members of Congress.

Some of the more important recent developments in political advertising are just vastly increased and improved versions of methods employed for some time now. Campaigning on television shows such as "Larry King Live" is a case in point. Politicians have come to understand that TV and radio talk shows can be used for free and very effective exposure. Ross Perot's 1992 campaign, for example, took off after his first appearance on the Larry King show (and fizzled out when he stubbed his toe on that show and then on a "60 Minutes" program.)

"Prefabricated" TV spots are another recent addition to the ad campaign arsenal. For example, in 1992, instead of spending $16,000 each on their TV spots,16 Democratic party candidates for state office in Connecticut spent about $1,250 each by developing a series of four generic spots that could be "personalized" so as to fit each candidate. Here is how *Campaigns and Elections* (January 1993) described the way it was done:

> The first 20 seconds of each ad featured a video segment on one of four topics chosen from focus group research: the environment, abortion, government spending, and jobs. The final 10 seconds of each spot showed a color slide of the specific candidate accompanied by a personal audio message to voters. . . .
>
> The first 20 seconds of the four videos was written and paid for by the Committee for a Democratic Majority, which then offered the spots as an in-kind contribution to each senatorial candidate.

A mere $16,000 for a 20- or 30-second spot, by the way, is a great bargain.

Another recent development, which hints perhaps at what the future on the "information superhighway" may be like, is the "interactive viewer opinion poll." One 1992 example is the CNN phone-in poll in which viewers were instructed, "If you think the economy is getting better, press one, then the pound sign. If you think the economy is getting weaker, press two and then the pound sign," and so on.

Still another recent development trades on the fact that whenever a legislative body considers a measure, some interests will be harmed and others served. So instead of employing mass ad campaigns on TV, PR experts influence legislation by direct mail-

---

*Chevron's "People Do" ad campaign, in which Chevron is portrayed as a friend of the environment, is perhaps the most successful of a growing genre of identification advertisements. Each Chevron ad describes some kind of environmental project. One, for example, was about their construction of wooden platforms on high-voltage wires to shield eagles from electrocution, ending with the question, "Do people really reach that high to protect a natural wonder? People Do" (displayed under the Chevron logo).*

*One point of these ads is to get environmentally conscious motorists to identify with Chevron and to switch to that brand of gasoline. Another point is to indirectly influence legislation by picturing Chevron, and the oil industry in general, as environmentally sound, thus blunting criticism based on the industry's actual environmental record, which is very poor.*

*Well, then, are these completely misleading ads effective? Hint: Chevron has been running this series of ads for ten years now.*

Courtesy *Indianapolis News*.

ings to those affected by proposed laws, counting on those contacted to lobby elected officials. Although always used in one way or another, modern methods for selecting just the right group to contact (computer files, etc.) have made this a favorite in the 1990s. Here is an example (taken from *The Washington Monthly*, September 1996):

> In 1990, auto industry lobbyists mounted a deceitful but effective grassroots campaign against stiffer gasoline mileage standards. The companies claimed that requiring them to increase the average miles per gallon of their products would force them to build nothing but small cars. Groups ranging from nuns to police deluged their representatives with protests.

The success of this ad rested with the advertiser's ability to target just those likely to drive large, gas-guzzling automobiles. (Notice that "grassroots" here refers to campaigns directed by powerful economic interests.)

The great increase in negative telephone advertising that has occurred in the past few years is one of the more unfortunate recent developments in political advertising. The device itself is old, perhaps first being used on a large scale in 1946 when Nixon first ran for Congress. A typical call in that telephone campaign went like this: "This is a friend of yours, but I can't tell you who I am. Did you know that Jerry Voorhis [Nixon's incumbent opponent] is a communist?" (Click.) Today's voters might be inclined to see that as a bit too dirty, so now the big item is "push polling," telephone calls disguised as opinion research, in which negative "information" about opposing candidates is revealed. Bob Dole's campaign team, for example, used push polling in the 1996 Iowa primaries to shoot down the candidacy of Iowa front runner Steve Forbes.*

---

*For more on push polling, see "When Push Comes to Poll," by Larry J. Sabato and Glenn R. Simpson, *Washington Monthly*, June 1996. The article also discusses push polling employed by, among others, Governor Lawton Chiles, Democrat, Florida; and Oliver North, Republican, Virginia.

The latest development in political advertising, as in advertising in general, results from the dramatic increase in those who regularly "surf the Net." During the 1996 presidential campaign, all candidates had Web sites dispensing "information" to Web browsers. The tremendous increase in the number of people who have access to computers also has provided political advertisers with a cheap, quick way to marshal loyal troops for rallies and to raise money, generate talk show callers, and so on. Telephone solicitations and direct mailing are much more expensive and time consuming than e-mail.

The upshot of all the new ways to advertise is that the 30-second TV spots that played the major role in elections to high office during the previous 30 years or so have now become just one of many devices for influencing the electorate (although still the most important). In 1996, over 100 million Americans tuned in to at least one presidential debate, and at least that many heard candidates give their spiels on TV talk shows. What this electronic age has in store for us next is an interesting and exceedingly important question to which politicians and their media masters would very much like to know the answer.

## Summary of Chapter 10

1. Most ads can be divided into two groups. *Promise ads* promise to satisfy desires or allay fears. *Example*: Use Old Spice deodorant and get rid of body odor. *Identification ads* sell the product by getting us to identify with the product. *Example*: The Virginia Slims cigarette ads, "You've come a long way, baby," tailored to specific audiences.

2. Although ads provide us with useful information about products, often in an entertaining way, they also are designed to manipulate masses of people via sophisticated ploys.
   a. They invite us to reason fallaciously. *Example*: Appeals to the authority of famous figures such as Ray Charles.
   b. They employ repetitive slogans and meaningless jargon: *Example*: "Nike: Just do it."
   c. They play on our weaknesses, prejudices, and fears. *Example*: The "ring around the collar" TV commercials.
   d. They use sneaky rhetoric, including fine-print disclaimers and weasel words. *Examples*: Using the word *free* when the product isn't free; weasely expressions like "fights bad breath."
   e. They play on our patriotism, loyalty, and identification with members of our own group. *Example*: The Archer Daniels Midland ad that begins with a video of President Kennedy delivering his famous line, "Ask not what your country can do for you but what you can do for your country."

3. Old marketing techniques have been improved with new wrinkles, including new qualitative and quantitative procedures. *Example*: The Tennessee department store direct-mail ads based on in-store records of specific customer purchases.
   What the future holds is, of course, uncertain. *Example*: Will the Internet become a big marketplace player in which customers can see ads and immediately buy products with a few mouse clicks?

4. Political candidates and issues are sold in pretty much the same way as any other products.
   a. In the age of television, elections are won or lost via exposure on the tube, whether in debates, paid 30-second TV spots, press conferences, or whatever. And it is *image*, not rationality, that generally wins in this arena. *Examples*: The Daisy/Girl TV spot that portrayed Barry Goldwater as too trigger happy to be trusted with the nuclear bomb button; Dukakis's "wimpy" response to Bernard Shaw's challenging question.

      In addition to exposure on television, some of the fringe benefits of office provide opportunities for elected officials to gain added exposure with voters. *Example*: Campaigning via franked mailings.

      When candidates are in trouble, there are ways in which they can sometimes beat the rap, one being by making a "totally insincere gesture." *Example*: Senator Bentsen resigning from private clubs that discriminated against blacks and rejoining them after the election.

      It also should be noted that the campaign rhetoric of candidates running for high office generally is guided by the results of polls. It's always safer to tell voters what they want to hear, not what candidates intend to do if elected. That is why we can expect candidates to lie when necessary to curry the favor of voters. (But savvy voters still can learn from political rhetoric by reading between the lines so as to figure out what candidates are likely to do if elected.)
   b. Politicians in a democracy "campaign" virtually all of the time, not just when actually running for office. They always have to be intent on projecting the right *image* to the voters, and once in office, they have several standard ways of doing this. One is by using their franking privilege to curry the favor of their constituents; another is by performing the ceremonial duties of their office well; still another is by holding press conferences.
   c. Views on issues now are advertised just like candidates. The point is to influence voter preferences and thus legislation that is before Congress or state or local legislatures. *Examples*: Philip Morris's promotion of a refendum that would weaken existing antismoking laws; the health insurance industry's multimillion-dollar ad campaign against President Clinton's health plan.
   d. The made-to-order TV spots that dominated campaigning during the past 30 years or so have received serious competition recently from TV talk shows that provide candidates with free exposure to mass audiences; prefabricated TV spots that save candidates tons of money; and interactive telephone polling of television audiences (with additional electronic campaigning marvels in the wings).

## EXERCISE 10-5

Write two letters to one of your senators or representatives in Washington, D.C., in one taking a short, strong stand on an issue of importance to you, in the other taking an equally strong but different stand (completely opposite, if possible) on the same issue. Compare the two replies that you get. (Remember that you can't expect instantaneous replies.) Send each letter from a different address and use different names (because some members of Congress keep track on computers).

## EXERCISE 10-6

These days, the mass media (in particular, newspapers and magazines) spend a modest amount of time and effort covering and evaluating the political advertisements, especially TV spots, of candidates for high office. Look into some of this reporting and then (1) present and explain the content of at least two such advertisements for candidates in your state or locality, and (2) evaluate the two ads for accuracy and cogency. (Did they appeal chiefly to reason, or to the gut?)

## EXERCISE 10-7

Recall Len Deighton's remark quoted on page 229 about straight teeth and blow-dried hair and consider what Andy Rooney had to say in his syndicated column (August 5, 1996) about what he called a candidate's "X-Factor"—what makes a person likeable. Rooney noted that Eisenhower, Kennedy, and Reagan had it, whereas Johnson, Nixon, and Bush did not, and speculated that if Dole lost the 1996 election, it wouldn't be "because of any one stand he took on an issue. The loser will be the one who, for some unfathomable reason, appears least attractive [he meant in the sense of being likeable] to the American public. Never mind the issues."

Rooney meant to imply that the X-Factor goes much deeper than what can be manipulated by makeup artists. Do you agree? Is Rooney right that being liked by voters is frequently more important than differences over issues or past records in determining who wins elections? Do you think personality was crucial in the victory of Bill Clinton over Bob Dole in 1996? Defend your opinions.

## EXERCISE 10-8

Here is an excerpt from a syndicated political column by William Pfaff that appeared in newspapers around the country in March 1990:

### The Threat of Demagogic Oligarchy

Chicago—**Pressure is mounting** for campaign reform in American politics. Campaigning in cities like Chicago has always been rough, but now character assassination has become the privileged instrument of political ambition in national as well as local politics, excluding virtually all serious debate on issues. . . .

We are in fact witnessing the decline of American democracy towards a form of demagogic oligarchy. Individuals and groups with access to the vast sums now essential in American politics manipulate to their electoral advantage powerful images, some latently violent, some xenophobic.

. . . What prompts fear about what is happening in the United States is the general substitution of irrelevant emotional appeals for debate. More than half the population now fails to vote in national elections and there is a clear trend towards political alienation among those who do vote. Combine that with the mounting rates of illiteracy and general ignorance in the society and the substitution of manipulative oligarchy for representative democracy comes steadily closer.

For once there is a simple solution. It is possible, at a stroke, to solve the campaign money problem and deal a severe blow to demagogic image-manipulation. This solution is to prohibit political advertisements on television and radio.

American political campaigns now are all but totally dominated by broadcast political advertising. The need to purchase time is responsible for the huge inflation of campaign costs in recent times. More than $250 million was spent on campaigns in the presidential year of 1988. Half a billion in current dollars will be spent during House and Senate campaigns in the 1990s. [The figures for 1992, 1994, and 1996 were much higher than for 1988 and 1990.]

The need for money to pay for advertising has made the single-issue political action committee the most powerful actor in American politics. It has made it all but impossible for an incumbent congressman or senator successfully to be challenged: the incumbent gets the PAC money because he can deliver what the PAC wants. Support for a challenger is speculation.

. . . No other serious democracy tolerates this. Virtually nowhere else is paid campaign advertising permitted. Ours is a mad system, perversely American, jeopardizing democracy itself. Banning advertising will hurt only the broadcasters. They are a powerful lobby, and one that politicians rightly fear, but even broadcasters not obsessed with their private interest must recognize the gravity of the situation.*

1. Summarize the part of Pfaff's column that explains his view as to what the problem is.

2. State his proposal to solve this problem in your own words.

3. State whether you agree or disagree with him about there being the problem that he describes. Explain.

4. Critically evaluate his solution.

---

Drawing by David Levine. Copyright © 1975 NYREV, Inc.
Reprinted by permission from *The New York Review of Books.*

*In this drawing, David Levine pictures the television-viewing audience as contented sheep. Do you agree?*

When covering the Capitol, the first
thing to remember is that every government is run by liars.
                    — I. F. Stone

Freedom of the press is guaranteed
only to those who own one.
                    — A. J. Liebling

Has any reader found perfect accuracy
in the newspaper account of any
event of which he himself had inside
knowledge?
            — Edward Verrall Lucas

Journalists separate the wheat from the
chaff . . . and then print the chaff.
                — Adlai Stevenson

I really look with commiseration over
the great body of my fellow citizens
who, reading newspapers, live and die
in the belief that they have known
something of what has been passing in
the world during their time.
                    — Harry S Truman

The headline of the Daily News today
reads BRUNETTE STABBED TO
DEATH. Underneath in lower case letters "6000 Killed in Iranian Earth-
quake." I wonder what color hair
they had.
                — Abbie Hoffman

*Chapter*

# 11

# MANAGING THE NEWS

The good news about the news is that there is more and better information available
concerning goings on in the world today than ever before in history. The bad news about
the news is that not all of the more is better. The trick is to know how to separate the
wheat from the chaff (and, thinking of the remark, above, by Adlai Stevenson, concentrating on the wheat).

## 1. THE MEDIA AND THE POWER OF MONEY

In France, the expression is "Cherchez la femme" (find the woman). In America, at
any rate, and maybe in France also, a more apt expression would be "follow the money."

## The Power of the People

The chief sources of news for most people these days are the mass media—ABC, *Newsweek* magazine, the *Chicago Tribune*, and their cohorts. And the one overriding fact about these news sources is that they are *businesses*. They exist to make *money*. They sell a *product* and we *buy* it. Or we don't, in which case they go out of business.

This means that we, the viewers of television programs, listeners to the radio, and readers of newspapers and magazines, have the most important say as to what sorts of news stories are reported in the mass media and how they are presented.

That is why, for instance, the mass media so often play up relatively unimportant events while slighting more important ones—most people tend to be more interested in certain kinds of relatively trivial goings on than in extremely important events.

*Item*: During the week in which the Soviet Union disintegrated and the Ukraine and other parts of the defunct Soviet Union declared a new union, TV news featured the William Kennedy Smith Florida rape trial.

Large audiences also tend to be quite provincial, so the mass media concentrate on national affairs and home-grown celebrities.

*Item*: Coverage of the 1996 Olympic Games in the United States featured American athletes such as Michael Johnson while slighting those of other countries. (For more on Olympic Games coverage, see the box on page 247 and the cartoon on page 248.)

---

### O. J. or President Clinton?

*On Tuesday evening, February 4, 1997, TV newsrooms around the country were faced with an ongoing crisis of major proportions: President Clinton's State of the Union address was on a "collision course" with announcement of the verdict in the second (civil) O. J. Simpson trial. What should be done if the verdict is announced before the president finishes his speech? And what about coverage of the drama being played out outside of the Los Angeles courtroom while the verdict was being awaited?*

*In San Francisco, CBS's KPIX solved the second problem in a way typical of stations around the country: it split its screen for the first 20 minutes of Clinton's speech and assured its audience after that that the jury's decision would be broadcast on KPIX "as soon as it happens." As it turned out, the verdict announcement coincided almost exactly with the end of Clinton's (as usual) overly long address; KPIX had to cut off only the last few words of the president's speech. Said the station's news director, Al Corral, "You go by your gut. I think viewers found the Simpson verdict more interesting. I know the State of the Union [address] is important. But traditionally, the overnights [TV ratings] on the State of the Union Address show that people aren't watching it."*

*Other TV outlets solved the problem in different ways, some going with the president all the way, but with occasional Simpson updates in a "silent crawl" at the bottom of their picture.*

*Interestingly, NBC's Tim Russert claims that Clinton's speech was originally to have been delivered on Wednesday, but was moved up to Tuesday so as not to compete with CBS's broadcast of the Miss USA beauty pageant. Naturally.*

*Calvin and Hobbes* by Bill Watterson. Copyright 1995 Universal Press Syndicate.
Reprinted with permission.

Mass audiences are more interested in light-hearted material, human interest stories, and fantasy than in hardheaded reality.

*Item*: The TV time given over to the O. J. Simpson trial and immediate aftermath was far greater than that given to all reports about the economy. Lance Ito may well have become the best-known jurist in American history. (Note, by the way, novelist E. L. Doctorow's remark that "The press, like the public, has room in its brain for only one story at a time.")

As mentioned in Chapter 6, large numbers of people are superstitious or believe in pseudosciences of one kind or another, and we all are wishful thinkers to one degree or another. That is why most prime-time TV programs are sitcoms and why TV features so many more pseudoscience programs than they do those concerning science.

*Item*: The February 1996 NBC program called "The Mysterious Origins of Man," hosted by the noted movie-star-cum-scientist Charlton Heston, in which absurd, even hilarious claims were made: for instance, that the human species is 60 million years old and did not evolve from earlier primates (the whole Darwinian theory of evolution was denied); frozen mammoths were explained by an almost instantaneous 2,000-mile continental shift supposed to have taken place about 12,000 years ago; and a South American civilization that was connected to ancient Egypt and the "lost continent of Atlantis" was said to have existed 17,000 years ago. (This very successful program was rebroadcast in June 1996. NBC is probably the worst offender of all TV networks when it comes to pseudoscientific and other fantasy junk programs.)

---

## News as Entertainment

In the 1980s, media mogul Rupert Murdoch (Fox TV network, N.Y. *Post*, *The London Times*, etc.), when criticized for buying the rights to the phony "Hitler Diaries," replied, "After all, we are in the entertainment business." More recently, Murdock's (London) *Sun* printed excerpts from the fake "Lady Di" (then Princess Diana Spenser) sex tapes. Murdock also is the publisher of perhaps the most ridiculous of the checkout counter tabloids.

And what is the reward for running so many "entertainment news" items? Murdock's media empire is one of the largest and most successful in the world. Well-packaged junk always outsells quality in the mass media.

*Revealing fact*: There is a science-fiction channel on some cable systems but no science channel.

The mass media also take account of the extremely short attention spans of mass audiences.

*Item*: Shorter and shorter "sound bites" have become the mainstay of all network daily news programs. In 1968, sound bites lasted a mere 40 seconds on average. By 1988, they had shrunk to an average of 10 seconds. Nothing, absolutely nothing, of any consequence can be dealt with in 40 seconds, much less 10. (On PBS, the news is presented in modestly larger and more sophisticated chunks, but the PBS audience is minuscule compared to that of the major networks. Similar remarks apply to NPR—National Public Radio.)

It is difficult for the mass media to tailor its material to its audience because mass audiences tend to be so diverse. News sources catering to smaller audiences are better able to take account of audience preferences and interests.

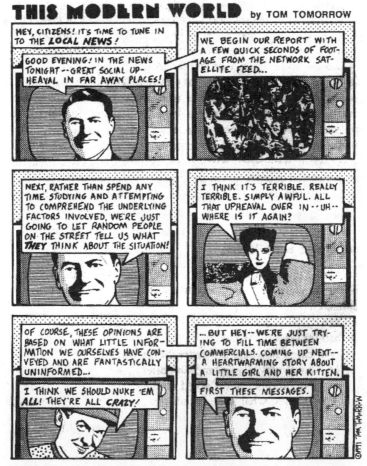

*This Modern World* by Tom Tomorrow. Copyright 1991. Reprinted by permission.

*Exaggeration used to make a point.*

*Anyone who wants to understand why television programs, including news programs, are as they are these days should carefully consider how NBC covered the 1996 Olympic Games held in Atlanta, Georgia. Here are a few examples:*

1. Over five minutes of air time were spent telling viewers about the American long-jump competitors, in particular, about how this was to be the last competition for "King Carl" Lewis. Less time was spent on the jumps themselves. Similar background "color" was provided about selected athletes in most of the events that NBC covered. For example, over five minutes was spent on a "human interest" story about the comeback of 800-meter competitor, Ana Quirot, who was very seriously burned 3 years before while 7 months pregnant (she lost the baby and spent 3 months in a hospital). Very little background information was provided about other competitors. (The 800-meter run itself, won by Russian Svetlana Masterkova, for whom no background information was provided, took just under two minutes of air time.)
2. Much more air time was given over to women's gymnastic competitions than to men's and women's track and field events combined. Ditto for women's swimming and diving. (The ancient Greek Olympic games were exclusively men's track and field competitions, as were the first modern Olympics, held in Athens in 1896.)
3. The men's 10,000-meter run final, won by the great Haile Gebrselassie of Ethiopia—Kenyan and Morrocan runners came in second and third—was simply passed over. (There were no Americans in that race, and it takes thousands of sound bites of time to complete.)
4. The shooting competitions, part of the Olympic program for over 50 years, were ignored.
5. In their "Olympic moments" finale, NBC gave us no shots of athletes doing great things on the track, in the ring, or in the water, but rather replays of moments of TRIUMPH—celebrations of VICTORY by gold medal winners. After the closing ceremony, NBC put on a totally nonsport bash.

*So why did NBC choose to present the games in this way? Here are excerpts from an article in* The New Yorker *that explain the philosophy behind NBC's fabulously financially successful coverage of the games:*

NBC executives . . . told [David Remnick, the article's author] . . . that their success was based on a scientific campaign to shape their broadcasts to a feminine sensibility. Bob Costas, the network's puckish anchor for the Games, said that in non-Olympic years the ratings for sports like track and swimming "can be detected only with a microscope." But by giving the audience a sense of occasion and a rooting interest in the Games, by establishing in the viewer a sense of empathy for an athlete and his or her trials (defeats, illness, accidents, etc.), the network would cause women, especially, to flock to the screen. (Men, being men, would be there already . . . .) The Olympic audience . . . has been fifty per cent women, thirty-five per cent men, and fifteen per cent children and teen-agers of both sexes. . . .

The World According to Rand-McNally Atlas...

The World According to NBC Olympic Coverage...

Bill Schorr, reprinted by permission of
United Feature Syndicate, Inc.

*Item*: The Black Press of America's "Man of the Year" for 1995 was Minister Louis L. Farrakhan. (See *Editor & Publisher*, February 24, 1996.)

Although the tastes and opinions of the people as a whole count the most in shaping news reporting, organized groups of people have clout out of all proportion to their numbers, just as an army has much greater power than a mob of similar size.

*Item*: In response to a letter-writing campaign directed by the National Rifle Association, all but one advertiser withdrew support from CBS's documentary "The Guns of August," which graphically portrayed the terrible carnage in World War I.

## The Power of Advertisers

The media are beholden not just to the people, organized or otherwise, but also to advertisers. Advertising revenue is the most important source of income for virtually all newspapers and magazines and also the principal source of funds available to television stations and TV networks. Since money translates into power, the media must cater to the interests of advertisers as well as to those of the general public. Commenting on this fact years ago, H. G. Wells, in his classic *Outline of History*, remarked:

> [T]hose fathers of America thought also that they had but to leave the Press free, and everyone would live in the light. They did not realize that a free press could develop a sort of constitutional venality due to its relations with advertisers, and that large newspaper proprietors could become buccaneers of opinion and insensate wreckers of good beginnings.

Wells would not be a bit surprised at the way things have gone on the tube.

*Item*: After Proctor & Gamble announced that it would withdraw all of its advertising from any TV station that ran a 30-second spot (produced by Neighbor to Neighbor, a grassroots political group) that publicized a boycott of Salvadorean coffee in general and P&G's Folgers brand in particular, only 2 of 30 local TV stations approached to run the spot were willing to do so. When television stations lose P&G advertising revenue, they fritter away millions of dollars in income.

## The Power of Government

Government has the right and often the power to regulate business activity. It thus can harass a news agency by being strict about the rules it sets up (it usually isn't) and the licenses it requires. The mere threat of government action has a "chilling" effect on the media.

*Item*: In April 1987, the Federal Communications Commission threatened to ask the Justice Department to consider criminal prosecution of station KPFK (a nonprofit Los Angeles FM station) for airing an allegedly obscene play about AIDS and gay love. Many other stations got the hint and decided to go easy on the topic of gays.

The United States Constitution guarantees freedom of the press as one of several freedoms necessary to make representative government function. But governments occasionally censor certain kinds of material anyway, perhaps the prime example being material alleged to be pornographic. At various times the courts have ruled that freedom of the press does not cover this kind of material.

Similarly, courts have upheld the federal government's right to forbid the publication of classified material—items, it is said, that need to be kept secret for "security reasons." In practice, this means that the federal government is able to keep all sorts of chicanery

---

*We the people, in our role as jurors in court trials, have been cooperating of late in the indirect censorship of the mass media by awarding increasingly large awards in libel suits, thus reducing our own access to news and opinion. These million-dollar awards have had a serious "chilling effect" on news reporting:* *

In *Sprague vs. Walter* (1990), the jury awarded $34 million, including $31.5 million in punitive damages, against the *Philadelphia Inquirer* for a 1973 (!) story that questioned a local prosecutor's handling of a homicide case.

*It used to be that large awards of this kind, especially to politicians and other public figures, were routinely overturned or dramatically reduced on appeal to higher courts, but recently the United States Supreme Court has refused to do so in several cases.*

*These cases reflect a conflict of two values, one being the right of citizens not to be unfairly defamed by the media, the other being the need of the people to know what is going on.*

*See Lee Levine and David L. Perry, "No way to celebrate," *Columbia Journalism Review* (July/August 1990).

*This Modern World* by Tom Tomorrow. Copyright 1991. Reprinted by permission.

secret simply by claiming that news stories about them would harm national security. (The "Freedom of Information" Act that grants individuals the right to see their own FBI dossiers sometimes is adhered to and sometimes isn't. Yes, the FBI does keep such files on lots of people who have never been charged with a crime.)

The federal government also has put a chill on freedom of the press via extremely liberal court interpretations of libel laws and by failing to protect the right of correspondents to keep their sources secret. Here is part of a *Columbia Journalism Review (CJR)* story (May/June 1992) about a very important case that has had a definitely chilling effect on media reporting:

> In June 1990, the Supreme Court ruled that a sports columnist's negative and factually challenged portrayal of a high school coach named Milkovich was not protected—even though it ran in the author's regular column. *Milkovich* was seen as exposing to new libel risk editorials, reviews, commentaries, and columns—areas widely thought to enjoy near-absolute protection under the First Amendment. . . .
>
> Andy Rooney was one of the first "victims." The CBS commentator had been sued for grousing that a product he had used on his windshield "didn't work." A pre-*Milkovich* court had found Rooney's grousing to be opinion, but on appeal, a post-*Milkovich* court decided that *Milkovich* had changed the standard, and ruled that Rooney's words were now an assertion of fact.

It's true that subsequent court rulings called into question the range of the *Milkovich* ruling, and probably (hopefully) true that sooner or later the ruling will be overturned. But meanwhile, media people have had a few more wings clipped. ("Did you notice the use of the euphemism "factually challenged" in the *CJR* account?)

Government officials also can, and do, manipulate the news by playing favorites among reporters, leaking only to those news people who play ball in return. Since leaks are such a large source of media information (see the discussion of news-gathering practices a few pages forward), reporters have to think twice before crossing their government informants. Similarly, reporters have to be careful in press conferences not to ask embarrassing follow-up questions; those who are too brash don't get called on in future.

Although many items leaked to the media are factually correct, the fact that their sources can be concealed gives government officials a good deal of power. They can rig stories to serve their own interest without being accountable.

*Item*: As reported in an *Extra! Update* (April 1995), "A Feb. 11 *New York Times* report from Mexico by Tim Golden was loaded with anonymous sources: 'government officials said,' 'one official said,' '. . . according to one official, . . .' " *Extra!*'s comment: "The article was about the alleged 'unmasking' of Zapatista leader Commander Marcos; how about unmasking the *New York Times*' sources?"

Of course, no U.S. government agencies have censoring powers that are anywhere near those regularly exercised in quite a few foreign countries. In China, Burma, Liberia, and many other countries, newspapers rarely are allowed to criticize governmental policies or actions. In some nations, reporters often are threatened, even with death, making the "news" from these places extremely unreliable. Reporters in Turkey, for example, have been subject to a reign of terror that is bound to intimidate all but the hardiest—one might say foolhardiest—of investigators. The very real threat of being murdered cannot just be sloughed off, and those who forge ahead anyway run the risk of ending up as did Ugur Mumcu, described in a *Columbia Journalism Review* (May/June 1993) item as "a gritty veteran investigative reporter . . . [for] one of Turkey's most respected newspapers," known "for his reports on Kurdish separatists, drug smuggling, and the rise of Islamic fundamentalism in Turkey, . . . killed this past January [1992] by a car bomb."

## The Power of the Media

The media are not simply beholden to the three powerful groups just discussed. They themselves are a genuinely separate power faction. Investigative reporters can, and sometimes do, unearth governmental chicanery as well as stories not in the best interests of advertisers, although we have gone to some pains to show why they often hesitate.

[The] journalist usually has a few hours to write and the perspective of last week. Why then expect the poor fellow to revise the history of the world?
— Lewis H. Lapham (editor of *Harper's*)

This doesn't mean that the media constitute a monolithic, organized group, but rather, that individual mass media organizations have a certain amount of power and that, taken as a whole, the mass media have great power. Cases such as the *Washington Post* Watergate exposés, which set in motion events that drove Richard Nixon from office, are well known. But plenty of less striking examples could be cited. With all of their shortcomings, the media are our first, and best, line of defense against government gone wrong and against the very advertising power that they themselves so often have to knuckle under to.

Of course, one media giant's power has to compete with that of the others. CBS's power to determine what will be shown on its network programs is held in check by the identical power wielded by NBC, ABC, CNN, and the rest of its competitors, not to mention competitors in the print media, just as the power of one politician may be reduced by the power of others, and by the power of the media. *Vive le competition!*

## The Power of Big Business

The days are long gone when most business in countries like the United States was conducted by individuals or small organizations. "Ma and pa" stores have given way to Walmarts and Krogers. Individual doctors hanging out their shingles have been replaced by group practices and HMOs. Most family farms have been replaced by huge agribusinesses. These days, virtually all industries are controlled by large corporations, in particular, by huge multinational conglomerates. Large corporations, individually and collectively, thus have great power, which they exercise almost exclusively in the interests of maximizing profits.

Corporate power affects the dissemination of news in two ways: first, by getting the viewpoints of big business reported favorably in the mass media and, second, by preventing conflicting viewpoints from being reported or stressed. This censoring power of large corporations stems in part from their power as advertisers (a point already discussed); large corporations are by far the largest advertisers in the mass media. But it also stems from the power money has in the political arena (a point to be discussed later). When the mass media cooperate with political power, they thus indirectly also cooperate with large corporate interests. Further, the mass media themselves have become controlled in large part by very large media conglomerates, which often are parts of even larger corporate structures (a point also to be discussed shortly). In general, the interests of media conglomerates coincide with those of other large businesses—for example, in favoring lower wages for on-the-line employees—so that the mass media tend to have a built-in bias in favor of big business.

The result is that news and opinion in the mass media tend to be skewed strongly to the interests of the rich rather than ordinary citizens or the poor. Of course, ordinary

---

*Have you ever noticed that the heads of labor unions frequently are referred to as "union bosses" but that expressions like "big business bosses" or "the boss of XYZ corporation" are almost never used in the mass media? Big business bosses go under nice labels like "CEO" and "President."*

people have great power in determining how the mass media portray the world—they can switch channels or otherwise tune out. They also can go to non-mass media news and opinion sources (yes, these will be discussed shortly). But most people do not do so, one reason being that the average person does not understand how the news is slanted in the interests of the upper class.* (Another reason, of course, is that large numbers of people, in particular, those in the lower half of the economic pecking order, tend to be indifferent about the crucial details concerning the important events that shape the economic and political arenas, concentrating their attention on more immediate personal concerns.)

*Item*: Most big city dailies have "business" sections that report goings on of large corporations and in the various financial markets—almost exclusively from the point of view of investors and other large money interests. But no daily newspapers have labor sections or report on business from the point of view of individual workers or, except on occasion, organized labor. Similarly, there are several business news programs on TV but no labor programs or programs regularly reporting from the point of view of ordinary workers.

This bias of the mass media is regularly commented on, with examples, in *Extra!* magazine, which has a feature called "Labor Media Watch." Its September/October 1996 Labor Media Watch, for example, dealt with the mass media's almost complete neglect of the meeting of some of the country's largest labor unions in June 1996 at which a new political party was formed—the first labor party in the United States since 1924. According to *Extra!*, neither of the two most influential newspapers in the nation, the *New York Times* and the *Washington Post*, covered the event, nor did network TV news programs mention it. Compare that lack of coverage with the media attention given to Ross Perot's runs for office in 1992 and 1996. Did you know that a national labor political party had been formed? (Anyone interested in the topic of media coverage of labor should take a look at the January/February 1996 issue of *Extra!*.)

*Item*: The media tell viewers about how Social Security payments and the nation's health expenses (in particular, for Medicare) need to be reduced if financial disasters lurking down the road are to be averted. But they don't often delve deeply into the extremely bloated military budgets that have hardly been reduced since the end of the Cold War (when there was supposed to be a drastic reduction in military spending). The rich don't depend on Social Security payments and can afford first-rate medical insurance policies that provide them with the kinds of coverage HMO policies don't allow.

It's also interesting that so much more attention is given to welfare for the poor than to welfare for the rich, yet government handouts and tax breaks for the rich total much more than do those granted to the poor. (Note that handouts to the rich rarely are referred to as "welfare" or as "handouts" in the mass media.) Here are a just a few examples of welfare designed primarily for the rich:

---

*The idea is widespread in America that there are no classes in the land of the free and the home of the brave. The truth in this idea is that in every generation some individuals move from lower into higher economic classes, even occasionally into the highest. The falsehood in this idea is that most of those born into rich families remain rich and most of those born into average- or lower-income households never become rich. Class membership in large industrial democracies is not carved in stone in the way it was in the monarchies of old, but this surely does not mean that there are any truly classless societies on this planet, other than in tiny hunting-and-gathering groups.

- Agribusinesses (most farms these days are run by large corporations) typically receive about $15–20 billion a year in subsidies and through the benefits of price-support programs, import restrictions, production and marketing programs, and special rates on grazing land and water. The ethanol subsidy alone came to $625 million in 1995 ($325 million to Archer Daniels Midland (ADM), sometimes called the welfare "king").

- Mining subsidies and programs cost the federal government untold billions every year. For example, an 1872 law, still on the books, requires the federal government to sell the rights to mine on federal land (it's called "patenting" mineral rights) at bargain basement prices; in one instance, the government signed away land containing an estimated $68 million in gold to a Canadian company for $540.

- Oil and many minerals are covered by depletion allowances, the idea being that extracting them from the ground depletes a company's reserves, for which they should be compensated (yes, it's just as ridiculous as it sounds). The oil depletion allowance alone comes to about $2.4 billion per year.

- There are all sorts of other subsidies, loopholes in laws, tax credits, and the like, whose exact value, again, is hard to calculate but which run into the billions every year. Examples are the synfuel (synthetic fuels) tax credit ($1.2 billion); timber subsidies (over $400 million); and insurance loopholes (over $7 billion—one, called "COLI," alone saves companies about $1.5 billion a year).

- Some of the largest giveaways are accomplished via tax breaks. Many of these also are available to the middle class but in much smaller amounts (the higher on the economic ladder, the greater the benefit). Some examples are accelerated depre-

---

*Although it's true that the media tend to skimp on the public interest when reporting about the business world, there are exceptions, in particular, when it can be presumed that there will be large-scale interest in a story. Here, for example, is an excerpt from a rather good item (San Francisco Chronicle, February 21, 1996) on an interesting way in which large banks have been nickel-and-diming depositors to swell profit margins:*

---

Banks are generating record profits and using excess cash to buy out competitors and repurchase their own shares. But don't expect a price break on your checking account. Fees imposed by the nation's top 250 banks and savings and loans have gone up more than 50 percent since 1990—or more than twice the inflation rate, according to the March issue of *Consumer Reports*. In addition, the minimum balance needed to avoid monthly fees is now 40 percent higher than in 1994.

---

*The article also mentioned another interesting recent bank ploy: advertising no-minimum, free checking accounts that, it turns out, charge a $5 fee during any month in which you use bank teller services for a transaction that could have been done via ATM machines. (The point, of course, is to replace employees with machines—machines don't earn salaries.)*

ciation (greater than true depreciation) of equipment, buildings, etc. (about $35 billion); tax deductions for interest on home loans ($58 billion); and what amounts to legal tax cheating allowed to corporations doing business both inside and outside of the U.S. ($12 billion)—for example, by means of "transfer pricing."

- But the biggest giveaway to the rich is via governmental waste and fraud that directly benefit primarily the rich. This waste occurs at every level of government, but the federal government's waste alone tops all the others combined. The most wasteful department of government is the military (interesting because virtually everyone agrees that we need a strong military defense), including contract overpayments and the procurement of unneeded equipment (often not even requested by the military), such as MILSTAR, more B-2 bombers, and so on).*

The point of all this, lest it be drowned in the details, is that the mass media spend relatively little time on welfare for the rich while regularly running feature stories on how welfare for the poor needs to be cut and on how Social Security and Medicare expenses need to be curtailed, without pointing out how the federal budget could easily be balanced without cutting any of these programs simply by cutting pork for the rich. And this point, of course, is made as part of the general topic of the power of big business to influence how the news is presented by the mass media.

## Power Tends to Cooperate with Power

Although the interests of big business and government often coincide with those of the media, sometimes they do not. Scandals may sell newspapers and increase TV news audiences, but they also tend to sink political careers. What is bad for Microsoft may be good for NBC. (But see the section at the end of this chapter on recent trends!)

In a majority of cases, however, it's better for the various power factions to cooperate rather than to fight. That is why, for instance, reporters covering the White House quickly learn which sorts of questions can be asked at presidential press conferences, how far follow-up queries can go, what sorts of editorial comments they can make in news reports, and the like. Journalists who don't play the game, who persist in challenging the standard self-serving replies to their questions, don't get called upon in future. Columnists who tear into an administration in Washington with a great deal of gusto are less likely to be the recipients of leaks or other tidbits.

When the interests of politicians and big business moguls coincide with those of the masses, coverage of interesting or important events will be automatic, perhaps even large-scale.

---

*Overpayments are one kind of waste that is occasionally featured in the media, because TV viewers easily comprehend that something is wrong when a hammer costs $435 or a toilet seat goes for $640. In addition, "60 Minutes" and some other TV shows have (very) occasionally run programs on the overpurchase of military items that gather dust and rust in huge military storehouses, benefitting the corporations from which they were purchased without increasing military security. Many of the figures and other items cited here were taken from *Take the Rich Off Welfare* by Mark Zepezauer and Arthur Nauman (Tucson, Ariz., Odonian Press, 1996), a book that contains an excellent list of information sources on the welfare topic. (We've omitted discussion here of the capital gains tax break [about $35 billion] so as to avoid controversies concerning its alleged offsetting benefits.)

*Example*: Every nook and cranny of the recent Gulf War was covered, *ad infinitum*, starting on day one—catering to the interest that masses of people were bound to have in this event. (An ongoing event that is newsworthy is the dream of everyone in the news business.)

But when there is doubt as to how people will respond or how one or another power faction's feathers may be ruffled, the media like to test the waters before taking the plunge. If large numbers of people are interested (and not offended!), additional coverage will be in order. Elected officials will sound off and the media will report their statements. How far this process will go, of course, depends on the degree of interest aroused. When interest lags, stories are forgotten or perhaps relegated to back pages.

*Example*: When 50,000 coal miners went on strike in 1989, initial local media accounts failed to generate interest in their middle-class audiences, and this fact, coupled with a paucity of outcries from powerful elected officials, convinced the national media to pretty much bypass the story. So even though the strike went on for months, and thousands of miners and their families were arrested (troops were called in, and so on), hardly any Americans outside of the affected areas knew anything about it.*

Of course, in practice, the system does not work in precisely this way every time. There is slippage due to inefficiency, middle-class interest is worth more (to advertisers, for instance) than is that of the poor, and it takes lots of audience interest to overcome serious political opposition. The media will generally buck political power only when buttressed by support from very large numbers of people or by competing powerful forces. But when all or most power blocks line up and the public is perceived to be receptive, the media will go for broke and public opinion will be moved.

*Example*: At the beginning of 1989, polls indicated that about 15 percent of the American public believed drug use was the most serious problem facing the nation. (This statistic itself was the product of previous "wars on drugs," media up-playing, and so on. Drug wars have been a standard diversion—modern day bread and circuses— since the Nixon presidency.) But when a newly elected President Bush made yet another war on drugs the focal point of his administration, the media, bowing to the power and authority of the presidency coupled with the receptivity of the American public to scare stories about illegal drug use, played up the drug problem for all it was worth. The result was that by September of that year, polls showed that about two-thirds of the American public listed drugs as the number one problem facing the nation.†

## 2. News-Gathering Methods Are Designed to Save Money

The all-important fact about the mass media, as we have been at pains to point out, is that they are in business to make money, not lose it. When they regularly spend more

---

*See, for instance, "The Silenced Majority," by Barbara Ehrenreich in *Z* magazine (September 1989).

†See "Viewpoint" by Hodding Carter, III, in the *Wall Street Journal* (September 14, 1989). Carter blames the media for their "overwhelming tendency to jump up and down and bark in concert whenever the White House—any White House—snaps its fingers," neglecting the reason for their doing so, namely, their fear of bucking public opinion. Note that the media have not always been kind to the Clinton administration.

"Hey, do you want to be on the news tonight or not? This is a sound bite, not the Gettysburg Address. Just say what you have to say, Senator, and get the hell off."

Drawing by Ziegler. © 1989 by The New Yorker Magazine, Inc.

money gathering the news than they take in, they go out of business. The result is that true investigative reporting tends to get slighted, because it is so very expensive in time, effort, and thus *money*. More "efficient" news-gathering techniques are used whenever possible, even though spending greater amounts of money might produce more accurate accounts, not to mention dredge up dirt the powerful are trying to hide. Media people generally do try to be careful in what they report, so as not to leave themselves open to libel charges, and (in most cases) because of a desire to adhere to professional ethics. But they rarely get to dig below the surface.

The principal way in which news is gathered is through established "beats." The major wire services, television networks, and a few top newspapers and magazines routinely assign reporters to cover the major news-developing institutions—the White

---

*Politicians want as much free media coverage as they can get, and television eats up hours of video footage every day. The upshot is that the two power factions cooperate with each other in the way described in the following passage:*

---

Late last month, on a picture perfect fall day, Republican Rep. John Hiler of Indiana strode across the grounds of the U.S. Capitol toward a television camera crew stationed near the building's southeast corner. That area, known as "the triangle," offers a breathtaking view of the Capitol rotunda as a backdrop.

Approaching his press secretary, . . . Hiler asked anxiously: "What am I going to say?" After a quick briefing by the aide, Hiler stepped in front of the camera and, with the poise that comes from years of practice, deftly delivered a 30-second attack on the House Democratic leadership for preventing him from offering an amendment to anti-crime legislation. . . .

That night, Hiler's constituents who watched the local news on Channel 28 saw their congressman being "interviewed" on the crime bill then pending before Congress. But by almost any definition it wasn't news and it wasn't an interview. Except for WSJV's cost for taking the segment off the satellite, the whole operation was financed by the National Republican Congressional Committee, the campaign organization of House Republicans. And the "interview" was conducted not by a reporter but by Hiler's press secretary.

. . . On the same day, the NRCC film crew performed the same ritual for close to two dozen other GOP lawmakers and their aides, just as they do almost every Wednesday afternoon. On a less frequent basis, the Democratic Congressional Campaign Committee provides the same type of service to incumbent House Democrats.

The satellite service is just one of an array of electronic media outlets—some paid for by the taxpayers—available to incumbent House members, providing them with almost instantaneous communication links with their districts. It also gives incumbent lawmakers a powerful reelection campaign tool that is seldom matched by their opponents.

—Excerpted from Tom Kenworthy, "Jive at Five: How Incumbents Get to Be News Makers," by Tom Kenworthy in the *Washington Post Weekly Edition* (October 22–28, 1990). © 1990, the *Washington Post*. Reprinted by permission.

Drawing by Wiley. © 1996 Washington Post Writers Group.
Reprinted by permission.

*It's true that the mass media have provided a modest amount of coverage of the mass layoffs that during the 1990s have played such a large part in the success of corporate America in generating very large profits. But the media only very occasionally make as graphic as does this Wiley cartoon what mass firings do to the lives of the workers who have been "downsized."*

House, Congress, and so on. At the local level, they cover city hall, the police, and the like. Roving reporters are assigned to cover breaking stories in business, medicine, and so on by interviewing interested parties—representatives of large corporations giving press conferences, "experts" in relevant fields, union leaders.* In effect, then, *most news is given to reporters by government officials or by others who have or represent power or wealth!* The news thus is bound to reflect established interests much more than those of the general public, given that it is the rich and powerful who have the means to call press conferences, provide video footage, or issue fancy press releases.†

That is why *very few important news stories in the mass media result from true investigative reporting!* It's much easier, quicker, and cheaper to interview heads of government agencies or representatives of big business than it is to find out what actually is going on by tedious digging. (It's also safer; recall the discussion a while back about the power of government and why power tends to cooperate with power.)

Anyway, there is a bit of good news on the topic of true investigative reporting. In recent years, newspapers, and occasionally TV and radio programs, have been recycling items from non-mass media magazines and from the major newspapers (which have set up syndicates for this purpose to compete with feature syndicates). Items from *Harper's, The Washington Monthly, The Atlantic, The New Republic,* and other nonmass media publications, as well as the *New York Times,* the *Washington Post,* and the *Los Angeles Times,* appear now and then in local rags and on network news programs.

---

*Experts can be found on every side of virtually all issues. Which experts are consulted depends on the way in which a story is to be slanted, and that, of course, usually is determined by the various factors we have been considering in this chapter.

†An important exception to this rule is that ordinary people often are interviewed to impart "human interest" to stories that otherwise reflect the opinions and viewpoints of power or money. Another exception is the coverage of local news events such as fires—reporters actually go to the scene and interview those affected by the event.

Another good bit of news is that the media are beginning to learn how to employ electronic marvels to lower the costs of true investigative reporting. For example, two *St. Louis Post-Dispatch* specialists in computer journalism, George Landau and Tim Novak, checked thousands of Missouri death certificates via computer and proved the locally well-known fact that citizens who have passed over into another constituency sometimes manage to register and vote. They also checked Missouri's computerized death certificate records to identify coroners who "repeatedly failed to investigate suspicious deaths," listing the cause as "unknown" when an autopsy might have revealed child abuse, elderly abuse, or other evidence of homicide.*

---

*Here is a summary of the contents of a typical TV national news program (the June 7, 1996, ABC TV evening news program with Peter Jennings):*

---

1. A report of Labor Department statistics on employment indicating an increase in jobs, followed by a Brit Hume comment and film of a President Clinton statement on new jobs, a stock market report, and a Bob Dole comment on the economy and jobs (this was during the 1996 presidential campaign, so the network was being "evenhanded" in its reporting). California employment was reported as up.
2. A Bob Dole campaign statement on abortion and so on, followed by a favorable Pat Buchanan comment and remarks by California Governor Pete Wilson at the governors' convention.
3. A Pentagon report on a plane crash in Bosnia.
4. A police report on a fire in a black church in North Carolina.
5. A report on a fire in Alaska in which husky sled dogs' lives were saved.
6. A story with the moral that students graduating from high school shouldn't drink and drive, describing a young woman who gives talks on the subject, based on personal experience.
7. A series of short items about Russia, including Boris Yeltsin comments and an interview with a Russian film director, and comments about new Russian fast-food chains.
8. A "Person of the Week" item on Sandra Hodge, who played on the Harlem Globe Trotters basketball team.

---

*Notice that most of these stories were given to ABC (for instance, by government officials), or report remarks by political candidates, or constitute relatively unimportant "human interest" stories (Sandra Hodge). Only one—the item about the Alaskan fire—resulted from anything remotely like true investigative reporting, and absolutely none were of the "muckraking" variety. That is, none reported on shady doings that the powerful were trying to cover up. (Video news releases are so common an item among large "Fortune 500" corporations that they have been given the acronym "VNR.")*

---

*See "Quantum Leaps: Computer Journalism Takes Off," in the *Columbia Journalism Review*, May/June 1992.

## 3. Misdirection and Lack of Proportion

An important lesson to be learned from what has been said so far in this chapter is that the news, as presented to us by the mass media, tends to misdirect our attention away from important, underlying, day-to-day occurrences and trends in favor of "human interest" stories and what the powerful want to tell us. That was one of the points of what has just been said about the way in which the two kinds of welfare, for the poor and for the rich, are dealt with by the mass media.*

The mass media also tend to play into the average person's lack of a good sense of proportion. That is why, for example, the media often pay just as much attention to an economic issue concerning, say, $100 million as to one about $10 billion. (It's well known that the average person is able to distinguish rightly between relatively small amounts, for instance, between $500 and $5,000, but tends to get hazy when the numbers get larger than the kind that directly relate to their own lives.)

Although satisfying the public's liking for human interest stories doesn't have to result in relatively trivial news getting a bigger play than more important items, in fact that is often the way it works. For instance, when an abandoned alligator turned up in a San Francisco lake in 1996, the local media had a field day (actually, several field weeks) with the story; relatively neglected were reports of increasing invasions of nonindigenous marine species into San Francisco Bay, causing million-dollar losses to local fishermen and threatening to wipe out several local marine species. The alligator and efforts to catch it were appealing to a large audience even though of trivial importance to anyone's life, while the more serious threat to local fishermen and the Bay Area economy lacked pizzazz.

## 4. News Reporting: Theory and Practice

People don't often stand back and look carefully at what they're doing from a wider perspective; they don't often theorize about their activities. On the whole, media workers do so more than most, but their theories frequently are self-serving.

### The Unusual Is News, the Everyday Is Not

Theory says that news is what is new—the unusual—not the commonplace. Yet what happens every day is generally more important than the unusual occurrences that make the headlines. For example, over the past 20 years or so, several kinds of bacteria slowly but steadily have been developing resistance to present-day antibiotics. Millions of people who would have been saved just a few years ago are dying, or being seriously impaired, and everyone is at an increasing risk from diseases once thought to be virtually conquered by miracle drugs (tuberculosis is an example). The media pretty much ignore this vitally important story, or relegate it to newspaper back pages, except every once in a while, when a news magazine or TV news program runs a story that turns a

---

*Another reason that the mass media spend much more time on welfare for the poor than for the rich is that the average person tends (for psychological reasons that go beyond the scope of this text) to be more interested in and more receptive to stories about welfare for the poor, especially unfavorable stories, than items about welfare for the rich. (How often, by the way, have you heard welfare for the rich called "welfare for the rich" on a TV news program?)

few heads for a short time and then disappears—buried in the minds of media audiences under a mass of information about relatively trivial, or quickly unimportant, events. (Without question, microscopic organisms—bacteria, viruses, etc.—constitute one of the two most serious threats to human life and health on this planet, the other being pollution and other swift environmental changes that threaten to unravel most, or at least an important part, of the ecological web on which human life depends.)

Another unfortunate consequence of the idea that only what is new constitutes news is that when a politician once is reported, say, as having lied on an important issue, the lie itself in most cases no longer counts as a new event, although the politician's denial generally does count as news. This sort of news practice tends to put politicians in the driver's seat, in particular at election time when any bad publicity received in the media can be buried under an avalanche of TV spots (recall the earlier discussion of the powerful effect of repetition). The moral here for critical reasoners is that long memories, appropriately brought to bear, are vital in the battle against the insidious effects of repetitive TV spots and of journalistic theories about what makes something newsworthy.

## News Reporting Is Supposed to Be Objective, Not Subjective

Those who work on the news often say that facts are objective, conclusions or value judgments subjective. Media workers are supposed to be objective—they are supposed to report only the facts.

But this theory of objectivity is erroneous. Reports of facts generally depend on somebody's judgment that they are facts. A reporter must *reason to the facts*, or at least report someone else's reasoning to the facts, just as one reasons to anything else. Facts do not generally grow on trees, to be plucked at one's leisure. We just mentioned, for example, the fact that mutant bacteria are becoming an extremely serious health problem, but there is no single observation, or series of observations, that demonstrate this truth. Medical experts have to reason to this fact from what they observe (for example, that syphillis, tuberculosis, and malaria cases sometimes do not respond to previously effective antibiotics).

Similarly, the idea that media hands should not make value judgments is foolish. They must make value judgments, if only about which items are important enough to be featured, which should be mentioned only briefly, and which tossed into the round file (where most items that go over Associated Press wires end up). The point is that *editing*, one of the chief tasks performed by media workers, requires value judgments about the relative importance of events.

In any case, theory is one thing, practice another. Practice is driven primarily by the various forces we have been at pains to describe and only to a small extent by abstract theory. The theory of objectivity serves as a convenient cover under which this can be done. Its cash value is that reporters are motivated to stay within the narrow social consensus when they make judgments or draw conclusions. So one effect of the theory of objectivity is to discourage the reporting of nonestablishment or nonconsensus points of view, satisfying instead the desires of media audiences, advertisers, and others who have great power. *Objectivity turns into not rocking the boat.*

It's also true, and worth noting, that journalists often confuse objectivity with its close relative—being *evenhanded*. It has become common practice, for example, for the major networks to present rebuttal from the "other side" when they carry major presidential addresses, so that both major parties get their say. Comments about the truth of whatever is at issue tend to get lost—they would be considered value judgments anyway, and so would not satisfy the criteria of the theory of objective reporting. Note how the expression "other side" masks the fact that there are many sides to most issues, and that the viewpoints championed by the two major political parties often run the range only from A to B. During the 1996 presidential campaign, for example, the mass media were more or less "evenhanded" in their coverage of Democratic and Republican candidates, but did very little reporting concerning Green party, Libertarian, and other candidates (except for billionaire Ross Perot's Reform party—ah, to be super rich).

## News Is Supposed to Be Separated from Analysis and In-Depth Reporting

The theory of objectivity requires that facts be reported separately from conclusions or evaluations (which are thought of as "subjective"). But this separation of news from analysis further aggravates a defect already in evidence in most media reporting: the failure to tie what happens to any *explanation* as to why it happened and why it is important.

Typically, when covering a story, a reporter consults those directly involved or affected by it. Writing, say, about civil service employee salaries, a reporter would very likely interview civil servants who, naturally, will say that their salaries are lower than for comparable jobs in industry, and critics who, having raised the issue, can be expected to say that the salaries in question are higher than in the nongovernment business world. In fact, this routine has been gone through several times in recent years. Most reporters, of course, have no idea which side is right—they don't know enough about the topic to make an intelligent judgment. They don't know, for example, whether

---

*Even though TV reporters arriving on the scene of a breaking story generally know very little about what is taking place, or about the topic that is at issue, they still must appear to be authoritative and not merely people reading someone else's news to us. That is why, for example, evening news anchors may turn up anywhere, reporting as someone "on the spot" and thus presumably knowledgeable about what is going on. So that is why on October 4, 1995, CBS evening news audiences were treated to Dan Rather reporting from the Florida panhandle during Hurricane Opal, with winds and water whipping past him as he was tied to a post to keep from blowing away. The double intent was to make coverage of the hurricane into high drama so that it had* human interest, *the essential ingredient of stories meant to interest a mass audience, and to wrap Rather in an "aura of authority"—make him appear to be much more than merely someone relating to us what others had told him about Hurricane Opal. Much more exciting than reading a prepared script in a TV studio, but at bottom pretty much the same thing.*

civil service job specifications truly describe what happens on the job day-to-day. (How could they, given that the topic they investigated the week before might have been water pollution in Pennsylvania, while next week's topic will be job flight to Mexico?)

But suppose they do indeed know about the job spec inflation gambit. Suppose, say, that they just happen to have read some of the many *Washington Monthly* articles decrying this practice. Nevertheless, the theory that news should be separated from "analysis"—that is, from evaluation for accuracy—makes it difficult for them to say something like, "According to civil servant spokespersons, civil servants are underpaid; witness higher salaries paid for comparable service in industry. But in fact civil service job descriptions almost always are grossly inflated." How often, for example, have you heard a TV reporter, having finished interviewing Senator Blowhard, conclude by remarking that what the good senator has just said borders on pure fiction? (And how often, by the way, *is* what the senator has just said merely self-serving political rubbish?)

Although the theory of objective news reporting often tends to deter journalists from saying what they believe or even know to be true, as just described, it doesn't absolutely forbid the mixing of news with evaluation or analysis. In fact, reporters have a modest amount of freedom to spout off, at least when no toes of the powerful are being stepped on. Nevertheless, the impossibility of being experts on every topic they must investigate, coupled with the need to seem authoritative, *whether they know what they are talking about or not*, often produces rather poor results. Consider, for example, the way in which the mass media handled the story about the possible discovery that there once was life on Mars. The news magazines ran feature stories, the evening news programs (for example, on August 7, 1996) played the story up to the hilt, and newspapers ran long articles about it. What generally was lacking in these mass media accounts was the balanced, questioning appraisal that could be found in non-mass publications, for example, in the October 1996 issue of *Scientific American* magazine. The story there was placed into its historical context (a similar 1961 story played up in the mass media turned out to be incorrect) and stressed the tentative, iffy nature of the August 1996 claim about Martian life, citing a great deal of contrary opinion by scientists in the field. (Note that the media played the story incorrectly even if it should turn out that there was indeed once life on the Red Planet.)

## The Opinions of the "Right" Authorities Take Precedence

Since the reporters who gather the news are not usually experts in the fields they have to cover, they must, and do, seek out expert opinion. The trouble is that experts can be

In a media-dominated world, children who insist upon the actuality of the Bermuda Triangle, the reality of pyramid power, or the accuracy of astrological projections are quick to refer to having seen it on TV, having read it in a book, or having seen it in the newspaper. This presents a problem for skeptical adults. When the media uses such terms as "Bermuda Triangle" freely, they are, in effect, creating an air of legitimacy. Logically, children conclude that there must be some truth to the matter if they see it in their local paper.

—Ray Hyman in *The Skeptical Inquirer.*

found on all sides of virtually every issue that is even mildly controversial. *Which* experts they consult thus becomes crucially important, and usually is determined by just a very few factors.

Perhaps the most important consideration is whether an expert's opinions might be unpopular either with the intended audience or with advertisers or other power groups. Experts with views that might raise too many hackles tend to be overlooked (or, sometimes, used as foils). Mainstream experts dominate the field. These days, for example, positions on race, gender differences, pollution problems, and so on, generally have to stay within bounds set by PC. There is, of course, still a great deal of racism in America, as in most other countries, but there also is an "official line" on the matter. Racism is definitely not PC. An expert who holds a contrary view is not going to be heard, except on very rare occasions. (One is reminded, on this score, of the many times in recent years that college audiences around the nation have hooted down scheduled speakers, denying them the right to have their say.) Books not in conformity to the PC line on race tend either to get trashed or to be ignored. A case in point is the publisher's withdrawal of the book *The g Factor: General Intelligence and its Implications*, by Chris Brand, a psychology lecturer at Edinburg University. The publisher, John Wiley & Sons, said that Brand had made "repellent" assertions in his book; for example, that "It is a scientific fact that black Americans are less intelligent than white Americans and the IQ of Asians is higher than blacks." (Note that the publisher's reason for squelching the book was not a belief that its claims about race were false but rather that they were repellent.)

## Self-Censorship

The theory that news reporting should be objective does not require that all of the news, even all of the very important news, be reported. During wartime, for example, national security takes precedence. But even in peacetime, the media sometimes voluntarily suppress news out of a sense of duty. Perhaps the most famous instance of this kind occurred during John Kennedy's time as president, when the *New York Times* decided not to print reliable information about the impending attack on Cuba by U.S.-trained forces intent on overthrowing Fidel Castro.*

But not all self-censorship has to do with national defense. A more common reason, mentioned before, is to placate advertisers. Here is a little item from *The Nation* (December 16, 1996) illustrating this point:

> As a protest against consumerism, the Media Foundation has for the past four years sponsored Buy Nothing Day on the day after Thanksgiving. This year the group wanted to run a thirty-second spot promoting its buy-out but was turned down by all three major networks. ABC said the ad violated its policy on "advertising of controversial issues"; CBS said it was an "advocacy ad"; NBC was more honest, saying that the ad was "inimical to our legitimate business interests."

---

*The invasion turned into a fiasco that was terribly embarrassing to the Kennedy administration. Kennedy himself is alleged later to have had the chutzpah to take the *Times* to task for this self-censorship on grounds that publication of the story by the *Times* might have resulted in the aborting of that ill-fated venture!

The other important reason for media censorship has to do with the power of media audiences to switch channels or not to buy a newspaper. Television, in particular, has to be sensitive to its audience, because its product comes into living rooms with such immediacy (and children may be watching). The way in which Elvis Presley was allowed to appear on an *Ed Sullivan* TV show in 1956 constitutes a classic example; Elvis was shown only from the waist up, so that TV audiences wouldn't be exposed to his pelvic gyrations. (That sounds silly today, but what is permissible and what isn't differs considerably from one time to another.) Another famous case occurred in 1952 when Lucille Ball became pregnant and the story line of the "I Love Lucy" show was adjusted accordingly: the TV Lucy could be said on camera to be "expecting" and *enceinte* (French for "pregnant") but the word "pregnant" could not be used. Even in the 1950s, this sort of censorship seemed ridiculous to lots of people, but to media moguls it was a very serious matter; too many viewers were likely to be offended by use of the term "pregnant."

Times change, of course, so that in the 1990s TV's Murphy Brown was allowed to be an unwed mother, and no one thought twice about referring to her as pregnant. But media self-censorship still is with us, as it always will be. It's just that standards and the topics subject to censorship change. Back in the 1950s a program about homosexuals would have been unthinkable—absolutely out of the question—so much so that the lack of such programs hardly could be considered to constitute self-censorship. Gays simply did not exist so far as television was concerned. But in the 1990s, they do, and yet programs featuring gays sometimes are censored by one segment of the media or other.

The 1994 PBS decision not to help fund a sequel to the very popular "Tales of the City" is a rather important case in point. PBS had received complaints about the portrayal of homosexuality and drug use in that mini-series and apparently gave in to right-wing pressure, abandoning the sequel.

But those who see self-censorhip as automatically evil might consider the right of individuals to privacy in their nonpublic life. A person in the public eye is still, after all, entitled to a private life. Anyway, things are not as bad here as in, say, England, where every move of the once Princess Diana is reported in daily newspapers and on television, and Prince Charles' private phone conversations become known to everyone.

Anyway, it was well known to media people that both before and after his marriage—as a congressman, senator, and president—John Kennedy was quite a lady's man. But the media, on the whole, chose not to divulge this feature of his private life. In those days, these matters were usually passed over, even though they would have found an eager audience. And yet, self-censorship of similar stories concerning Kennedy's brother, Ted, may well have been a mistake, given what happened at Chappaquiddick.* Knowledge of a person's sex life *may*, in some cases, be relevant to character and thus to potential performance as a public figure.

---

*Those unfamiliar with what happened there would profit a great deal from finding out—first, because of the way in which it was handled by the media, and second, because the affair nicely illustrates how the rich and powerful sometimes are above the law in ways that the rest of us are not.

# Last year, 300,000 Americans were arrested for smoking an herb that Queen Victoria used regularly for menstrual cramps.

It's a fact.

The herb, of course, is *cannabis sativa*. Otherwise known as marijuana, pot, grass, hemp, boo, mary-jane, ganja—the nicknames are legion.

So are the people who smoke it.

By all reckoning, it's fast becoming the new national pastime. Twenty-six million smokers, by some accounts—lots more by others. Whatever the estimate, a staggeringly high percentage of the population become potential criminals simply by being in possession of it. And the numbers are increasing.

For years, we've been told that marijuana leads to madness, sex-crimes, hard-drug usage and even occasional warts.

Pure Victorian poppycock.

In 1894, The Indian Hemp Commission reported marijuana to be relatively harmless. A fact that has been substantiated time and again in study after study.

Including, most recently, by the President's own Commission. This report stands as an indictment of the pot laws themselves.

And that's why more and more legislators are turning on to the fact that the present marijuana laws are as archaic as dear old Victoria's code of morality. And that they must be changed. Recently, the state of Oregon did, in fact, de-criminalize marijuana. Successfully.

Other states are beginning to move in that direction. They must be encouraged.

NORML has been and is educating the legislators, working in the courts and with the lawmakers to change the laws. We're doing our best but still, we need help. Yours.

Used with permission of NORML.

---

*Ad censorship. NORML marijuana ad rejected by* Time *and* Newsweek, *accepted by* Playboy.

*Calvin and Hobbes* by Bill Watterson. Copyright 1992 Universal Press Syndicate.

## 5. DEVICES USED TO SLANT THE NEWS

So far, we have been considering why the media slant the news and how that affects story selection. Now let's take a brief look at a few of the many devices used to accomplish this task. (The examples are taken primarily from newspapers and magazines, but television and radio have their analogs.)

### Stories Can Be Played Up or Down

If you like something in a story, or believe your audience will be interested, you can play it up. If not, you can bury it by placing it on page 59 or by packing the undesirable material toward the end of an otherwise acceptable story. Back pages are relatively unread and readers tend not to get past the first few paragraphs of anything—including, alas, material in school textbooks, but that is another matter. (If you've read this far, place an "X" at the end of this sentence.) On TV, stories get buried by being run toward the end of a news program (although not, interestingly, at the very end), when attention may be wandering, and by being cut to run for just 10 or 15 seconds.

The way in which the 1993 and 1994 debates concerning health care reform were covered in newspapers provides an interesting example. Opinion polls at the time showed that a small majority of Americans favored a "single pay" plan much like the Canadian system; but this happened to be the plan that powerful factions in the United States (in particular, the health insurance industry) most strongly opposed. For whatever reasons (readers are invited to draw their own tentative conclusions), newspapers typically ran stories whose headlines and first few paragraphs were hostile to Canadian-style systems, although buried further down they often provided a great deal of favorable information.

Of course, the chief way in which TV buries a story is simply to pass it over. TV news programs, by their very nature, are able to deal with many fewer items than daily newspapers, so that it is easier to get away with failure to report a news event. But even newspapers omit items for one reason or another. For instance, they often inform readers about which movies are drawing the largest audiences, which records are selling best, and so on. But the *New York Times*, for obscure reasons of its own, routinely excludes religious books (Bibles, etc.) and romance" ("Harlequin") paperbacks from its lists of best selling books, even though together these two kinds of publications account for a very large slice of the book market. (According to an item in the February 1994

*Harper's Index*, romance novels alone account for about 47 percent of all paperback sales.) Any thoughts as to why the *Times* engages in this practice?

## Misleading, Sensational, or Opinionated Headlines Can Be Used

Many more people read the headlines on stories than read the accounts that follow. So even if an account itself is accurate, a misleading or sensational headline (generally

---

The shock of Dec. 7 [1941] can be well imagined. When the last Japanese plane roared off, five American battleships had been sunk and three damaged, three cruisers and three destroyers badly hit, 200 planes destroyed, and 2344 men killed. For the loss of only 29 planes, Japan had virtually crippled the U.S. Pacific Fleet at a single blow.

The American service chiefs immediately decided that news of a disaster of such magnitude would prove unacceptable to the American people, and steps were taken to ensure that they did not learn about it. So effective were these measures that the truth about Pearl Harbor was still being concealed even after the war ended. The cover-up began with an "iron curtain" of censorship that cut off the United Press office in Honolulu from San Francisco in the middle of its first excited telephone report.

So drastic was the suppression of news that nothing further, except for official communiques, came out of Pearl Harbor for another four days. These claimed that only one "old" battleship and a destroyer had been sunk and other ships damaged, and that heavy casualties had been inflicted on the Japanese. It cannot be argued that these lies were necessary to conceal from the Japanese the extent of the disaster they had inflicted on the U.S. Pacific Fleet. The Japanese knew exactly how much damage they had done, and reports in Tokyo newspapers accurately stating the American losses meant that the Americans knew that the Japanese knew. The American censorship was to prevent the American public from learning the gravity of the blow.

After flying to Hawaii on a tour of inspection, the Secretary of the Navy, Colonel Frank Knox, held a press conference in New York at which, with President Roosevelt's approval, he gave the impression he was revealing the full extent of the American losses at Pearl Harbor. Colonel Knox told correspondents that one United States battleship, the *Arizona*, had been lost and the battleship *Oklahoma* had capsized but could be righted.

This must have made strange reading for anyone actually at Pearl Harbor, who had only to lift his eye from his newspaper to see five United States battleships— the *Arizona*, the *Oklahoma*, the *California*, the *Nevada*, and the *West Virginia*— resting on the bottom.

—From *The First Casualty*, © 1975 by Phillip Knightley.

---

*In wartime, truth is the first casualty, censorship the first expedient.*

Reprinted by permission of Harcourt Brace Jovanovich, Inc., and Andre Deutsch, Ltd.

not written by whoever wrote the news report itself) distorts the news for many readers. Here are a few examples:

In July 1990, during the time when President Bush's son was big news because of his involvement in the S&L scandal, *USA Today* slanted a headline by the simple, and sneaky, use of quotation marks:

### Bush defends his son's "honor"

The quotes implied that Bush's son's honor wasn't up to snuff.

The *San Francisco Chronicle* headlined one of its rather interesting and accurate stories:

### Chiapas Peasants Start Big Land Grab

The article itself revealed that the Mexican Chiapas Indians had retaken land stolen from them centuries ago—land that in 1993 had been verified by court proceedings to belong to them—an edict that was simply ignored by Mexican authorities, motivating the rightful owners to take matters into their own hands. Ah, those grabby Indians.

By Handelsman for the *Times-Picayune*, New Orleans. Reprinted with permission.

*Once a story gets going, it's hard to squelch. The fiction that jets circulated for 20 minutes over Los Angeles International Airport while President Clinton, in a plane on the ground, was given a trim made front page "news," and generated countless jokes on late-night TV shows. The correction—no flights were delayed—appeared days later and was confined, pretty much unnoticed, to newspaper back pages.*

Those who read more than one newspaper occasionally are treated to the sight of contrary, even contradictory, headlines on what essentially are the same account of some event or other; for example:

**AMA to Be Neutral on Health Plan**
—*Los Angeles Times*, September 30, 1993
**Doctors Rebel Over Health Plan in Major Challenge to President**
—*New York Times*, same day.

## Follow-up Stories Can Be Omitted

Follow-up stories rarely make headlines, primarily for three reasons. The first is that they are more difficult to obtain than breaking news stories. It takes much less time and effort to record the fact that a bank has failed than to follow up details of an ensuing court case against its directors. The second is that the public (and media) conception of "news" is what is *new*, and follow-up stories are more of the same.

However, the principal reason for the paucity of follow-up stories is that most of us have short attention spans. Except for "ongoing" stories—wars providing the best examples—people tend to tire of any topic quickly (the truth behind Andy Warhol's remark, "In the future, everyone will be famous for 15 minutes"). When bored, it's all too easy to flip the switch to another channel or to put down the newspaper and instead watch Roseanne do her thing on the tube.

Well, no one can be in favor of boredom. The problem is that in the vast majority of cases it is the time-consuming details that make all the difference. Ten-second news sound bites aren't all that different from "Chevrolet—the heartbeat of America" or "Magnavox—smart, very smart." Short and easily remembered usually drives out long and complicated. That may well be the chief reason relevant background information and follow-up tend to be in short supply on TV news programs.

## Points of View Can Be Conveyed via Cartoons and Comic Strips

According to the old saying, a picture is worth a thousand words, which may account for the ability of cartoons and comic strips to effectively—*graphically*—make a point. In any case, it most certainly accounts for the large number of these handy little devices that have been reprinted in this particular textbook. A clever practitioner of the cartoonist's art can puncture prejudices and force us to open our eyes to unpleasant truth in a way that few others can match. The Tom Meyer cartoon on the next page, for example, forcefully brings home the point that the so-called "three strikes and you're out" laws—mandatory life sentences for those convicted of a third felony—don't really get at the nub of the crime problem, and it ironically suggests what needs to be done if we are to make a serious dent in that problem.

The *Doonesbury* strip deserves special mention here because it has been in the forefront of a minor trend on newspaper comic pages to feature strips that at least occasionally touch on social or political issues. (That is why, for instance, so many *Calvin and Hobbes* strips appear in this text; they deal with serious matters instead of just tickling the funny bone.) A particular favorite of the authors of this text (one of whom is a U.C.L.A. alum) is the 1994 *Doonesbury* series that poked fun at the hiring of junk

Cartoon by Tom Meyer. © *San Francisco Chronicle*. Reprinted by permission.

bond ex-con Michael Milken to teach a business course at U.C.L.A. In one panel, Milken is pictured saying, "Who is Professor Milken, the genius who created a new world of financial instruments? Well, I'm many things, of course. But most of all, I'm a survivor. After a 98-count indictment and a 6-count plea bargain, I'm still here—and with $1 billion to show for it!" after which students repeat his code: "Greed works! Crime pays! Everybody does it!" In another strip, Milken states what must certainly be his actual opinion on the matter, that government attempts at regulation are a joke and government employees no match for "a true visionary and his defense team." Students are shown booing the student who has the temerity to ask the pertinent question: "As the key player of the greatest criminal conspiracy in the history of finance, do you think justice was served by your brief stay in a country club prison?"

Unfortunately, this ability of comic strips to graphically make a point sometimes results in their being censored. *Doonesbury*, of course, bites the dust now and then. But even normally nonpolitical strips occasionally get the axe. For example, when a young boy in the *For Better or for Worse* comic strip summoned the courage to tell his parents that he was gay the resulting furor came as a shock to the strip's creator, Lynn Johnston. The series of strips on this theme ran for just 10 days in 1993, but was censored during that time in 40 papers, with 20 more canceling the strip outright. In Memphis, Tennessee, to cite just one city, about 2,000 readers canceled their subscriptions to the *Commercial Appeal* because that paper ran the strips they objected to. Johnston was flooded with mail, both pro and con, and stung by the anger and hate some letters exhibited. She wrote the series, she said, because several friends have died from AIDS, and one of her closest gay friends recently had been robbed and killed. "He was nothing more than a wonderful person and a good friend to me," she said. "My intent was to show that Lawrence [the gay boy in the strip] was different but that he's still the kid next door, still a member of the community, someone who should be judged on his moral character, not his genetic code."*

## 6. TELEVISION: THE ONLY TRULY MASS MEDIUM (SO FAR)

Although still a relative baby, television is by far the most important of the mass media. More households own television sets than bathtubs or showers. (Interesting fact: One family in four in the United States has three or more television sets.) TV gives us the closest thing we have to a way of bringing a whole diverse nation together. It is the town crier, certifier, authenticator, and grapevine of modern life. That's why political campaigns are fought, and won or lost, on it; the news is broadcast on it; and a nation's mood and tone are set by it.

It would be hard to overestimate the effects of television on everyday life. (One thinks, for a parallel, of the ways in which the automobile has transformed the world.) When film shot from a privately owned camcorder caught police in the act of beating up Rodney King, pictures of their brutality on TV news programs had a profound effect on the way in which police everywhere thenceforth carried out their duties (fear of being filmed in the act constitutes a powerful deterrent). Similarly, the way in which the Los Angeles police department took it on the chin during the O. J. Simpson trial undoubtedly did much to improve police crime procedures everywhere.

All of the media, of course, have the power to force dramatic changes—to expose the bad and publicize the good. But television's power to expose and publicize is vastly greater and more immediate than all of the other mass media combined. Its power, therefore, is awesomely—indeed, frighteningly—greater.

Consider, for example, what Americans know about Nazi Germany's extermination camps compared to what they know about Soviet labor camps. Only a few Americans know that many more civilians died in Soviet labor camps than were murdered by the Nazis. The names *Auschwitz, Buchenwald*, and *Treblinka* are familiar to us, while few Americans have heard, say, of *Kolyma*. (Speaking of Nazi camps brings to mind another medium that has great graphic power—motion pictures. The film *Schindler's List* powerfully conveyed the inhumanity of the German attempt to exterminate *untermensch*, and it did so in a way—by reducing the horror of the actual events —that masses of people could tolerate, and hence digest.)

---

Television is the first truly democratic culture—the first culture available to everybody and entirely governed by what people want. The most terrifying thing is what people do want.

— Clive Barker

---

*See, for instance, the *San Francisco Examiner*, April 25, 1993.

*Calvin and Hobbes* by Bill Watterson. Copyright 1991 Universal Press Syndicate. Reprinted with permission.

We also shouldn't forget the way in which news reporting has helped break down prejudices. It was a very important event indeed when the first woman, Barbara Walters, read the evening news to us on national TV and an equally important event when the first African American, Max Robinson, did so.

But perhaps the most graphic illustration of television's power to change the world is in its effect on the nature of war and associated diplomacy. It is a commonplace today that television shortened American involvement in the war in Vietnam through its living-room coverage, but insufficient notice has yet been taken of the way in which TV influenced the conduct of the recent Gulf War. The American government and its coalition allies were exceedingly careful to reduce the number of casualties, not just of their own forces but also of enemy civilians, in a way that (in the long history of warfare) has rarely, if ever, been true. Compare that, for instance, with the American and British record of mass bombings of civilians in World War II, when television was not peeking over every general's shoulder.

Even sitcoms and the other prime-time entertainment programs sometimes have positive effects—in addition to providing entertainment—a case in point being their role in reducing ethnic and gender prejudice, one of the great improvements that has taken place in the United States (and most other democratic nations) since World War II. African Americans are portrayed holding middle-class jobs, not just as janitors; women as business executives, not just housewives. "The Cosby Show" was the top-rated sitcom for quite a few years; Jessica Fletcher solved crimes on "Murder, She Wrote," one of the longest-running programs in TV history.

## TV Is the Best News Source for Many People

When we think of the *mass* media, it's important to remember that at least one-third of American adults are or come close to being functionally illiterate. For them, and for many others, a picture is worth *more* than a thousand words. So for the mass of people, by default, television is the best news source.

But capturing and informing this kind of mass audience requires extremely tight editing (matched in print only by advertisements). The average attention span is short and comprehension limited. TV does a better job than the other media in editing the news so that it can be understood, somewhat, by most Americans.

## 7. The Non–Mass Media to the Rescue

The mass media are a reasonably good source of information about breaking stories—speeches made by important officials, fluctuations in the Dow, bills passed by Congress (but not about a bill's value or who benefits and who is harmed!), and so on. Television does these stories rather well, at least when it can get good visuals. But for detailed, sophisticated, in-depth accounts, and for analysis that doesn't just parrot what powerful people are saying, the non–mass media are indispensible.

The commercial networks do feature one excellent investigative, in-depth program, namely, "60 Minutes," and run several other good investigative programs, including "Nightline," "20/20," and "48 Hours." But PBS, the Public Broadcasting Service, is the best everyday television news source—best, without doubt, for in-depth reporting and analysis. Indeed, in most ways, PBS is perhaps the brightest spot on the television spectrum. But those viewers who are on the cable, which means an ever-increasing majority, also can click to the Discovery channel, the Arts and Entertainment channel, C-Span, and, of course, CNN, which still gives its viewers a good deal more news and analysis than the major networks. (Lots of young people prefer to watch channels like MTV, alas.)

Nevertheless, TV still easily is eclipsed by the few excellent daily newspapers and especially by small-circulation magazines and journals. The mass media, even the big-city newspapers, focus on what is current, in the air, neglecting the underlying forces that ultimately determine what will be big news at a later date. *Time*, *Newsweek*, and *U.S. News and World Report* do do a bit of this sort of thing, but they tend to sensationalize what is going on, and to be flighty, blowing with the winds of public opinion (although a late 1996 change in the editorship of *U.S. News and World Report* seems to have improved the quality of its news and analysis). But it is precisely the underlying forces that are the bread and butter of small-circulation periodicals, some of which deal with these matters very well indeed. (See the annotated list of publications at the end of the book for examples and for the opinions of the authors of this text concerning some of these important information sources.)

But understanding what is going on isn't so much a matter of mass versus non–mass media as it is of learning how to be selective—learning how to separate pearls from schlock. Those interested in science, for example, would do well to avoid newsstand magazines that pander to the appetite so many people have for stories about ESP and other matters on the edge of legitimate science and that try to sensationalize science to increase sales.

The non–mass media contain lots more pearls per square inch and are, on the whole, a good deal more sophisticated in their discussions of what is going on in the world than are newspapers, TV, and even mass-sales books. Best-selling books, for instance, concerning politics, economics, and the like tend to be shallow and, often, sensationalist.

---

Thoughtfully written analysis is out, "live pops" are in. . . . Hire lookers, not writers. Do powder-puff, not probing, interviews. Stay away from controversial subjects. Kiss a___, move with the mass, and for heaven and the ratings' sake don't make anybody mad. . . . Make nice, not news.

— Dan Rather (of CBS's "Evening News")

*Example*: The best seller *Megatrends: Ten New Directions for 1990*, by John Naisbitt and Patricia Aburdene (Morrow, 1990), is a klinker as a source of insight compared to the so-so seller *Entangling Alliances: How the Third World Shapes Our Lives*, by John Maxwell Hamilton (Seven Locks Press, 1990).*

Of particular note are the self-serving memoirs of "distinguished statesmen" such as Henry Kissinger, which are nothing but baldfaced attempts to rewrite history in their favor. Presidential memoirs, supposedly written by former presidents, are perhaps the most offensive of these tomes. *Example*: Ronald Reagan's *An American Life* (Simon & Schuster, 1990), apparently written by Robert Lindsey (whom Reagan credits by saying "Robert Lindsey, a talented writer, was with me every step of the way").

Famous "authors" of horn-tooting books generally don't admit how small their part was in the actual writing process, but O. J. Simpson apparently found it prudent to do so when testifying during his 1996 civil trial about one of "his" books: *Question*: "And you wrote that, quote, 'I tried all the images.' . . . True?" *Simpson*: "I don't recall that, no." *Question*: It's in your book, . . . ." *Simpson*: "I didn't write the book. . . . In general, I O.K.'d the book, . . . I *think* [italics added]. I read the galley of the book before it went to press."

We should note, by the way, that National Public Radio (NPR) does a better job of presenting the news and analysis than does any television channel or any other radio outlet. Some examples of their regular programs are "All Things Considered," "Talk of the Nation," "BBC World News," "News Hour with Jim Lehrer," "Fresh Air," and "Science Friday." There is even at least one major network entertainment program, "Law and Order," that provides a good deal of information about how the legal system really works, as opposed to how it is supposed to work (more will be said about this topic in the next chapter) in addition to straight entertainment. (Note, however, that this first-rate program didn't attract enough viewers during prime time so that NBC relegated it to the 10 P.M. slot in its lineup.)

Finally, a word or two more about newspapers and magazines. The best of the muckraking newspapers is very likely the *Philadelphia Inquirer*; for example, their seven-part series (April 1993) on the major nonprofit, and thus tax-exempt, organizations in the United States, and how they cost the U.S. Treasury about $36 billion but pay out only about $9 billion in grants (lots of the rest goes to pay high executive salaries, country club dues, etc.). But the best newspapers, overall, probably are the *New York Times* (unfortunately sans comic strips, which means no *Doonesbury*), the *Los Angeles Times*, and the *Washington Post*. Even so, most large metropolitan areas have at least one reasonably good newspaper that is a better source of information than any of the major networks, or than CNN for that matter.

## 8. RECENT DEVELOPMENTS

During the past ten years or so, dramatic changes have been taking place in the news business. Perhaps the most important of these is the ever-increasing concentration of media ownership, and thus power, in fewer and fewer hands.

The first and much smaller concentration of media power occurred way back in the nineteenth century with the development of newspaper chains, the most important,

---

*See James Fallows' review of these books in the July 1990 *Atlantic Monthly*.

*As stated a few paragraphs back, PBS and the other non–major network channels air a lot more high-quality programs than do CBS, ABC, NBC, and Fox. Here are a few of the very good programs they have run in the past few years:* *

- A December 1993, January 1994 PBS discussion of rap music and its political messages. (Programs on PBS often are shown on different dates on different PBS outlets.)
- A "Bill Moyer's Journal," January 1994 account of how big money buys "access" and manipulates government in the interests of big business and the rich.
- A 1996 PBS "Frontline" program, "Why Americans Hate the Media," which went into some details discussed in this text (so we liked it).
- The two-part 1996 "Nova" special "In Search of Human Origins," a nice anti-dote to the many inaccurate TV programs on the subject run on the major net-works (for instance, the horrendous program featuring Charlton Heston mentioned earlier).
- An April 1993 PBS special, "The Longest Hatred," about anti-Semitism through the ages.
- The March 15, 1994, "Firing Line" debate "Resolved: Welfare Has Done More Harm Than Good," which featured sensible people on both sides of the debate and permitted them time to make their cases.

*We also should mention the often fascinating interviews with authors of interest-ing and important books on C-Span's* Booknotes.

*Even though news programs on the major networks tend to be second rate—recall the remarks by insiders Dan Rather and Ted Koppel cited a while back—good things do occasionally get aired on these channels, including occasional stories on "20/20," "48 Hours," "Dateline," and in particular on CBS's "60 Minutes." Here are two examples:*

- The December 22, 1996, "60 Minutes" story about the Clinton administration "giveaway" to defense contractors, managed by subsidizing mergers of defense conglomerates. (The Clinton people, by the way, called this new subsidizing policy a "clarification" of the old policy, not a new one.)
- The October 27, 1996, "60 Minutes" story on how public nonprofit hospitals are being bought by for-profit corporations, recounting how, according to "60 Minutes," Columbia HCA offered "golden parachutes" to top executives and board members of nonprofit Blue Cross/Blue Shield of Ohio as induce-ments to sell at a bargain price to Columbia HCA, thus enabling that for-profit megacorporation to control both the insurance end of health care as well as a great many Ohio hospitals and, via insurance HMOs, control thousands of doc-tors and nurses in that state. (The program mentioned several other shady-ap-pearing takeovers by for-profit hospital groups.)

*Transcripts and videos of these and similar programs are available for a modest fee.

perhaps, being the one put together by William Randolph Hearst and fictionalized in the movie classic *Citizen Kane*. The power of these early media magnates is illustrated in that film by a scene in which a journalist sent to Cuba in 1898 reports back that there is no sign of war in Cuba, only to be told that Kane (Hearst) would supply the war. The scene is a takeoff on what is held by many to be true: that the United States' involvement in the Spanish-American War was in large part due to the Hearst publications' sensationalistic journalism. The power of the Hearst media empire was illustrated again in 1941 when Hearst forced RKO, the producer of *Citizen Kane*, not to show that film in its theaters nationwide. The threat was to refuse ads listing any RKO theater offerings in Hearst's many newspapers around the country, which would have caused RKO a tremendous financial loss.

This blacklisting of *Citizen Kane* nicely illustrates the great censorship potential of concentrated media power. But back in those days, all big cities had more than one newspaper so that no small group or individuals could effectively control the newspaper business. (It was not until about 1950 that television usurped the role of newspapers as the principal news source for a growing majority of people in the United States and Canada.)

Today's media conglomerates are a good deal more worrisome than were the newspaper chains of old, because they concentrate power into an extremely few hands in *all* of the major news media—television, radio, mass-circulation magazines and newspapers. (Independent newspapers still exist in some cities and towns, but their number shrinks every year, and most big cities now are down to just one daily paper, usually owned by a large and powerful chain.) So today, a single individual may control quite a few TV outlets as well as newspapers and magazines, as does, for example, Rupert Murdoch (the Fox TV network, the New York *Daily News*, and many other newspapers, including the *London Times*, and magazines worldwide).

Equally frightening is the fact that the new giant media empires are parts of even larger conglomerates whose primary interests tend to be elsewhere than in the mass news media, and whose ruling principle is the bottom line, not the best possible dissemination of the news. Here is a list of some of the holdings of four of the megaconglomerates that have large media holdings:

**Time Warner** owns or controls Turner Broadcasting (CNN, TNT, TBS, Turner Entertainment*), HBO, Cinemax, Six Flags Cable franchises, TCI Cable, Warner Brothers, Comedy Central, Turner Publishing, Turner Classic Movies, *Sports Illustrated*, *Time*, *Life*, *People*, and dozens of other magazines, the Book-of-the-Month Club, and Warner Brothers Television ("Murphy Brown," "ER," etc.). Oh, yes, Time Warner also owns the Atlanta Braves and the Atlanta Hawks and has a 14.5 percent share of Seagrams (liquor). (We've listed fewer than half of TW's holdings, by the way.)

**General Electric** owns NBC (NBC Network News, nine NBC local stations, "Dateline NBC," the "Today Show," CNBC, etc.) and a large slice of Court TV, Bravo, the Arts and Entertainment (A&E) channel, the American Movie Classics (AMC) channel, the History channel, Romance classics, and several regional sports channels. It's listed, by the way, as number one (tied with General Motors) in the Forbes 500 corpo-

---

*Which owns the rights to MGM, RKO, and pre-1950 Warner Brothers films.

rate rankings. GE manufactures aircraft engines, power generators, appliances, bulbs, etc., and owns an important insurance division.

**Disney/Cap Cities** owns ABC ("ABC Network News," "Prime Time Live," "20/20," TV stations serving one-fourth of U.S. households; radio stations serving 24 percent of U.S. households, etc.), over a dozen newspapers, three record companies, two book publishers, Miramax Film Corp., Walt Disney Pictures, and five magazine publishers, not to mention Disneyland, Disneyworld, etc. Disney/Cap Cities also runs over 400 Disney stores nationwide, selling Disney products, and has a nice slice of Berkshire Hathaway, Inc., one-third of A&E, 80 percent of ESPN, and a small part of Sid R. Bass (crude petroleum and natural gas). (They're number 48 on the Forbes 500 list.)

**Westinghouse** owns CBS ("60 Minutes," "CBS Evening News," etc., and dozens of local CBS TV stations). It is heavily involved in nuclear power plant design and maintenance, insurance, financing (Bankers Trust, for example), radioactive waste disposal, telephone, and other communication systems.

So all four major networks, plus CNN (and thus all TV news channels of consequence) are owned by huge many-product megacorporations. Oh, yes, we've forgotten to mention the gigantic newspaper and media service corporations such as Gannett, Knight-Ridder, Times Mirror, New York Times, Tribune Company, Newhouse, etc.— groups that control an ever-larger portion of the newspaper business in America today.*

Well, then, why should the rest of us care about this concentration of media power into fewer and fewer hands? Doesn't size, after all, yield efficiency? Aren't large news companies better able to afford large staffs of reporters gathering news items around the world? The answer to both of these questions may well be yes. But three other nagging questions immediately arise. Will being *able to afford* larger staffs automatically translate in practice into larger staffs? Will greater efficiency generally translate into better news reporting or simply into greater profits? Will media moguls resist the temptation to further their own interests, including the interests of their own nonnews subsidiaries, at the expense of news quality and fair evaluation? The answer to all of these questions, unfortunately, seems to be no.

*Item*: After the Winston-Salem (North Carolina) *Journal* was taken over by the huge Media General Corporation, efficiency experts placed news stories into categories, determining, for example, that A-1 stories were to be limited to six column inches or less of space and that reporters were to spend no more than 0.9 hours per story and were to produce 40 items of this kind per week. Longer stories, labeled B-3, were to be limited to six to twelve column inches of space, and a good reporter was to research and produce seven such stories per week. Clearly, this sort of efficiency is bound to reduce reporter thoroughness and discourage true investigative reporting, which happens, unfortunately, to require a great deal of reporter time and effort and isn't often reportable in six to twelve column inches of space.†

*Item*: In 1996, ABC devoted the entire two hours of a "Good Morning America" program to a show on Disney World; ran a special program "Disney's Most Un-

---

*A great deal has been written of late about this ever-increasing concentration of mass media power. Of particular interest is the entire June 3, 1996, issue of *The Nation*.
†For more on this, see *The Washington Spectator*, July 1, 1996, or the University of North Carolina *Journalist*.

likely Heroes"; and featured footage from the Disney film *The Hunchback of Notre Dame* as well as a special program on the making of that film. (Responding to criticism for promoting Disney products as news, a Disney spokesperson told the *Wall Street Journal* [July 12, 1996], "I think we would have been faulted for *not* using that kind of synergy.")

*Item*: Jim Hightower, described as a "sharp-tongued Texas populist," was one of the more popular radio talk-show hosts. His program reached an estimated 1.5 million listeners on some 150 radio stations nationwide before it was canceled by ABC on September 5, 1995. On his August 19 program, Hightower had criticized Disney/Cap City for replacing full-time employees with contract workers who had to pay for uniforms and tools out of their $4.25-per-hour salaries while Disney's CEO made $78,000 per hour (that's 16,000 times as much as $4.25 per hour!). On his September 4 program, Hightower chastised ABC for caving in to tobacco company lawsuit threats and remarked that ABC "had just merged with the Mickey Mouse empire of Disney, Inc." (In defense of ABC—sort of—it should be noted that Hightower's attacks on big businesses had been losing advertisers for stations carrying his program. For more on this story, see *Extra! Update*, December 1995.)

If you think about it for just a moment, it should become clear that it isn't reasonable to expect, say, NBC to look for and to present news of chicanery engaged in by its parent company, General Electric, or to wait for CBS to blow the whistle on Westinghouse. Indeed, we should expect that every major media interest will tread lightly when reporting the doings of any of the other powerful media groups (recall the remarks before about the way in which power tends to cooperate with power).

Having just mentioned Disney/Cap City several times brings to mind one of the few definite advantages of mass media control by powerful megacorporations. As you might imagine, Disney/Cap City would like very much to get a nice slice of the growing Chinese market for films and other entertainment products. So Disney was con-

---

*The media watchdog magazine* Extra! *is an excellent source of information about the media of the kind that rarely appears in mass media publications or on TV news programs. Here, for example, is an interesting item from their February 1996* Extra! Update:

---

*Time* magazine (12/18/95) ran an article applauding Channel One, the video service that delivers a mix of commercials, infotainment and headline news to a captive audience of high school students. *Time* claimed that "more than 90 percent of teachers in Channel One schools approve of the show"—citing an "independent study" that was actually funded by the company which until recently owned Channel One, a company that was 40 percent controlled by Time Warner (a connection unmentioned in *Time*'s report). While the magazine mentioned that "Channel One still raises hackles in some quarters," it didn't mention that these quarters include the National Education Association (representing 2.2 million teachers) and the national PTA. *Time*'s article contained not one word from these critics about why it might be a bad idea to force students to watch commercials in school.

fronted with a very tough choice when Chinese authorities warned Disney executives in late 1996 that China would be forced to "reconsider" Disney investment plans in that country if Disney failed to put the kibosh on a movie that portrayed the current situation in Tibet from the point of view of the exiled Tibetan Dalai Lama. Smaller companies might well have felt unable to withstand the threat of being shut out of the Chinese market and have caved in to the threat, but Disney, to its great credit, stood fast and continued production of the film—which, of course, will not be allowed to be shown in China. (For more on this, see, for example, the November 26, 1996, *New York Times*.)

Another important recent development in the news business is a direct offshoot of the one just discussed: The megacorporations that now dominate the news industry are under much greater pressure to produce very large profits than were the news organizations of old. In particular, institutional investors, owning very large blocks of stocks in these huge corporations, demand high profit margins—the threat being to sell shares and seriously lower stock prices. Here is an excerpt from a July 29/August 5, 1996, article in *The Nation* on how market forces led to the demise of a fine big-city daily newspaper:

> A stunning recent example comes in the person of Mark Willess, chairman, president and CEO of the Times Mirror Company [*L.A. Times*, etc., who] had no experience in journalism before joining Times Mirror from General Mills [food products] last year. He followed the usual regimen of new managers, slashing thousands of jobs and imposing lofty profit targets. He terminated *New York Newsday*, a fine but insufficiently profitable alternative voice to the city's three daily papers [New York once had almost a dozen dailies]. All this stimulated "euphoria" on Wall Street, . . . and Times Mirror was rewarded with a nearly doubled stock price (which put millions in the pocket of Willess, who had cleverly tied his compensation to the company's stock price).*

Perhaps the least expected recent development is Oprah Winfrey's use of her TV pulpit to convince audiences that *reading books* can be both fun and informative.† When Oprah selects a book for discussion on her program, it usually rises quickly onto best-seller lists. People write to her about how they have started reading and love it. Hooray for Oprah Winfrey! (On the negative side, Winfrey engages in some of the shoddy news practices that are routine on TV and radio talk shows—for example, concerning health news.)

Which brings us to the Internet, interactive television, and the other electronic wonders. At this time (May 1997), no one knows how these new media will work out with respect to the news and other kinds of information. Bill Gates, for example, says that within a few years people will regularly be watching TV programs on their computer screens. TV sets now are available that can do some of the simple things done by computers. HDTV (high-definition TV) is on the horizon. Most computers these days are programmed to handle CD-ROMs containing whole dictionaries, almanacs, encyclopedias, and the like. Billions are being wagered one way or another in the attempt to get in on the ground floor of the new ways in which the electronic marvel industry is going to change our lives.

---

*For more on this topic, see the *Columbia Journalism Review*, September/October 1996.
†See, for instance, Caryn James's "Critics Notebook" (*New York Times*, November 21, 1996).

*Here is an excerpt from a January 31, 1997, syndicated column by the well-known journalist Molly Ivins, which illustrates how many journalists feel about the recent "conglomeratization" of the mass media:*

I'm apparently up for sale, along with my newspaper, the *Fort Worth Star-Telegram*. Our corporate masters have put us on the bidding block, and here we stand, waiting for prospective buyers to come along and inspect our teeth, as it were.

As a veteran of this experience (this is my fourth time on the block) I prefer it when the corporate masters announce the results abruptly after the deed is done. That way, you don't have time to worry about which Simon Legree might come along and snap you up as a bargain at the price. "Could have been worse," we say to one another after the done deal is announced. "We could have gone to Rupert Murdoch." Mr. Murdoch is widely regarded as the worst plantation owner producing our line of crops.

Trouble is, the news business is rapidly becoming one big plantation. I'm looking over the list of potential bidders the same way they're looking over us. Si Newhouse is on the list. Murray Kempton once observed, "I think Si Newhouse has lost his moral compass since Roy Cohn died"—the single meanest thing I've ever heard said about anyone.* . . .

We're on the block because our division is producing a profit of *only* $200 million a year. That barely covers Michael Ovitz's golden parachute. Wednesday, the Walt Disney Co. announced a 33 percent increase in its net income in the first quarter of fiscal '97. . . .

I'm teaching a course [at the University of California at Berkeley] to some of the world's brightest graduate students, trying to convince them that journalism is an honorable and important craft.

We discuss ethical traps and libel and fairness, the morality of writing about the private lives of public figures, and the corruption of politics by money. We talk about how to report on the public's business without squeezing out all the life and suspense and juice and joy and humor of it. And, of course, we study the media and the concentration of media ownership and its effect on what we do. . . .

I've never had much use for management myself. I've worked for a wide variety of managements, and the result is that I always join a union if there's one available. When management was the art of getting a whole bunch of people together to do something in the best way possible, I had some interest in it. But now that it has become an endless quest for increased quarterly profits, I find it boring and a menace to quality. . . .

—Reprinted by permission of Creator's Syndicate.

---

*If you don't know about Roy Cohn, try *Citizen Cohn* by Nicholas Von Hoffman (New York: Doubleday, 1988).

Perhaps the biggest threat to current news dissemination of these new electronic devices has to do with advertising and the Internet. Newspapers get most of their revenue from ads, including classified ads. If a good deal of this advertising revenue is diverted to the Internet, newspapers will suffer greatly, and many, perhaps most, could go out of business.

It also has been argued that the Internet is going to increase the division in large, industrial countries between the resources available to the rich as compared to the poor. Libraries, for example, have traditionally been free sources of all kinds of information; the Internet seems to be headed more and more toward information provided at a price that may seriously limit access by the poor.

But many, on the contrary, see the Internet as a wonderful democratizing force, counteracting the concentration of media power now taking place. The Internet, some say, provides a megaphone for ordinary people, allowing all of us to tell the world what is on our minds. (Whether the world will be tuned in is another matter.) Correspondence via e-mail also seems to have great promise as an information source. But so far, the now-traditional media (television, radio, newspapers, periodicals, libraries) still remain the principal news and information sources for the vast majority of people.

## SUMMARY OF CHAPTER 11

1. The mass media are businesses intent on making money. So they have to satisfy their audiences, advertisers, and governments.

   They cater to their audiences by simplifying the news to make it more easily understood—by breaking news items into small "sound bites" that stay within the average attention span in length and by arranging coverage of news so as to conform to audience interests and prejudices. *Example*: The 1996 Olympic Games coverage on NBC, larded over with human interest stories. (Note that organized groups of people—for instance, the NRA—have more clout than do isolated individuals.)

   The media cater to advertisers by suppressing news that reflects badly on them or their products and by touting advertisers' products free as "news" items. *Example*: Proctor and Gamble pressuring TV stations into not running an item critical of Folger's coffee.

   They also bow to the power of government to harass by rescinding licenses or censoring anti-CIA exposés, by playing favorites in the dissemination of news, and by awarding damages for alleged cases of libel. *Example*: The *Milkovich* court decision that exposed the media to new libel risks concerning what is said in editorials, commentaries, and columns. The media often give in to this power of government by treading more carefully in criticizing government actions. *Example*: Reporters at press conferences who are careful not to ask overly pointed follow-up questions. (Note that the power of government to censor is much greater in many other countries than in the United States and in most other industrial democracies.)

   But the mass media have a good deal of power of their own, stemming from their ability to expose and publicize whatever they care to. *Famous example*:

The *Washington Post*'s dogged exposé of the Watergate scandal that forced President Nixon to resign in disgrace.

The business world—in particular, very large corporations—have a large say in the dissemination of news, which they use, first, to suppress stories unfavorable to their interests and, second, to get favorable stories included in media presentations. This power of big business stems from its power as advertisers (to withdraw advertising), from its ability to influence politicians and governments (principally through "campaign contributions"), and from its ownership of a good deal of the mass media. *Example*: Disney/Cap Cities media outlets touting Disney products.

Of course, in practice the media tend to try to satisfy all of the various power factions and to not needlessly throw their weight around. It almost always is more profitable to cooperate with power than to fight it. *Example*: Politicians and the media cooperating to produce sound bites: The pols get exposure and the media get footage to show on the evening news.

2. Since the bottom line is, as they say, the bottom line, news-gathering methods tend to be designed to save money, which means that regular beats are set up to gather the news from those able to regularly supply it (the rich and/or powerful and the government). True investigative reporting is very costly and so relatively less common than a mere gathering of the news from other sources. *Example*: The regular attendance at presidential press conferences as compared to the amount of journalistic digging below the surface.

3. One lesson to be learned from what has been said so far is that the media tend to misdirect audience attention away from important, underlying issues and events to human interest stories. Another lesson is that the media tend to take advantage of the average person's lack of a good sense of proportion.

4. What happens every day is not new, and therefore not usually considered to be news. *Example*: The ongoing and extremely serious threat posed by bacteria and viruses that tends to get only sporadic coverage.

The media's theory of objectivity, to which lip service is widely paid, requires that news stories be separated from speculations, judgments, evaluations, and the like, which are considered to be subjective. But this theory is off the mark. Facts don't just lie around waiting to be picked up; reporters must reason to the facts. Similarly, decisions as to what will be covered and what will not depend in part on value judgments, so that news and evaluations cannot be separated.

In practice, however, the theory of objectivity simply keeps the media from straying too far in their judgments and evaluations from the mainstream social consensus. *Example*: Their attempts to be objective by being "evenhanded" merely result in our hearing what the Democrats have to say as compared to the Republicans.

Because the theory of objectivity says that news reporting must be separated from judgments, speculation, and background information, the mass media tend to be short on explanations as to why things happen as they do. *Example*: Reporters covering stories about civil service wages who don't have any idea whether they are too high or too low.

Of course, reporters cannot be expected to be experts on every topic they cover. But they still want to appear to be authoritative—to appear to know what they are talking about whether they do or don't. *Example*: Dan Rather reporting from the midst of a hurricane.

The media generally want to play it safe when featuring expert opinion. They want to satisfy all relevant power factions, if possible. So they tend to consult establishment figures, including media bigwigs, and not annoy their audiences. The result often is silly pontificating. *Example*: The political correctness of almost all political discussion.

Note that the media sometimes act as self-censors, either out of patriotic intent (as in wartime), or in order to placate their audiences or advertisers, or to avoid the possibility of libel. *Example*: Showing Elvis Presley doing his stuff only from the waist up on the old Ed Sullivan show.

5. The media need to slant the news can be accomplished in quite a few different ways: playing a story up or down, using a misleading or sensational headline, omitting or playing down follow-up stories, using (or not using) emotive language, and using cartoons to convey a point of view. *Example*: Burying reports on the virtues of the Canadian single-payer health care system at the end of articles after presenting critical material at the beginning.

6. The most important mass medium these days is television, which serves as town crier, certifier, and grapevine. It is the chief medium on which political contests are fought and news about major events such as wars is disseminated. No other medium comes close to television in the size of its audience or the immediacy of its offerings.

The result is that the television industry has greater power than the other media and indeed can and does influence the course of events in the world on which it reports. *Example*: The way in which TV coverage of war affected the recent War in the Gulf.

Even prime-time television entertainment sometimes has positive features. *Example*: It has helped to break down prejudices against ethnic and religious groups and women—portraying blacks and women in important jobs in the business community, and so on. Note also the positive effects of employing African Americans and women on TV news programs. (TV also is superior in explaining the news to ordinary people on the street.)

7. Although the mass media are a modestly good source of breaking news, smaller-scale outlets are much better at analysis, at supplying background information, and at investigative reporting. *Example*: "Bill Moyers' Journal" PBS story on how money buys "access" to government.

While PBS and CNN are good sources of news, background information, and analysis, lots of small-circulation magazines are significantly better, being crafted so as to appeal to a more sophisticated audience. *Example*: The *Atlantic Monthly* article "Rubbish."

But the point is selectivity, not mass versus non–mass media. This is true not only with respect to television, newspapers, radio, and magazines, but also to books. Popular books tend to be lighter weight than some that are less popular, because mass audiences tend to be rather unsophisticated. *Example*: *Discover* and *Omni* magazines, which hoke up science in the attempt to make it interesting to a mass audience. (Note that presidential memoirs often are particularly shoddy products. *Example*: President Reagan's rearrangement of facts called *An American Life*.)

8.  The intense concentration of media power in the hands of giant conglomerates is one of the more ominous recent developments in the media business. *Example*: Westinghouse owning CBS, dozens of local stations, nuclear power plants, etc. Although size can yield efficiency and better news coverage, in general it hasn't worked that way so far. *Example*: Disney/Cap Cities' firing Jim Hightower for criticizing Disney/Cap Cities. But large scale at least once enabled a news source to resist pressure to censor by foreign governments, namely, Disney/Cap Cities standing up to Chinese pressure to censor. Finally, what the Internet and computers hold for the future is an interesting and as-yet-unanswered question.

## Exercise 11-1

1.  Evaluate the coverage in your local newspaper of a particular event or issue of national importance, with respect to (a) objectivity, (b) original versus second-hand reporting, (c) use of headlines, (d) establishment or mainstream point of view compared to minority opinions, and (e) any other matters discussed in this chapter.

2.  Do the same for a recent issue of *Time*, *Newsweek*, or *U.S. News and World Report*.

3.  Do the same for an ABC, NBC, or CBS national evening news program.

4.  Get a recent copy of *The Economist*, a British news magazine that widely circulates in the United States and Canada. Select a story in it about a particular event and compare how it is handled with the way it is dealt with in one of the major American news magazines.

5.  Compare news reporting on the BBC world news program carried on National Public Radio (NPR) with news reporting on any commercial TV or radio station. Which is better, and why?

6.  Watch several TV episodes of "ER" and of "Chicago Hope" and explain how doctors and the medical industry are portrayed. Be sure to explain how their portrayal is like and how different (if it is) from the real medical world. Do you think these programs influence how viewers tend to see doctors and medical care?

7.  How are the elderly and teenagers portrayed on network TV programs, both in news stories and, especially, in popular entertainment programs? Back up your conclusions with details.

8.  Check the front page of a single issue of your local newspaper and determine as best you can the sources of their stories. (In the case of wire stories—Associated Press, Reuters, and the like—try to determine their sources.) How many

of these stories are based primarily on a single handout or speech, how many were compiled from several such sources, and how many from reporters going out and finding for themselves what is going on?

9. Read through a single issue of three non–mass media magazines, one liberal (for instance, *The Washington Monthly*), one conservative (say, the *National Review*), and one libertarian (for example, *Reason*). Are their points of view evident? How do you think they compare to mass media magazines such as *Time* or *Newsweek*, or to national TV news programs?

10. There were lots of complaints, chiefly from men, about how NBC "skewed coverage" of the 1996 Olympic Games so as to appeal to women as well as men. The complaints centered on the increase in human-interest background material at the expense of coverage of the events themselves and on the concentration on women's events and those that might appeal more to women. (Recall the discussion of this earlier in the chapter.) But shouldn't coverage be made to appeal to women as well as men? Doesn't fair play and equality require that this be the case? So shouldn't the media be applauded rather than criticized for this? Doesn't it constitute better coverage if it interests more people? Defend your answers against likely objections. (By the way, in your opinion, was NBC right about what sort of sports coverage most women prefer?)

11. How do you think the news would be presented to us if the federal government controlled and managed the mass media? Be specific and defend your answer with some thoughtful analysis.

12. Suppose that you owned a local television station or newspaper, or a whole television network. Would you report the news any differently than the outlets in your area do now? If so, how, and why? If not, why not? (Assume that, while rich, you can't withstand losses forever. And be realistic, not goody-goody.)

13. There are many more women working in the mass media than in the old days, but fewer women than men rise to the top. Perhaps one reason for this is the desire of many media women to have a career and also raise a family, given the fact that the industry is not set up to accommodate this. In a letter to the editor of *Editor & Publisher* (February 24, 1996), Marcia Meier described the extremely long hours required and how, even with 16 years in the media, 10 with the same newspaper, and having risen to editorial page editor, she still was "chewed out for not working more than 8 hours a day" and, during one news "redesign," was chastised because she left for home after "only 12 hours" on the job. Her lament was that the industry doesn't practice what it preaches for other industries: "more humane hours, job sharing, flex time when possible, support around pregnancy and birth issues, and corporate compassion."

It would be interesting to speculate about whether it wouldn't be a good idea not to require anyone, men or women, to work extremely long hours, have to bring home work problems, etc., and whether society as a whole doesn't need to institute better mechanisms so that both men and women can have careers as well as family lives. But the question here has to do with how the news is packaged and disseminated now. Do you think the fact that men hold so many of the top positions in the mass media and thus make most of the important policy decisions seriously influences work conditions and news content in ways that would be different if women were equally represented in news media high management? If so, how? If not, why not?

14. *For the energetic*: Go to the library and dig through back issues of some mass media publication (guided perhaps by referring to the *Reader's Guide to Periodical Literature*) and evaluate its coverage over time of some important, underlying, or long-term national issue or problem (for example, under- and unemployment, crime, pollution, etc.). Defend your evaluation.

15. *Also for the energetic*: Write your own news story about a personal event that truthfully makes you look bad. Write it as though it were to appear in your local, or school, newspaper, including headlines and the rest. Now rewrite the story to show your part in it in the best light possible without actually lying. Compare the two. Was this little exercise educational? (Answer: Very definitely, *if* you did it well.)

16. When confronted with the claim of bias implicit in ABC TV's "Good Morning America" having spent a whole two-hour program solely on Disney World, owned by ABC's parent corporation, Mark Burstein, executive producer for "Good Morning America," is quoted in *The Nation* (October 28, 1996) as responding: "You hope people are smart enough to know we're not going to let the ownership issue interfere with our editorial decisions." Well, then, what is your opinion on this matter? Would ABC not let the "ownership issue" interfere with editorial decisions? Defend your answer.

17. When you were in high school, did your class get Channel One, the video news and commercial program that is tailored for high school students? If so, what was your opinion of it? It has been frequently criticized for exposing students to commercials without their consent. What do you think about this?

18. Recall the discussion earlier about how Disney/Cap Cities stood up to a Chinese threat and continued production and distribution of a film the Chinese didn't want produced. As this edition of *Logic and Contemporary Rhetoric* was being printed, it was unclear just how China would respond or whether Disney might change its mind. So what was the upshot of this confrontation between China and Disney/Cap Cities? (If you don't know the answer to this question, do some research. If you think you do know, do some anyway.)

19. The thrust of the discussion about the recent intense concentration of media power into fewer and fewer hands was that on the whole this is bad for the effective dissemination of the news. We noted, for example, that the chief concern of these large corporations is the bottom line, not the best presentation of the news. But isn't it possible, perhaps even likely, that these megacorporations will find that the highest profits are obtained by best satisfying their audiences, thus putting all of us (collectively) into the driver's seat—being given the sort of news coverage we most prefer? And if so, isn't that all to the good? So why worry about the concentration of media power that has been taking place lately?

20. A January 1994 "Prime Time Live" TV program criticized the Independent Insurance Agents of America (IIAA) for treating some congressional staff mem-

bers to a Key West holiday. (Yes, lobbying does go on among congressional staffers.) But as *The New Yorker* pointed out (September 12, 1994), several months before that the IIAA had paid Sam Donaldson, co-anchor of "Prime Time Live," a $30,000 "lecture fee." (No, they didn't mention this on "Prime Time Live.") Donaldson's defense, according to *The New Yorker* article, was that journalists are different from members of Congress, "because we don't write the laws." (1) Does this justify Donaldson's taking the money? Defend your answer. You might even want to check the magazine article in question for more information on the topic. (But note the interesting fact that the "Prime Time Live" program criticized the IIAA, rather than tooting its horn, so that news coverage doesn't seem to have been distorted by Donaldson's having taken the money.) (2) How do you feel, in general, about media stars receiving large lecture fees from organizations that the media are supposed to cover in an unbiased way?

21. Your reward for diligently answering the previous 20 questions is this give-away question. Write a comment to go below this Feiffer cartoon, tying it, in the best way you can, to the topics discussed in this chapter. (Your model might be how this was done in the case of the cartoons on pages 246 and 270.)

Feiffer © Jules Feiffer. Reprinted with permission of Universal Press Syndicate.
All rights reserved.

# Dependence Day, 1993

EDWARD SOREL

This July 4, Senator Dole has a special reason for celebrating. The American political system has been good to him. According to reports filed with the Federal Election Commission, his campaign receipts for 1991-92 totaled $2,362,936—almost all from special interests. His agribusiness contributors include Philip Morris, Dow Chemical, John Deere, Kellogg, General Mills, Archer Daniels Midland and Farmland Industries. (Dole is a senior Republican on the Agriculture, Nutrition and Forestry Committee.)

Finance and real estate interests also contribute. These include Equitable Life, Goldman Sachs, American Express, Glendale Federal Savings and Loan, PaineWebber, First Boston, Chemical Bank, Mutual of Omaha and Prudential Insurance, among others. (Dole is *the* senior Republican on the Finance Committee.)

Senator Dole insists that his interventions on behalf of his contributors are perfectly legal, and while being interviewed by *The Wall Street Journal* was surprisingly frank about how Congress operates: "When these political action committees give money, they expect something in return other than good government."

From *The Nation*. Reprinted by permission of Edward Sorel.

*T*his drawing (with comment) by Edward Sorel, whose excellent work frequently graces the pages of The New Yorker, The Nation, *and* Atlantic *magazines, nicely illustrates the point that lobbying in the United States today is quite different from, and a good deal more insidious than, the lobbying described in public school textbooks.*

*Not to know what has happened before one was born is always to be a child.*

— Cicero

*A high school teacher, after all, is a person deputized by the rest of us to explain to the young what sort of world they are living in and to defend, if possible, the part their elders are playing in it.*

— Emile Capouya

*A child educated only at school is an uneducated child.*

— George Santayana (see also the *Calvin and Hobbes* cartoon on page 274)

*The less people know about how sausages and laws are made, the better they'll sleep at night.*

— Otto von Bismarck

*Germany has taught me that an uncritical view of the national past generated an equally subservient acceptance of the present.*

— Hans Schmitt (who grew up in Nazi Germany)

*If a nation expects to be ignorant and free, . . . it expects what never was and never will be.*

— Thomas Jefferson

*Chapter*

# 12

# TEXTBOOKS: MANAGING WORLD VIEWS

Public schools are one of the earliest sources of information about the world that most of us are exposed to. So it is important to have a good idea about how accurate what we have been told while growing up might be.

One way to get an idea of the way a subject is presented in public school classrooms is to examine the way it is dealt with in typical textbooks adopted for those classes. The good news here is that textbooks that have been coming off the presses in recent years are on the whole probably the best of their kind that have ever been published—anywhere.

> He that reads and grows no wiser seldom suspects his own deficiency, but complains of hard words and obscure sentences, and asks why books are written which cannot be understood.
>
> — Samuel Johnson

## 1. HISTORY AND SOCIAL STUDIES TEXTBOOKS

Textbooks don't stay the same for very long. Ups and downs in quality and content are bound to occur every so often. But since about 1960, the quality of history and social studies textbooks used in public schools in America has improved in ways that are both dramatic and radically different from anything that had ever happened before.

The first of these improvements was in the portrayal of African Americans in United States history and civics texts. Blacks had been close to invisible in texts published before that time. They were mentioned, of course, with respect to slavery and its elimination via the Emancipation Proclamation, and reference generally was made to two "token" Negroes, Booker T. Washington and George Washington Carver. (It wasn't unusual, by the way, for publishers to print two versions of their American history texts, one that fitted Southern attitudes toward the Civil War and nonwhites, the other in tune with the rest of the country.) But by some time in the 1970s, virtually all history and civics texts had been revised to include more, and fairer, material about African Americans and their place in American history and everyday affairs.

Improved treatment of other minority groups and of women quickly (as these things go) followed, reflecting changing attitudes and roles in the body politic. Today, virtually every high school history textbook mentions the "Trail of Tears" (the forced move of the Cherokee Indians from their homeland in the South to the Oklahoma territory), the illegal incarceration of loyal Japanese citizens in concentration camps during World War II, and so on.* Today there are no textbooks for "home economics" classes—classes intended to help turn young girls into good housewives—because there no longer are any such classes. (Students today would very likely find the old "home ec" texts rather amusing, even hilarious.)

Coupled with the improved treatment of minority groups has come a moderately large step toward objectivity in the portrayal of the darker side of American history and of the current social system. Imperialistic interference in the affairs of other countries—for example, of the so-called "banana republics"† of Central and South America—sometimes is hinted at (although the nasty details are never gone into in any

---

*Interestingly, hardly any texts mention homosexuals (about 5 percent of the population?), and, while Jews are referred to, anti-Semitism in this country rarely is discussed except in connection with the Ku Klux Klan. Some books do mention the discrimination against the Irish that was common in times past, but never with more than a line or two. (The paucity of textbooks that talk about homosexuals has made the selection of texts quite difficult in the very few places—the most prominent being San Francisco—where gays have a certain amount of political clout.)
†The expression derives from the way in which the United Fruit Company dominated the political affairs of many of these countries for many years.

depth), a few of the shortcomings of the American court system are mentioned, and so on.

Oh, yes—the bad news. The bad news is that these improvements tend to be buried under a mass of dull verbiage, so that only the brightest and most diligent students who do a good amount of reading between the lines are apt to learn much from them about the true history of their country or about the way in which social institutions actually work (as opposed to how they are supposed to work). Very little in these texts is likely to raise student interest in these matters. Most of the better-selling senior high school history textbooks now run to at least 800 large pages of double-column type (some contain more than a thousand pages), with endless "learning aids," questions, special features, and the like.* (Social studies texts are a bit shorter.) The small amount of negative material are easily overlooked. Students are snowed by the mountains of facts ladled out one after the other in an "and then this happened and then that happened" style that is completely devoid of what English teachers refer to as *voice* or *tone*. Names that even professional historians would not always be able to identify—for example, of some of the failed early-nineteenth-century vice-presidential candidates— pile up one after the other as details concerning the election of 1816, the election of 1820, the election of 1824 . . . are described. Interesting topics have the guts wrung out of them. Even accounts of the good features of the American social system tend to fall flat.

It also is true that in the past several years a great many textbooks have been "dumbed down" with respect to vocabulary and sentence construction, although more linguistically sophisticated texts still are available. (One interesting consequence of this dumbing down is that these texts contain fewer obscure and inconsequential facts for students to memorize—hopefully more understanding thus can take place.)

That detailed facts spewed out one after another don't easily become part of the working knowledge of students is supported by all sorts of surveys (in which, for instance, students identified J. Edgar Hoover as a nineteenth-century president and Jefferson Davis as a guitar player). But students also don't seem to grasp the general, or approximate, kinds of knowledge that are more important than most precise facts. It's more important, for example, that students know the approximate size and population of their country rather than precise statistics on this matter, and the evidence indicates the ideas of most students concerning these important statisics are either way off the mark or nonexistent.

As evidence of this, consider a 1990 Gallup poll of 1,225 adult Americans, most of whom were educated in public schools. When asked about the current population of the United States, 17 percent answered less than 50 million people; 26 percent less than 200 million; 27 percent between 200 and 300 million; and 15 percent over 500 million; with 30 percent being unwilling even to venture a guess. (There was some overlap in the figures.) (And what percentage of respondents had the right answer?) The average respondent in this survey believed that Latinos constitute 21 percent of

---

*Interestingly, units labeled "critical reasoning" now tend to occur here and there in most of the newer social studies and history textbooks.

*Here are typical responses of twenty African American professional baseball players to the question "What does Jackie Robinson mean to you?" as reported in* Sport *magazine (January 1990—team affiliations are those of 1990):*

Fred McGriff, Toronto Blue Jays: That's kind of tough [to answer] because I've never seen him play.
Barry Bonds, Pittsburgh Pirates: I know very little about [Robinson].
Chili Davis, California Angels: I don't know much about [Robinson]. All I know is that he was the first black [major league player].
Dwight Gooden, New York Mets: I didn't follow Jackie Robinson's career.
Ricky Jordan, Philadelphia Phillies: Sorry, I can't help you.
Ricky Henderson, Oakland Athletics: The success of Jackie Robinson is the reason I wear his number. The man was a great player.

*Half of the 20 ballplayers had next to no idea who Jackie Robinson was. (And who* was *Jackie Robinson?)*

the population in the United States, Jews 18 percent, and African Americans 32 percent (the average black person in the survey thought the right figure was 48 percent).*

It's true, of course, that there are some specific facts that every adult person who intends to participate in the political process ought to know, and one unfortunate general fact is that large numbers of adult Americans do not know them. (The same is true of Canadians, Germans, etc.—Americans are not a unique case by any means.) For instance, 22 percent of the respondents to a 1995 Gallup poll of 1,020 adults did not know about our having dropped two, or any, atomic bombs on Japan during World War II (35 percent didn't know that Hiroshima was thus destroyed). Indeed, about one-third of respondents to a CBS news poll could not name a single country that the United States fought against in that indescribably terrible war. (Let's hope that George Santayana was wrong when he said that "Those who do not remember the past are condemned to relive it.")

## 2. TEXTBOOKS AND INDOCTRINATION

The obvious question to ask is why public school textbooks are written in the way just described. There is no easy answer to this question, but one thing is clear. The ultimate purpose of public schools is to educate the young to fit into adult society. This means, first, giving them the knowledge they will need to be productive citizens and, second,

---

*It is very important that members of various ethnic and racial groups have some rough idea as to their strength in the general population, if for no other reason than that they then can gauge their organized clout in the social/political arena. Jews, for example, in fact constitute less than 2 percent of the American population, African Americans about 12 percent. Were these two groups represented as poll respondents believed, the political scene in the United States would be much different from what it is.

*From about the time just after World War II until very recently, science textbooks steadily improved both in accuracy and in content. But the "dumbing down" of public school textbooks mentioned before has affected some science texts, just as those concerning history and social studies. The idea seems to be to make science texts easier to read (by shortening sentences and limiting vocabulary), more interesting (by making science "relevant" and by pandering to pseudoscience) and, of course, politically correct (by fudging facts of geography, anthropology, etc.). There still are a great many excellent textbooks available, but there also are some that seriously cross over the line. An example is Prentice-Hall's* Exploring Earth Science.* This science text goes out of its way to discuss astrology (without ever using that term) in a chapter dealing with astronomy, leaving the impression that astrology has some scientific merit, or at least some truth to it. (Interestingly, the account of astrology is historically false.) At the end of the short discussion, students are asked: "Under what sign were you born? Do you know how your emotions are supposed to be affected by your sign?" No mention is made of the fact that emotions are not affected by signs of the zodiac. (This text also contains a gratuitous discussion of the completely unscientific Oriental theory of yin and yang—included to make the text "multicultural"?).***

*Upper Saddle River, New Jersey, 1995.
**For more about this and two other poor-quality science textbooks, see the September October 1996 issue of *The Textbook Letter*. Every issue of this excellent publication discusses and evaluates recent public school textbooks in the various disciplines.

inculcating in them the values, attitudes, and practices that will make them good citizens. Education thus inevitably involves a certain amount of *indoctrination*.*

Applying these thoughts to public school textbooks yields some tentative conclusions as to their likely content, conclusions that are borne out by examining these works. The first is that noncontroversial topics, like mathematics, will be presented in a more or less straightforward way, with indoctrination at a minimum. Society wants just about everybody to be able to do arithmetic. (But see the comments on pages 298–299 concerning math textbook adoptions.)

The second is that history and social studies texts are bound to distort their material. The history of every nation has its dark spots as well as bright, and no system works the way it is supposed to. Public school history and civics texts therefore inevitably distort their subject matter so as to make "Our Great Nation" appear better than it really is. No society wants disaffected citizens. Embarrassing matters have to be papered over somehow or other; exactly how depends on social and political factors that

---

*Although the primary intent of the adults who write and adopt public school textbooks is indeed to educate the young of their society, human nature being what it is, they also have another motive—to defend their own collective contribution to the history of their nation and to deny or play down their collective mistakes and misadventures. It's always difficult to notice how this creeps into the content and tone of the works of one's own group, but becomes more evident when we examine those of other societies.

change from time to time. Today, these factors are more favorable for providing students with greater accuracy and less indoctrination than ever before. (But not all is sweetness and light by any means, as we shall see shortly.)

A third tentative conclusion is that controversial topics such as lobbying, immigration, and social justice or its lack will be approached gingerly, or simply not discussed at all.

## 3. TEXTBOOKS AND POLITICS

When discussing the mass media in the previous chapter, we pointed out how the various interested parties—media owners, governments, big business, readers, and viewers—exert their power both in the political and the business arenas. The textbook arena also is the scene of power encounters, although, as should become evident, the various strengths and roles of the players are modestly different from what they are in the mass media. The players in the textbook political arena are (in the order of their relative power?) voters, in particular, parents of school children and organized groups of interested individuals; teachers, educators, and other scholars; and textbook manufacturers. Governments, of course, in particular, on the state and local level, have a large say in the matter, but they more or less act in response to guidance and pressure from the interested parties, and in particular to voter demands. There is nothing new in the fact that politics plays an important role in determining textbook content. It has always played a big role in the field of education. Even the idea of universal literacy was once fought over in the political arena. Until well into the nineteenth century, education in Europe and America was confined to the upper classes, with very few exceptions. Indeed, the dominant upper-class world view held that the masses of people were easier to control if they remained ignorant. (It also self-servingly held that the lower classes were too loutish to be able to learn to read and write with any facility.) The push for universal literacy began only with the nineteenth-century growth in the size and political power of the middle classes. Textbooks, in fact, themselves are an invention, more or less, of nineteenth-century educators. In Shakespeare's day, for instance, grammar school students were taught primarily from the great classical writings and other treatises.

In the United States today, textbooks are selected and purchased on the local level: School boards either select the texts to be used or provide teachers and school principals with lists of approved books. In practice, of course, local boards follow the advice of teachers, except when under political pressures or higher-level direction of the kinds about to be described. (Similar remarks, by the way, apply to the way things work in most other democratic countries, including Canada and most of the European democracies.)

School boards, elected by the public or appointed by elected officials, tend to be rather vulnerable to lobbying by politically active groups. These groups thus indirectly influence textbook publishers intent on satisfying the requirements of local and state boards. This is perhaps the most important reason for the textbook revisions in the treatment of class, gender, and race briefly described a while back. Publishers today wouldn't dream of using a title like *Man and His Changing World*, to cite a 1930s example, any more then they would illustrate a textbook exclusively with pictures of white, middle-class males. Minority groups with increasing political power are insisting that textbooks reflect more accurately the historical and cultural experiences and contributions of nonwhites, of women, and of other minority groups. Women's rights organizations have successfully reduced the use of sexist language in textbooks, and the hotly debated traditional canon of Western literature has been broadened to include a wider selection of multicultural writers. All of these changes have been politically driven.*

Another skirmish currently being fought on the textbook battlefield concerns the liberal versus conservative interpretation of traditional values. In 1995, for instance, the decision to use textbooks depicting nontraditional families (including homosexual parents) in certain San Francisco public schools sparked a controversy that threatened government funding. There also still is a good deal of infighting going on over the issue of evolution versus creationism (more about that later). Nor should we overlook the political fights over ideological issues concerning the quality and standards maintained in textbooks. Over the past two decades, the American school system has been intensively scrutinized and extensively criticized. Textbooks have come under fire, in particular, for being "dumbed down" both in content and linguistic sophistication. Educators are under pressure to raise textbook standards, to standardize content, and to link material to an increasing number of state and national achievement tests.

In times now long gone, funds spent by local boards in America came exclusively from local taxes—chiefly property taxes—and each district controlled its own choice of textbooks. Nowadays, a great deal of school money comes from state coffers, and even from the federal government, with the inevitable consequence that school boards are restricted from above as to their textbook choices. Political power concerning education thus has been dispersed from being almost exclusively local into entire states and even, to a lesser extent, to the nation as a whole. Nearly half of the states in America now have state textbook adoption committees that screen publisher offerings, in particular, those concerning basic or "sensitive" topics and books intended for the first six school grades. Local boards in states with textbook committees must choose books from lists approved for adoption within their state. Inevitably, politicking on the state (and to a much lesser extent) national levels increasingly shapes the content of the textbooks from which local boards must choose.

All of this means, by the way, that big business has less power in determining textbook content than it does in shaping the news offered by the mass media. But textbook publishing companies still exert a good deal of power in the textbook arena. State and local boards, after all, are forced to choose from the books offered to them by textbook publishers (whose number grows smaller every year because of the same market-driven forces that have been shrinking the number of mass media outlets). But publishers, in their turn, are guided by the demands of state and local agencies, especially of textbook committees in two key states—California (by far the largest buyer) and Texas (where pressure groups are the strongest).† That is why publisher power

---

*Of course, as in most cases of this kind, success very likely also depended on a readiness to change on the part of many ordinary citizens, the point being that perhaps organized groups can succeed only to the extent that the times are ripe, even though, without organized political pressure, little change might take place. In any case, organized political agitation surely was (and is) an important cause of widespread changes in attitude concerning minorities and women.
†A state committee in California approves all books used in kindergarten through the eighth grade; in Texas, through grade twelve. But California does lay down requirements that all texts used in every grade must meet.

*Here is part of what Texas textbook laws stipulate concerning the selection of texts to be used in Texas public schools:*

Illustrations and written materials shall avoid bias toward any particular group or individual and should present a wide range of goal choices. Particular care should be taken in the treatment of ethnic groups, roles of men and women, and the dignity of workers, and respect for the work ethic. [Textbooks] shall present examples of men and women participating in a variety of roles and activities and shall further present the economic, political, social, and cultural contributions of both men and women, past and present. . . . Traditional and contemporary roles of men, women, boys, and girls shall be included. . . .

Textbook content shall promote citizenship and understanding of the essentials and benefits of the free enterprise system, emphasize patriotism and respect for recognized authority, and promote respect for individual rights. [They shall not] include selections or works which encourage or condone civil disorder, social strife, or disregard of the law, [nor shall they] contain material which serves to undermine authority . . . or which would cause embarrassing situations or interference in the learning atmosphere of the classroom. . . . [They] shall not encourage life styles deviating from generally accepted standards of society.

derived from their role as commodity supplier is not as large as one might suppose.* A textbook that makes neither the California nor the Texas list is going to have a hard time hanging around long enough to find a sufficiently large constituency in other states, and so the major publishers pretty much have been forced to tailor their offerings accordingly. (Low-budget books intended for use in a single state or locality are obvious exceptions.) Further, because local boards also generally specify a pool of potential texts from which individual schools in their districts must select, publishers also have had to take these boards' preferences into account. The requirements of big city school boards (remember the extent to which the United States has become an urban society) thus are an important influence on textbook publishers.

But the large textbook conglomerates, just like other large corporations, can and do influence the marketplace for their products in another way, namely, by lobbying. (Interestingly, one of the important defects of social studies textbooks is that they must pussyfoot around controversial issues such as the effect of lobbying on the political process.) In 1996, for example, after intense lobbying by publishers, the California State Board of Education voted six to one to approve three new series of math textbooks for use in California schools even though they had been given very low scores by a special review committee of math instructors. Eliminated from the approved list, and thus ineligible for adoption in any California public school, was the rigorous math series developed by the

---

*If the idea that the supplier of a commodity has great power in determining the nature of those goods is foreign to you, think only of the way in which Microsoft, by gaining a controlling portion of the computer software market, has been able to influence the computer revolution.

University of Chicago and adopted by many prestigious private schools (including, interestingly, Sidwell Friends Academy, the school attended by Chelsea Clinton).

Authors and experts in the various fields also inevitably have a say as to textbook content. Although under the thumb of political and market forces of the kind just discussed, authors do generally have scruples concerning truth telling and do tend to be constrained by professional standards. They aren't inclined to stray from the straight and narrow (as they see it!) any more than they are forced to do so. (There no doubt are rotten apples in this barrel, just as in every other, and let's pass over the charge occasionally heard that some authors of public school history and social studies texts do not have a realistic grasp of their subject matter.) But they rarely, if ever, have a genuinely free hand to "write it as they see it."

Oh, yes, students also have an indirect say in textbook content, particularly as to style and level of difficulty. Unliked books, or those that are too difficult, tend to be unread

---

*Here is an item taken from the December 1994* Extra! Update *that illustrates what can happen when school material is provided by corporations that have non-educational irons in the fire:*

---

### Smoke Signals

"Do Cigarettes Have a Future?" a *Weekly Reader* cover asked (10/14/94, sixth-grade edition), illustrated by tobacco workers carrying signs saying "No More Taxes" and "Freedom of Choice." "Taxes and bans have caused many tobacco growers and workers to lose their jobs," the cover noted. The article inside played down the health risks of smoking—and didn't mention that the demonstration pictured had been organized by the tobacco industry. Nor did it mention that *Weekly Reader* is owned by K-III Communications—a division of Kohlberg Kravis Roberts and Co., which is the largest investor in tobacco giant RJR Nabisco.

---

*In any case, the* Weekly Reader *is old stuff on the education scene. The new potential king of the hill is "Channel One," a twelve-minute TV program seen daily by over eight million students. "Channel One," according to individuals quoted in the* New York Times *(January 22, 1997, Education section) provides students with "oversimplified political stories [and] frivolous contests" to go with product commercials that are the financial support for this intrusion of big business into public school classrooms. The* Times *article points out that "Channel One" provides schools with 19-inch television sets, two VCRs, and a satellite link in exchange for the requirement that their program be shown every day. The profit for "Channel One" in this venture comes from the big businesses that advertise their products to the millions of captive students. (For more on "Channel One," in particular, concerning how the news is "managed" in the interests of big business advertisers, see the January/February 1997 issue of* Extra!*)*

> *Political correctness has had a dramatic effect on college texts and classrooms, just as it has on teaching in grades "K through 12" (to use the current phrase). Most of this effect has been to the good, as mentioned before. But sometimes the attempt to be politically correct has surprising results. Shakespeare's play* The Tempest, *for example, was taught recently at Stanford University as "a moral lesson on culture clash and Western Imperialism," which no doubt would have surprised Shakespeare himself and greatly amused Globe Theatre audiences. (O.K., students, what was the Globe Theatre and where was it?)*

books. Teachers want the textbooks they select to be read, indeed, to be *studied*.* Anyway, that's why, in the case of public school textbooks, the term *indoctrination* isn't far off the mark. In the case of the mass media, the ultimate users of the commodity wield great power (as should be evident from the discussion in the last chapter). In the case of public school textbooks, the ultimate users, students, have relatively little say. (But then, most mass media audiences consist of "responsible" adults, while public school textbook audiences are considered to be just "children" or, extrapolating from other currently popular lingo, just "pre-adults.")

## 4. CENSORSHIP

It's very difficult to determine in particular cases whether or not books have been censored, but the discussion above about the ways in which local and state boards influence textbook content should make it clear that censorship does occur. Government agencies do in fact force changes in the content of public school texts (and also nonprint materials). Authors definitely are not free to write the books that they might prefer to; at least they cannot do so with any serious hope of having their efforts published and adopted. Textbook writers these days try very hard to tailor their works so as to be politically correct, just as, you will recall, do writers in the mass media.

### The Controversy Concerning the Teaching of Evolution: An Instructive Example

All even remotely controversial topics are subject to censorship, or at least to serious attempts at censorship. The theory of evolution is an interesting case in point because, perhaps more than any other scientific theory, it goes against the grain of many deeply held world views.

Starting in 1859 with the publication of Charles Darwin's great work *On the Origin of Species*, the theory of evolution has been challenged and denied countless times and for several different reasons. But the most important of these reasons has always been

---

*Occasionally, students make their dislike of texts known via direct political activity, for example, as some Latino and Asian "ESL" (English as a second language) students did in 1994 in San Francisco. But flurries of activity of this kind are unusual.

Cartoon by Tom Meyer.© *San Francisco Chronicle*. Reprinted by permission.

that evolution theory runs counter to literal interpretations of the book of Genesis in the Old Testament. In a famous 1924 court case, commonly referred to as the "Scopes Monkey Trial," John Scopes was convicted of violating a Tennessee law against the teaching of the theory of evolution in public school classrooms. In more recent times, however, courts have systematically struck down laws like the old Tennessee statute, notably in 1962 when the United States Supreme Court declared unconstitutional an Arkansas law that banned the teaching of evolution.

After the 1962 Supreme Court decision, fundamentalists invented the theory they call "creation science" in an attempt to make their Biblical view at least be taught alongside that of evolution theory in science classes. But in 1987, the Supreme Court declared creation science to be religious advocacy, not science, and thus not to be taught as science in public school science classes. Although this has dealt a blow to those advocating creationism as science, it has not stopped attempts at state and local levels to flout the law; in fact, creationism is still espoused in some schools where community sentiment is highly in favor of this being done, and evolution theory is slighted in many others because of that pressure. (Interestingly, because of the Supreme Court's ruling, fundamentalists now often eschew the terms "creation" and "creation science," instead employing the euphemism "intelligent design.") Fundamentalists still attempt to picture evolution as just one theory (as the name "theory of evolution" implies to those who don't quite grasp scientific lingo) and to get the Biblical account in Genesis taught alongside it. In Alabama, for instance, textbooks must warn students that evolution is

*Although the vast majority of biology textbooks in use today in public schools in America hold the line, more or less, against fundamentalist censorship demands, they do so in different ways. In some cases they teach evolution theory as a very well-confirmed scientific theory and simply ignore creationism entirely. That is the way the problem is handled, for instance, in one of the best biology textbooks:\* In other texts, creationism is briefly mentioned and then dismissed, as illustrated by this excerpt from a rather good, although "linguistically simplified" text:†*

When [H.M.S.] *Beagle* sailed from England [in 1831, Charles] Darwin, like most people of his time, believed in creationism. . . . According to creationists, God designed each kind of animal and plant to match its particular habitat. Thus, places with similar environments have similar kinds of plants and animals. Moreover, creationists believe that species are unchanging.

During his journey Darwin often left the ship to collect specimens of animals, plants, and fossils. His observations led him to doubt creationism and its assumption of unchanging species.

*This text then describes some of Darwin's findings, including those concerning the famous finches on the Galapagos Islands, findings that provided Darwin with very good evidence for what became his theory of evolution and natural selection.*

*Another way in which biology texts respond to religious challenges to evolution theory is illustrated by this excerpt from a somewhat better-than-average high school biology textbook:\*\**

Creation science is not science because its working assumptions cannot be examined by scientific methods. The word *creation* is associated with religion and a supreme being. It is, therefore, a matter of faith—not of scientific investigation. Furthermore, creationists are not willing to modify their model even when observations fail to support it. That . . . does not exclude creationism from a place in the school curriculum, but rather it strongly suggests that creationism should be taught as a religious belief and not as a scientific theory coequal with evolution theory.

\**Modern Biology*, by Albert Towle (Austin, Texas: Holt, Rinehart & Winston, 1993).
†*Biology: Visualizing Life*, by George B. Johnson. (Austin, Texas: Holt, Rinehart & Winston, 1994.)
\*\**Biological Science: A Molecular Approach*, 6th ed., 1990. D.C. Heath. The revision is by a team of seven writers from Colorado College, Colorado Springs.

"controversial" and an "unproven belief."\* (In fairness, it needs to be said that at least some advocates of creation science mistakenly believe it to be scientific.) Their failure

---

\*For more on these recent trends, see "Monkey Business," by Eugenie C. Scott, in *The Sciences* (January/February 1996) or the November-December 1996 issue of *The Textbook Letter*.

> *It is an interesting fact about the education of American youth that, in spite of the general excellence of high school science textbooks, most students do not obtain an adequate understanding either of scientific method or of the basic scientific view of the world. Indeed, similar remarks apply to college textbooks and to college graduates. This has been proven over and over again by surveys of both high school and college graduates. The seriousness of this educational failure is hard to exaggerate, given the fact that science intrudes everywhere in daily life and into virtually every social or political issue.*

to make large inroads into public school classrooms has not reduced their efforts; indeed, in the 1990s pressure on state and local school boards and on individual schools has increased, no doubt due to the increase in enthusiasm for fundamentalist religion in the United States (as in many other countries).*

Interestingly, Darwin himself did not believe that his theory of evolution was antithetical to belief in the existence of a creator. In fact, the last sentence in his classic book *On the Origin of Species* affirms such a belief:

> There is a grandeur in this view of life, with its several powers, having been originally breathed by the Creator into a few forms or into one; and that, whilst this planet has gone cycling on according to the fixed law of gravity, from so simple a beginning endless forms most beautiful and wonderful have been, and are being evolved.

It is difficult to be sure why the very well-organized fundamentalists are not winning more battles than they do, but one reason has to be the pressure exerted by an aroused scientific community, worried that a generation of scientific illiterates will be raised in the United States. Eminent scientists, for example, testified in the court cases mentioned before that creation science is not a science and convinced courts to hold that this is the case. Nevertheless, fundamentalists have not given up the fight by any means and, indeed, have had success at the local level in many places where large numbers of parents do not want students to be taught that evolution theory is a fact. Winners in these ongoing battles tend to be those with the most political clout, either because they constitute a majority of interested citizens or because of superior organization.

Interestingly, religious fundamentalists are largely responsible for one of the important improvements in recent public school textbooks, namely, the treatment of the topic of religion in American life. After World War II, and up to just a few years ago, religion tended to get mentioned only in the Colonial period, except for accounts of the Mormons' great trek west in the nineteenth century and the inauguration of the first (and so far only) Catholic president, John F. Kennedy, in 1960. Most of the newer texts today

---

*Note, however, that there are other sorts of books espousing the creationist viewpoint that sometimes are used in public schools, especially in states such as Louisiana and Texas, where fundamentalist interepretations of the Bible are widely accepted. Also of interest is the fact that the influence of fundamentalist Jewish and Muslim groups on public school education has been comparatively slight because these groups constitute a tiny minority in America today.

provide much more information than that about the role religion has played in American life, even if their accounts still have a bit of the flavor of a token gesture.

## Publisher Self-Censorship

Given what has been said so far, it shouldn't come as a surprise that publishers have become exceedingly cautious in the editing of public school textbooks, or that they try very hard not to offend powerful special-interest groups. This is especially true with respect to grade school textbooks, as might be expected. (We tell tiny tots that there is a Santa Claus and a tooth fairy, but after age six or so falsification is of a more subtle nature, its point often being to initiate the young into the harsher realities of life rather slowly.) A West Coast publisher's illustrator, for instance, was forced to remove the stem from a picture of a plum because it cast a shadow that might be construed as phallic. Harcourt Brace had an artist remove a mother's apron from a drawing picturing a typical eighteenth-century family scene because the apron was seen to be "demeaning to women." (Never mind that the portrayal was accurate.) Some publishers no longer allow udders on drawings of cows or flies on the trousers of little boys.

In the old days, when Dick and Jane reigned supreme, the world was portrayed as having a gardenlike quality. Slums did not exist, nasty people were restricted to

---

### "Make Sure It's Not Iceberg"

*Irene Trivas, an artist, stopped accepting assignments to illustrate children's readers partly out of frustration over publishers' efforts to be "everything to everybody," as she put it.*

*Here is her account of the instructions she received for one book:*

---

It's etched in acid in my mind. They sent 10 pages of single-spaced specifications.

The hero was a Hispanic boy.

There were black twins, one boy, one girl; an overweight Oriental boy, and an American Indian girl.

That leaves the Caucasian.

Since we mustn't forget the physically handicapped, she was born with a congenital malformation and only had three fingers on one hand.

One child had to have an Irish setter, and the setter was to be female.

The Hispanic kid had two parents. The father has a white-collar job. The mother is an illustrator and she works at home.

At one point, they are seen through the kitchen screen door making dinner, having spaghetti and meatballs and a salad. The editor appended a note that said: "Make sure it's not iceberg; it should be something nice like endive."

They also had a senior citizen, and I had to show her jogging.

I can't do it anymore.

—Copyright © 1990 by the New York Times Company. Reprinted by permission.

---

### Housebroken

School authorities in Green Cove Springs, Florida, have barred the 1941 children's classic, *My Friend Flicka*, from fifth- and sixth-grade optional reading lists
because parents complained that the book contains the word "bitch" in reference to a female dog.

—Item from *The Progressive* magazine (January 1991)

---

fairy tales, almost everyone was white, and women were primarily pictured as housewives and mothers. The pressures on publishers were different, so the product was
different.

## Other Books Also Are Censored

Books that are not explicitly textbooks often are subjected to censorhip. The censor in
most of these cases is the local school board, but state boards have been getting into
the act in recent years.

Almost any kind of book may be censored, but most that are contain passages that
are alleged to be obscene, that are seen as racially or ethnically biased, that slight or
demean women, or that favorably portray a lifestyle claimed to be immoral. A Tennessee county school board, for example, removed the old standby *Drums Along the
Mohawk* from an assigned list because it contained words judged to be obscene, such
as *hell* and *damn*. Shakespeare's *The Merchant of Venice* is sometimes censored because
Jewish groups object to its portrayal of Shylock.

A bit sillier was the removal from California's annual English exam list for tenth
graders of the short story, "Am I Blue," by Pulitzer Prize–winning author Alice
Walker—removed primarily because it was "anti-meat-eating." But perhaps silliest of
all, one of the most frequently censored books is *The Adventures of Huckleberry Finn*.
Sam Clemens would have been amused, but not surprised. The Clemens classic has
two groups on its back: fundamentalists and others offended by its portrayal of religion and by the way Huck flouts conventional morality, and African Americans
offended by its protrayal of Negroes and by the racist language it puts into the mouths
of bigoted slave owners. Irony of ironies: one of the schools that has censored *Huck
Finn* turns out to be Mark Twain Intermediate School in Fairfax County, Virginia.

Censoring *Huck Finn* also is ironic, of course, because Clemens intended his great
work to expose the evils of slavery—precisely what civil rights groups today want every
American to remember. It would be provincial, however, to conclude that public school
book censoring is a uniquely American phenomenon. On the contrary, this sort of censorship, like most other kinds, is less frequent and less severe in the United States than
in most, perhaps all, other countries. Every nation dolls up its past, for the same reasons that we do so in the United States, and many censor on religious grounds or out
of a sense of propriety. In Germany, starting after World War II and continuing to a
lesser extent to this day, history texts have understandably played down the atrocities
committed by Germans during that most horrible of all wars (so far!). And, needless to
say, Soviet texts didn't bother to mention the millions killed during Stalin's reign of

*The number of books and magazines censored out of public school class-rooms and libraries runs into the thousands every year. Here are a few striking examples.* *

---

*The Sun Also Rises* (Ernest Hemingway)
*The Catcher in the Rye* (J. D. Salinger)
*The Grapes of Wrath* (John Steinbeck)
*Andersonville* (McKinley Kantor)
*Look Homeward Angel* (Thomas Wolfe)
*The Invisible Man* (Ralph Ellison)
*Native Son* (Richard Wright)
*Brave New World* (Aldous Huxley)
*Slaughterhouse Five* (Kurt Vonnegut, Jr.)
*Marjorie Morningstar* (Herman Wouk)
*The Naked Ape* (Desmond Morris)
*I Know Why the Caged Bird Sings* (Maya Angelou)
*Ms.* magazine
(*The American Heritage Dictionary* was banned because it includes "gutter words" like *ball*, *nut*, and *tail*, and cites certain uses of the term *bed* as a transitive verb)

---

*Oh, yes. Perhaps in an attempt to prove that George Orwell is the Nostradamus of the twentieth century, lots of school districts have banned use of . . . 1984.*

*See the American Library Association's *Newsletter on Intellectual Freedom*.

---

terror, or the smaller but still significant number of people worked to death in Siberia even after his death.

In this country today, the censoring of books outside of public schools (and of some schools that are religiously sponsored) is much less common than it is within educational walls. But it does occur, and it obviously limits what students as well as adults can read. Favorite targets are books with sexual content and those affecting national security. In the long history of censorship, however, all sorts of things have been banned. In 1933, for example, the U.S. Customs Office confiscated copies of "obscene photo books" it described as "Ceiling Sistene Chapel Filles Michael Angelo" [sic]. In 1961, Canadian customs officials confiscated as obscene the official report of the trial in England in which D. H. Lawrence's *Lady Chatterley's Lover* was held to be not obscene.

---

*To limit the press is to insult a nation; to prohibit reading of certain books is to declare the inhabitants to be either fools or slaves.*

— Claud Arrien Helvetius

Way back in 1526, the first English translation of the New Testament was banned and printed copies burned; in Spain, a similar fate awaited the first translation into Spanish. Indeed, the Bible may be the most censored book in history.

In more recent times, several states have banned *Fanny Hill* as obscene. (Not too many years ago, advertisements sometimes boasted, "Banned in Boston.") And the U.S. government still occasionally forces the censorship of books dealing with clandestine activities, past or present, of the Central Intelligence Agency.

# 5. Textbooks Distort History

As stated before, public school history textbooks in the United States are more accurate today than every before. But they still don't provide students with a true picture of the history of their nation. One reason they don't, of course, is the dull way in which they ladle out facts one after another, without providing students with a good grasp of *why* things happened that way. But another reason has to do with the need to make students into loyal, proud citizens.

## United States History Is Sanitized

History texts "clean up" our past so as to maintain student pride in America. As much as possible, our leaders are pictured as better than human, all dressed up and minus their flaws (except, of course, for a very few Benedict Arnolds whose transgressions can't be papered over). Take the way in which Theodore Roosevelt, affectionately referred to as *Teddy* (the teddy bear was named after him), is spruced up in virtually all public school texts. Typically, he is portrayed as an energetic, hard-driving, exuberant, brave, trust-busting conservationist, reformer, and progressive, who was against monopolistic big business—a great man deserving of his place on Mount Rushmore.*

And perhaps he was. But no textbooks the authors of this text have ever seen, or even heard of, tell students about another side of good old Teddy. They don't describe him as a bloodthirsty bigot who, though unusually brave, reveled in the slaughter he personally engaged in and witnessed during the Spanish-American War; a man who expressed pleasure after 30 men had been shot to death in the Civil War draft riots ("an admirable object lesson to the remainder"); a man who justified slaughtering Indians on the grounds that their lives were only "a few degrees less meaningful, squalid, and ferocious than that of the wild beasts," and who said that "All the great masterful races have been fighting races. . . . No triumph of peace is quite so great as the supreme triumph of war." Not exactly a teddy bear, this Teddy Roosevelt. (History texts also falsely pump up the part played by Roosevelt's "Rough Riders" in the famous charge up San Juan Hill in Cuba during the Spanish-American War.)

---

*But Roosevelt's role in the machinations that went on before construction of the Panama Canal, now seen as definitely not politically correct, sometimes are mentioned as a minus, whereas his role in the building of the canal previously was cited as one of his more glorious achievements. (*The more things stay the same, the more they change.* —Harold Gordon)

## America's Role in History Is Distorted

Although outright lying is frowned upon, the writers of public school textbooks have other devices at their disposal enabling them to satisfy the various kinds of social and political demands described before. The most commonly employed of these devices is the complete *omission* of embarrassing historical events. For example, most of the CIA interference and "dirty tricks" over the years in several foreign countries get passed over. (Interestingly, the "Irangate" scandal that occurred during President Reagan's administration usually is mentioned.) Similarly, although all textbooks expend dozens of pages on World War II, most omit reference to the terrible firestorm bombing of Tokyo that killed more people than either of the atomic bombs we dropped on Japan, and they frequently fail to mention the deliberate policy of the American and British air forces to bomb German civilians, mostly women and children, as a way of breaking down German will to continue fighting.*

Embarrassing events also sometimes are papered over by carefully controlled *emphasis*, especially by simply expending relatively little space on a topic. For example, although most history textbooks these days, unlike those of times past, do tell readers about the war that occurred between American troops and Philippine guerrillas intent on gaining independence after the United States annexed the Philippine Islands at the end of the Spanish-American War, they do so quickly, so as to mask the extreme nastiness of the way in which the Filipinos were subjugated. The war with Spain gets relatively lots of space in most texts; the war against Filipino patriots extremely little, even though many more deaths and much greater destruction resulted from the war to force the Philippine people to knuckle under than from the war against Spain (itself quite a blot on the American escutcheon).

Textbooks also distort history by playing up the American role in foreign affairs at the expense of others. The part played by the United States in World Wars I and II always is puffed up in this way. In the Second World War, for example, the principal fighting, and dying, against the Germans was done by Soviet troops, not American or British; but student readers of any of the current history textbooks are bound to draw the opposite conclusion.

These devices are very hard for uninformed or unsophisticated readers to see through, particularly because we all want very much to believe in the greatness of our own society and tend to see national warts only after a good deal of experience has forced us to do so.

Even though the role of the United States in World War II is puffed up and cleansed, it might be supposed that the suffering and dying of American fighting troops would

---

*Absolutely no texts provide anything like an accurate depiction of the nature of these cataclysmic bombings of German cities and of Tokyo (although there are hints of the horror of the atomic bombings of Hiroshima and Nagasaki). Only a very few even mention the infamous firestorming of Dresden in which about 100,000 civilians were killed, an extremely ugly blot on the American and British escutcheons because Dresden had next to no military importance, and in any case the war was all but won when the thousands of bombers turned that once architectural gem into an inferno. (An accurate count of the dead was impossible because all that was left of many people were heaps of ashes or a layer of gelatine covering the floors of cellar air raid shelters. See, for instance, *Target: Hitler's Oil,* by R. C. Nesbit (Kimber, 1985) or *Brute Force: Allied Strategy and Tactics in the Second World War*, by John Ellis (New York: Viking, 1990).

*Here is an example of the way in which a typical textbook ladles out a seemingly endless stream of tens of thousands of facts to students who have few pegs on which they can be hung:* *

---

In 1880 the Republican party had three factions. The Stalwarts, followers of New York senator Roscoe Conkling, defended the spoils system. The Half-Breeds followed Maine senator James G. Blaine and tried to balance the need for reform of the spoils system with loyalty to the party. Independents opposed the spoils system altogether. They were sometimes called "googoos," a derisive term that was short for *good government.* In the 1880s, when independents left the party to support a Democrat, they also became known as *Mugwumps.* An Algonquin word for "renegade chief," the term stuck when a newspaper editor joked that it really meant "unreliable Republicans," men whose "mugs" were on one side of the fence and "wumps" on the other.

President Hayes had announced at the beginning of his presidency that he would not seek a second term. In 1880, Republicans selected James A. Garfield, a member of Congress from Ohio, as their presidential candidate. Because Garfield was linked to the Half-Breeds, who were only somewhat loyal to old-time Republican policies, the vice-presidential slot went to Chester A. Arthur, a Stalwart.

In the 1880 election, Garfield won a narrow victory against Democratic candidate General Winfield S. Hancock. His term was cut short. . . .

---

* *America: Pathways to the Present*, by Andrew Cayton, Elisabeth Israels Perry, and Allan M. Winkler (Needham, Mass.: Prentice Hall, 1995).

---

be explained in a way that would let students understand the extent of their sacrifices and the terror they endured, as they did, for instance, on June 6th, 1944 ("D-Day"), when several thousand American troops lost their lives on the beaches of Normandy, in France.* After all, this would show how brave and self-sacrificing American troops have been. But telling students about this would require explaining what modern warfare really is like: about what it means to advance into concentrated machine gun fire that is certain to mow down most of those who find themselves in this terrible and terrifying circumstance; about flying on bombing missions with the knowledge that sooner or later most bombers in your unit are likely to be shot down†; about suddenly being covered with the splattered brains of a buddy who has just been hit by an unseen sniper; about the last moments of men drowning on submarines; about incinerated tank crews or the soldiers blasted into thousands of tiny pieces by enemy shelling. (Back in high

---

*A great many died or were permanently maimed, by the way, because of a lack of cooperation between air and ground forces. But even most reasonably good histories of that great invasion gloss over this disgraceful fact, so we can't realistically expect public school textbooks to mention it. Similarly, no textbook can be expected to mention the large number of men who deserted during World War II, as in every major war fought by this country.

†That is one of the important points made in the well-known and excellent novel *Catch 22.*

Drawing by David Levine. Copyright © 1969 NYREV, Inc.
Reprinted by permission from *The New York Review of Books*.

## Hamburger Hill

*David Levine's drawing of Hamburger Hill (a hill in Vietnam on which many soldiers lost their lives) pictures two American presidents as jolly mass murderers. Would the Texas State Textbook Committee give its approval to a book containing this*

school did you notice the total omission of pictures of dead American soldiers in history textbooks or of anything that graphically conveys the true horror of modern warfare?)

Before passing on to other matters, perhaps we should point out that the worst distortion of American history occurs in grade school texts and that as students move up in grade level textbooks become less goody goody and quite a bit more accurate. The idea seems to be that tiny tots are not ready for unvarnished truth and need to be gently introduced into the "facts of life" over time. What we have stressed here is that even in high school, students are provided a dolled-up version of reality, an account that fails to square with the true history of the United States. (Similar remarks apply to the social studies—civics, government, politics—texts about to be discussed.)

## 6. TEXTBOOKS MINIMIZE THE GREAT GULF BETWEEN THEORY AND PRACTICE

In the constant struggle for power and wealth that goes on in every country, national ideals, customs, and laws get violated. Thus, a great gulf always exists between the official story about how a system is supposed to work and actual, everyday practice. It is extremely important that we know the extent of this gulf if we are to have at least a modestly good idea about what is likely to be in store for us as we go through life. We need to know, for example, what our chances are of getting justice if we have to go into

---

*Although students are provided facts about thousands of events, they generally are not given sufficient information about them to arrive at a true understanding of the import of these events. Here, for example, is the way in which one very good history text describes one event:*

---

### The Pentagon Papers

At about the same time as the Laos invasion, a former employee of the Defense Department, **Daniel Ellsberg**, delivered to the *New York Times* a set of secret documents that he had photocopied from classified files in the Pentagon. They contained an internal history of the American involvement in the war, written by officials of the Johnson administration. Known as the **Pentagon Papers**, they attracted wide attention. Millions of readers were shocked by what these documents revealed about the way the United States had entered the war. The Nixon administration, outraged at *what it considered* [italics added] a major breach of security, tried unsuccessfully to convict Daniel Ellsberg of criminal behavior. It also tried to prevent the *New York Times* from publishing these papers. The Supreme Court, however, ruled in favor of the newspaper.*

---

*An account like this one leaves all sorts of questions unanswered, questions that a perceptive, interested, and awake (!) student might raise, such as: What did the Pentagon Papers say that so shocked the public? Was this a major and important breach of security? Why did the Supreme Court rule as it did? Why was Ellsberg not tried and convicted? Was Ellsberg right to have done what he did? Is it necessary for me and my fellow students to know about this apparently less-than-earthshaking event?*

---

*American Voices: A History of the United States.* (Glenview, Ill.: Scott Foresman, 1992).

*Here is a passage from a book that absolutely never will find its way into public school classrooms. It describes how a great many of the American GIs who fought in the front lines against the Germans in World War II felt about it at the time:*

## "The Real War Will Never Get in the Books"

What was it about the war that moved the troops to constant verbal subversion and contempt? [This was described earlier.] It was not just the danger and fear, the boredom and uncertainty and loneliness and deprivation. It was rather the conviction that optimistic publicity and euphemism had rendered their experience so falsely that it would never be readily communicable. They knew that in its representation to the laity what was happening to them was systematically sanitized and Norman Rockwellized, not to mention Disneyfied. They knew that despite the advertising and publicity, where it counted their arms and equipment were worse than the Germans'. [The author doesn't mention here that GIs had a much larger supply, at any rate, of weapons than did their opponents, and that American and British airplanes were as good as or better than those of the Germans.] They knew that despite official assertions to the contrary, the Germans had real smokeless powder for their small arms and that they did not. They knew that their automatic rifles . . . were slower and clumsier, and they knew that the Germans had a much better light machine gun. . . . They knew that their own tanks, both American and British, were ridiculously under-armed and under-armored, so that they were inevitably destroyed in an open encounter with an equal number of German panzers [tanks]. . . . And they knew that the greatest single weapon of the war, the atomic bomb excepted, was the German 88-mm flat-trajectory gun, which brought down thousands of bombers and tens of thousands of soldiers. The Allies had nothing as good, despite one of them designating itself The World's Greatest Industrial Power. The troops' disillusion and their ironic response, in song and satire and sullen contempt, came from knowing that the home front then (*and very likely historiography later*) could be aware of none of these things. (Italics added.)*

---

*Paul Fussell. *Wartime: Understanding and Behavior in the Second World War.* (New York and Oxford: Oxford University Press, 1989).

court,* how far we can trust the leaders of our nation to consider our economic interests, and to what extent elected officials are influenced by lobbyists to do what is not in our, or the nation's, best interests.

---

*It may very well be true, as some have suggested, that many young people learned more about the difficulty of getting justice when going to court from television and newspaper coverage of the two O. J. Simpson trials—in one of which he was declared innocent of murder while in the other guilty—than from anything they learned in public schools.

For example, one of our official myths is that no one is above the law—that a Rockefeller can't break into someone else's property with impunity any more than you can. Civics texts try as much as possible to stress the positive and play down the negative, so they don't tell students that this particular official myth really is a myth—that the rich and/or powerful frequently are above the law in ways we common folk never are, and that a Rockefeller can (because one actually did) sometimes break into someone's else's property and get away with it. Here, for instance, is a *Washington Post* (December 1, 1981) tidbit you're not likely to run across in any public school texts, although it reveals a great deal about privilege differences between the "aristocracy" and the rest of us:

## Rules Are Made to Be Broken, for Some People

Late one night in Kansas City, [Nelson] Rockefeller [later, by the way, one of the two unelected vice presidents in American history] couldn't find his Water Pik. "He had dental work that debris would catch in sometimes," recalls Hugh Morrow, the former Rockefeller spokesman. "So with the aid of the local police, [aide] Joe [Canzeri] broke into a drugstore, got the Water Pik and left the money on the counter . . . ."

During the 1968 New York City garbage strike, [then New York Governor] Rockefeller was once in all-night negotiations with the union. By 5 A.M. the group was tired and hungry. Canzeri broke a kitchen lock at the nearby Gotham Hotel, then made bacon, scrambled eggs, coffee and toast for the group of 30.

Other cases in which the rich, or the politically powerful, are known to violate the law and still get away with it quickly come to mind. Think, for example, of the way in which Senator Ted Kennedy was treated after his escapade at Chappaquiddick; almost certainly guilty of negligent homicide and quite likely of more serious crimes, he received no legal punishment whatsoever.

Nevertheless, today's textbooks are miles better than the ones in use until the last 15 or 20 years. In the old days, civics texts restricted themselves almost entirely to descriptions, detailed and quite accurate, as to the theory of American government and social practices, more or less ignoring everyday reality. A typical text went on for pages about the "checks and balances" of government, minute details concerning the Constitution, the various departments and bureaus of the federal government, and so on, but hardly ever discussed the ways in which the system fails in actual practice to operate as it is supposed to. Today's textbooks, unlike those in the past, often at least hint at everyday reality; for example, mentioning ways in which bribery, graft, and incompetence reduce and skew the performance of government. Here, for instance, is an example from a social science textbook typical of those on the market today:

Why would voters want to remove the "Ins" and replace them with the "Outs"? Sometimes . . . a political scandal of some kind may cause voters to wonder whether officials at city hall or at the state or national capital are honestly serving the public. In a democracy, elections provide the people with a powerful means of "cleaning house" and ridding government of those who, in their opinion, are not properly fulfilling their duties.*

---

*Government for Everybody*, by Steven L. Jantzen. (New York: Amsco School Publications, 1992).

*The near invisibility of African Americans in public school textbooks until some time in the 1960s certainly was disgraceful. The improvements that have occurred since then were long overdue. But as in many other cases in which error is rectified, things sometimes have gotten a bit out of hand. For example, in the guise of rectifying "errors of Eurocentric" scholars, a few African-American scholars have rewritten history so as to puff up the role in world history played by sub-Sahara Africans—peoples generally thought of as black, or Negroid.*

*One of the first to do so was Martin Bernal in his widely cited book* Black Athena.* *Bernal claimed that the ancient Egyptians were black (he says that they "might usefully be called black") and that their civilization was the source of the ancient Greek culture that was so influential in the development of Western (European) societies. His ideas have been championed by a few other African-American scholars and are being taught in one form or another in quite a few public schools in America—especially in many inner-city schools that have pre-dominately African-American student enrollments. (The Portland, Oregon, "Baseline Studies"† are often used in courses in which this general historical line is taught.)*

*The problem, of course, is that there is no evidence supporting the idea that ancient Greek culture had it basic origins in ancient Egypt and very little to the idea that the ancient Egyptians were black.** Students thus are being taught doctrines that are almost certainly false—theories that have almost no acceptance among historians and anthropologists—outside of a very small coterie of black academics.*

*One is reminded of the way in which American history has always been distorted so as to portray the United States in the best possible light, thus further-ing the aim of making students into good citizens. In this case, the point seems to be to instill pride of origin in African-American students. But is it a good idea to completely falsify history in this way for that or for any other purpose?*

---

*Black Athena: The Afroasiatic Roots of Classical Civilization.* (Rutgers University Press, Volume I, 1987; Volume II, 1991). [Bernal is a Chinese scholar and has no professional standing (to put it politely) in the fields he addresses in these books.]

†Asa Hilliard and Carolyn Leonard (eds.). *African American Baseline Essays.* (Portland, Oregon: Portland Public Schools, 1990).

**The little in this idea is that skin color in ancient Egypt ranged from typical "light Mediterranean"—the skin color, say, of Greeks and Italians—to darker shades that occur in other groups generally thought of as white—for example, Iranians and Pakistanis. But there is no historical connection between the ancient Egyptians and sub-Sahara Africans (Bantus and so on) generally thought of as racially black—the groups from which African Americans today are partially descended. (Most people considered to be African Americans, by the way, are at least in part descended from Europeans generally classified as white, indeed, often primarily so descended. Black and white in America today are cultural concepts.) It's also true that a great many anthropologists today refuse to employ the racial terms "caucasoid," "negroid," and "oriental" on grounds that no sharp divisions exist justifying this sort of classification, but they do believe that the ancient Egyptians did not spring from sub-Sahara African populations. Note also that almost all scholars distinguish between the Nubians, who were descended from sub-Sahara Africans, and the ancient Egyptians, as did the ancient Egyptians themselves.)

> Who controls the past controls the future; who controls the present controls the past.
>
> — George Orwell (*1984*)

Note that the bad news about occasional scandals is followed by the good news about how the guilty can be voted out of office.

And what about corruption due to the power of big business? Here is what the same text has to say on that score:

> Another issue that challenged and changed the two [political] parties was the rising power of big business. For a while [!!], it seemed that railroad companies and other businesses could buy votes in a state legislature. Big businesses could use their money and influence to pass laws that gave them special privileges. When a politician accepts bribes from rich supporters, it is known as corruption.
>
> In the early 1900s, a Republican president, Theodore Roosevelt, made himself popular with voters by trying to regulate big business. Later, a Democratic president, Woodrow Wilson, did much the same thing. Because of their leadership, the two major parties became less corrupt. Also, businesses came to be regulated by laws enforced by the national government.

In most other social studies textbooks, even the better ones, the issue of bribery via "lobbying" and corruption in general are even more sanitized than in the one just discussed. Here, for instance, is how one venerable text that has been much improved in recent years discusses lobbying:

> The typical lobbyist of today is a far cry from those of an earlier day—and from many of the fictitious ones still found on television and in novels and the movies. The once fairly common practice of bribery and the heavy-handed use of unethical practices are almost unknown. Most present-day lobbyists work in the open, and their major techniques come under the heading of friendliness, persuasion, and helpfulness.
>
> Lobbyists are ready to do such things as buy lunches and dinners, provide information, write speeches, and prepare bills in proper form. The lunches and dinners are good, the information usually quite accurate, the speeches forceful, and the bills well drawn [!!]. Most lobbyists know that if they behaved otherwise—gave false information, for example—they would damage, if not destroy, their credibility and so their overall effectiveness. . . .
>
> Lobbying abuses do occur now and then, of course. False or misleading testimony, bribery, and other unethical pressures are not common, but they do exist. . . .*

---

*\*Magruder's American Government*, the latest edition by William A. McClenaghan. (Needham, Mass.: Prentice Hall, 1995.) This book has been a popular one since 1917. The quotes here are from a four-page account of lobbying that almost in its entirety is a whitewash of the topic. Still, anyone who wants to see how much better today's texts are than those of even 20 years ago would do well to look at earlier editions of this work.

[W]hen American scholars talk about . . . Soviet texts which blatantly indoc-
trinate, they are called brainwashing. When our own texts are biased, prejudiced, one-sided and unfair, it is called "transmitting a favorable view of
our democracy."

— S. Samuel Shermis

Obviously, textbook accounts of this nature don't come close to revealing the way
in which legislators are bought by the rich and powerful. (Recall then-Senator Dole's
unusually candid comment, quoted by Sorel in the drawing at the beginning of this
chapter: "When these political action committees give money, they expect something in
return other than good government.") But most of today's public school textbooks do
at least hint at something close to the truth, and this is a great improvement over the way
in which the topic of graft was discussed in times past. Students carefully reading
between the lines now may be able to get at least a vague idea as to how the system
works in practice.

## 7. TEXTBOOKS FAIL TO GIVE STUDENTS GENUINE UNDERSTANDING

From what has been said so far, it should be clear that public school textbooks fail to
give students true understanding of the history and workings of their society. They fail
primarily because of defects in style and content of the kinds we have been at pains to
describe. These defects, we have suggested, result from the various forces at work shaping the finished products, in particular, conflicting pressures from interested social
groups coupled with professional considerations.

It is important to understand that these defects do not result from something peculiar to the American system. The textbooks of any democratic society are bound to

*If you're still wondering whether all that much progress has occurred in text-
book quality in recent years, this snippet from a really bad textbook still in circulation as late as 1970 should provide a bit of evidence:*

As you ride up beside the Negroes in the field they stop working long enough to
look up, tip their hats and say, "Good morning, Master John." You like the
friendly way they speak and smile; they show bright rows of white teeth. "How's
it coming, Sam?" your father asks one of the old Negroes. "Fine, Marse Tom,
jes fine. We got more cotton than we can pick." Then Sam chuckles to himself
and goes back to picking as fast as he can.

—Mentioned in *The New Republic* (July 25, 1970); the book's title is best omitted here.

*If that sort of writing doesn't make every current textbook look wonderfully good,
nothing will.*

*There are two related, interesting facts about public school history and social studies textbooks. One is that money strapped local school boards around the country, and in many foreign countries, spend large amounts of money for huge, glossy, feature-packed, multicolor textbooks even though smaller, more modest, less-expensive texts are available. The second is that among these less-expensive, black-and-white texts are to be found most of the best books* with respect to content—*best in particular because they present a more realistic picture, often with interesting discussions of serious political theories, about what goes on in the political arena, than do their expensive, glossy counterparts. Very few of these smaller, more accurate books sell as well as do their big, glossy competitors. Here, for instance, is a short excerpt from one of the best of these smaller texts concerning two conflicting theories about politics:*

The pluralists state that politics in America is democratic, with widespread participation in decisions that most people agree with. The elitists say that politics is dominated by an elite that controls and manipulates the rest of us in its own interest. . . .

The pluralist and elite approaches can . . . be seen as two ends of a range of theories about American politics. Recent modifications have discussed a *plural elitism*. This stresses that politics is divided into different policy arenas. Here special interest elites dominate in specific arenas, usually at the expense of the public interest. So, for example, when it comes to deciding on public spending for the military, a trio of military leaders, defense businesses, and congressional representatives on key armed forces committees dominate the decision making. The general public is confused by ideology and patriotic symbols from clearly seeing the elite dominance that is occurring in these narrow arenas.

There is then according to this view no "right" answer to the argument between pluralists and the power elite school. It may depend on which political conflict we are talking about. Sometimes, as in the town meetings held in many New England towns, we can see a number of views being expressed on an issue and a fairly democratic decision being reached by the community. In other areas, such as the making of foreign policy, a small number of high officials meeting behind closed doors decides policies that will affect the lives of millions. . . .*

*Although this text implies, but never states, that plural elitism comes closest to the truth, it does have to make the inevitable move: asking students "What do you think?" as a way of protecting itself from the charge of taking sides on a controversial topic.*

*By the way, does what this text says about a power elite conform to Texas textbook adoption requirements (mentioned on page 298)?*

*The Basics of American Politics, 7th ed., by Gary Wasserman. (New York: HarperCollins, 1994).

reflect the different opinions and interests of its citizens. To have it otherwise would be to surrender control of this important part of our lives to others, as is the case in most authoritarian societies around the world. While fighting to make textbooks better than they are today, we should not forget how much they have improved since, say, when the authors of this college text went to school (light years in the past, when dinosaurs stll roamed the earth).

One final comment. The praise that has been somewhat grudgingly given to today's public school textbooks* in this chapter should not cloud the fact that the writers of this college text do not care for the large doses of indoctrination they contain. This text was written in a completely different spirit. A student who accepts its contents uncritically has missed its main point, which is that in important or controversial matters, free men and women must become their own experts, or at least must be able to judge for themselves the opinions and advice of those who call themselves experts. The success of a free society depends on an informed *and thinking* electorate, not on an indoctrinated one.

## 8. Postscript on College Texts

The question naturally arises about college textbooks: Do they distort American history and practice as do public school texts? If the forces at work are the same in both cases, we should expect the results to be roughly the same (taking into account the greater maturity of college students). If they aren't, we should expect the finished products to be different. What do our world views tell us about this question?

Note first that the publishers of college texts have exactly the same motives as those who produce public school textbooks. In fact, many, perhaps most, publishers in one field also publish in the other. Second, most college texts are adopted by the teachers who will use them in their own classes (or, in the case of courses having several sections, by group faculty decisions), not by school boards or state agencies. (Students buy them but can't choose which ones to buy.)

The reason for this important difference is the history and the current funding of higher education in the United States as compared to primary and secondary education. Primary and secondary school traditions are largely "homegrown" and intended for a mass audience. Public school teachers have always had their rights to academic freedom infringed upon by local school boards, or, more accurately, never had such rights. But American colleges and universities evolved on the model of their European counterparts (chiefly in Germany and England), which were intended for an elite clientele. Professors, at least, were granted a great deal of academic freedom. (Of course, this was not the case during the Nazi period in Germany!) The result of transplanting this tradition to the United States, the freest Western society, has been academic freedom for almost all faculty members; thus, college teachers have always had the privilege of selecting the books they and their students will use.† It follows, then, as night follows

---

*The history and social studies books used in private schools are, with rare exceptions, quite similar to those discussed here, except for some of the textbooks used in schools run by organized churches. Of course, in some of the very best private schools, original sources—books intended for adult readers—are more in evidence than are texts designed explicitly for schoolroom use.

†More precisely, almost all *tenured* faculty members. Nontenured faculty still have to worry about offending those who determine who will be rehired and who "terminated." This benefit of the tenure system often is overlooked, but is of great importance.

day, that college textbook publishers will try to produce books that please college teachers—their potential adopters.

College teachers, however, do not operate in a vacuum. They, too, have an audience to consider—their students—and many students, unfortunately, are not as well prepared to do college work as typical students were, say, 40 years ago. (This obviously is less true of students in "elite" colleges and universities.) One reason for this fact is that a larger proportion of young people go to college today than in times past, when only brighter students (and a few who were merely rich) went to college. But another reason is that over the years, more and more students have become victims of the "dumbing down" of grade and high school texts mentioned a while back and find it difficult to comprehend some of the more high-powered college texts; they are more easily intimidated by thick books or those written in past centuries in a dense or a different style. College teachers, being human, often react (consciously or unconsciously) to the problem this raises by selecting textbooks and works of literature that are relatively brief and more easily understood. Reading lists have been shortened; books perceived as "weighty tomes" tend to get neglected in introductory courses.*

Anyway, college texts, wherever they may rest on an absolute scale, are genuinely unlike their public school counterparts. College teachers want widely differing textbook content and levels of difficulty, creating a market in which all sorts of views and qualities find a constituency. College texts even tend to be less dull than their lower-level counterparts, a happy note on which to end this particular—immensely interesting and entertaining—college textbook.

## SUMMARY OF CHAPTER 12

Public school textbooks in America have improved a great deal in the past 25 years or so.

1. History and social studies texts are more accurate in their portrayal of minorities and women, and in the way in which they deal with the dark side of the social system and history of the United States. But textbooks still are written in a dull, one-fact-after-another style that makes true understanding, and also retention of specific facts, quite difficult. They also have reflected the general "dumbing down" that has occurred in public schools and colleges during the past several years.

2. The ultimate purpose of public schools is to educate the young to fit into the adult world. Textbooks are intended to provide students with the knowledge they will need to be productive citizens and to inculcate the values, customs, and attitudes of the society as a whole. (That is why it is accurate to speak of *indoctrination*.)

---

*There also is the fact that what is "in" at one time may well become "out" at another; textbook selection tends to reflect these changes, especially the dramatic changes in course offerings. Forty years ago, for example, there were no courses in critical reasoning. Most schools required courses in formal logic, usually taught in philosophy or math departments, and these obviously did deal with the principles of good conclusion drawing; critical reasoning was taught by English department instructors primarily in the context of the writing of argumentative essays. That is why there was only one true critical reasoning textbook (Monroe Beardsley's *Thinking Straight*, mentioned in Chapter 7) in common use prior to *Logic and Contemporary Rhetoric*'s appearance on the scene in 1971.

We can expect, then, that noncontroversial topics will be presented in a more-or-less straightforward manner, while topics that are controversial, or sensitive—in particular, those connected to the history and social practices of society—will tend to pull punches and portray matters in the best light possible.

3. Just as in the case of the mass media, politics enters into the textbook business. Because they are a commodity, textbooks are written so as to satisfy potential buyers, which means primarily local school boards, state agencies, and the professional educators who are empowered to make selections. Political considerations enter in at every level—local, state, and national.

   Although the details change from time to time, there is nothing new in this intrusion of politics into the educational arena. Even the very idea of public school education is political, there being no public schools whatsoever in the United States until some time in the nineteenth century.

   Big business, of course, has some power over textbook content, but less than it does, say, concerning how the news is presented in the mass media. But it does have some power, including power derived from its ability to lobby state legislatures and local school boards.

   The most important of the state agencies concerned with textbook selection are those of California and Texas, California because it is the largest textbook market and Texas because of very effective lobbying by several pressure groups, in particular, Christian fundamentalists.

4. Pressure groups have been rather successful, indeed, sometimes oversuccessful, with respect to their demands that textbooks be politically correct by increasing coverage of minorities, women, and religion in American history and life, leading publishers to tailor their products to fit expected pressure group preferences. But attempts to have discussions of creation science included in biology texts, either alone or alongside evolution theory, on the whole have not been successful.

   It should be noted that nontextbooks also sometimes are censored by public schools, including classic works of literature (by Hemingway, Mark Twain, and many others) as well as dictionaries listing four-letter words.

5. History texts tend to bombard students with almost endless lists of forgettable facts that tend to bury important information. They also distort reality so as to satisfy the various interested pressure groups and to mold students into good, loyal citizens. For example, they portray American presidents and heroes in a one-sided manner (for instance, not mentioning the vicious, bloodthirsty side of President Theodore Roosevelt). They also exaggerate the American role in world affairs (as in World War II) and play down the nasty side of U.S. history (for instance, in putting down the Filipino attempt to gain independence).

   High school texts, it should be noted, are more accurate and less propagandistic than those used in junior high, which in turn are much better in this way than typical grade school texts.

6. Although today's social studies texts are light years better than those of even 30 years ago, they still say relatively little about the large gulf between theory—how the American social system is supposed to work—and practice—how it actually works in everyday life. For example, they don't tell students about the preferential treatment often given to the rich and powerful (how they are sent

to cushy jails when they are convicted of crimes, for instance) and play down the corruption that is common in government (for example, at best only hinting at the extent to which governments are corrupted by lobbying and by campaign contributions).

7. The result is that textbooks fail to provide students with genuine understanding or even, because of their dull styles and piling on of facts, knowledge of particular facts that is retained for any length of time. They do, however, reflect what organized groups and professional educators want students to read, which is as it should be in a democratic society.

8. But college texts, having a different sort of clientele, are different. *(Vive la difference.)*

## EXERCISE 12-1

1. Here is a famous quote by Northrop Frye: "Censorship is to dissent (and democracy) what lynching is to justice." Evaluate this quote, in particular, discussing the charge that it contains a fallacy.

2. Now here is a (fortunately) much less famous quote by Mel Gabler, Educational Research Analysis (a pressure group that has had success, in particular, in the state of Texas):

    When a student reads in a math book that there are no absolutes, suddenly every value he's been taught is destroyed. And the next thing you know, the student turns to crime and drugs.

    a. What is Gabler's (unstated) point? What is he advocating, and why?
    b. Evaluate his argument, again considering the charge that his reasoning is fallacious.

## EXERCISE 12-2

1. At what point in their educational careers do you think students are ready to be taught the biological facts concerning human sex and reproduction? Or do you think these topics should not be broached in public schools? Defend your answers.

2. Recall the excerpt on page 312 from Paul Fussell's book about GIs in World War II and the textual remarks about the horrors or war (soldiers being blown apart, etc.).
    a. In your opinion, should high school students be exposed to books that tell students things like this about war? Defend your view on this.
    b. In fact, they never are told these things. Why do you think this is so? Again, defend your answer.

3. It has been forcefully argued that very young children are tender shoots who need to find out the bad features of their society (as of life in general) rather gradually, so that it would be wrong to tell them too quickly that quite a few presidents (including such "heroes" as Franklin Roosevelt and John Kennedy)

had mistresses; that the bribes taken by the "Keating Five" were just the tip of the iceberg; or that America's history is filled with nasty deeds and steeped in blood and conquest. The point of these arguments is that we don't want to destroy the pride and loyalty of the young, and we don't want to make future citizens into cynics.

a. Do you agree or disagree with this line of reasoning? Defend your answer.

b. Does it tend to undercut one of the themes of this chapter—that less indoctrination means better education?

c. At what age, if ever, should students be given a completely accurate and balanced account of these matters?

d. It has been argued that, in a society such as exists today in the United States, where several religions flourish and there is no single moral code accepted by all, public schools should not attempt to teach students about alleged values, customs, or traditions of the culture. What is your opinion on this question and, of course, why do you think so?

*4. Does the term "creation science" ring a bell with respect to a topic discussed in an earlier chapter in this book? Explain.

5. Recall how the Boston Massacre was described in your history textbooks back in high school. Then look up that event in a first-rate history book and describe the differences. (Hint: If there are no differences, either your high school history text was the best ever published or your memory is poor or your new source is not a first-rate book.)

6. In the box on page 314, claims about the Egyptian origins of ancient Greek culture were objected to on the grounds that there is next to no evidence in their support. It would be extremely difficult for nonexperts to refute these "Afro-centered" (we all can play language games) claims in their entirety, but it should be relatively easy to refute the specific claim that the ancient Greek philosopher Aristotle—often admiringly called, by the way, "the philosopher"—derived his ideas from a study of African books he read in the famous library in Alexandria (northern Egypt). So go to your close-by library (the one at Alexandria is not available at this time) and prove this claim to be false.

## EXERCISE 12-3

This is an extremely difficult exercise, whose correct answer without doubt is in dispute (so perhaps it would make a good class project). Although difficult, it should be an interesting one because it concerns the textbooks college students are required to buy for most of their classes. Anyway, here is the exercise:

During the past 30 years or so a minor revolution, hardly noticed by most people, has taken place in the way that textbooks are sold to students in most colleges. One large change resulted from the rise of used textbook companies that buy used books from students at the end of each semester. They do so if there is a market anywhere in the United States for a particular book, whereas in the old days student bookstores would buy back used copies only if they were to be assigned in the next semester at that very college. Another change was in the management or ownership of college bookstores themselves. They used to be owned and managed by the colleges themselves. Faculty ordered books through their college bookstores and the bookstores filled the orders from two sources: (1) textbook publishers (new copies) and (2) used copies bought back from students who used them in the previous semester (obviously they could do this only if a book was used in the previous semester and students sold their copies back to the bookstore). Most college bookstores now are managed, and often owned, by outside companies (for example, by Barnes and Noble) that pay schools for the right to profit from the running of their bookstores. Orders now go from teachers to these companies and are filled by new books ordered from publishers and by used books bought back from students around the country. School administrators find the new arrangement congenial because now bookstores typically yield a guaranteed profit to the school, eliminating the risk, as of old, that bookstores will lose money. The new system would appear to be better also from the point of view of students because used, and thus cheaper, copies of textbooks would be more likely to be available for them to buy, and their used books would be more likely to be bought back by bookstores, thus saving students money. (The theory behind the "privatization" of college bookstores obviously is the same as the one we hear about, for example, for health care and for public utilities.)

The question you are to answer, then, is how in fact the new system operates at your school. (If your school still operates its own bookstore, your problem is to find out why it has resisted outside offers.) In particular, do students on average pay less for books than they would under the old system? To help you answer this question, here are two facts about the pricing of textbooks in the old days: (1) New copies typically were sold at a 25 percent markup, so that, say, copies costing the bookstore $24 would be sold to students for $30; and (2) used copies were typically bought from students (when they were to be used in the next semester at that school) for a good deal less than half the original price and sold to students for about 25 percent more than that amount. (Policy on used texts varied somewhat from school to school, but new-book pricing policies were as indicated in a large majority of schools nationwide.)

You need to think very carefully about this exercise and do some "real-life" research. Start by going to the company manager of your school bookstore to try to determine some facts about its operation, in particular, about the way in which faculty orders are filled and the percentage markup usually charged on new and used textbooks. (Hint: Ask about the typical ratio of new to used books—whether new copies always are available for those students who want them—and draw a useful conclusion from the answer you receive.) You might also consider the managers of nearby bookstores that sell college textbooks and think carefully about how publishers have reacted to all this. You also might find it interesting to try to find out from your college administrators what sort of contract has been made with the company running your bookstore and why the college doesn't run its own bookstore as in days of old. Good luck.

## *Exercise for the Entire Text

This text, like all others, is based on certain presuppositions (only some made explicit) and no doubt contains fallacious reasoning, in spite of the authors' best efforts to reason cogently. So, as the final exercise, write a brief critique of this textbook with respect to: (1) its major presuppositions (that is, the world views of the authors as stated or implied in the text); (2) possible fallacious arguments; (3) biased selections of material; and (4) rhetorical devices used to persuade readers to accept the authors' opinions on this or that. (Be sure to defend your findings, including examples to back up your claims.)

*Dennis the Menace.* © 1984 North American Syndicate, Inc.
Reprinted by permission of Hank Ketcham.

"It'll stop, Joey. It always has before."

*A youthful inductionist at work.*

*The object of reasoning is to find out, from the consideration of what we already know, something else which we do not know.*

      — Charles Sanders Peirce

*A simple person believes every word he hears; a clever one understands the need for proof.*

      — Proverbs 14:15

# APPENDIX: MORE ON COGENT REASONING

Recall from Chapter 1 that good (cogent) reasoning, as opposed to bad (fallacious) reasoning, must satisfy three conditions. It must (1) contain warranted (justified) premises (reasons); (2) include all relevant information; and (3) be valid (correct), which means roughly that the premises offered in support of the conclusion must truly support that conclusion.

Let's say a few more words on the third of these conditions.

## 1. DEDUCTIVE VALIDITY: A REVIEW

We stated in Chapter 1 that if the premises of a *deductively valid argument* are true, then its conclusion must be true also (because its conclusion already is contained in its premises, although usually only implicitly). We also pointed out that different arguments may have the same *form*, or *structure*, as do these two deductively valid arguments that have the form *modus ponens*:

(1)  1. If the president acts forcefully, then he'll gain points in the polls.

     2. He will act forcefully.

∴3. He'll gain points in the polls.

(2)  1. If you gave money to that homeless person, you felt virtuous.

     2. You gave money to him.

∴3. You felt virtuous.

The form these two argument share is this:

    1. If *A* then *B*.

    2. *A*.

∴3. *B*.

In Chapter 1, we also mentioned several other deductively valid argument forms, including *modus tollens, disjunctive syllogism,* and *hypothetical syllogism.*

In daily life, arguments having these valid forms, and others, tend to get strung together into larger arguments leading up to a point, a grand conclusion or *thesis.* Here is an example (with logical structure exhibited to the left) in which the conclusion of the first argument is used as a premise in the second, and the conclusion of the second is used as a premise in the third, and final, argument:

|  |  |
|---|---|
| 1.  If *A* then *B*. | 1.  If a world government doesn't evolve soon, then wars will continue to occur. |
| 2.  If *B* then *C*. | 2.  But if they continue to occur, then nuclear weapons will proliferate. |
| ∴3.  If *A* then *C*. | 3.  So if a world government doesn't evolve soon, then nuclear weapons will proliferate. |
| 4.  If *C* then *D*. | 4.  But if they proliferate, then a nuclear war will be inevitable, sooner or later. |
| ∴5.  If *A* then *D*. | 5.  Which proves that if a world government doesn't evolve soon, we'll end up fighting a nuclear war sooner or later. |
| 6.  Not *D*. | 6.  But it's ridiculous to think we'll actually have a nuclear war (that is, it's false that we'll have such a war). |
| ∴7.  Not *A*. | 7.  So a world government is going to evolve soon (that is, it's false that a world government won't evolve soon). |

## 2. SYLLOGISMS

We said before that arguments having the form called *hypothetical syllogism*:

1. If *A* then *B*.
2. If *B* then *C*.
∴3. If *A* then *C*.

are only honorific syllogisms—syllogisms by extension—although those having the form:

1. All *A*s are *B*s.
2. All *B*s are *C*s.
3. All *A*s are *C*s.

are of the full-blooded variety. What makes one the genuine article and the other not quite the real thing? The explanation is contained in the following little exposition as to the nature of true syllogisms in traditional syllogistic logic.*

In traditional syllogistic logic, a **categorical proposition** is a subject-predicate proposition that asserts or denies a relationship between a **subject class** and a **predicate class**. There are exactly four kinds of categorical propositions (with one variation): **uni-**

---

*Obviously, something has changed since days of old, and that is why, for example, argument forms such as *hypothetical syllogism* now sometimes are thought of as the genuine article. The point is that Aristotle and Aristotelians, until recently, would not have considered these other forms to be syllogisms.

versal affirmative (**A propositions**), having the form "All *S* are *P*" (*Example*: "All sinners are betrayers."); **universal negative (E propositions)**, having the form "No *S* are *P*" (*Example*: "No chess players are imbeciles."); **particular affirmative (I propositions)**, having the form "Some *S* are *P*" (*Example*: "Some men are chauvinists."); and **particular negative (O propositions)**, having the form "Some *S* are not *P*" (*Example*: "Some logicians are not nitpickers."). The one variation is that statements such as "Socrates is a man," having as their subject a particular item rather than a class of items, are honorifically considered to be *A* propositions.

A **syllogism** is an argument containing three categorical propositions, two of them premises, one a conclusion. Here is one of the original examples (dechauvinized):

| *Syllogism* | *Traditional Symbolization* |
|---|---|
| All humans are mortals. | MAP |
| All Greeks are humans. | SAM |
| ∴ All Greeks are mortals. | ∴ SAP * |

The term *P*, the predicate of the conclusion, is said to be the syllogism's **major term**; the term *S*, the subject of the conclusion, its **minor term**; and the term *M*, which occurs once in each premise but not in the conclusion, its **middle term**. Every syllogism has exactly three terms (none used equivocally), each one repeated twice but not in the same proposition. There are hundreds of different syllogistic forms (figure out how many), but, of course, only some are valid. The one given above is valid, whereas the syllogism "All Greeks are humans; All humans are mortals; therefore, "All mortals are Greeks" is not.

## EXERCISE A-1

1. Invent a deductively valid syllogism that has the same form as the valid syllogism just mentioned.

2. Invent another deductively valid syllogism having some other form. (You should be able to do this without first seeing an example.)

3. Now invent a deductively invalid syllogism, and explain why you think that it is not valid.

4. Explain why *disjunctive syllogisms* are only honorific syllogisms.

## A Misconception About Deduction and Induction

There is a widespread but erroneous idea about the difference between deductive and inductive validity. This is the idea that in deductively valid reasoning, we go from the

---

*In traditional accounts, this syllogism is said to have the form AAA-1 (the "1" indicating that this AAA syllogism is in the "first figure"). In the Middle Ages, students determined the validity of syllogistic forms by reciting a chant containing a name for each of the valid cases in each figure. For example, the name "bArbArA" occurs in the chant for the first figure, indicating that the form AAA-1 is valid. For more about syllogisms, including an explanation as to how a syllogism's figure is determined, see Howard Kahane and Paul Tidman, *Logic and Philosophy,* 8th ed. (Belmont, Calif: Wadsworth Publishing Company, 1998).

general to the particular, while in inductively valid reasoning, we move from the particular to the general. But there is little to be said for this idea. For instance, the deductively valid argument

1. All Republican politicians are to the right of Al Gore.
∴2. All who are not to the right of Al Gore are not Republican politicians.

moves from the general to the equally general, while the inductively valid argument

1. Bill Clinton made promises during the 1992 campaign that he didn't intend to keep.
∴2. Bill Clinton probably made promises during the 1996 campaign that he did not intend to keep.

moves from the particular to the equally particular. And the inductively valid argument

1. So far, all Republican party presidential candidates have been male.
∴2. The next Republican party presidential candidate will be male.

moves from the general to the particular, not the other way around.

So there isn't much truth to the old idea that deductive reasoning moves from the general to the particular, while inductive reasoning moves from the particular to the general. More accurately, when we reason deductively, we reason to conclusions already contained (implicitly or explicitly) in our premises; when we reason inductively, we move to conclusions by extending patterns or resemblances from one set of events to another set.

Some of those who argue otherwise claim that the idea of deduction moving from the general to the particular is intended to be true only for syllogistic reasoning. Thus, the valid syllogism "All humans are mortals; Socrates is human; therefore, Socrates is mortal," does indeed move from the general to the particular. The trouble, of course, is that this is not true for a great many other valid syllogisms, including the one mentioned a while back, whose conclusion is that all Greeks are mortal.

## 3. INDIRECT OR REDUCTIO AD ABSURDUM PROOFS

Another common everyday kind of reasoning is called an **indirect** or a **reductio ad absurdum proof**. We reason in this way when we assume the opposite of what we wish to prove and then deductively derive a conclusion claimed to be false, indeed, often contradictory or otherwise absurd. The point is that if we validly reason to a false conclusion, then our original assumption must be false and hence its negation—the thing we wish to prove—must be true. Here is an example:

> Assume for the moment that President Clinton offered a night's stay in the Lincoln Room in the White House in return for campaign contributions. Then, since doing so would definitely be at least shady, if not illegal, Clinton would have done something shady if not illegal. But Clinton is an honorable man, so we can be sure that he did not do anything shady or illegal. Therefore, the assumption that Clinton offered a stay in the Lincoln room in return for money must be false.

There are two ways in which an indirect proof can be defeated. One is by showing that there is a mistake in reasoning. (In our example, there is no mistake in reasoning.) The other way is to show that at least one of its premises (other than the assumed premise) is false. (In our example, the likely premise would be . . . ?)

## 4. TAUTOLOGIES, CONTRADICTIONS, AND CONTINGENT STATEMENTS

A **tautology** is a statement that is logically, or necessarily, true or is so devoid of content as to be practically empty (and thus true because completely empty statements, making no claim, cannot be false).* *Example*: "O. J. did it, or he didn't." A **contradiction** is a statement that is necessarily false (because it contradicts itself). *Example*: "O. J. did it and he didn't do it." (Contradictions, you will recall, were discussed early in the book in the section on the fallacy of inconsistency.) All other statements are said to be **contingent**. *Example*: "O. J. denied doing it."

We can determine the truth value of a contradiction or of a tautology by logical means alone, without the need for any empirical investigation. But to determine the truth or falsity of a contingent statement, we need to do some sort of investigating or other. For example, to determine whether it is true that O. J. denied being guilty, we need to consult court records or other evidence of his denial (or, of course, to have been in court when he declared his innocence).

## EXERCISE A-2

Which of the following are tautologies, which contradictions, and which contingent statements? Defend your answers. (Be careful; at least one of these is sneaky.)

1. Either Hubert Humphrey almost became president of the United States, or a lot of newspapers were mistaken.

2. Either Humphrey almost became president of the United States, or he didn't.

*3. Humphrey didn't campaign in 1969 both for the presidency and the vice presidency.

4. Snow is always white, except, of course, when it isn't.

5. The media always report accurately.

6. No politicians ever keep any of their campaign promises.

7. Those who laugh last, laugh best.

8. I learned in school that $2 \times 2$ always equals 4, but I don't believe it.

9. Either you're in favor of an equal rights amendment to the Constitution or you're against it.

---

*Note that logicians often use the term *tautology* in a more restricted manner, so as to cover only the logical truths provable by means of what is called "sentential logic."

*10. Trespassers will be shot, or they won't.

11. If you don't play the state lottery, you can't win it.

## 5. POSSIBILITIES, IMPOSSIBILITIES, AND NECESSITIES

Something is **logically possible** if it does not violate a principle of logic, **physically possible** if it does not violate a law of nature, and **technically possible** if we actually know how it could be done. *Examples*: It is logically possible (because not contradictory) to fly to the nearest star in one second, although *physically impossible* (because of the law of nature that says nothing can move faster than the speed of light). It is physically possible to get to the nearest star in ten years (light can get there in four), although *technically impossible* (because so far we haven't figured out how to get a space vehicle to fly at the required speed). But it is technically possible to send a space ship to Neptune (meaning simply that we know how to do so and have the necessary means). Similarly, it is logically necessary that two plus two equal four, and physically necessary that copper conduct electricity under normal circumstances, but neither logically nor physically necessary that we actually run a current through a copper wire.

The point of mentioning these matters here is that in everyday life people often confuse one kind of possibility or necessity with another. So whenever in daily life someone uses the terms *possible*, *impossible*, or *necessary*, we need to get clear as to which sort is intended and which sort might make a statement true, which false.

## 6. REASONING COGENTLY VERSUS BEING RIGHT IN FACT

Reasoning correctly and getting a true conclusion are unfortunately not the same thing. We can reason correctly and get a false conclusion, and we can reason fallaciously and get a true conclusion.* *Examples*: Scientists in times past reasoned correctly from what was then known to the conclusion that superconductivity occurs only at temperatures very close to absolute zero, but we now know that this conclusion is false. Astrology buffs often reason incorrectly that they will have a good day from the fact that a newspaper column says they will, and then do have a good day (for completely different reasons having nothing whatever to do with astrology).

On the whole, it's a lot better to reason incorrectly to true—right—conclusions than it is to reason well to false ones.† But *the most likely way to be right, in the long run, is to reason correctly!* When people who follow astrology columns do well, they're just lucky, not smart. In daily life, however, people often lump together being smart and being successful, as though success proves reasoning has been cogent. It doesn't, nor does having failed prove reasoning fallacious. That's life. Smart people, as they say, "play the odds"—they try to reason well to good conclusions, and take their chances in this not quite best of all possible worlds, and in the long run in most cases, they do better than those who reason fallaciously.

---

*In philosophical jargon, we can be *epistemologically right* although *ontologically wrong,* and we can be *epistemologically wrong* but *ontologically right.*

†Philosophical slogan: "I'd rather be epistemologically wrong and ontologically right than vice versa.

# 7. MORE ON CAUSE AND EFFECT

In Chapter 1, we said a few words about how inductive reasoning is used to discover causal relationships—to discover how one thing causes another. But just as in the case of most interesting concepts, that of causation is really a cluster of related concepts, mostly with blurred edges. When we call one thing the cause of another, we can mean simply the **sufficient condition** for bringing it about. In this sense, the cause of Marie Antoinette's death was being guillotined—having one's head cut off certainly suffices to bring about death.

On the other hand, we often mean by the cause of a thing or event whatever is a **necessary condition** for bringing it about. Striking a match on a rough surface (thus heating it) can be thought of, for example, as a necessary condition of the lighting of a match, even though it is only part of what must be true for the effect—the lighting of the match—to occur. It is a necessary condition, but not a sufficient condition: Matches also need to be dry and struck in the presence of oxygen if they are to light. Being in the presence of oxygen and being dry and being heated together constitute both the necessary and the sufficient conditions for a match to light.

The point here is that, even though striking a match (heating it) cannot alone cause a match to light, we still in everyday life talk as though striking a match is what makes it light. It usually makes perfectly good sense to say, for instance, that the match lit because it was struck on a rough surface (which heats the match to the required temperature), even though a match struck in a vacuum will not light (because of a lack of oxygen). But we would not say, for example, that it lit because it was in the presence of oxygen. The difference, roughly speaking, is *human agency*—in everyday life, it's easy to *make* a match light by striking it (heating it), but we can't usually make it light by providing oxygen (for one thing, the oxygen already is there and for another the match still won't light because ordinary air temperatures are too low).

Also of interest is the fact that we sometimes need to distinguish between **proximate causes** and those that are more **remote**. Suppose that a truck jackknifes on an icy highway, blocking three of four lanes, and that an auto, call it auto A, has to swerve into the unblocked lane and that another auto, B, then crashes into auto A. The ice on the road would be said to be the *proximate cause* of the truck's jackknifing but a much more remote cause of the accident between autos A and B. The difference between proximate and remote causes can be important in everyday life, in particular in legal cases. Clearly, auto A's swerving into the last unblocked lane is a proximate cause of the crash between A and B, yet the driver of A may well not be held responsible, since his need to go into that lane was caused by more remote events. The guilty party more likely will be held to be the driver of the truck for driving without sufficient care on an icy highway.

This example brings to mind the fact that, in everyday life, a given effect can be explained in terms of more than one cause. Which one we select usually depends on our particular interest in that effect. In assessing blame, say, in the case of a knife murder, we don't care about the neural and muscular causes of the murderer's arm movement, but, we do care very much about his having consciously willed to do the act. A biologist, on the other hand, might be very interested indeed in neural firings in the guilty party's body, and in a court of law might well testify to neural and muscular causes of the knife blow. So it makes sense to say either that the willing caused the event or that the neural firings and muscle contractions did so.*

## 8. CALCULATING PROBABILITIES AND FAIR ODDS

Billions of dollars are legally wagered on games of chance each year in the United States, and billions more are wagered illegally. The popularity of Atlantic City, Reno, and Las Vegas testifies to the fact that many millions of people in America gamble every year. Yet most who gamble have no idea how to calculate fair odds, one reason almost all gamblers lose in the long run. (Another reason, of course, is that the odds on all legal gambling games, including in particular slot machines and state lotteries, are rigged against the player—the odds *always* favor the house.)

Legitimate, fair odds depend on the *likelihood* (*probability* or *chances*) that a given outcome will occur. For example, when you flip a symmetrical coin, the chances are *one out of two*, or $\frac{1}{2}$, that the coin will land heads up because there are two possibilities, and both are equally likely. **Fair odds** on heads thus should be even money— one to one—and someone who bets a dollar and wins should win a dollar.

Most games of chance are designed to present players with a specific number of equally likely alternatives, or combinations of alternatives, on which they must wager. To find the **probability** of combinations of outcomes, simply divide the number of favorable outcomes by the total number of possible outcomes, favorable or unfavorable. (Remember, though, that this works only in cases where all individual outcomes are equally likely and outcomes are independent of each other—a matter to be discussed soon.)

Suppose we want to calculate the chances of getting a 7 on the next toss of an honest (symmetrical) pair of dice. There are exactly 36 possible outcomes on each toss, of which exactly 6 add up to 7 (namely, the combinations 1 and 6, 2 and 5, 3 and 4, 4 and 3, 5 and 2, and 6 and 1). So the probability of getting a 7 on a given toss equals $\frac{6}{36}$, or $\frac{1}{6}$. Out of 6 tosses, the average wagerer will win once and lose five times. That is why fair odds on 7 in a dice game are 5 to 1, and why someone who wins a dollar bet should win $5. (At a casino, someone who bets a dollar is required to place it on the table, so that, if winners were paid fair odds, they would get back $6—their own dollar plus five in winnings. But no casino in history has ever paid fair odds. Gambling establishments are in business to make money, not to run fair games of chance!)

State lotteries probably offer the worst odds of any popular games of chance, since they pay back in winnings only from one-half to at best two-thirds of what they take in.†

At Las Vegas and other places where gambling is legal, perhaps the best odds for average players are at the dice tables. Slot machines provide the worst odds (except for wagers on sporting events or horse races). Yet the slots are without doubt the most popular way to lose money at every legal gambling casino.

---

*For more on causation and related matters, see Howard Kahane and Paul Tidman: *Logic and Philosophy*, 8th ed. (Belmont, Calif.: Wadsworth Publishing Co., 1998).

†That is why playing a state lottery amounts to paying a voluntary state tax. Thomas Jefferson, among other illustrious figures, favored lotteries for that very reason. Ordinary taxes are compulsory; lottery "taxes" are completely voluntary. Good point. Of course, human nature being what it is, plenty of people who regularly toss money away on state lotteries complain bitterly about having to pay state sales and income taxes.

Anyway, probabilities being what they are, when the odds are less than fair, virtually everyone who gambles must lose in the long run. But people being as so many of us are, all sorts of foolish theories have gained wide currency among those who like to gamble. The most foolish theory, of course, is that there is something called luck and that in certain situations luck is on our side—an idea that was discussed earlier.

But there are also two other, more sophisticated theories that should be mentioned. One is the belief that doubling a bet after a losing play, say, at the dice table, assures victory in the long run even when the odds are stacked against you. After all, you must win sooner or later, thereby recouping all losses plus a nice profit. Alas, there is no gambling Santa Claus. First of all, the odds are against you on every play; doubling the bet cannot change that fact. Second, unless you are a Bill Gates or a Warren Buffett, the house always has a much larger pile of reserve cash than you do and therefore can withstand a greater run of losses. In the battle between house and gambler, the gambler thus almost always gets wiped out first by a streak of bad luck. (There are old stories and even a song about "the man who broke the bank at Monte Carlo," but if it ever happened, it wasn't in living memory.)

According to a variation of the double-the-bet gambit, a bet made after previous losses should cover just what has been lost so far plus just a small amount extra—say, the amount of the first bet—so that if you bet $2 on the first play and lose, the second play is for $4, the third for $8, and so on until you win, at which point you start over with a $2 bet. This method certainly increases the average number of plays until a gambler will get wiped out, but it still can't change the inevitable failure lurking in the distance. This method also has the disadvantage that, even if you beat the odds and end up a winner, you've just won the tiny amount of your initial wager. (A friend of the authors of this text actually tried this system at Las Vegas a few years ago—at $10 a pop—and actually lasted over two hours before losing her bankroll.)

The other cute fallacy that gamblers fall for is to believe that the less often, say, a 7 has shown up lately at the dice table, the more likely it is that it will show up on the next toss of the dice. The odds, gamblers are fond of saying, have to "even out." Wait until 7 has not shown up for a specified number of tosses, say, 10 in a row, and then bet heavily on 7.

The trouble with this system is that each toss of the dice is *independent* of every other toss, which means that what happens on one toss is independent of what happens on any other. The point is that the dice don't know (or care!) what has shown up on previous tosses. The conditions that determine the odds on any given toss determine them to be the same for all tosses, no matter how previous tosses turned out. The dice, after all, are still the same symmetrical devices obeying the same laws of physics on every toss.

True critical reasoners, of course, don't need to know anything about correct odds to be sure that systems like this don't work. The house is in business to *win*; if they let you play, you can bet your system is no good.*

---

*There have been very few exceptions to this rule. One occurred many years ago when "card-counting" systems were devised for blackjack that changed the odds so that they were in favor of adept card counters. At first, casinos refused to let card counters play—they actually kept lists—but then they simply increased the size of blackjack decks or used mechanical devices spewing out an endless series of cards, thereby ruining the card-counting game.

Another exception also occurred many years ago when college students discovered the tiny bias of a particular Las Vegas casino roulette wheel by patient observation over several days. They were allowed to win several thousand dollars, because of the great publicity, before the house ruined the game simply by changing the wheel.

Anyway, although the theory about how to calculate fair odds is quite complicated, there are a few simple rules that cover many common cases. Using the lowercase letter *a* to stand for a first event or outcome and *b* for a second, and *P* as shorthand for probability, here are four such rules:

*Restricted conjunction rule:*

If two events are independent of each other (the occurrence of one has no effect on the occurrence of the other), then the probability of both occurring is equal to the probability of the first times the probability of the second. In symbols, this reads:

$P(a \ \& \ b) = P(a) \times P(b).$

For example, the probability of getting two 7s in a row with a fair pair of dice is equal to the probability of first getting a 7 ($\frac{1}{6}$) times the probability of 7 on the second toss ($\frac{1}{6}$), and thus is $\frac{1}{6} \times \frac{1}{6} = \frac{1}{36}$.

*General conjunction rule:*

$P(a \ \& \ b) = P(a) \times P(b, \text{ given that } a \text{ occurs}).$

For instance, the probability of drawing two spades in a row out of an at-first-complete deck of cards is equal to the probability of drawing the first spade ($\frac{13}{52}$, because 13 of the 52 cards in a deck are spades) times the probability of drawing a second one, given that the first spade is not replaced in the deck ($\frac{12}{51}$), and thus is $\frac{13}{52} \times \frac{12}{51} = \frac{1}{17}$.

*Restricted disjunction rule:*

If *a* and *b* are mutually exclusive events (an outcome cannot be both *a* and *b*), then

$P(a \text{ or } b) = P(a) + P(b).$

For example, the probability of drawing a spade or a heart on a given draw is equal to the probability of drawing a spade ($\frac{1}{4}$) plus the probability of drawing a heart ($\frac{1}{4}$), and thus is $\frac{1}{4} + \frac{1}{4} = \frac{1}{2}$. (Drawing a spade and drawing a heart are mutually exclusive because no card can be both a spade and a heart.)

*General disjunction rule:*

$P(a \text{ or } b) = P(a) + P(b) - P(a \ \& \ b).$

For instance, the probability of getting at least one head in two tosses equals the probability of getting a head on the first toss ($\frac{1}{2}$) plus the probability of doing so on the second toss ($\frac{1}{2}$) minus the probability of getting heads on both tosses ($\frac{1}{4}$), and thus is $\frac{1}{2} + \frac{1}{2} - \frac{1}{4} = \frac{3}{4}$. (Note that we can't just say it is equal to $\frac{1}{2} + \frac{1}{2}$.)

It should be obvious, by the way, that the probability of a contradiction equals zero and of a tautology (logical truth), one.

## EXERCISE A-3

   *1. What is the probability of getting either 2 or 12 on a given toss of an honest pair of dice?

   2. How about one or the other in two tosses?

3. What is the probability of getting a red jack, queen, or king with an ordinary deck of cards on one random draw?

*4. If a state lottery paid fair odds, how much should a $2 wager pay a winner who picked the correct five-digit number?

5. Can we use the general disjunction rule in cases where the events are mutually exclusive, as in the spade/heart example just mentioned? Explain your answer, and give an example.

## EXERCISE A-4

Here is a "system" promoted in a book on gambling.* (A tiny part of the system has been omitted here.) Explain why it doesn't work (hard question, but well worth figuring out).

> There is only one way to show a profit. Bet light on your losses and heavy on your wins.
>
> *Bet minimums when you're losing.*
>
> You recoup losses by betting house money against the house, not your own. When you win with a minimum bet, let the winnings ride and manage to come up with a few more wins. . . .
>
> *Bet heavy when you're winning.*
>
> Following a win with your minimum bet, bet the original minimum plus the amount you won. On a third win, drag [keep?] the minimum and bet the rest. You now have a one-minimum-bet profit on the round, regardless of what happens. . . . As soon as you lose, go back to the minimum bet. . . .
>
> *Always make your heavy bets with the other fellow's money, not your own.*
>
> The worst thing you can do betting house money against the house on a bet is break even on that particular wager. Actually, you've lost money on the round—but it was money that you got from the other fellow, not part of your original venture money. . . .
>
> *Don't limit your winnings.*
>
> Always ride out a winning streak, pushing your skill to the hilt. . . .
>
> *Quit on a losing streak, not a winning streak.*
>
> While the law of mathematical probability averages out, it doesn't operate in a set pattern. Wins and losses go in streaks more often than they alternate. If you've had a good winning streak and a loss follows it, bet minimums long enough to see whether or not another winning streak is coming up. If it isn't, quit while you're still ahead.

## 9. SCIENTIFIC METHOD

Scientific method is just common sense writ large, sharpened, fine-tuned, and applied (in the best cases) with creative persistence and patience. There is nothing mysterious or impenetrable about how scientists go about justifying their hypotheses.

---

*Clement McQuaid, editor, *Gambler's Digest: The World's Greatest Gambling Book,* 2nd ed. (Northfield, Ill.: DBI Books, 1981).

Common sense requires that beliefs about the nature of the world be justified, more or less, by cogent arguments, as discussed in earlier chapters. Scientists have no other way, no magic formulas or wands, for coming to justified beliefs about the nature of the world. Science's "secret" lies in the persistent accumulation of knowledge by thousands (now literally millions) of practitioners who have required of each other the elimination so far as is possible of the shoddy, wishful thinking that peppers everyday reasoning. The rules of the scientific game force scientists to reject unjustified theories* and to give up their most cherished ideas when experience shows that they are false (or unsupported by good evidence).

Typical scientific theories result from a complicated mixture of deductive and inductive arguments, but the key arguments are inductive. Good scientists try to find *patterns* in what they have observed so far, in particular in their scientific experiments,† and project these patterns via inductive reasonings to larger slices of reality. In everyday life, common sense reasons by inductions from past experiences that sugar sweetens, vinegar sours, bread nourishes, and drought kills crops. Scientists, using the same common sense methods, but much more persistently and stringently, conclude that copper conducts electricity, cigarette smoking causes cancer, the Earth's path around the sun is an ellipse, and radioactive substances have half-lives. (They also, of course, use viewing instruments they have learned to construct by means of inductive reasoning— telescopes, microscopes, X-ray machines, and so on—that we ordinarily don't have at our disposal in daily life.)

So science is just the accumulated knowledge gained by huge numbers of individuals observing nature, proposing theories (patterns) that explain what has been observed, and testing by additional observations to confirm their theories (hypotheses). When scientists claim to have discovered a new pattern, others will try to duplicate their findings; when they succeed, a theory tends to be accepted into the scientific canon; when they cannot successfully duplicate the findings, a theory will be discarded, or at least modified so as to take account of what has been learned by the failure to confirm. It is this that distinguishes science from pseudoscience: A scientific theory predicts what will be experienced under certain conditions; if it is not experienced, the theory must be rejected, or revised to conform to what has been discovered. Those who believe in pseudosciences—for example, extrasensory perception—cling to theories that are disconfirmed by experience and that do not make successful predictions about what will be experienced in future.

Speaking of pseudoscience brings to mind the fact that a truly scientific theory must conform not just to evidence directly supporting it but also indirectly to all scientific theories whatsoever. Pseudosciences, on the other hand, never conform to the whole body of scientific knowledge or even, sometimes, to ordinary everyday thoughts. Creation

---

*Scientists use the terms *theory* and *hypothesis* in at least two ways. In one sense, both of these terms refer to untested speculations or to insufficiently confirmed patterns. In another, they refer to well-established, well-confirmed, and accepted patterns. The second sense is synonymous with the expressions "scientific law" and "law of nature."

†A scientific experiment is just a kind of deliberately arranged experience. Instead of waiting for an event to happen, scientists arrange for it to happen, perhaps in their laboratories. For instance, they may mix two chemicals in the laboratory that rarely, if ever, are found mixed in nature, in order to see the result. But whether an event is "found" in the laboratory or found in "nature" is irrelevant to scientific procedure.

science, for example, asserts that all human beings except for Noah and his family perished about 5,000 or so years ago in the Biblical flood. This means that all of the human genetic variety we see today—all racial differences—must have evolved in just a few thousand years from the common Noah family stock, and this contradicts everything we know about how human beings, or any mammals, evolve and propagate. So anyone who accepts creation science on this point must reject virtually everything known about genetics, along with a great deal of the rest of modern biology.

Note, by the way, that failure to confirm a proposed scientific theory does not mean that the attempt to do so was of no value. On the contrary, failure can be very revealing; indeed, it often is more enlightening than success. For example, the failure of experiments conducted in the 1880s to prove the existence of an "ether," believed in those days by scientists to be the medium through which light (and other electromagnetic waves) traveled through space, led to a crisis in Newtonian physics that was finally resolved by Einstein's special theory of relativity. So, in a sense, one of the most important scientific advances of the twentieth century grew out of the failure to confirm a previously widely accepted scientific theory.

Students often misunderstand this aspect of scientific investigation. They often object, for example, to biological research done on animals because what works with respect to other animals frequently does not do so in the case of human beings; students often see this as proof that animals were made to suffer with no offsetting increase in knowledge about how human diseases can be conquered. They don't understand that failures of this kind may lead investigators away from a wrong path and on to a right one. (They also often overlook the many cases in which, say, drugs that work well on close mammalian relatives also do so when tried on human beings.) Note, by the way, that those who champion pseudosciences generally do *not* learn from failures to confirm their theories; they tend simply to sweep this sort of counterevidence under the nearest metaphorical rug.

Pseudoscientists also tend to ignore ways in which their theories run counter to simple facts and ideas about how things work that we all hold in everyday life. Creation science, for example, fails to take account of what we all know about the abundance of species in today's world. There are thousands of mammal species, thousands of bird species, thousands of amphibian and reptilian species, and millions of insect species, all of which could not have fitted into one ark that even today's technology might with great effort construct. So even forgetting that lions can't be expected to lie down with lambs; forgetting that the ark would have had to be stocked with an incredible amount and variety of food so animals would not starve; forgetting that literally millions of plant species would have had to be collected; forgetting the physical impossibility of Noah and his family going around the world to collect all of these animals and plants and food; forgetting about bacteria and viruses; and forgetting fussy details about getting rid of huge amounts of fecal material, it should be clear that the creation science story violates not just dozens of extremely well-confirmed, high-powered scientific theories but also all kinds of everyday ideas about how the world works, *while predicting nothing about what sorts of (earthly!) experiences the future may hold for us!* The scientific theory of evolution, on the other hand, is consistent with every other well-confirmed scientific theory and has predicted all sorts of things that have been and continue to be discovered to be true, including how and where fossils might be found, and so on.

Finally, let's take a look at a rather simple and truly scientific theory—the "sea-of-air" hypothesis—and at how scientists test and confirm their hypotheses. The theory was proposed by the seventeenth-century mathematician and physicist Evangelista Torricelli, a disciple of Galileo. It was well known then that water can be pumped from a well only from about a depth of 34 feet (without the aid of auxiliary power); Torricelli proposed to explain this and other facts by his theory that a sea of air surrounds the surface of the Earth and presses down on it because of the force of gravity, just as water presses down on something at the bottom of the ocean. Pumps thus can raise water from a well (at most) to a height of about 34 feet, Torricelli theorized, because of this *air pressure*.

Torricelli's theory can be, and was, confirmed by performing several different sorts of experiments. For instance, if the limit that water can be pumped from a well is about 34 feet, and if mercury is about 14 times heavier than water (it is), then if the sea-of-air theory is correct, it follows that air pressure will hold up a column of mercury only $\frac{1}{14}$ as high as a column of water. So we can confirm the sea-of-air hypothesis by constructing a mercury device (we call these things barometers) and finding that this is the case. Torricelli's followers also confirmed his theory by testing at higher-than-sea-level elevations where, according to the sea-of-air theory, a column of mercury should be held up a lesser amount than at sea level, because there is less air pressing down on the mercury. (We now use this fact in other ways, for instance, in measuring fluctuations in air pressure at a given elevation, part of the knowledge needed to predict changes in the weather.) Notice, by the way, that had the results of experiments not conformed to Torricelli's theory, his hypothesis would not have been accepted by the scientific community.

The point of all this is twofold. First, scientific method is not some mysterious entity; and second, although in practice it leads to extremely complicated experiments and arguments, the basic underlying patterns of scientific enquiry are rather simple. We also should mention that it is the incredibly diverse evidence that supports scientific theories that is the reason why they are so reliable and why we should not reject what science has to say on any subject without having *extremely good reasons* for doing so.

# ANSWERS TO
# STARRED EXERCISE ITEMS

These answers certainly are not presented as revealed truth. They represent the authors' thoughts on the matter, which it is hoped will prove useful to the reader.

## Exercise 1-1 (pp. 3–4)

4. *Premise*: We are sinners all.
   *Implied premise*: All sinners should forbear to judge (others).
   *Conclusion*: We all should forbear to judge (others).

6. *Premise*: Marijuana has many medical benefits.
   *Premise*: Marijuana is less harmful than many legal drugs.
   *Implied premise*: Anything beneficial that is less harmful than already legal drugs should be made legal.
   *Conclusion*: Marijuana should be made legal.

9. *Premise*: I never heard of most of the people and events you talk about in class.
   *Premise*: The textbook is way over my head, also talking about people and events I've never heard of.
   *Implied premise*: You can't expect students (me) to understand material about people and events I've never heard of.
   *Conclusion*: You (the instructor) should not expect me to understand the material in this class.

   (The remaining portions of this excerpt are explanation, not argument.)

## Exercise 1-2 (pp. 4–6)

1. *Premise*: At the present rate of consumption, the oil will be used up in 20 to 25 years.
   *Premise*: We're not going to reduce consumption in the near future.
   *Conclusion*: We'd better start developing solar power, windmills, and other "alternative energy sources" pretty soon.

3. No argument. Just a list of things the student doesn't like.

5. *Premise*: Animal research takes money away from research into other new technologies.
   *Conclusion*: Animal research impedes scientific progress.
   *Premise*: Animal research impedes scientific progress.
   *Implied premise*: Whatever impedes scientific progress is bad.
   *Conclusion*: Money spent on animal research is bad (wastes billions of dollars).

10. *Premise*: We all think ourselves so abundantly provided with good sense that we don't desire any more.
    *Implied premise*: If everyone is satisfied with the amount of good sense they have, then good sense must be equally distributed.
    *Conclusion*: Good sense is equally distributed.

    (The bit about it being the most equally distributed item is, we can assume, a rhetorical flourish. By the way, do you suppose Descartes was being a bit ironic?)

## Exercise 2-2 (pp. 29-30)

1. *Relevant background beliefs that underlie George Will's reasoning:*
(1) Will is against a "giving government," that is, one that gives the poor welfare money. (He doesn't give us clues about welfare for the rich.) (2) Will is not a good democrat (small "d"); he doesn't believe all adults should have the vote, or perhaps he believes just that we shouldn't make it easy for the poor or disenchanted to vote. (3) He generally favors Republicans over Democrats for elected office.

## Exercise 3-1 (pp. 58-61)

1. *Appeal to authority.* Doctors are specialists in medicine. They don't necessarily know anything more about moral issues than anyone else. Anyway, don't we all need to make up our own minds about moral matters?

2. Johnson came very close to being *inconsistent.* If he meant that under no circumstances should the right to dissent be exercised, then he was indeed inconsistent. But if he meant that under the actual circumstances at the time, dissent was not warranted, then he was not inconsistent. (Whether he was then guilty of a questionable belief—that things then were as they should be—is another story.)

14. *Evading the issue.* Aunt knew very well that dryness of the mouth results from insufficient saliva production. She wanted to know why her salivary glands were not functioning correctly—producing sufficient saliva.

15. *Suppressed evidence.* Most of us are in our own home a lot more than we are in these other places. The rape rate *per unit of time* is much greater in the other places mentioned by Dr. Brothers than in one's own home.

20. *Inconsistency.* Doesn't the phrase "heritable disposition" mean a disposition caused by a genetic inheritance?

22. *Reverse appeal to authority.* If *Pravda* said they're bad, they must be good. In fact, lots of things *Pravda* knocked back then when there was a Soviet Union were indeed bad.

## Exercise 4-1 (pp. 74-77)

4. *Irrelevant reasons.*

6. *Slippery slope.*

13. *Equivocation.* You don't have to make the past or future present in thought. What you make present, the "it," is *thoughts* about the past or present. The term *it* is used equivocally, the first use denoting the past or present and the second the thought of the past or present.

22. *Equivocation.* To imagine our own death is to visualize what it would be like to experience it. In this sense we can and do imagine our own death. Freud changes the meaning of *imagine* so that to imagine it we would have to *not* visualize it, which, of course, is impossible.

## Exercise 5-1 (pp. 97-99)

5. The student is wrong. Suppose, to make the figuring simpler, that stopping smoking reduces the risk of heart attack by 50% and taking aspirin also reduces the risk by 50%. We can't then just add 50% and 50% and conclude that by stopping smoking and taking aspirin the risk of heart attack is completely eliminated. If, for instance, the initial risk of having a heart attack in a given year is 1 in 100 (it's actually much lower), then stopping smoking reduces that risk by 50%, or to 1 in 150, and also taking aspirin by an

additional 50%, or to 1 in 225. Similarly, losing weight, lowering cholesterol intake, and so on would further reduce but not eliminate the risk of heart attack. (We've also simplified by ignoring possible synergizing factors—for example, losing weight may change the risk reduction from taking aspirin—and passed over ambiguities in the statements of risk percentage reduction as well as the fact that most people are unlikely to run all of the risks—for example, most people don't smoke—because these considerations are not relevant to the student's mistake.

## Exercise 5-2 (pp. 99–101)

10. The student is wrong. It's true that, taken literally, the sayings he mentions are contradictory, but they are not intended to be so taken. The point is to get good at knowing when one of an apparently inconsistent pair applies and when the other does.

13. Not the fallacy of *common practice* or *two wrongs*. Diplomatic practices have evolved over the centuries as a way to facilitate peaceful relations among nations. The United States appealed to these practices merely to get the Russians to accept the note, not as a reason for granting the compensation.

16. *Suppressed evidence*. Perhaps the most important thing to do when evaluating rhetoric is to bring background beliefs to bear. In this case, think about how the hundreds, perhaps thousands, of items in this text must have been gathered. This should bring to mind the author watching television and listening to the radio, reading all sorts of magazines and newspapers, and so on. Wouldn't it be quite natural for him to read the publications he likes best a good deal more than those liked less well? Specifically, wouldn't it be likely that he would spend more time reading *The Washington Monthly* than the *National Review*?

18. If LaPierre intended his analogy to prove anything, then he was guilty of the fallacy *questionable analogy*. But since he then provided reasons for believing gun bans do not reduce crime rates, we have to assume he meant his analogy to be illustrative, not demonstrative.

## Exercise 5-3 (pp. 101–105)

1. This is one of those cases where different people should see the matter differently, depending on their value judgments concerning the quality of television programs (and of Ming vases?). The authors of this text, television fans in spite of their intense dislike for most major network programs, find the analogy quite questionable. They would like very much to be able to see programs with sharper pictures. (The fact that the picture on American television programs has been less sharp over the years than in European and many other countries around the world has always rankled. It's no doubt true that plans to introduce HDTV in a way that will ultimately make all present-day TV sets obsolete can be argued against, but that's not relevant here.)

2. *Suppressed evidence*. In a nation where most people live in cities, where pigs cannot be kept, forbidding the sale of pork, bacon, and such is tantamount to forbidding the eating of these items. *Inconsistency*. So Rabbi Shapira came close to being inconsistent when he claimed that the ultrareligious Jews in Israel want the sale but not the eating of these kinds of meat to be forbidden, since the one is tantamount to the other.

4. *Questionable statements*. (Or *straw man*?) It's unlikely that Dr. Warren bases his moral position just on the New Testament, to the exclusion of the Ten Commandments and other precepts in the Old Testament, and unlikely that Dr. Barnhart's position was as stated (not indicating, for instance, *whose* pleasure is to count—we can suspect, for example, that the pleasures of convicted felons might weigh less heavily with him than the gratification of upstanding citizens). *False dilemma*. In any case, both of these

theories may be wrong. All sorts of other moral theories have been championed at one time or another, and one of them may be the right one (assuming that there is just one right moral theory).

6. *Questionable statistics.* Having extolled scientists for their generally correct handling of statistics, here is a case where they goofed. The problem isn't that a rough statistic did not follow from their evidence but rather that precise ones such as 968.1 billion tons of carbon stored 18,000 years ago did not. Note, for instance, that they *estimated* how much carbon dioxide was locked within plants, and so on.

8. *Suppressed evidence.* (1) Superstition is more accurately defined, in part, as belief without good evidence or in the face of contrary evidence. (So the article changed the meaning of the term *superstition*, and some readers may have been guilty of falling for the fallacy *equivocation*.) (2) Some of the greatest scientists may have been superstitious, Isaac Newton being perhaps the best candidate. But the parts of their beliefs that became incorporated in science were not superstitions, Newton again furnishing perhaps the best example. (3) In addition, a great deal of what scientists once accepted, *on good evidence*, they now reject, or have modified or sharpened, because of better evidence (for example, the rejected ether theory). Rejecting or modifying well-supported theories because of better evidence in favor of more accurate theories is the heart of science and is definitely not superstition.

11. No fallacy. His analogies are apt.

14. *Suppressed evidence.* Isn't it very likely indeed that those who don't take the trouble to register are more likely not to vote, even if no registration were required, than those who do take the trouble? *Hasty conclusion.* But the evidence cited does lend some support to the conclusion; it's just insufficient evidence. To clinch the point, evidence would need to be presented showing that the likelihood just mentioned in fact is false.

16. *Hasty conclusion.* The evidence cited certainly is relevant to the question and favorable to Peirce's claim that the ads caused a rise in teen smoking, but it is not conclusive. Many other factors were at work (was there a similar increase in the use of other harmful drugs such as alcohol or marijuana?) and need to be evaluated along with the ads. *Questionable statement.* Why isn't banning cigarette ads a First Amendment issue? It's true that we don't think a ban on ads for illegal substances would violate the First Amendment prohibition on censorship of speech, but, on the other hand, we wouldn't be inclined to agree that nothing can be advertised which causes serious illnesses (for instance, high-fat foods).

17. *Hasty conclusion.* There certainly are plenty of good background reasons for concluding that raising the speed limit will increase traffic fatalities. But we can't automatically credit the 55-mph speed limit with reducing fatalities (for one thing, that limit was generally flouted anyway; for another, cars have been made safer, and perhaps drivers on average are more sober). Still, it would have been a good guess, based on background beliefs, that increases in speed would result in increases in fatalities. (Experience so far is mixed as to whether in fact the new higher maximum speed limits have resulted in increased highway deaths.)

18. *Irrelevant reason.* How does being mentioned in the Constitution (he meant that his position—being a member of Congress—is so mentioned) make one not be an employee of the federal government?

20. This is a very questionable use of statistics. Why subtract the Arab-Israeli vote? They were legal voters after all. Analogy: Clinton really lost the 1992 election. If the votes of all women had been subtracted from the totals, Bush would have won more electoral votes than Clinton.

# Exercise 7-1 (p. 156)

3. *Translation*: Printed on paper that is at least 10 percent recycled, with a minimum of 40 percent new material.

    Is there something sneaky about this? Yes, indeed. Starting out with the statement "Printed on recycled paper" leads one to suspect that the item is printed on 100 percent recycled paper, thus playing to those who like to use recycled materials. The bit about post- and preconsumer materials is bound to be confusing to most of these people, who will then rely on the (misleading) first statement—the one they can understand. At the same time, the manufacturer is protected from fraud by the statements about pre- and post-consumer materials.

6. What the good admiral said in militaryese was that Navy teams had gone around the country trying to find ways to get naval installations to spend more money. (It was close to the end of the fiscal year and the Navy had not used up its appropriation for that year. Yes, bureaucracies, with very few exceptions, do work this way.)

# Exercise 7-3 (pp. 157–158)

2. Actually, two of the sayings might be challenged. Charles Beardsley's quote may be thought to be doublespeak, and the Chinese proverb clearly does use the pronoun *he* when people in general are meant. But Beardsley deliberately employed "pompous prolixity" in order to rail against that very kind of language. And it makes not a great deal of sense to change ancient sayings (or should we commit to flames the King James version of the Bible with its sexist sayings, such as "Let him who is without sin cast the first stone"?).

    Confucius's precept does exaggerate the slipperiness of the slope he describes. But it is slippery!

8. The item is included because it contains a kind of *fine print take back*, in which what is implied by the headline and first few paragraphs is extremely modified by the last paragraph. Any item that either the five-person board or the president of the United States wanted to keep secret could always be said to be withheld because its publication "might [note that weasel word!] damage U.S. foreign relations, disclose intelligence sources or methods or invade an individual's privacy." (In fact, so far—June 1997—the commission has been doing a reasonably good job with little evidence of unreasonable withholding of documents.)

# Exercise 8-1 (pp. 165–168)

3. *Thesis*: None of the historical or anecdotal parts of the Bible are the word of God.
    *Reason* (premise): What I've seen (or know?) needs no revelation.
    *Conclusion*: Revelation is that which reveals what we don't know (haven't seen) before.
    *Reason*: Revelation is that which reveals what we don't know (haven't seen) before.
    *Conclusion*: Revelation can't tell us about earthly things men could witness.
    *Reason*: Revelation can't tell us about earthly things men could witness.
    *Conclusion* (thesis): None of the historical or anecdotal parts of the Bible count as revelation. (Paine assumed an equation between revelation and the word of God.)

6. *Reason* (premise): Legal separation of the races usually is interpreted as denoting the inferiority of Negroes.
    *Reason*: A sense of inferiority affects the motivation of a child to learn.
    *Conclusion* (thesis): Legal separation of the races retards development of Negroes and deprives them of the benefits of a racially integrated school.

## Exercise 8-5 (pp. 169–171)

1. The *thesis* of Ms. Wilkinson's letter is that smoking does not hasten or deter the inevitable (death) one whit. She presents three reasons for her thesis (the material in the last paragraph about fear of death and the many causes of death is irrelevant.)

   *Reason 1*: Statistics from a 1955 survey of 100 lung cancer patients showing 82 percent were nonsmokers. Fallacies: *Small sample* (100 cases is not very many) and *suppressed evidence* (the many and much larger and better samplings showing a connection between cigarette smoking and cancer, heart disease, and so on).

   *Reason 2*: Wilkinson has been smoking for 50 years and is still healthy (and has had her hyperactivity curbed by cigarette smoking). Fallacies: *Small sample* (but it does show that cigarette smoking alone is not sufficient to cause the disease) and *questionable cause* (how does she know that it has been cigarette smoking that has controlled her hyperactivity?—nicotine generally is a stimulant).

   *Reason 3*: Someone standing on a street corner inhales more toxic material in five minutes than a cigarette smoker inhales in a year. Fallacy: *Irrelevant reason* (whether or not—and we are inclined to question this—her statistic is accurate, it is irrelevant to the question of whether cigarette smoking may or may not hasten death by causing disease. (Analogy: It would make little sense to deny that long-term hypertension causes heart disease on grounds that eating too much fatty food is even more likely to do so.)

## Exercise 9-4 (pp. 201–202)

It is very difficult to construct margin notes or a summary for material such as these excerpts from *Mein Kampf*, because confusion and ambiguities abound. Nevertheless, here is a reasonably accurate summary (omitting Hitler's anthropomorphization of laws of nature):

1. It is a law of nature that animals mate only with members of their own species.

2. Breeding higher with lower within a species produces a medium that will lose out eventually to the higher.

3. If a law of nature did not exist forbidding breeding higher to lower, still higher could not develop.

4. The struggle for food and mates results in a higher development of a species.

5. Just as mating stronger with weaker *individuals* goes against nature, so does mating higher with lower races.

6. Proof: Aryans in North America remained pure and became masters of the continent; Latins in Central and South America mixed with the natives and produced an inferior culture, of which they are not complete masters. (This isn't exactly what Hitler says, but it is what he means. Remember that a good deal of Latin America was still in a colonial status in the 1920s when Hitler wrote his tome.)

## Exercise 10-1 (pp. 222–224)

3. *Suppressed evidence.* Jergens Lotion and Vaseline Intensive Care Lotion are intended to be used for other purposes. *Faulty comparison.* So the correct comparison would be with other antiitch medications, but all of them that contain cortisone (most of them) are equally effective.

14. *Irrelevant reason.* The Transamerica slogan trades on the fact that their headquarters in San Francisco is in a very famous building shaped as an elongated pyramid that is often refered to as "The Pyramid." The bit about the *power* of the pyramid is a takeoff on the pseudoscientific baloney about pyramid power that got its start from various archeological goings on in Egypt.

16. *Begged question.* Saying they've got it down to a science doesn't tell us how they did it. (By the way, is Kleenex any softer than it used to be? Products regularly say things like this without actually making any significant change in the product. Over the years, Kleenex has gotten softer so many times, according to ads, that by now it should be as soft as down.) *Jargon*: The slogan "We've got it down to a science" is just empty jargon.

20. This Nike commercial wins the *Logic and Contemporary Rhetoric* "Most Offensive Commercial of the Decade" Award for telling those who have just proved to be the second best at an activity (perhaps by the tiniest margin) among the several billion people on the planet that they are losers, instead of crediting them with their great accomplishment. (The underlying offensive message is captured by Vince Lombardy's famous remark, "Winning isn't everything; it's the only thing." Compare that to "It isn't whether you win or lose but how you play the game.")

21. *Questionable statements.* Everything those who have their eyes wide open have observed indicates that Dean Witter plans first and foremost for its own benefit, not for any client's future, and measures success in terms of their own profits (as do virtually all corporations?)

24. *Appeal to authority.* Agronsky is no authority on the subject. *Straw man.* No one claims coconut oils are "poisoning" America. *Suppressed evidence.* (1) While some fats are healthier than others, coconut oil is low on the healthy list. (2) It is total amount of fat intake that is most important. (3) No single fat source supplies more than a small portion of total intake of fat, so that "only" 1.5 percent coming from coconut oil proves nothing. The point is that it's prudent to reduce one's total amount of fat intake well below the national average and to reduce intake of some kinds of fat—coconut oil being a prime example—more than others. (4) If true that the fatty acids in coconut oil are beneficial, that would be a good reason to prefer this oil to others—say, when cooking. But this claim is generally not accepted by the medical profession. On the contrary, it is fats such as olive oil that seem to be the most beneficial.

## Exercise 10-2 (pp. 224–225)

3. This commercial points to a profitable use of air travel—to foster face-to-face business relationships. That is why this has been an extremely successful ad—it reminds business executives of the value of catering to customers in person. But the commercial gives no reason to fly United instead of other airlines. (The implied reason that United flies to over 200 locations is not a good reason for choosing United. For one thing, some other airlines fly to that many cities; and for another, what difference does it make if you intend, say, to fly to Chicago, whether the airline you choose also flies to 199 other cities or just to half that many?) *Jargon type slogan.* "United. Come fly the friendly skies." *Identification.* Casting the right actors for TV commercials is crucial and this ad does it beautifully. Ben is someone most people in business will identify with.

## Exercise 12-2 (pp. 321–322)

4. The topic is the one discussed in Chapter 7 entitled "Those Who Control the Definitions"—defining oneself into victory. Those who favor teaching the Biblical account of creation in science classes were trying to define themselves into victory by calling the Biblical account "creation science," very much like businesses do who call employees "subcontractors."

## Exercise for the Entire Text (p. 323)

You didn't really expect an answer to this one, did you? (If you did, go back to page 1 of Chapter 1 and start reading—carefully this time.)

## Exercise A-2 (pp. 329–330)

3. *Contingent.* It certainly is not a contradiction, and it also is not a tautology because there is no law of logic that forbids one from running for both president and vice president in the same election. (Is there a legal law of the land?)

10. *Tautological.* It's true whether trespassers happen to be shot or not.

## Exercise A-3 (pp. 334–335)

1. Since it isn't possible to get both 2 and 12 on a given toss, we can use the restricted disjunction rule. And given that the probability of getting a $2 = \frac{1}{36}$ and of a $12 = \frac{1}{36}$, the probability of getting 2 or $12 = \frac{1}{36} + \frac{1}{36} = \frac{2}{36} = \frac{1}{18}$.

4. There are 100,000 five-digit numbers, each one equally likely to be picked. Thus, the odds on any given number are 100,000 to 1. So a winning $2 bet should pay $200,000 plus the $2 wagered. (None do. But note that in lottery cases of this kind, how much is paid to winners usually depends on how many people pick the correct number and whether there was a winner of previous plays. When there is no winner for several plays and the pot becomes very large, the number of people who play increases dramatically (people are not always rational!), so that, even though the amount of prize money increases, the probability that there will be several winners increases, thus dividing each winner's share. Of course, when the odds against winning anything are 100,000 to 1, the chances of winning are so miniscule that it is a waste of time to play. It almost never makes sense to wager at such poor odds, even if they are statistically in your favor; doing so loses you the opportunity to profit in some more likely ways. Human irrationality makes most of us see things differently, but that's just one of the tendencies that a good rational thinker fights against.)

# BIBLIOGRAPHY

## Cogent Reasoning

Carroll, Lewis. *Symbolic Logic and the Game of Logic*. New York: Dover, 1958.

Dewey, John. *How We Think*. Lexington, Mass.: D. C. Heath, 1910.

Kahane, Howard. "The Proper Subject Matter for Critical Thinking Courses." *Argumentation*. Vol. 3, 1989.

* Kahane, Howard, and Tidman, Paul. *Logic and Philosophy*, 8th ed. Belmont, Calif.: Wadsworth, 1998.

Lemmon, E. J. *Beginning Logic* (revised by G. N. D. Barry). Indianapolis, Ind.: Hackett, 1978. (A strictly formal logic text.)


## Fallacious Reasoning

* Bentham, Jeremy. *The Handbook of Political Fallacies*. New York: Harper Torchbooks, 1962. (A reprint of a classic nineteenth-century tract.)

Broad, C. D. "Some Fallacies in Political Thinking." *Philosophy* 29 (April 1950). (Interesting article by an important twentieth-century philosopher.)

* Cerf, Christopher, and Navasky, Victor. *The Experts Speak: The Definitive Compendium of Authoritative Misinformation*. New York: Pantheon Books, 1984.

* Dixon, Paul. *The Official Rules*. New York: Delacorte, 1978.

Ekman, Paul. *Telling Lies: Clues to Deceit in the Marketplace, Politics, and Marriage*. New York: W. W. Norton, 1992. (Fascinating book that will help readers to perceive when they are being lied to.)

Hamblin, C. L. *Fallacies*. Newport News, Va.: Vale Press, 1986. (A reprint with new preface of the definitive history of fallacy theory.)

Huff, Darrell. *How to Lie with Statistics*. New York: W. W. Norton, 1954.

* Kahane, Howard. "The Nature and Classification of Fallacies." In *Informal Logic: The First International Symposium*, ed. by J. Anthony Blair and Ralph H. Johnson. Inverness, Calif.: Edgepress, 1980.

Miller, James Nathan. "Ronald Reagan and the Techniques of Deception." *Atlantic Monthly*, February 1984. (Nice illustration of how statistics can be misused for political advantage.)

Morgan, Chris, and Langford, David. *Facts and Fallacies: A Book of Definitive Mistakes and Misguided Predictions*. Exeter, England: Webb & Bower, 1981. (One of several excellent books illustrating expert feet of clay.)

Morgenstern, Oscar. "Qui Numerare Incipit Errare Incipit." *Fortune*, October 1963. (Still one of the best explanations of how government statistics on business and such can be and are manipulated for political purposes.)

Smith, H. B. *How the Mind Falls into Error*. Darby Books, 1980. (Reprint of the 1923 edition.)

Thouless, Robert H. *Straight and Crooked Thinking*. New York: Simon and Schuster, 1932.

Wheeler, Michael. *Lies, Damn Lies, and Statistics: The Manipulation of Public Opinion in America*. New York: Dell Laurel Edition, 1977.


## Impediments to Cogent Reasoning

* Bentham, Jeremy. *The Handbook of Political Fallacies*. New York: Harper Torchbooks, 1962. (A reprint of a classic nineteenth-century tract.)

---

*Asterisks indicate items mentioned in the text.

*French, Christopher C., Fowler, Mandy, McCarthy, Katy, and Peers, Debbie. "Belief in Astrology: A Test of the Barnum Effect." *Skeptical Inquirer*, Winter 1991.

Gardner, Martin. *Science: Good, Bad, and Bogus*. Buffalo, N.Y.: Prometheus, 1981. (Debunking of pseudoscience.)

———. *Fads and Fallacies in the Name of Science*. New York: Dover, 1957. (The classic debunking of pseudoscience.)

*Gilovich, Thomas. *How We Know What Isn't So*. New York: The Free Press, 1991.

*Goffman, Erving. *The Presentation of Self in Everyday Life*. New York: Anchor Books, 1959. (A classic.)

*Goleman, Daniel. *Vital Lies, Simple Truths*. New York: Simon and Schuster, 1985. (The best understandable explanation of recent scientific ideas about self-deception, its biological functions, and the unconscious.)

MacKay, Charles. *Memoirs of Extraordinary Popular Delusions and the Madness of Crowds*. New York: Harmony Books, 1980. (Reprint of 1841 edition, with foreword by Andrew Tobias. An excellent account of several disasters—the Crusades, the seventeenth-century Dutch tulip madness, the South Sea Bubble—driven by mass hysteria.)

Nickell, Joe. *Inquest on the Shroud of Turin*. Buffalo, N.Y.: Prometheus, 1982. (An example of sanity on a foolishness-provoking topic.)

Nisbet, Robert. *Prejudices*. Cambridge, Mass.: Harvard University Press, 1986.

Peirce, Charles Sanders. "The Fixation of Belief." *Popular Science Monthly*, 1877. (A classic article by America's premier philosopher.)

Sagan, Carl. *The Demon-Haunted World*. New York: Random House, 1996. (A protest by an eminent astronomer against superstition and the uncritical acceptance of pseudoscientific claims.)

Shermer, Michael. *Why People Believe Weird Things: Pseudoscience, Superstition, and Other Confusions of Our Time*. New York: W. H. Freeman, 1997.

Twain, Mark. *Mark Twain on the Damned Human Race*. Edited by Janet Smith. New York: Hill and Wang, 1962. (The great American humorist on all sorts of human foibles. If you think of Sam Clemens as just a writer of stories, you should read this book. For one thing, it will make evident to you how ridiculous it is to censor *Huckleberry Finn* on grounds of racism.)

Vyse, Stuart A. *Believing in Magic: The Psychology of Superstition*. New York: Oxford University Press, 1997.

## Language

*American Philosophical Association (APA). "Guidelines for Non-Sexist Use of Language." (Publication of the APA, available from their national office.)

*Caroll, Lewis. *Alice's Adventures in Wonderland*. New York: New American Library, 1960. (Reprint. The Rev. Dodgson, by the way, was a first-rate logician.)

"Guidelines for Equal Treatment of the Sexes in McGraw-Hill Book Company Publications." (Eleven-page, in-house statement of policy that has been generally adopted in the publishing business.)

Hall, Edward T. *The Silent Language*. New York: Doubleday, 1973.

Lutz, William. "Notes Toward a Description of Doublespeak." *Quarterly Review of Doublespeak*, January 1987.

*Orwell, George. *Nineteen Eighty-Four*. New York: New American Library, 1949. (Shows how language control helps control thoughts, and thus behavior.)

*———. "Politics and the English Language." Reprinted in *A Collection of Works by George Orwell*. New York: Harcourt Brace Jovanovich, 1946.

Postman, Neil. *Amusing Ourselves to Death: Public Discourse in the Age of Show Business*. New York: Penguin Books, 1986.

Solomon, Norman. *The Power of Babble: The Politician's Dictionary of Buzzwords and Double-talk for Every Occasion*. New York: Bantam Doubleday Dell, 1992.

## Evaluating and Constructing Extended Arguments

Cavender, Nancy, and Weiss, Len. *Thinking/Writing*. Belmont, Calif.: Wadsworth, 1987.
Flew, Antony. *Thinking Straight*. Buffalo, N.Y.: Prometheus, 1977.
Lanham, Richard. *Revising Prose*. New York: Charles Scribner's Sons, 1979. (A good guide to clear writing.)
St. Aubyn, Giles. *The Art of Argument*. Buchanan, N.Y.: Emerson Books, 1962. (A beautifully written little book on argument.)

## Evaluating and Constructing Cogent Essays

*Hayes, John R., and Flower, Linda S. "Writing as Problem Solving." *Visible Language* 14: 396–398.
*Kahane, Howard. *Contract Ethics: Evolutionary Biology and the Moral Sentiments*. Lanham, Md: Rowman & Littlefield, 1995. (Helpful in bringing value judgments to bear when evaluating arguments.)

## Advertising

Baker, Samm Sinclair. *The Permissible Lie*. Cleveland, Ohio: World Publishing, 1968.
* Beiler, David. *The Classics of Political Television Advertising: A Viewer's Guide*. Washington, D.C.: Campaigns and Elections, 1986. (Companion guide to 60-minute videocassette containing some of the great TV campaign spots. Great fun and educational too.)
Benn, Alec. *The 27 Most Common Mistakes in Advertising*. New York: AMACOM, 1978.
* Clark, Eric. *The Want Makers*. New York: Viking, 1988.
* Collins, Thomas L. *Beyond Maximarketing*. New York: McGraw Hill, 1994.
Faucheux, Ron. "How to Win in '94." *Campaigns and Elections*, September 1993. (Interesting to compare with how campaigns were run in 1994.)
* Feldstein, Mark. "Mail Fraud on Capitol Hill." *Washington Monthly*, October 1979.
Glatzer, Robert. *The New Advertising: The Great Campaigns from Avis to Volkswagen*. New York: Citadel Press, 1970.
Hopkins, Claude. *Scientific Advertising*. New York: Crown, 1966. (Reprint of one of the classics on advertising.)
Iyengar, Shanto, and Ansolabehere, Stephen. *Going Negative: How Political Advertisements Shrink and Polarize the Electorate*. New York: Free Press, 1996.
Jamieson, Kathleen Hall. *Dirty Politics: Deception, Distraction, and Democracy*. Oxford University Press, 1992. (How campaigns dominated by 30- and 10-second TV spots fail to provide voters with adequate information.)
———. *Packaging the Presidency: A History and Criticism of Presidential Campaign Advertising*, 2nd ed. New York: Oxford University Press, 1992.
*Lemann, Nicholas. "Barney Frank's Mother and 500 Postmen." *Harper's*, April 1983.
McGinnis, Joe. *The Selling of the President 1968*. New York: Trident Press, 1969. (Still the best inside account of a presidential campaign—Nixon's successful run for the presidency.)
*Ogilvie, David. *Confessions of an Advertising Man*. New York: Atheneum, 1963.
Preston, Ivan. *The Great American Blowup: Puffery in Advertising and Selling*. Madison, Wisc.: University of Wisconsin Press, 1975. (Interesting account of what legally counts as mere puffery rather than false advertising.)

Rowsome, Frank, Jr. *They Laughed When I Sat Down.* New York: Bonanza Books, 1959. (Perhaps still the most interesting book on the history of advertising.)

*Sabatim, Karry J., and Simpson, Glenn R. "When Push Comes to Poll." *Washington Monthly,* June 1996.

Savan, Leslie. *The Sponsored Life: Ads, TV and American Culture.* Philadelphia: Temple University Press, 1995.

Stauber, John, and Rampton, Sheldon. *Toxic Sludge Is Good for You: Lies, Damn Lies, and the Public Relations Industry.* Monroe, Me: Common Courage, 1995.

(In addition to the books listed above, there are several excellent videocassettes available from Campaigns and Elections, Washington, D.C., including the June 1986 *The Classics of Political Advertising* [with an accompanying booklet by David Beiler]; *Prime Time Politics,* a 1989 cassette primarily concerned with the 1988 elections; and *The 25 Funniest Political TV Commercials* [actually, not all that funny, but instructive]. There also are several other modestly interesting videocassettes available, including *30-Second Seduction,* a 1985 cassette by *Consumer Reports.*)

## Managing the News

Bagdikian, Ben. *The Media Monopoly,* 4th ed. Boston: Beacon Press, 1992.

Bennett, James, "The Flack Pack: How Press Conferences Turn Serious Journalists into Shills." *Washington Monthly,* November 1991.

Cohen, Jeff, and Solomon, Norman. *Adventures in Medialand: Behind the News, Beyond the Pundits.* Monroe, Me: Common Courage Press, 1993.

Cohen, Richard. "Making Trends Meet." *Washington Post* magazine, September 28, 1986. (How *Time* and *Newsweek* exaggerate and invent trends and fashions.)

Crossen, Cynthia. *Tainted Truth: The Manipulation of Fact in America.* New York: Simon and Schuster, 1994.

Croteau, David, and Hoynes, William. *By Invitation Only: How the Media Limits Political Debate.* Monroe, Me. Common Courage Press, 1997.

Day, James. *The Vanishing Vision: The Inside Story of Public Television.* Berkeley, Calif.: University of California Press, 1995. (A good account of how and why public television [PBS] succeeds in some ways and comes short in others.)

Fallows, James. *Breaking the News: How the Media Undermine American Democracy.* Pantheon Books, 1996. (Important book by the now [1997] editor of *U.S. News & World Report.*)

Faludi, Susan. *Backlash: The Undeclared War Against American Women.* New York: Bantam Books, 1991.

Fineman, Howard. "The Power of Talk." *Newsweek,* February 8, 1993. (How "call-in democracy"—TV and radio talk shows —are influencing elections and the legislative process.)

Hess, Stephen. "Television's Self-Fulfilling News." *Washington Post, National Weekly Edition,* October 30–November 5, 1989. (How TV shops around for expert opinion that conforms to the view they want to air.)

Hitt, Jack. "Warning: CIA Censors at Work." *Columbia Journalism Review,* July/August 1984.

*Jensen, Carl, and Project Censored. *Censored: The News that Didn't Make the News—and Why.* New York: Seven Stories Press, 1996. (A [hopefully] yearly publication about censored news stories.

*Knightly, Phillip. *The First Casualty.* New York: Harcourt Brace Jovanovich, 1975. (The first casualty in war is, of course, truth.)

Levine, Richard M. "Polish Government versus the Workers: Why TV Is the Prized Weapon." *TV Guide,* November 7, 1981. (An illustration of how important TV has become for politics everywhere.)

Lieberman, David. "Fake News." *TV Guide,* February 22, 1992. (How video press releases, created by public relations firms, are surreptitiously slipped into TV news programs.)

McChesney, Robert. *Corporate Media and the Threat to Democracy.* Seven Stories Press, 1997. (Interesting critique of corporate media power, plus some suggestions for improving the fairness and accuracy of the mass media.)

Perkins, Ray, Jr. *Logic and Mr. Limbaugh.* Chicago: Open Court Press, 1995. (A nifty account of how Rush Limbaugh mangles truth and logic.)

* Perry, David L. "No Way to Celebrate." *Columbia Journalism Review*, July/August 1990. (On how increasingly large jury awards in libel cases are putting a chill on investigative reporting.)

Smiley, Xan. "Misunderstanding Africa." *Atlantic Monthly*, September 1982. (How government intimidation and interference mangles news from Africa. An old article, but not that much has changed.)

Waters, Frank. *The Earp Brothers of Tombstone.* Lincoln, Neb.: University of Nebraska Press, 1976. (The most accurate account of the exploits of the famous "Wild West" Earp brothers (Wyatt and Virgil), including a reasonably accurate account of the so-called "gunfight" at the O.K. Corral. A good antidote to the baloney the media dish out on this and other aspects of Western U.S. history.)

* Zepezauer, Mark, and Naiman, Arthur. *Take the Rich Off Welfare.* Tucson, Ariz.: Odonian Press, 1996.

(In addition to the books just listed, there are several excellent videocassettes on managing the news, perhaps the most revealing being *Fear and Favor in the Newsroom*, distributed by California Newsreels, dramatically illustrating how corporate power influences news coverage.)

## Textbooks: Managing World Views

American Indian Historical Society. *Textbooks and the American Indian.* San Francisco: Indian Historical Press, 1970. (Shows how textbooks in those days—pre-1970—covered up the horrible treatment of Native Americans by European invaders.)

Barzun, Jaques. "The Wasteland of American Education." *New York Review of Books*, November 5, 1981. (Still very relevant.)

Black, Hillel. *The American Schoolbook.* New York: William Morrow, 1967.

Chubb, John E. *Politics, Markets, and America's Schools.* Brookings Institution, 1990.

* Elson, Ruth M. *Guardians of Tradition: American Schoolbooks of the 19th Century.* Lincoln, Neb.: University of Nebraska Press, 1964.

* Fussell, Paul. *Wartime: Understanding and Behavior in the Second World War.* New York: Oxford University Press, 1989.

Henry, Jules. *On Sham, Vulnerability, and Other Forms of Self-Destruction* . (Unfortunately out of print.)

"History/Social Science Framework for California Public Schools, Kindergarten through Grade Twelve." (The basic document governing California schools.)

Kasarda, John D. "The Jobs-Skills Mismatch." *New Perspectives Quarterly*, Fall 1990. (The economy needs highly educated workers; schools produce "low achievers.")

Loewen, James W. *Lies My Teacher Told Me: Everything Your History Textbook Got Wrong.* New York: New Press, 1995. (Terrific book explaining how and why public school textbooks distort history the way they do. Probably the best book on the topic ever written.)

* Nelson, Jack, and Roberts, Gene. *The Censors and the Schools.* Boston: Little, Brown, 1963. (The best book on the topic up to 1963.)

Paulos, John Allen. *Innumeracy: Mathematical Illiteracy and Its Consequences.* New York: Hill & Wang, 1988.

Schrank, Jeffrey. *Understanding Mass Media*, 2nd ed. Skokie, Ill. 1986. (One of the best public school social science texts.)

* Shenkman, Richard. *Legends, Lies and Cherished Myths of American History.* New York: William Morrow, 1988.

Washburn, Katharine, and Thornton, John. *Dumbing Down: Essays on the Strip-mining of American Culture*. New York: W. W. Norton, 1996. (Several fascinating essays on how the dumbing down of American public schools is harming society.)

Zinn, Howard. *A People's History of the United States*. Harper & Row: New York: l980. (Perhaps the easiest to understand antidote to the history learned via public school history texts.)

## Selected List of Periodicals

One of the themes of this text is that good reasoning requires reasonably accurate background beliefs, and one of the best ways to acquire a good stock of general information and theory is by reading some of the literally thousands of periodicals—magazines and journals—that are readily available these days. Here is a selected list of (primarily) non–mass media periodicals, the majority concerned mostly with social/political issues, the media, or science, which the authors of this text happen to dip into at least now and then. (The comments represent our opinions and are not to be taken as some sort of revealed truth.)

*AIM Report*. A right-wing media watch of dubious accuracy published by Accuracy in Media. *Examples*: The February 1997 article on the "White House conspiracy" to conceal the "true facts" concerning the death of Clinton White House aide Vince Foster; an awful 1992 article that branded the recently deceased journalist I. F. Stone as a KGB agent while failing to produce a shred of satisfactory confirming evidence.

*American Heritage*. Perhaps the most interesting history magazine, featuring fascinating articles about American history. A good antidote to dull public school history texts. *Examples*: The entire November 1996 issue "100 Years of the Automobile in America"; the December 1996 story about General Stonewall Jackson, "Lee's Greatest Lieutenant."

*American Spectator*. Wild-swinging right-wing publication. *Examples*: The September 1996 article on recent antievolution books and arguments; the March 1992 article "The Real Anita Hill"; the April 1997 item on how mob-controlled unions "deliver the goods for Bill Clinton."

*Amnesty Action*. Publication of Amnesty International reporting on government torture around the world (reading this publication makes one appreciate living in a democratic society). *Examples*: The Winter 1996 articles on the execution of Nigerian government opponents, including Ken Saro-Wiwa, and on the conviction for alleged treason of Chinese dissident Wei Jingsheng.

*Atlantic Monthly*. One of the best general magazines, with some fiction. *Examples*: An August 1996 article, "The Next Church," on a new trend in Protestant churches to large, "full-service" facilities with pop culture. The May 1994 article on how the inner-city environment fosters a need for respect and a self-image based on violence. Also prints occasional stinkers. *Example*: The February 1992 article entitled "The Extinction of Darwinism."

*Bible Review*. Concerned with the Bible and biblical history. *Examples*: The October 1992 article arguing against Mary Magdalene having been a whore; a fascinating December 1992 article on "How the Alphabet Democratized Civilization."

*Black Enterprise*. A business magazine oriented towards African Americans in the business world. *Examples*: The February 1993 article on the 40 most powerful black executives; a May 1994 article entitled "Hot Cities for Black Business," which contained interesting statistics on black/white incomes, unemployment, and so on, as well as ways in which the cities discussed have improved business opportunities for black-owned or black-run enterprises.

*Business Week*. Good business magazine, written for those in business and much better than, say, *Money*, written for the masses. *Examples*: The May 12, 1997, article on the booming U.S.-Mexican border; the May 5, 1997, article on how the Internet is shaping electronic commerce.

*Campaigns & Elections*. Meant for those in the trade, important for the rest of us to read to find out what the political experts are up to. *Examples*: The May 1994 article providing a step-by-step guide for developing a winning campaign message.

*Campus America's Student Newspaper*. Written by and for college students. *Examples*: The Spring 1997 articles "Banning the Bard While Boosting the Banal" and "Is It Weird? You May Get College Credit," decrying the dumbing down and "PCing" of college courses.

*Civil Liberties*. Publication of the American Civil Liberties Union (distributed to members). *Examples*: A Spring 1992 article arguing against the Pornography Victims Compensation Act intended to blame legally the producers and distributors of works determined to be "obscene" that are judged to have caused serious sex crimes to be committed; and a report on how the U.S. government thwarted attempts by Haitians to gain political asylum in the U.S.

*Columbia Journalism Review*. One of the better journalism publications. *Examples*: Monthly "Darts & Laurels" awards; the July/August 1996 issue, which had an article on what's at stake (plenty) in the awarding of new space on the TV spectrum and an article on the lack of credibility of the *Wall Street Journal* editorial page; and a May/June 1994 article suggesting term limits on the media people who cover the federal government.

*Common Cause* magazine. Liberal magazine sent to Common Cause contributors. *Examples*: The excellent Spring/Summer 1996 article on how big business, unions, and the superrich control politics through campaign contributions; the Spring 1994 article on the battle for control of "cyberspace"; and one on how "a little-known government program helps defuse racial tensions in communities across America."

*Conservative Chronicles*. A compendium of conservative opinion expressed in political columns, cartoons, and so on. *Examples*: The November 3, 1993, article by Thomas Sowell on how educators are "scared of school vouchers," and one by Phyllis Schlafly on "Hillary's totalitarian health care proposal."

*Consumer Reports*. Publication of Consumers Union, an unbiased, nonprofit organization; a very good source of information about consumer products. *Examples*: Any one of the several articles every year on new cars; the January 1994 article on where to go, and when, to get things fixed. The back page of every issue on advertising and product chicanery to watch out for.

*Discover*. Perhaps the best of a bad lot of mass media, popular science magazines. *Examples*: The February 1997 article on how galaxies form; the very good February 1994 article "How Africa Became Black"; the not-so-hot October 1993 cover story "Hawking's Challenge: Can the Future Exist if a Black Hole Swallows the Past?"

*The Economist*. Quite good British news weekly concentrating on business news, but containing more general news than *Time*, *Newsweek*, or *U.S. News and World Report*, plus in-depth essays. *Examples*: The November 2, 1996, article on the catastrophe in Zaire; the April 16–22, 1994, 20-page survey of Poland; the March 5–11, 1994, survey of manufacturing technology.

*Editor & Publisher*. Important trade magazine. A good source of information as to how those in the business see things. *Examples*: Several articles in the January 27, 1996, issue on the need for efficiency in the print media.

*Environmental Nutrition*. A very good publication on diet, nutrition, and health. *Examples*: A May 1994 article on how, by switching from chocolate to cocoa, when baking, you can get the chocolate flavor without the fat (recipes included), and one containing some sensible thoughts about alleged dangers of microwave ovens; a February 1994 article on whether "your coffee habit is grounds for health concerns."

*Extra!* The best magazine on the media. *Examples*: The March/April 1997 articles blasting media coverage of the Social Security system fix via privatization and downsizing; the October 1996 "Update" on the disgracefully biased media reporting that unfairly attacked the accuracy of the *San Jose Mercury News*'s important story about the "CIA-Contra Crack Connection" (e.g., the *New York Times* going out of its way to cover up for the CIA); the July/August 1995 article on how the media initially, without any facts, assumed that Mideast Muslim terrorists were responsible for the Oklahoma City bombing.

*Free Inquiry*. Secular humanist publication. *Examples*: The Spring 1996 article arguing that we don't need God to be moral, and one defending the "wall between church and state"; the Fall 1996 article deflating Mother Teresa.

*Harper's*. Very good general monthly; the "Harper's Index" has become very popular, and editor Lewis Lapham's monthly columns often are very enlightening. *Examples*: The February 1997 article on American investments in peon-wage industries around the world; the August 1996 issue discussion on abortion.

*Harvard Health Letter*. A publication of Harvard University containing reasonably reliable medical information. *Example*: The March 1997 article on the top ten medical advances of 1996. (A good antidote to the trendy stuff you hear about in the mass media.)

*Index on Censorship*. Chronicles censorship around the world. *Example*: November 1992 articles on censorship in the recently liberated (from Soviet rule) Baltic states.

*Intercollegiate Review*. Conservative journal of scholarship and opinion. *Example*: The Spring 1994 article on cultural norms, family ties, and the like in Third World countries and, by comparison, in the "Four Little Dragons."

*In These Times*. Left-wing socialist publication. *Examples*: The May 26, 1997, food issue articles on how African-American farmers get a raw deal from the U.S. Department of Agriculture; how factory fish trawlers are replacing independent fishermen and ruining the marine ecosystem; and how independent dairy farmers are losing out to giant corporations.

*Linguafranca*. A reasonably good journal of academic life. *Examples*: The November 1996 article "Casting Out the Gods from Religious Studies," and a piece on "Out of Africa" author Martin Bernal; the March/April 1994 articles on how athletic departments have become university powerhouses and on an extremely dubious sexual harassment case in New Hampshire.

*Mother Jones*. Successor to *Ramparts*; radical left viewpoint, with occasionally very good exposés. *Examples*: The January/February 1997 articles on how federal regulators are not adequately protecting consumers and farmers from corporate machinations; the May/June 1994 article on how environmental toxins cause breast cancer, and how scientists tend to look the other way; and one on how the CIA is "spying on foreign competitors of American companies."

*Movieguide*. A movie magazine that discusses and rates films from the point of view of fundamentalist Christian doctrine. *Examples*: Panning *Mrs. Doubtfire* because it flouts the admonition in Deuteronomy 22:5 that men not wear women's clothes.

*The Nation*. Long-established left-wing magazine, recently very much improved under a new editor, and now very good indeed. *Examples*: The July 15–22, 1996, article on the "corporatization of the world"; several stories and many statistics in the excellent June 3, 1996, issue on the increasing concentration of media power in the hands of a very few megacorporations; the November 18, 1996, article on how Columbia/HCA and other huge corporations are taking over previously nonprofit hospitals and making tons of money by eliminating care of the poor and by reducing staff.

*National Geographic*. The long-established, special-topic magazine. Tends to make the world look somewhat better than it is, but nevertheless has interesting articles, with very good, sometimes stunning, visuals about interesting places around the world. *Examples*: The special August 1996 issue "Energizing Mexico"; the January 1994 article on the Rabari sheep herders of northwest India.

*National Review*. Perhaps the most interesting conservative magazine. *Examples*: The April 21, 1997, article on the privatized British electric system's better service and how privatization would do well in America, and an article on the benefits of tying the value of the dollar to gold.

*Natural History*. A publication of the American Museum of Natural History. *Example*: The April 1994 article on the evolution of carnivores; the May 1994 article on the excavation of an ancient Peruvian crypt.

*Nature Conservancy.* Magazine sent to contributors to The Nature Conservancy, an organization that purchases land in the attempt to preserve natural habitats. *Examples*: The July/August 1996 article "Ten Things . . . You Can Do to Save Life's Diversity"; the May/June 1994 article on the purchase of a critical watering ground for Colorado elk.

*New Internationalist.* Excellent, very left-wing publication intent on reporting "issues of world poverty and inequality; [and] the unjust relationship between the powerful and the powerless." *Examples*: The January/February 1997 article showing the "transfer of resources between rich and poor," and an article on the high maternal mortality rate among the poor around the globe; the May 1997 issue devoted to Bombay, India (soon to surpass New York City in population), showing how the poor live in misery while a few others become very rich.

*New Republic.* Long-established liberal (sort of) political magazine. *Examples*: The October 28, 1996, article "The World of the New Urban Poor"; the January 31, 1994, article on the case against "language mavens," such as William Safire, who tell us when our speech and writing are "correct" and when not.

*Newsletter on Intellectual Freedom.* American Library Association newsletter containing lists of censored books.

*Newsweek.* Mass media, general news weekly. Trendy, generally fails to scratch the surface. *Examples*: A May 16, 1994, article, "Sexual Politics and Cyberspace"; an April 18, 1994, cover story on the suicide of Kurt Cobain and teen suicides, and one on the Singapore flogging debate; an April 4, 1994, article on Whitewatergate; the May 2, 1994, article "The Legacy of Richard Nixon," on the death of this most disgraced of all American presidents, ending with the statement: "In the postmortems, the eulogists and even many of his enemies saw him as he wished to be seen, as a statesman."

*New Yorker.* A very good general magazine, with funny cartoons (several reprinted in this textbook), great photos, plus information on goings on in New York City. *Examples*: The May 19, 1997, profile of Donald Trump; an October 16, 1995, article on how the rich have been getting much richer since 1973, while most of the rest of us have been getting poorer or just holding our own; a March 28, 1994, review of the movie *The Wonderful, Horrible Life of Leni Riefenstahl*, about Hitler's favorite filmmaker (she did *Triumph of the Will*, an extolment of the 1934 Nazi rally at Nuremberg and perhaps the best propaganda film ever made). Also nifty covers by the likes of Edward Sorel and J. J. Sempé. (TV commercials tout the *New Yorker* as "perhaps the best magazine that ever was," something no magazine could possibly be. Anyway, anyone interested in perusing what may well be the best single issue ever of any magazine should hunt down the July 1939 issue of *Fortune* magazine, ironically entirely about New York City.)

*New York Review of Books.* Very good left-wing publication with excellent, indeed, sometimes superb, lengthy reviews and articles. *Examples*: The April 24, 1997, review of recent books about Thomas Jefferson that picture a much less perfect person than do public school textbooks, and a review of a book about the rise of Western Christendom. Also, fascinating letters to the editor combat, for example, the March 6, 1997, letters concerning Carl Sagan's *The Demon-Haunted World*. Also, David Levine's great caricatures.

*Nucleus.* Quarterly report received by members of the Union of Concerned Scientists (UCS). *Example*: The Summer 1996 article on how scientists are attempting to explain to the rest of us what is wrong with "junk" (pseudo) science; the Winter 1993–1994 article about how the Nuclear Regulatory Commission "continues to turn a blind eye to potentially serious safety problems at U.S. nuclear plants."

*Nutrition Action Health Letter.* Publication of the Center for Science in the Public Interest. An excellent source of information about food and health. *Examples*: The July/August 1996 articles on how to avoid food poisoning; the May 1994 article on why chocolate, alas, is an "artery-clogger," and one on the extremely high fat content of movie popcorn, no matter what oil is used in popping.

*Omni.* A mixed-bag science magazine meant for the masses. *Example*: The six-part 1994 series of articles on "The UFO Conspiracy"—an extremely unlikely government conspiracy they claim exists to squelch information about the real evidence for UFOs.

*Quarterly Review of Doublespeak.* An excellent publication of the National Council of Teachers of English. *Examples*: January issues containing their annual Doublespeak and Orwell Award winners; the April 1994 reprint of the still-relevant 1973 Richard Wynn article, "The Wynn Principle"; tons of examples of doublespeak in every issue (many of which are reprinted in this textbook). Reprints of relevant cartoons. Indispensable for anyone seriously interested in how language can and is used to con.

*Reason.* Perhaps the most interesting of the libertarian (pro free enterprise, con big government) publications. *Examples*: The August/September 1993 article on how the mayor of Indianapolis is trying to revolutionize city government by cutting back on city hall; the June 1994 article on how private enterprise management may revolutionize public schools and a review of a book by philosopher Robert Nozick.

*Science News.* Very good weekly on what's new in science. *Examples*: The June 15, 1996, article on using the sun's energy to generate electricity; the April 13, 1991, article on the Big Bang, which can be understood by lay readers.

*The Sciences.* Very good science publication of the New York Academy of Sciences. Interesting reviews and articles about what is happening in science, most of which can be understood by intelligent lay readers. *Examples*: The July/August 1996 article on the ecological crisis arising from the serious decline in numbers of honey bees and other pollinators; several March/April 1997 articles on race, including one about how ancient Egyptians were Caucasian.

*Scientific American.* Excellent science monthly, often difficult going for lay readers, but worth the effort. *Examples*: The April 1997 article on the African evolution of modern *Homo sapiens* (that's us); the May 1994 debate on biology and homosexuality, and one on the possibility of retrieving information from black holes; a March 1997 article discussing the rise in worldwide sea levels.

*Secular Humanist Bulletin.* Addendum to *Free Inquiry* that will amuse nonbelievers and infuriate fundamentalists, in particular, with their accounts of Biblical passages that appear to be contradictory when taken literally. *Example*: The Summer 1994 article "The Amazing Livestock of Egypt," describing how, in the account in Exodus, Egyptian livestock get wiped out in plagues, only to reappear later.

*Skeptical Inquirer.* Publication of the Committee for the Scientific Investigation of Claims of the Paranormal. The best periodical on pseudoscience. *Examples*: The Spring 1994 articles on the threat of "antiscience" and an article about philosopher David Hume's writings on miracles; a Summer 1989 article on the New Age nonsense. Indispensable for anyone seriously interested in pseudoscience.

*Textbook Letter.* The best source of information about the quality of new public school textbooks. *Examples*: The January/February 1997 article on a new human biology text designed for honors courses and scathing reviews of a new United States history text described as "far-left propaganda that fosters anti-intellectualism" that romanticizes and sanitizes non-Western cultures while denigrating Western civilizations (in an attempt to make the book PC?).

*Time.* Mass media general news weekly. Trendy, generally fails to scratch the surface, often with a misdirected slant. *Examples*: The May 5, 1997, cover story on how we get addicted and might be cured; the April 21, 1997, cover story on "The Most Influential People in America, 1997"; the April 18, 1994, excerpts from a Soviet memoir containing the unsupported (and almost certainly false) claim that several key and world-renowned scientists who worked on the U.S. atomic bomb project during World War II were Soviet spies; the December 27, 1993, cover story on "The New Age of Angels," with a cover picture of an angel, wings and all; a series of three articles in the May 2, 1994, issue legitimizing Richard Nixon in *Time*'s eulogy at his death.

*TV Guide*. Lists each week's TV offerings, plus sometimes interesting articles on TV programs and personalities. *Example*: A June 29–July 5, 1996, item on the 100 most memorable moments in TV history.

*Utne Reader*. Reprints "the best of the alternative press," and perhaps itself the best of the magazines that reprint material from other magazines. *Examples*: The May/June 1994 reprints of three articles on "the legacy of Ellis Island"; a reprint of a *Sojourners* magazine article on the problem with cultural globalism; and reprints from *The Nation* and *American Prospect* on the question "Why blame TV for violence?" (No, the authors of this textbook hadn't heard of *Sojourners* before, either, but finding out about "alternative" publications is one benefit gained by subscribing to the *Utne Reader*.)

*U.S. News and World Report*. A mass media general news weekly that for many years tilted a bit to the right, now under liberal editor James Fallows expected (time will tell) to tilt a bit to the left. *Examples*: The May 19, 1997, cover story on how Americans should be more concerned about premarital sex and an article on how to improve public schools; the April 14, 1997, article on the 1990s Wall Street bull market; the (pre-Fallows) May 2, 1994, eulogy to Richard Nixon on his death.

*Washington Monthly*. Neoliberal. Our favorite magazine on how our political system works and might be improved. *Examples*: The March 1997 article arguing against billions of dollars spent preparing for a "two-front war that will almost certainly never occur," and an article arguing against the current proliferation of easy bankruptcies; a January/February 1994 article on how to get the federal government back on track.

*The Washington Post National Weekly*. A compendium of articles, columns, and cartoons from the *Washington Post*. *Examples*: The June 3, 1996, articles on AT&T's firing of 40,000 employees and on the battle between large corporations for control of the Internet and the change from free to for-fee information on the Internet.

*The Washington Spectator*. Four-page political pamphlet continuing the tradition of *I. F. Stone's Weekly*. *Examples*: The January 1, 1996, article showing that all six depressions in American history have followed balanced federal budgets, arguing that balancing the budget is bad for the economy; the May 15, 1994, issue devoted to the poor and how the U.S. does less for them than other industrial countries, and on the tremendous income and wealth disparity between rich and poor.

*Wired*. Nerd's magazine on computing, the Internet, and so on. *Examples*: The November 1996 article on Bill Gates' Corbis, billed as the first on-line for-profit library, and an item about Mattel taking Barbie into cyberspace.

*Women's Health Watch*. A very good Harvard University health letter for women. *Examples*: The April 1994 article on breast cancer and environmental influences and one on evidence implicating hormone replacement therapy and gallbladder disease. Interesting question-and-answer regular feature.

*Working Woman*. Typical of some of the recent additions to the women's magazine market. *Examples*: The July/August 1996 articles on the "hottest careers for women" and on giving your HMO a "checkup."

*World*. A weekly news magazine reporting from a right-wing "Christian perspective." *Examples*: An April 5, 1997, article on a private meeting between church leaders and President Clinton; the June 8–15, 1996, report on a conversation with "pro-life stalwart" Congressman Charles Canady.

*Z magazine*. An interesting leftist political monthly. *Examples*: A May 1994 article on the way Israel treats its Arab citizens less well than its Jewish citizens, and an article arguing that the "white-black" model of racism in America no longer fits a nation that, they claim, soon will be almost one-third Latino and Asian American.

# Topic Index

# Name Index

## Index of Magazine, Newspaper, Television, and Radio References